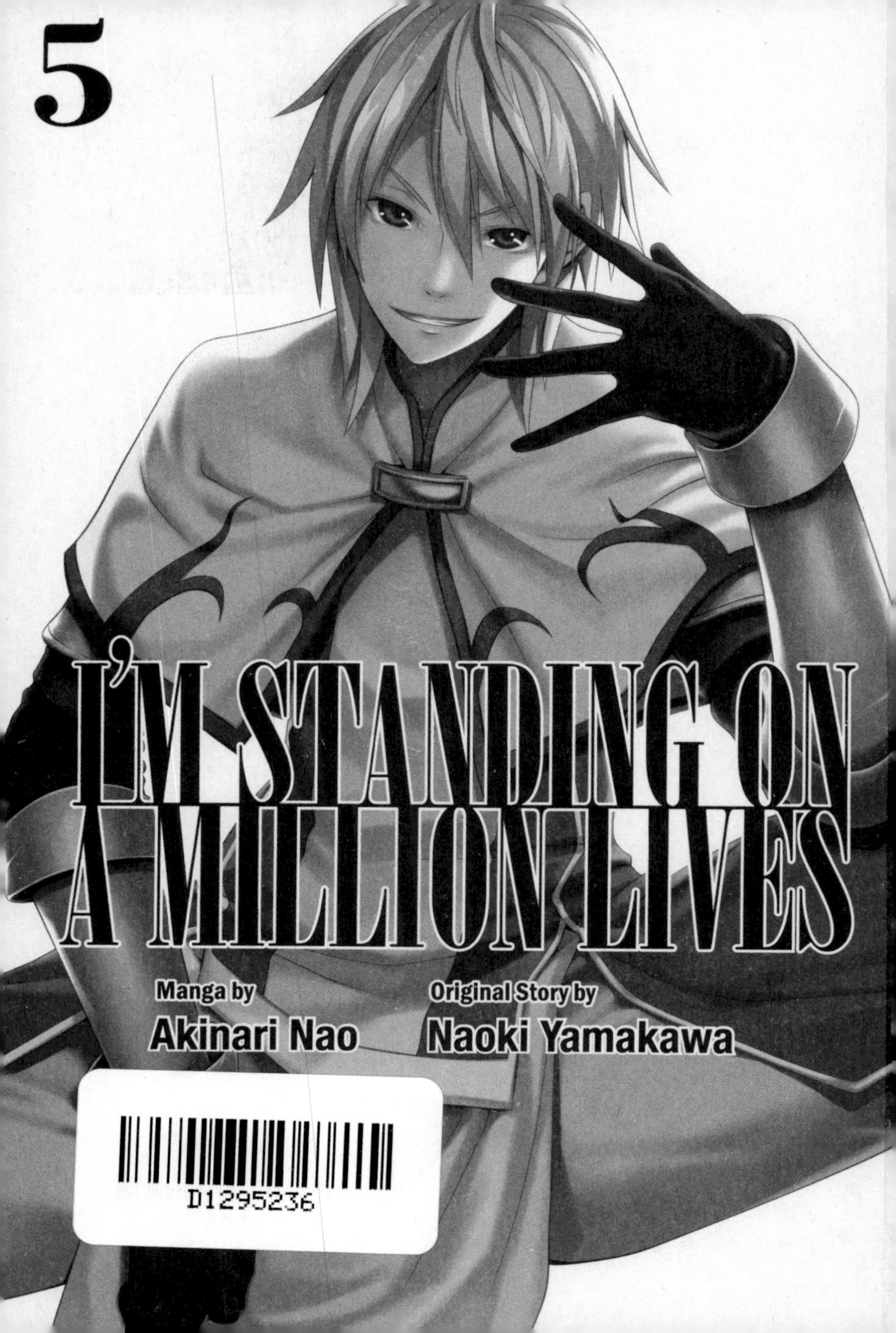

5

I'M STANDING ON A MILLION LIVES

Manga by
Akinari Nao

Original Story by
Naoki Yamakawa

❧ C O N T E N T S ❧

#20 The Throbbing Indoor Battle

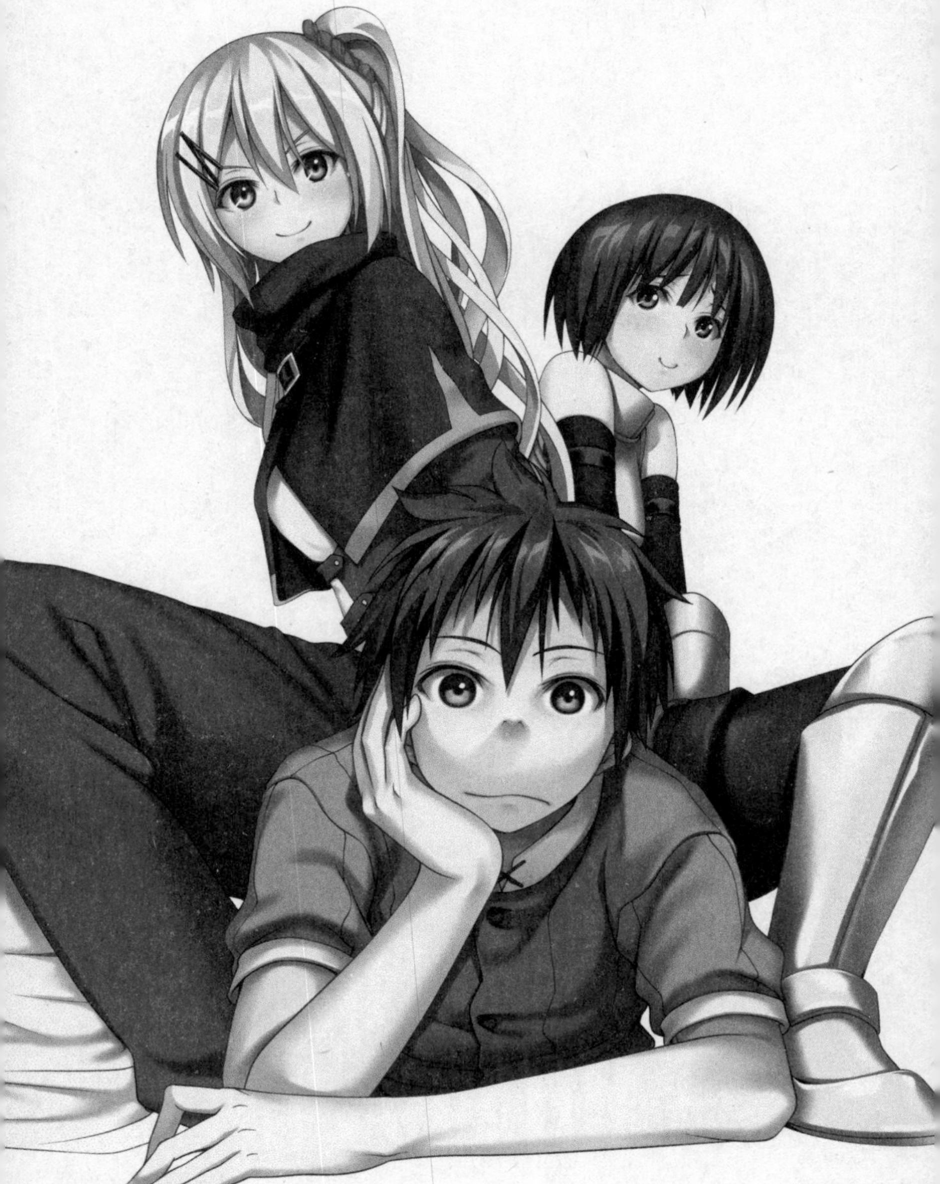

I'M STANDING ON
A MILLION LIVES

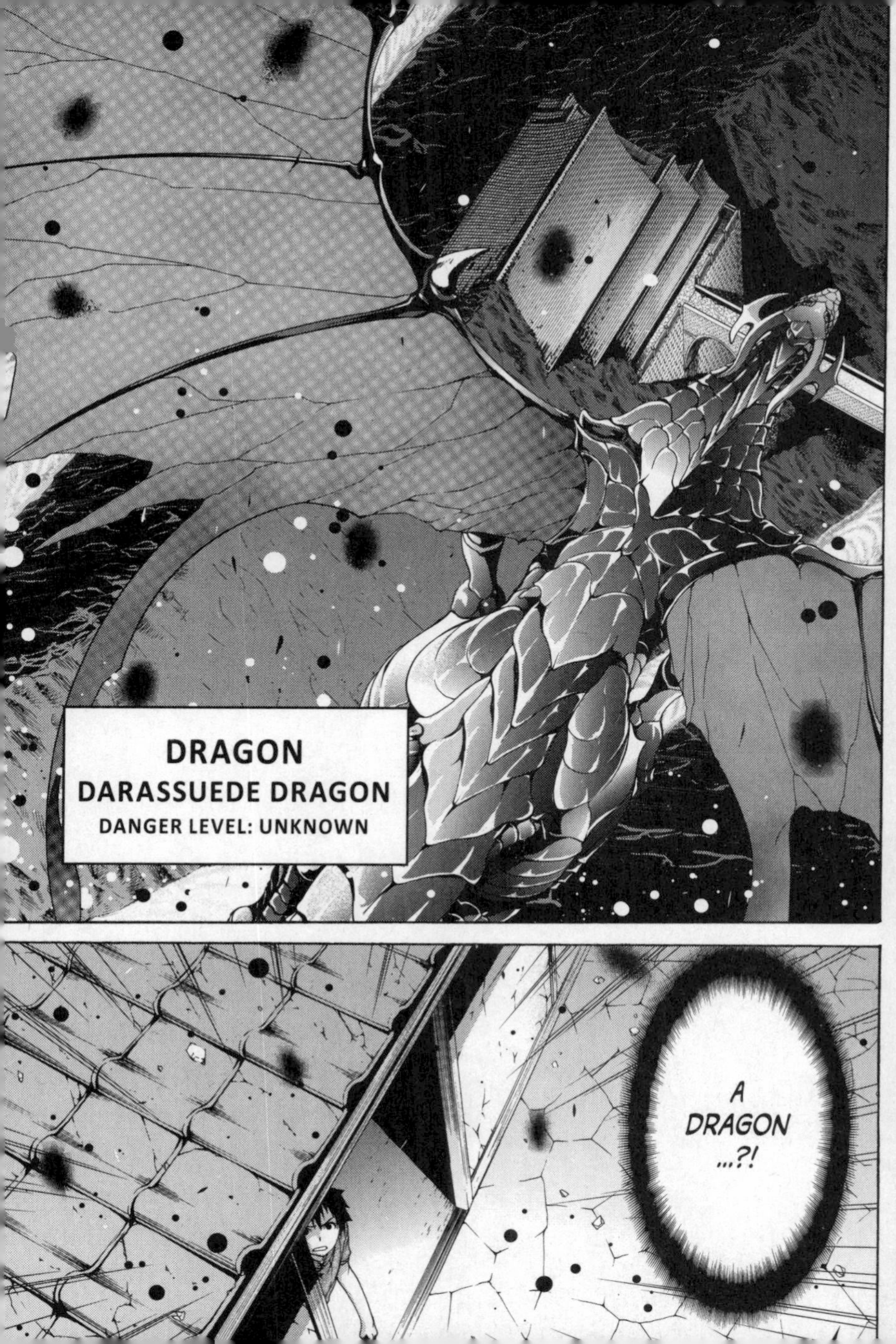
DRAGON
DARASSUEDE DRAGON
DANGER LEVEL: UNKNOWN
A DRAGON ...?!

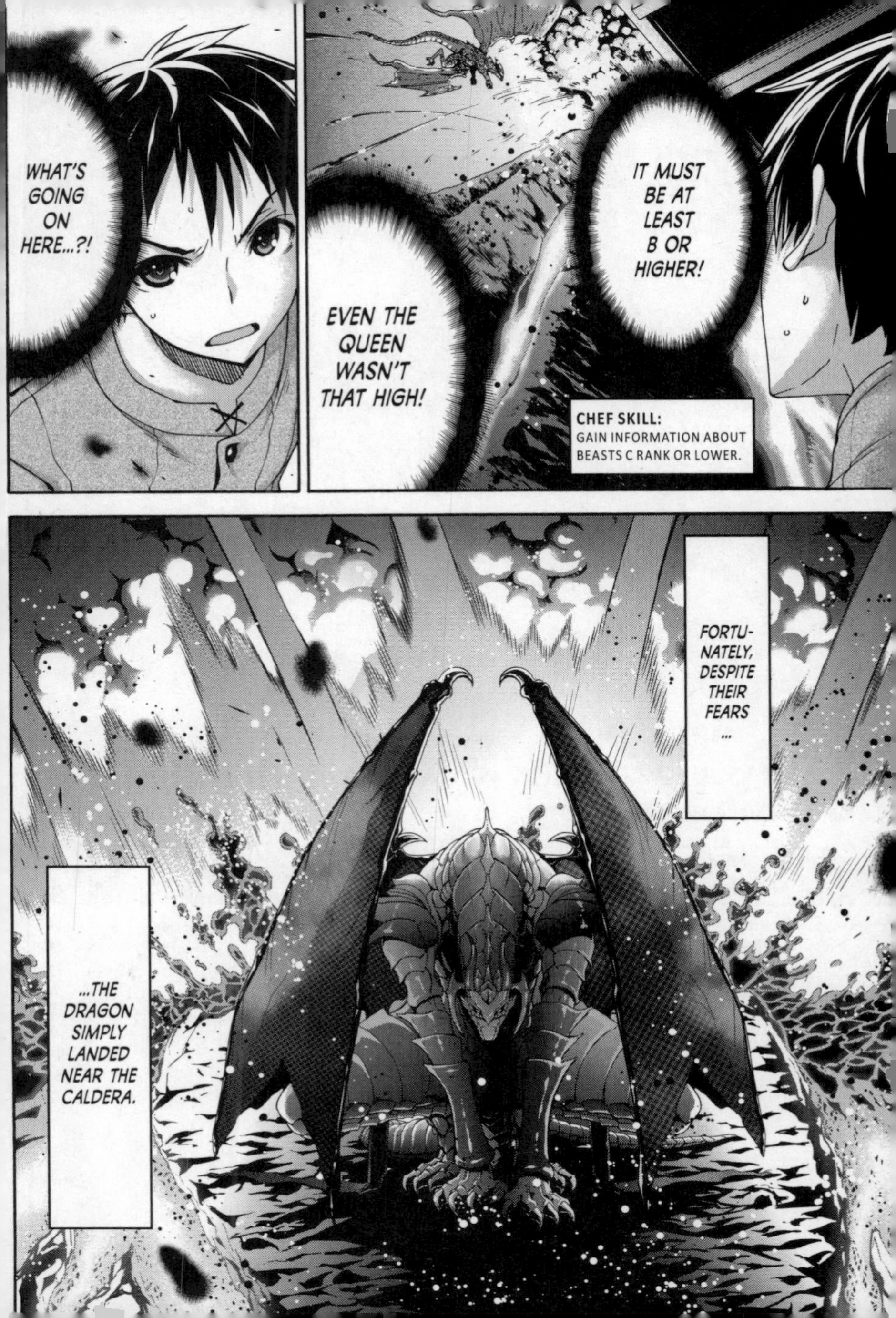
IT MUST BE AT LEAST B OR HIGHER!
EVEN THE QUEEN WASN'T THAT HIGH!
CHEF SKILL: GAIN INFORMATION ABOUT BEASTS C RANK OR LOWER.
WHAT'S GOING ON HERE...?!
FORTUNATELY, DESPITE THEIR FEARS ...
...THE DRAGON SIMPLY LANDED NEAR THE CALDERA.

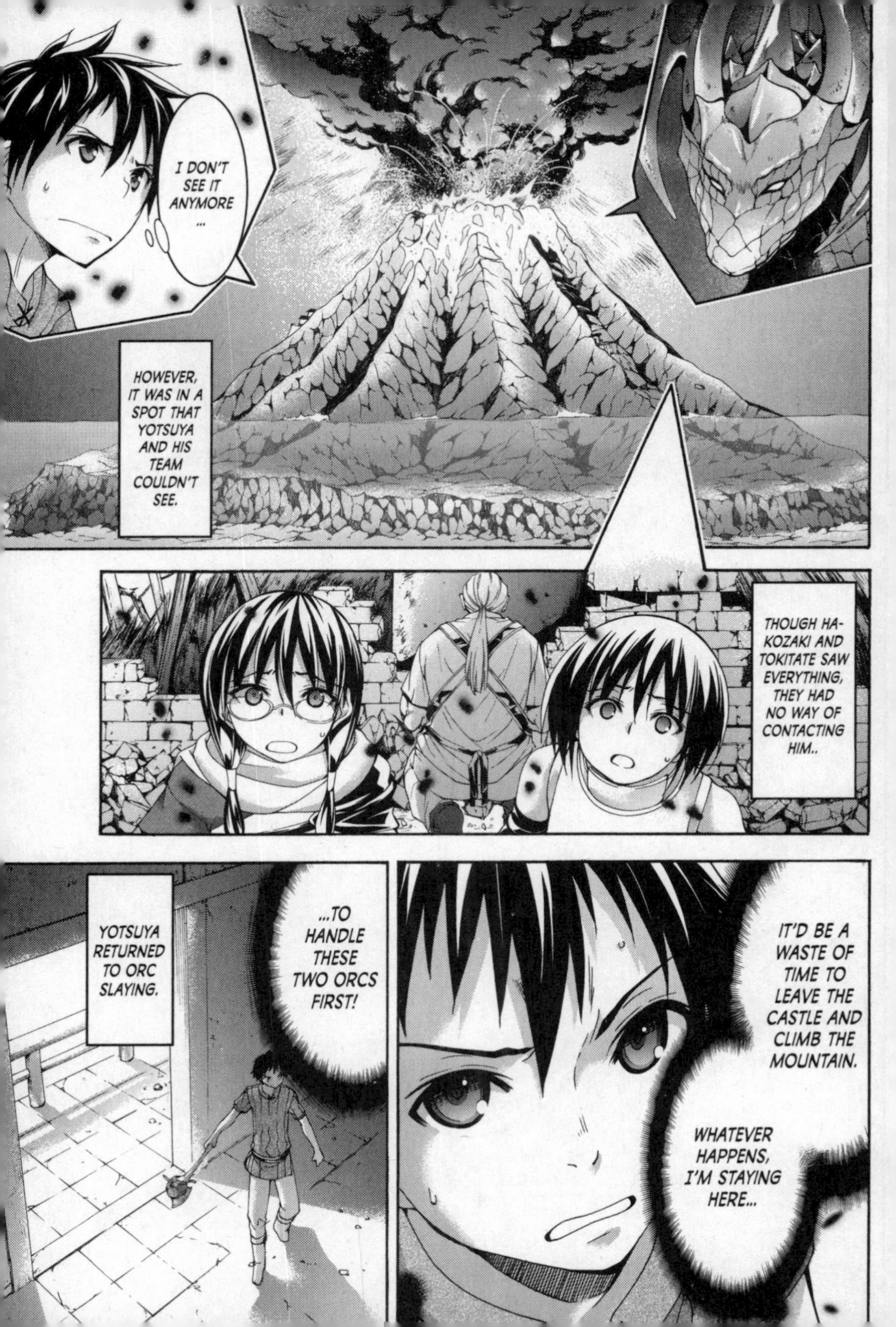
I DON'T SEE IT ANYMORE ...
HOWEVER, IT WAS IN A SPOT THAT YOTSUYA AND HIS TEAM COULDN'T SEE.
THOUGH HA-KOZAKI AND TOKITATE SAW EVERYTHING, THEY HAD NO WAY OF CONTACTING HIM..
IT'D BE A WASTE OF TIME TO LEAVE THE CASTLE AND CLIMB THE MOUNTAIN.
WHATEVER HAPPENS, I'M STAYING HERE...
...TO HANDLE THESE TWO ORCS FIRST!
YOTSUYA RETURNED TO ORC SLAYING.

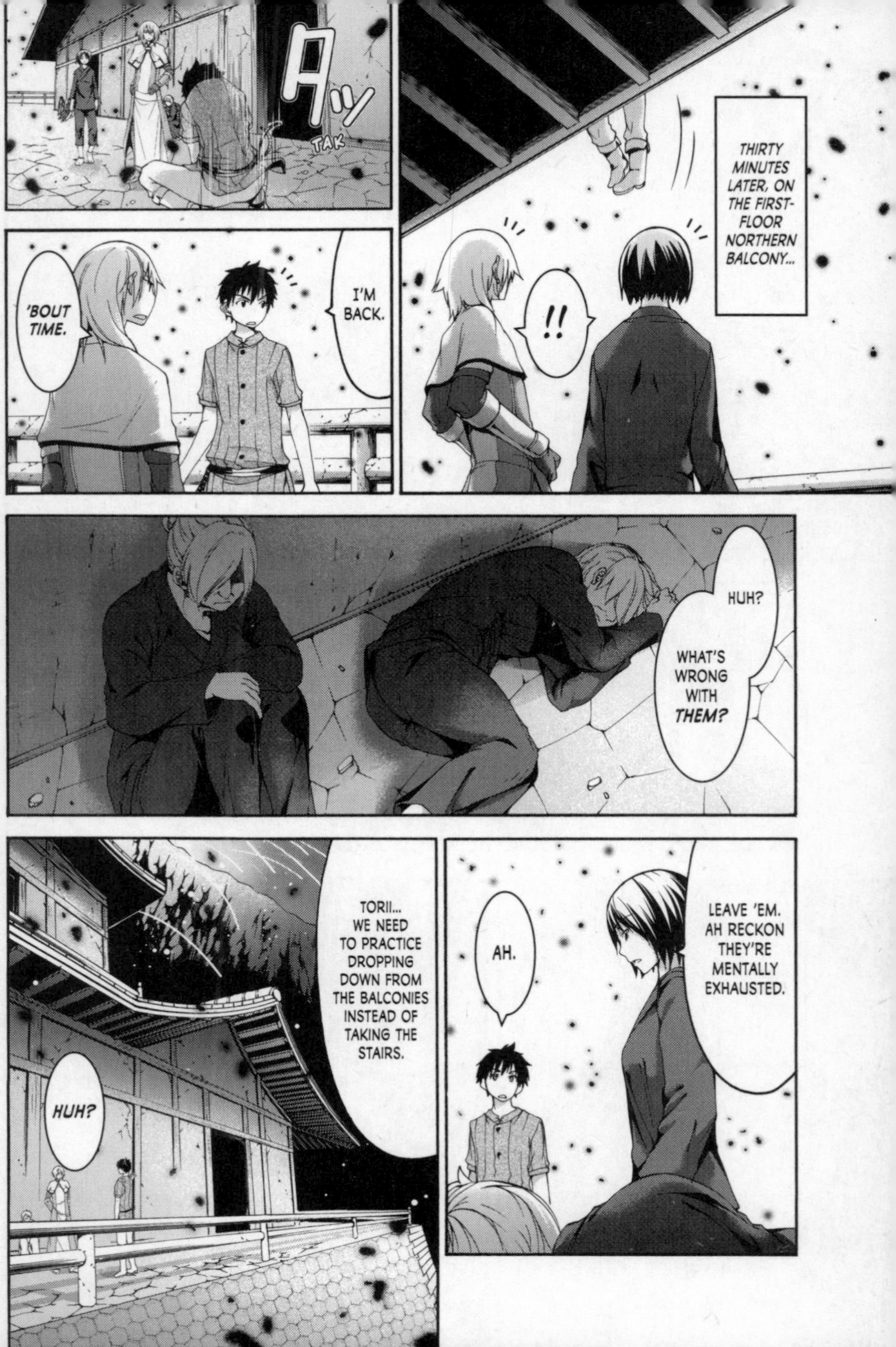
THIRTY MINUTES LATER, ON THE FIRST-FLOOR NORTHERN BALCONY...
!!
TAK
I'M BACK.
'BOUT TIME.
HUH?
WHAT'S WRONG WITH *THEM?*
LEAVE 'EM. AH RECKON THEY'RE MENTALLY EXHAUSTED.
AH.
TORII... WE NEED TO PRACTICE DROPPING DOWN FROM THE BALCONIES INSTEAD OF TAKING THE STAIRS.
HUH?

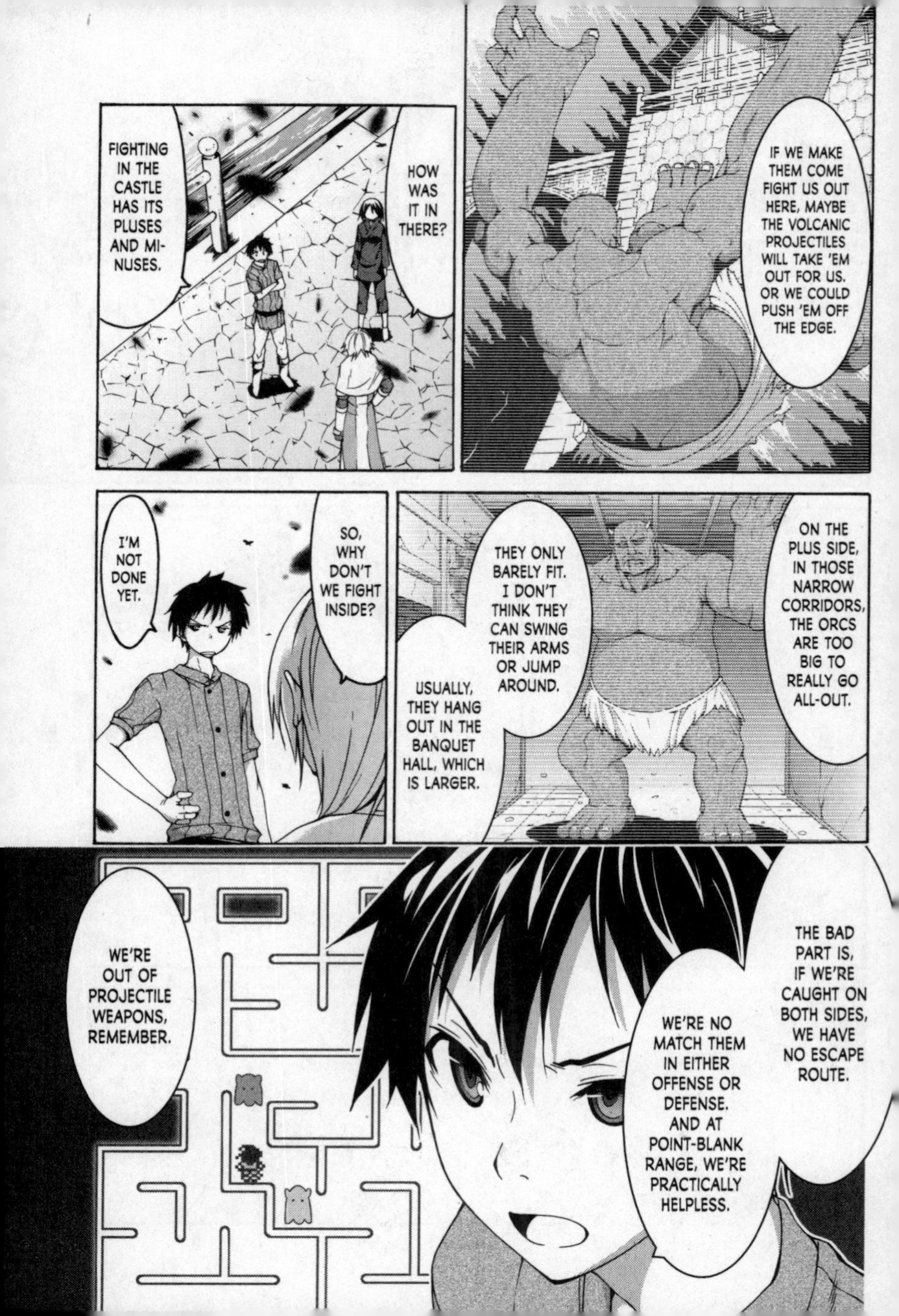
IF WE MAKE THEM COME FIGHT US OUT HERE, MAYBE THE VOLCANIC PROJECTILES WILL TAKE 'EM OUT FOR US. OR WE COULD PUSH 'EM OFF THE EDGE.
HOW WAS IT IN THERE?
FIGHTING IN THE CASTLE HAS ITS PLUSES AND MI-NUSES.
ON THE PLUS SIDE, IN THOSE NARROW CORRIDORS, THE ORCS ARE TOO BIG TO REALLY GO ALL-OUT.
THEY ONLY BARELY FIT. I DON'T THINK THEY CAN SWING THEIR ARMS OR JUMP AROUND.
USUALLY, THEY HANG OUT IN THE BANQUET HALL, WHICH IS LARGER.
SO, WHY DON'T WE FIGHT INSIDE?
I'M NOT DONE YET.
THE BAD PART IS, IF WE'RE CAUGHT ON BOTH SIDES, WE HAVE NO ESCAPE ROUTE.
WE'RE NO MATCH THEM IN EITHER OFFENSE OR DEFENSE. AND AT POINT-BLANK RANGE, WE'RE PRACTICALLY HELPLESS.
WE'RE OUT OF PROJECTILE WEAPONS, REMEMBER.

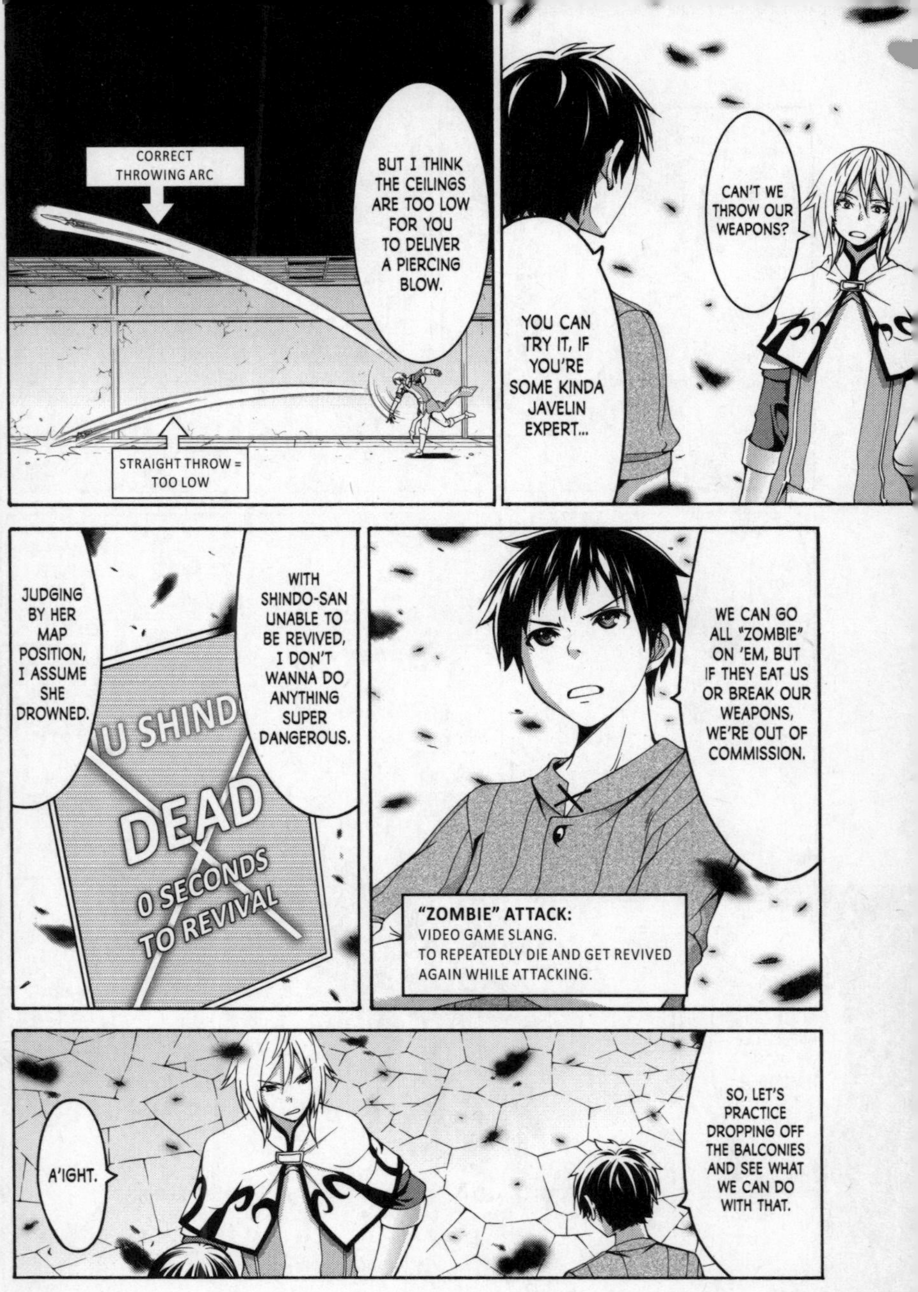
CAN'T WE THROW OUR WEAPONS?
YOU CAN TRY IT, IF YOU'RE SOME KINDA JAVELIN EXPERT...
BUT I THINK THE CEILINGS ARE TOO LOW FOR YOU TO DELIVER A PIERCING BLOW.
CORRECT THROWING ARC
STRAIGHT THROW = TOO LOW
WE CAN GO ALL "ZOMBIE" ON 'EM, BUT IF THEY EAT US OR BREAK OUR WEAPONS, WE'RE OUT OF COMMISSION.
"ZOMBIE" ATTACK:
VIDEO GAME SLANG.
TO REPEATEDLY DIE AND GET REVIVED AGAIN WHILE ATTACKING.
WITH SHINDO-SAN UNABLE TO BE REVIVED, I DON'T WANNA DO ANYTHING SUPER DANGEROUS.
JUDGING BY HER MAP POSITION, I ASSUME SHE DROWNED.
U SHIND
DEAD
0 SECONDS TO REVIVAL
SO, LET'S PRACTICE DROPPING OFF THE BALCONIES AND SEE WHAT WE CAN DO WITH THAT.
A'IGHT.

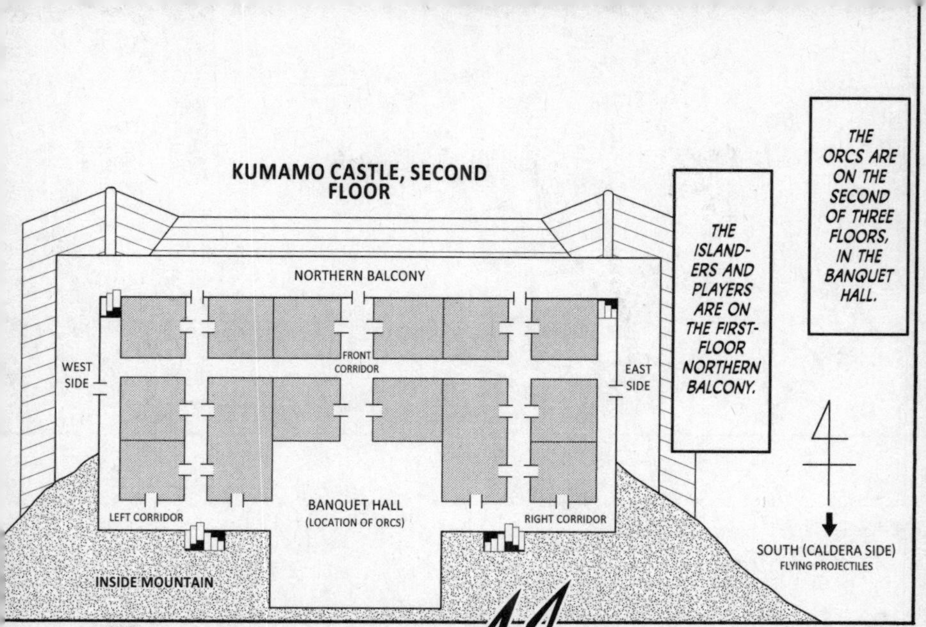
THE ORCS ARE ON THE SECOND OF THREE FLOORS, IN THE BANQUET HALL.
THE ISLANDERS AND PLAYERS ARE ON THE FIRST-FLOOR NORTHERN BALCONY.
KUMAMO CASTLE, SECOND FLOOR
NORTHERN BALCONY
FRONT CORRIDOR
WEST SIDE
EAST SIDE
LEFT CORRIDOR
BANQUET HALL
(LOCATION OF ORCS)
RIGHT CORRIDOR
INSIDE MOUNTAIN
SOUTH (CALDERA SIDE)
FLYING PROJECTILES

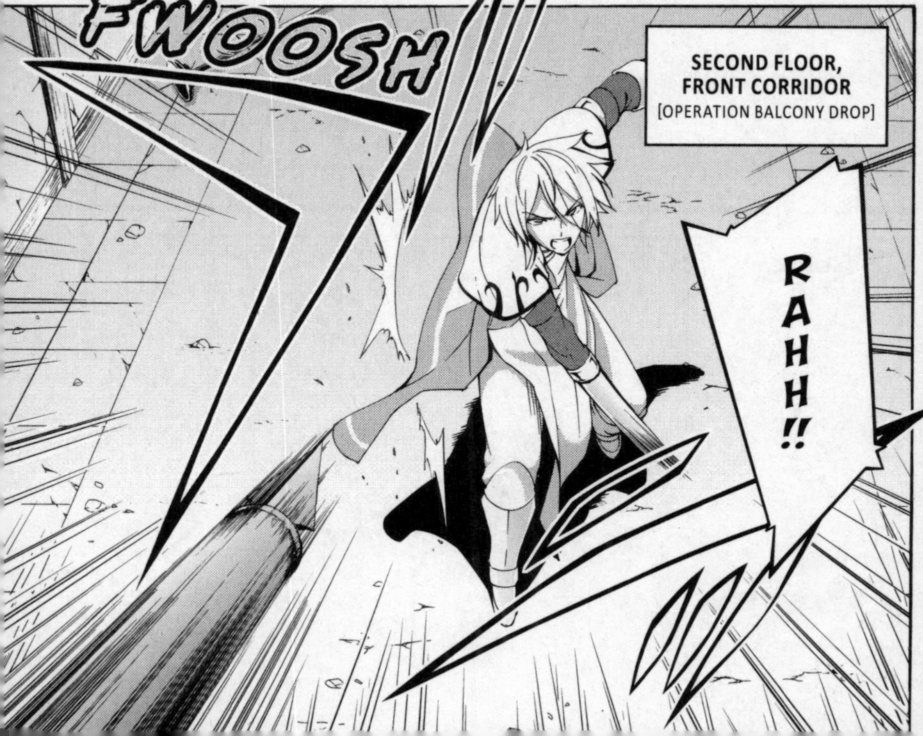
SECOND FLOOR, FRONT CORRIDOR
[OPERATION BALCONY DROP]
RAHH!!
FWOOSH

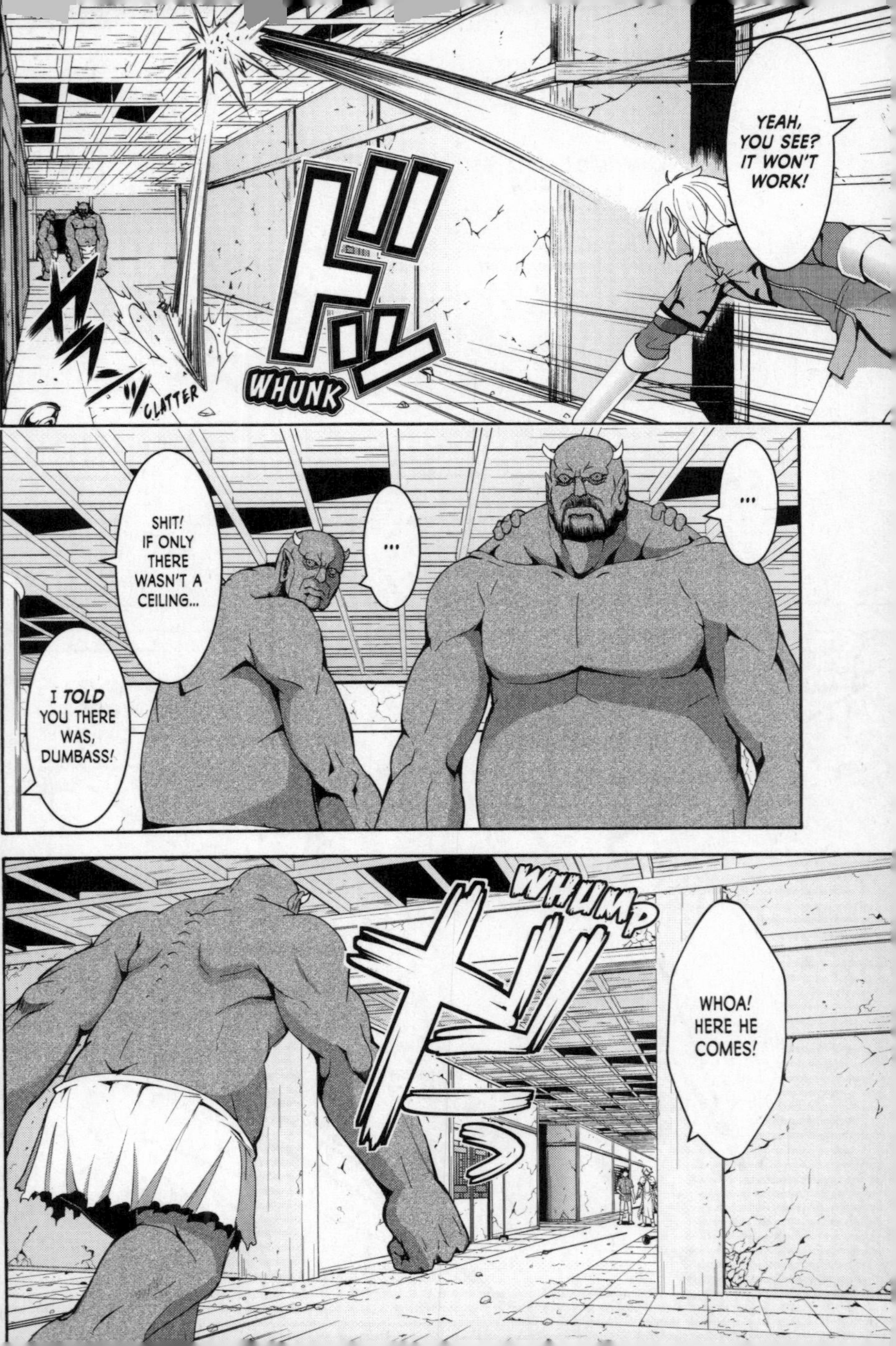
YEAH, YOU SEE? IT WON'T WORK!
WHUNK
CLATTER
...
...
SHIT! IF ONLY THERE WASN'T A CEILING...
I *TOLD* YOU THERE WAS, DUMBASS!
WHUMP
WHOA! HERE HE COMES!

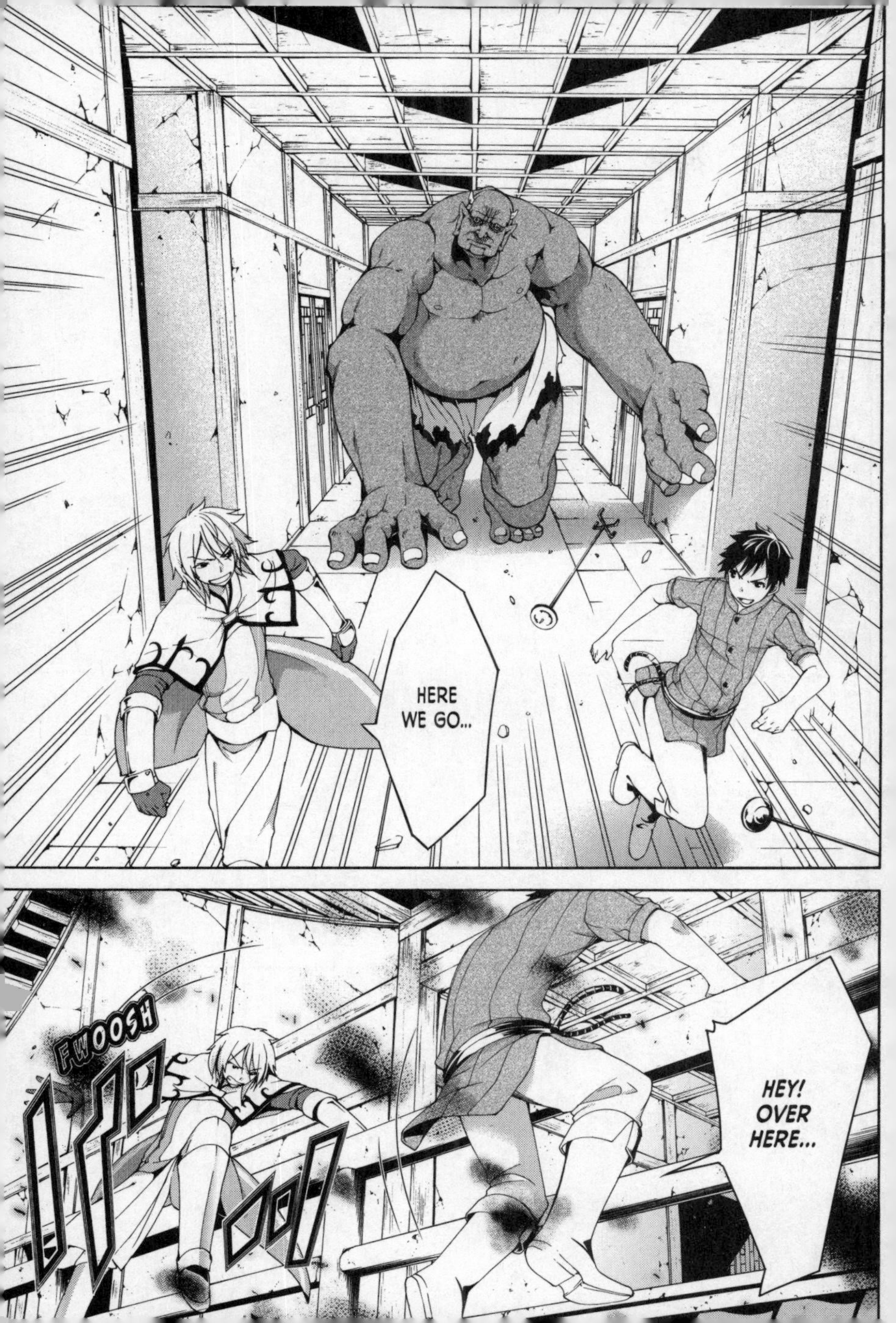
HERE WE GO...
HEY! OVER HERE...
FWOOSH

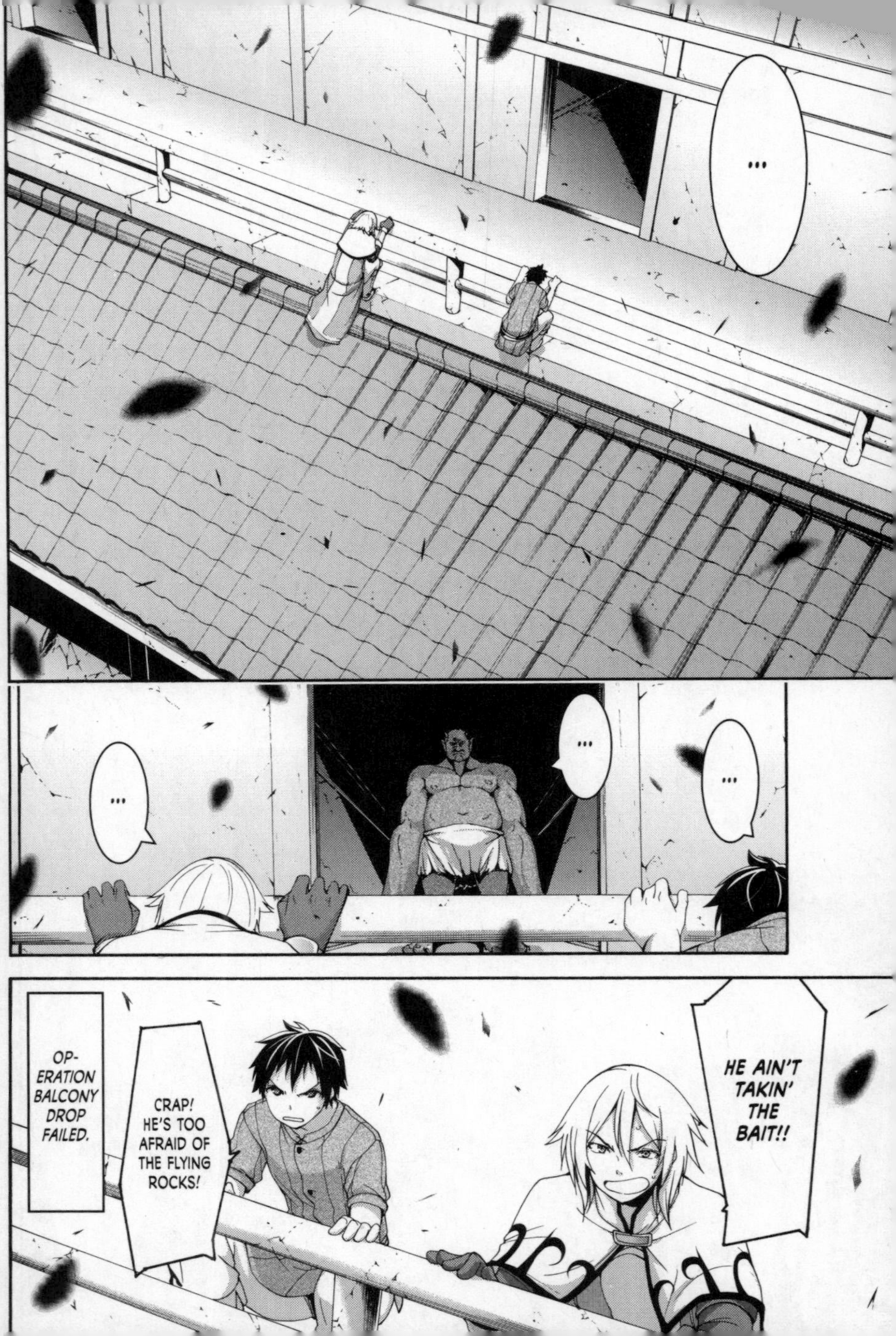
...
...
...
...
HE AIN'T TAKIN' THE BAIT!!
CRAP! HE'S TOO AFRAID OF THE FLYING ROCKS!
OP-ERATION BALCONY DROP FAILED.

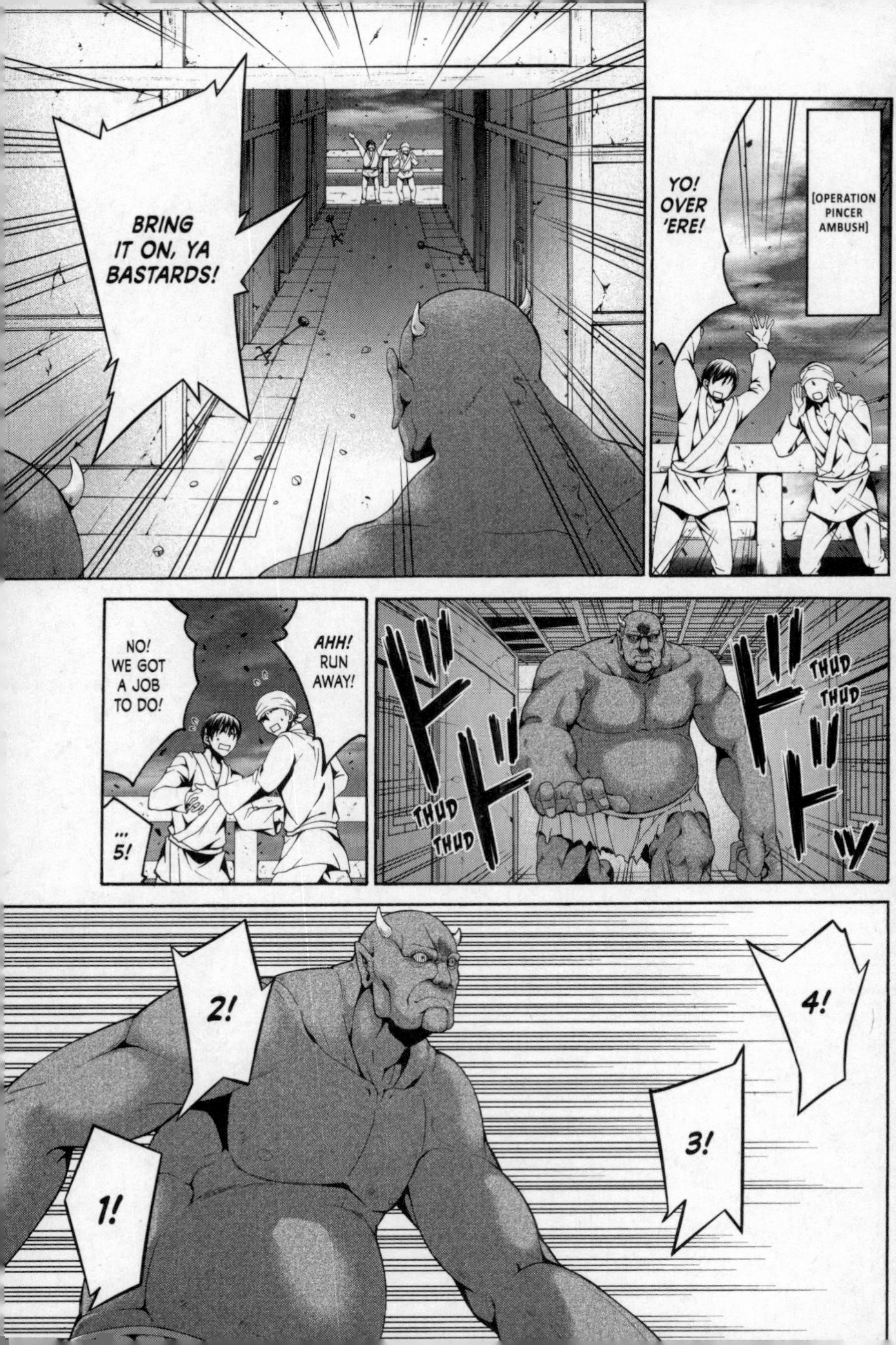
[OPERATION PINCER AMBUSH]
YO! OVER 'ERE!
BRING IT ON, YA BASTARDS!
ドドドッ
THUD THUD
ドドド
THUD THUD
AHH! RUN AWAY!
NO! WE GOT A JOB TO DO!
...5!
4!
3!
2!
1!

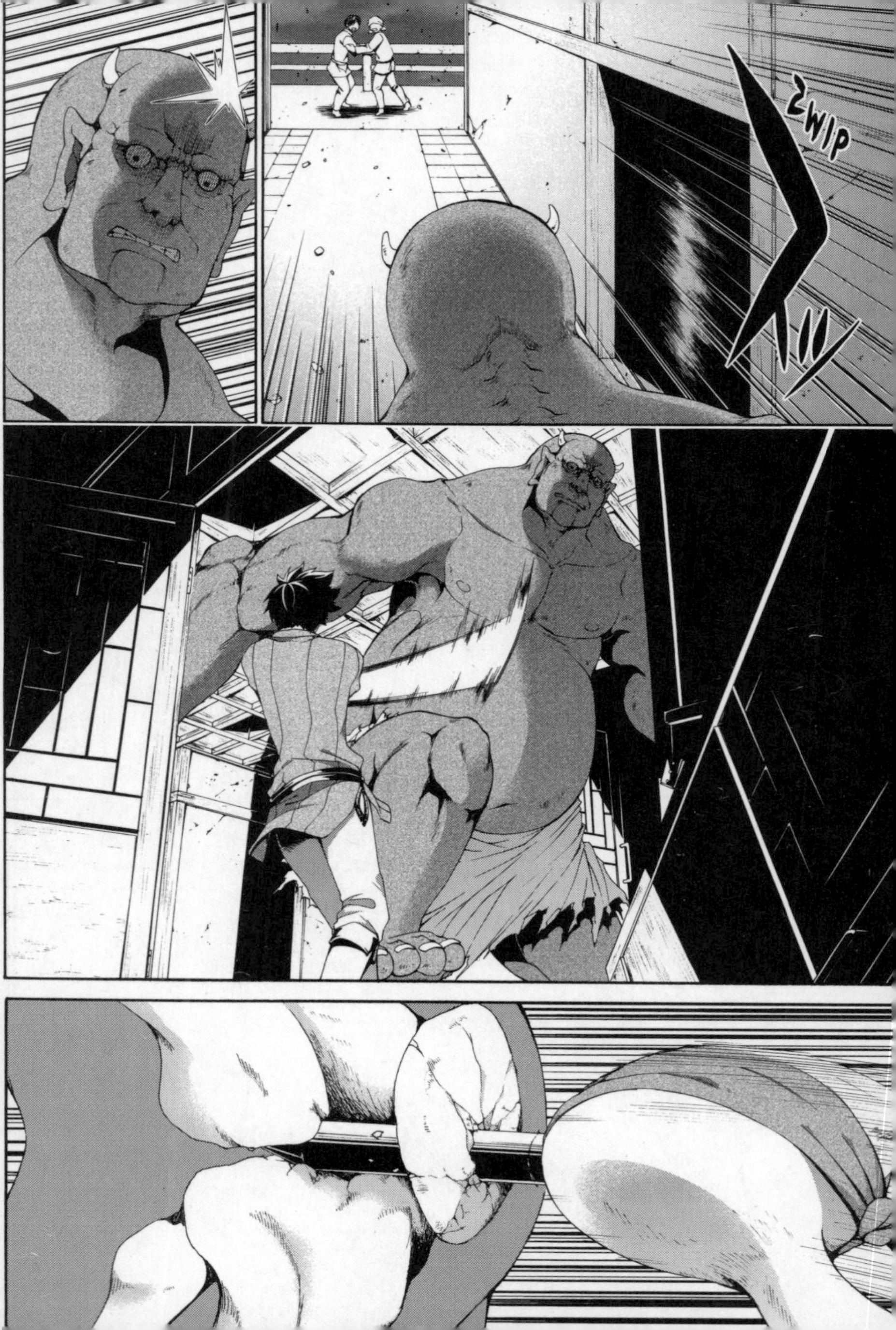
ZWIP

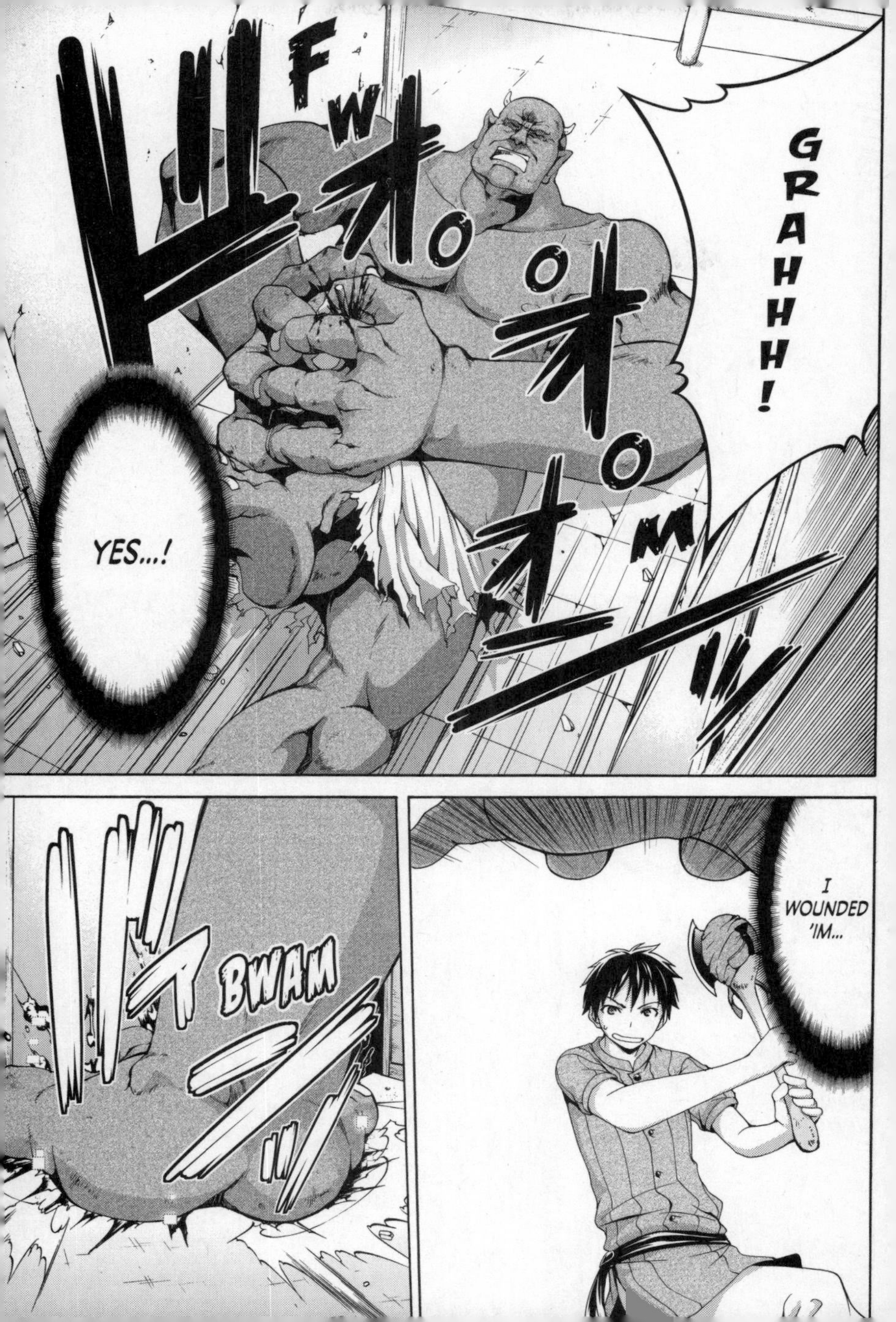
GRAHHH!
FWOOOM
YES...!
I WOUNDED 'IM...
BWAM

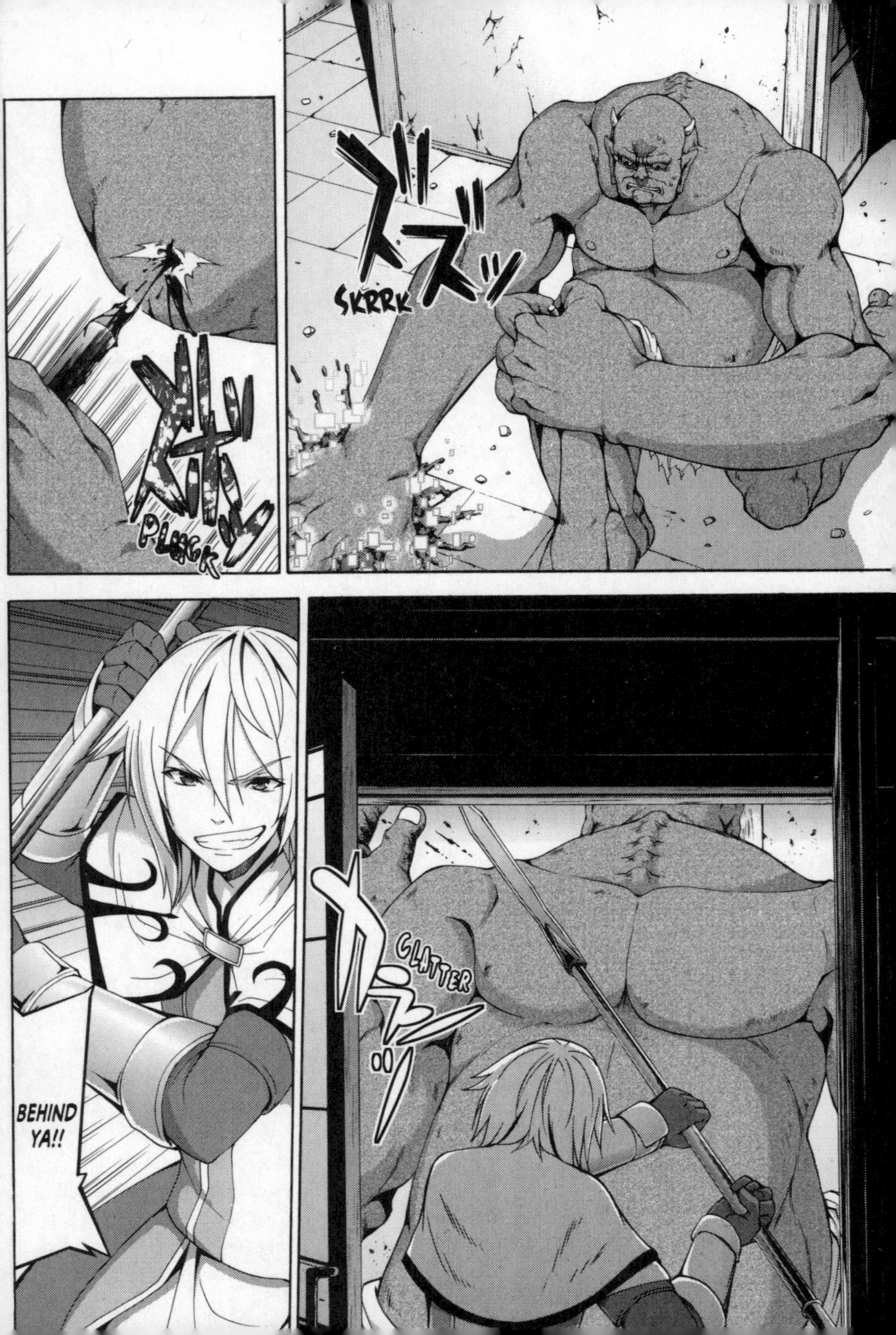
SKRRK
PLUCK
CLATTER
BEHIND YA!!

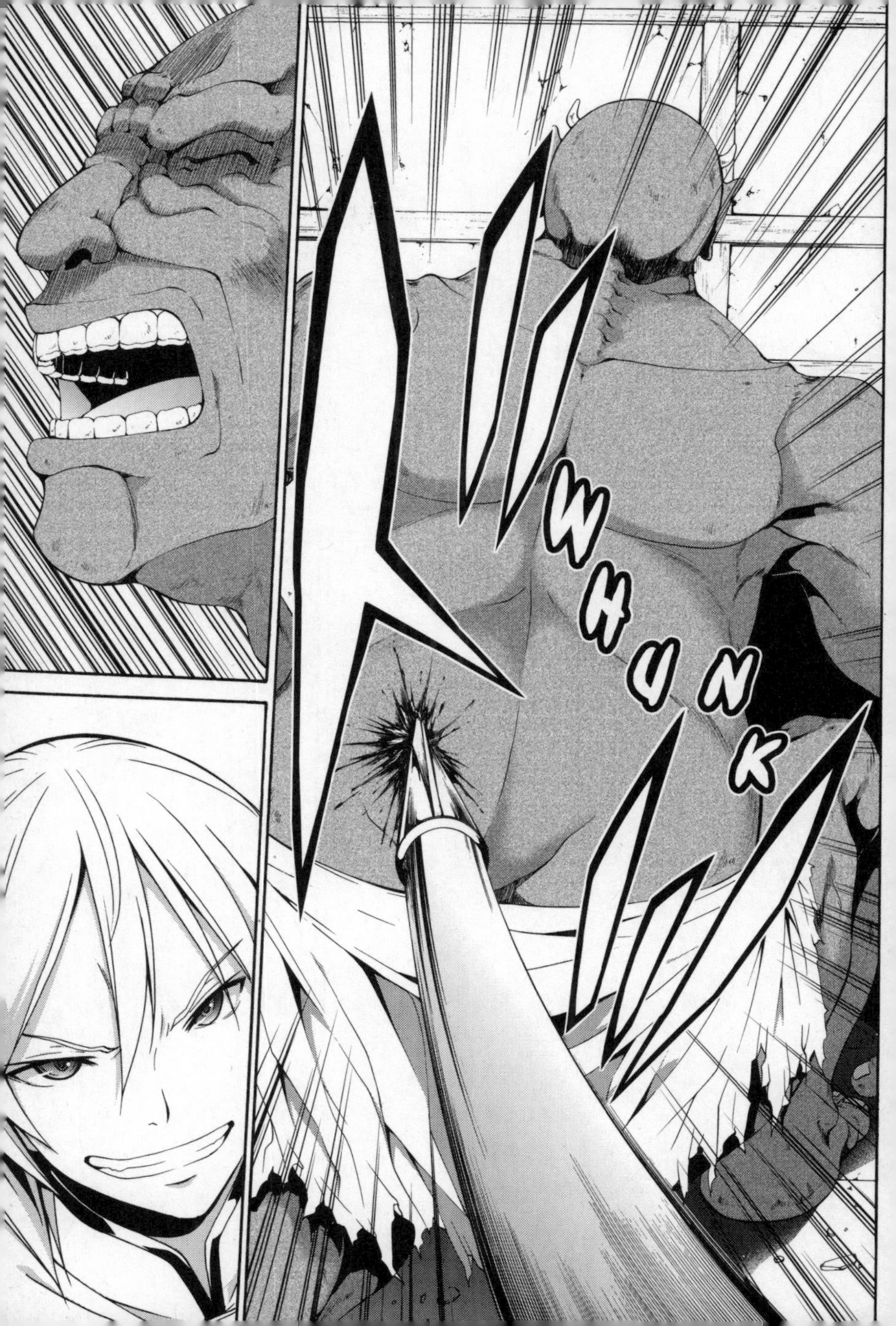
WHUNK

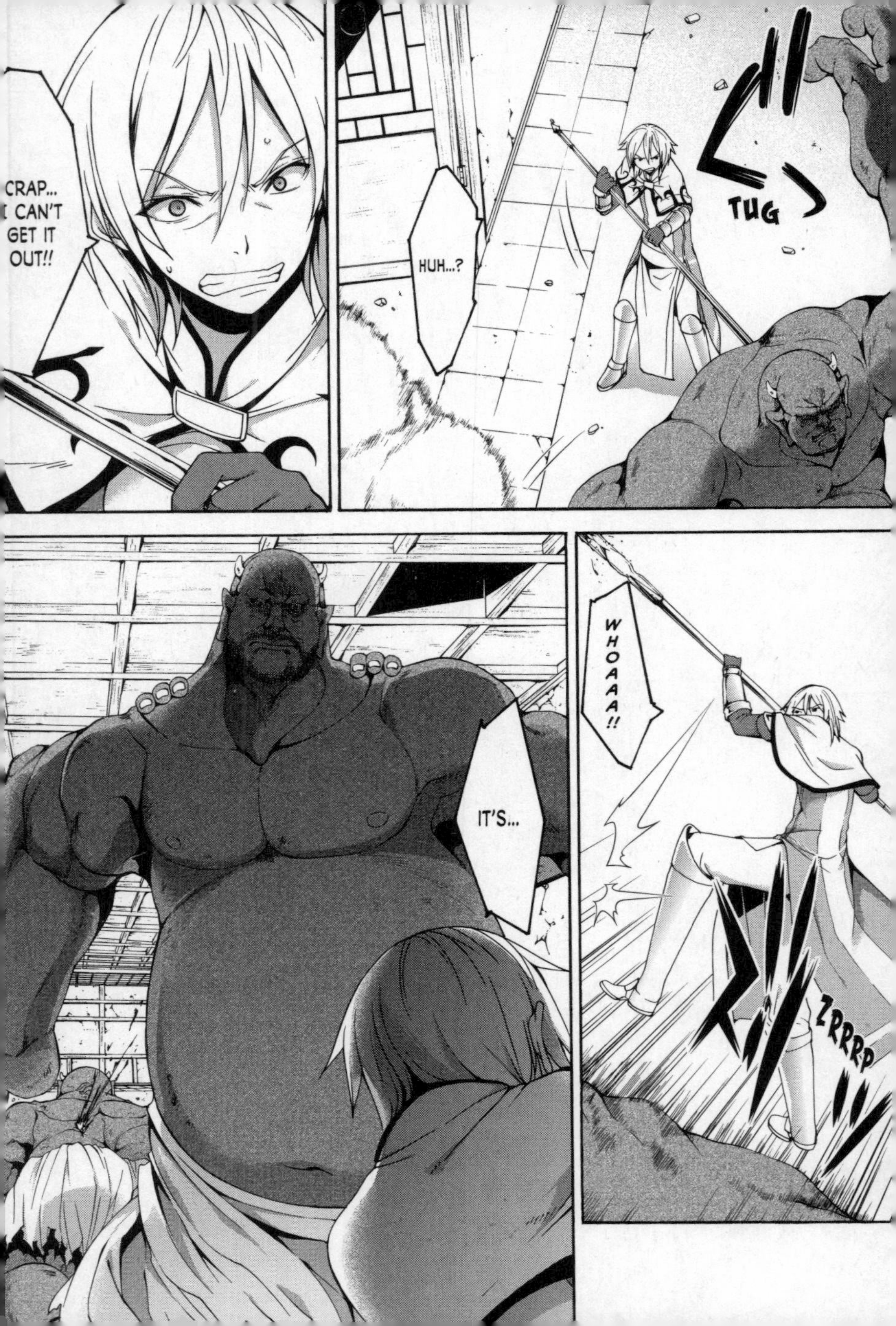
TUG
HUH...?
CRAP... I CAN'T GET IT OUT!!
WHOAAAA!!
ZRRRP
IT'S...

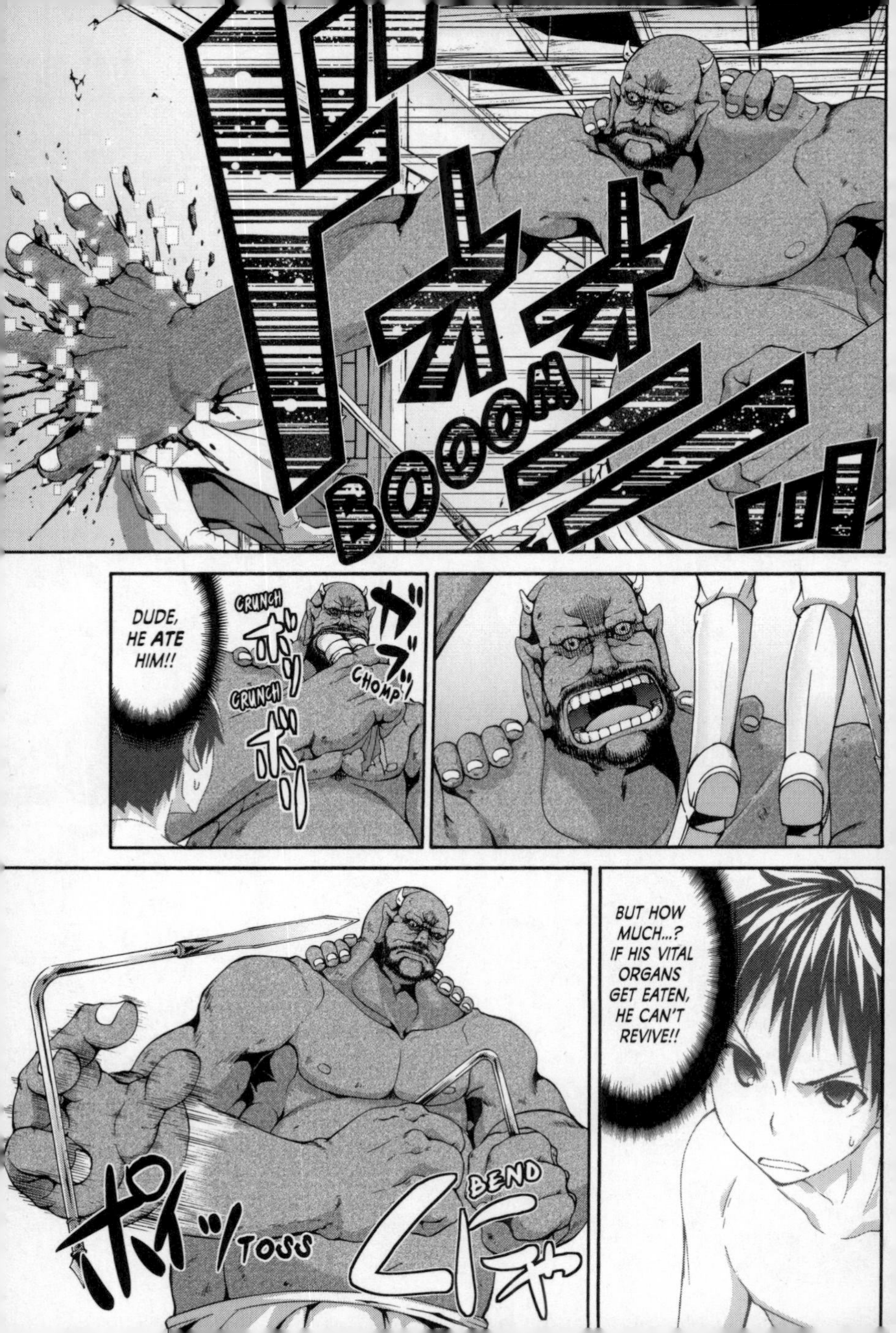

BOOOOM
CHOMP
CRUNCH
CRUNCH
DUDE, HE ATE HIM!!
BUT HOW MUCH...? IF HIS VITAL ORGANS GET EATEN, HE CAN'T REVIVE!!
BEND
TOSS

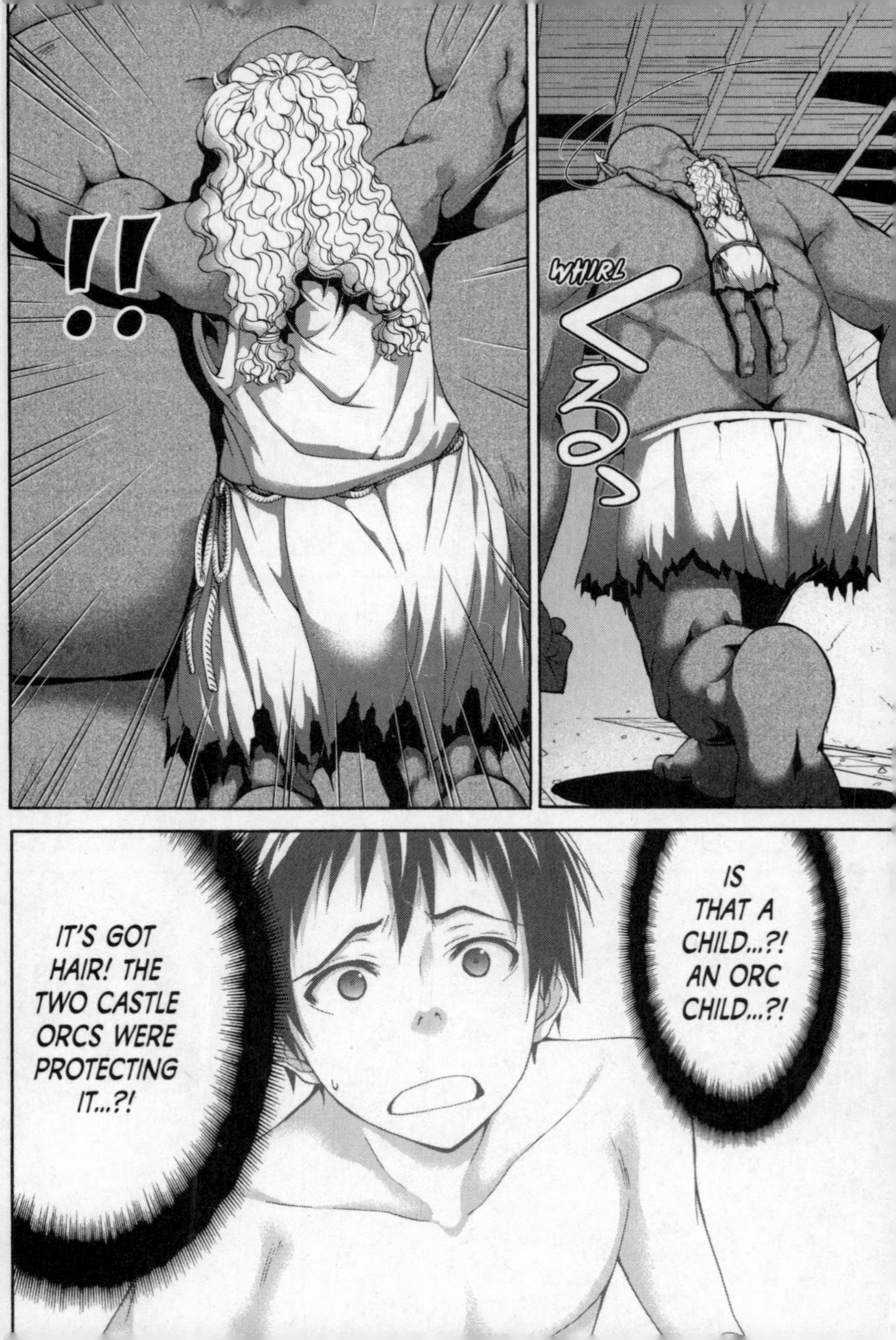
WHIRL
くるっ
!!
IS THAT A CHILD...?! AN ORC CHILD...?!
IT'S GOT HAIR! THE TWO CASTLE ORCS WERE PROTECTING IT...?!

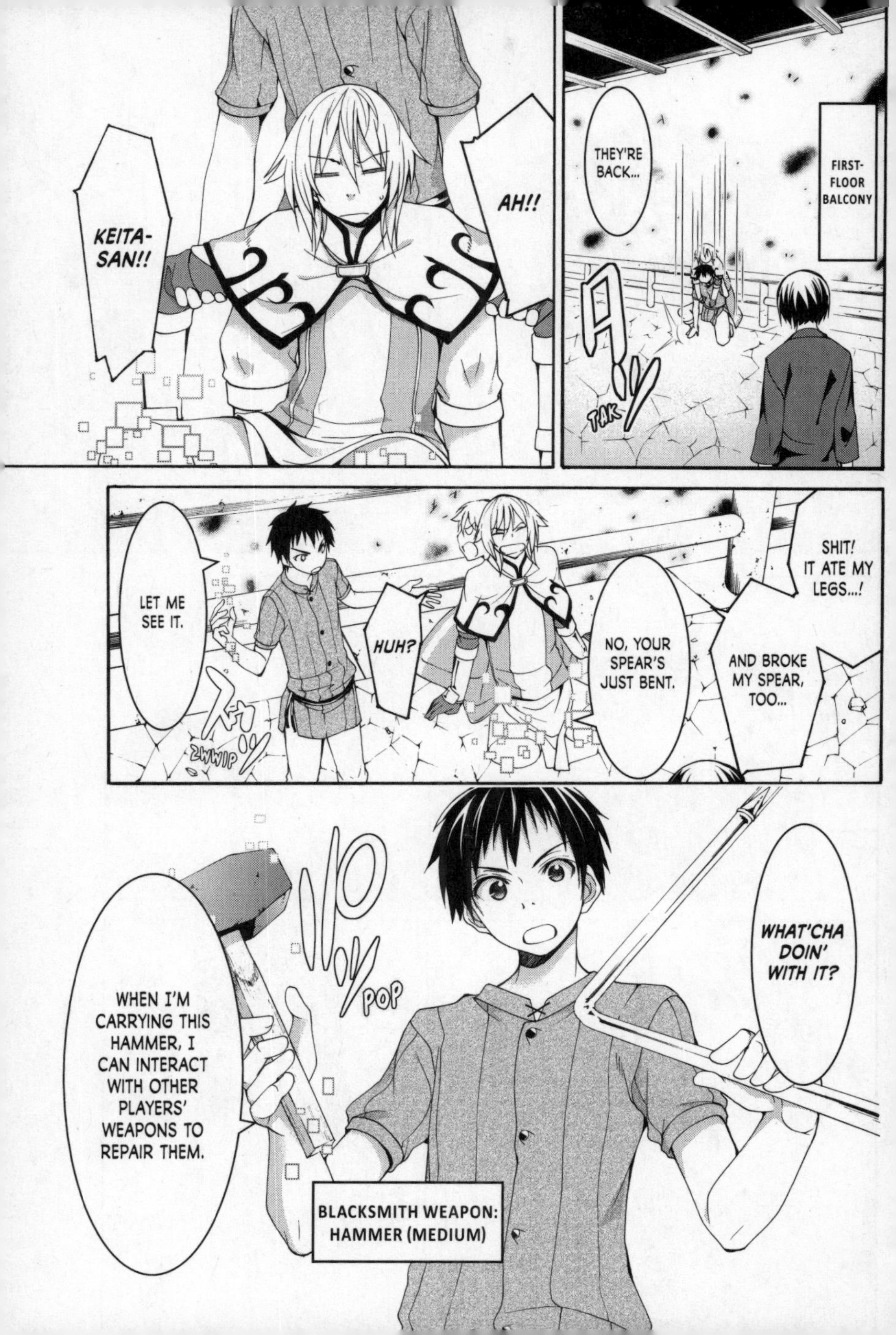
FIRST-FLOOR BALCONY
THEY'RE BACK...
TAK
AH!!
KEITA-SAN!!
SHIT! IT ATE MY LEGS...!
AND BROKE MY SPEAR, TOO...
NO, YOUR SPEAR'S JUST BENT.
HUH?
LET ME SEE IT.
ZWWIP
WHAT'CHA DOIN' WITH IT?
POP
WHEN I'M CARRYING THIS HAMMER, I CAN INTERACT WITH OTHER PLAYERS' WEAPONS TO REPAIR THEM.
BLACKSMITH WEAPON: HAMMER (MEDIUM)

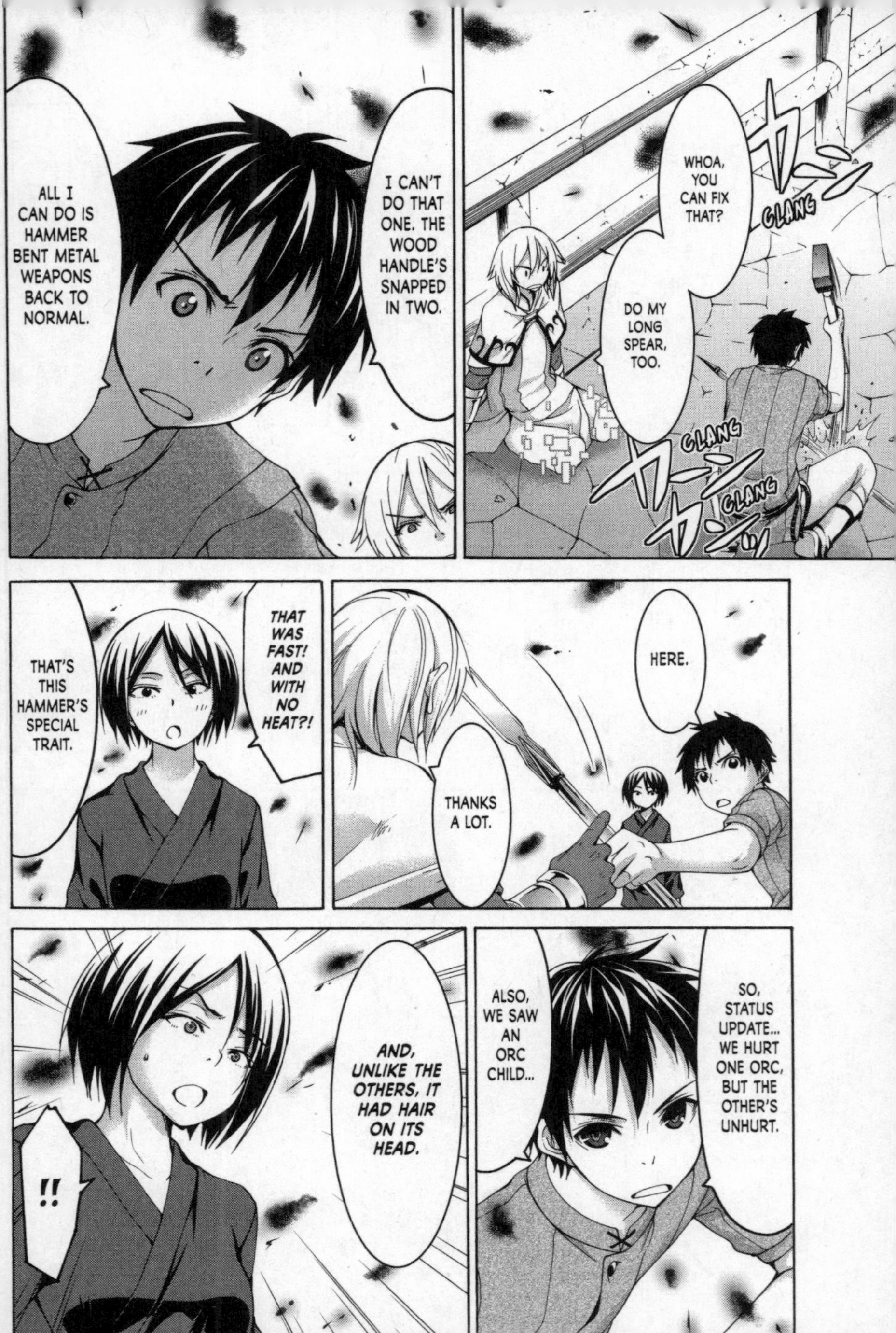
WHOA, YOU CAN FIX THAT?
CLANG
DO MY LONG SPEAR, TOO.
CLANG
CLANG
I CAN'T DO THAT ONE. THE WOOD HANDLE'S SNAPPED IN TWO.
ALL I CAN DO IS HAMMER BENT METAL WEAPONS BACK TO NORMAL.
HERE.
THANKS A LOT.
THAT WAS FAST! AND WITH NO HEAT?!
THAT'S THIS HAMMER'S SPECIAL TRAIT.
SO, STATUS UPDATE... WE HURT ONE ORC, BUT THE OTHER'S UNHURT.
ALSO, WE SAW AN ORC CHILD...
AND, UNLIKE THE OTHERS, IT HAD HAIR ON ITS HEAD.
!!

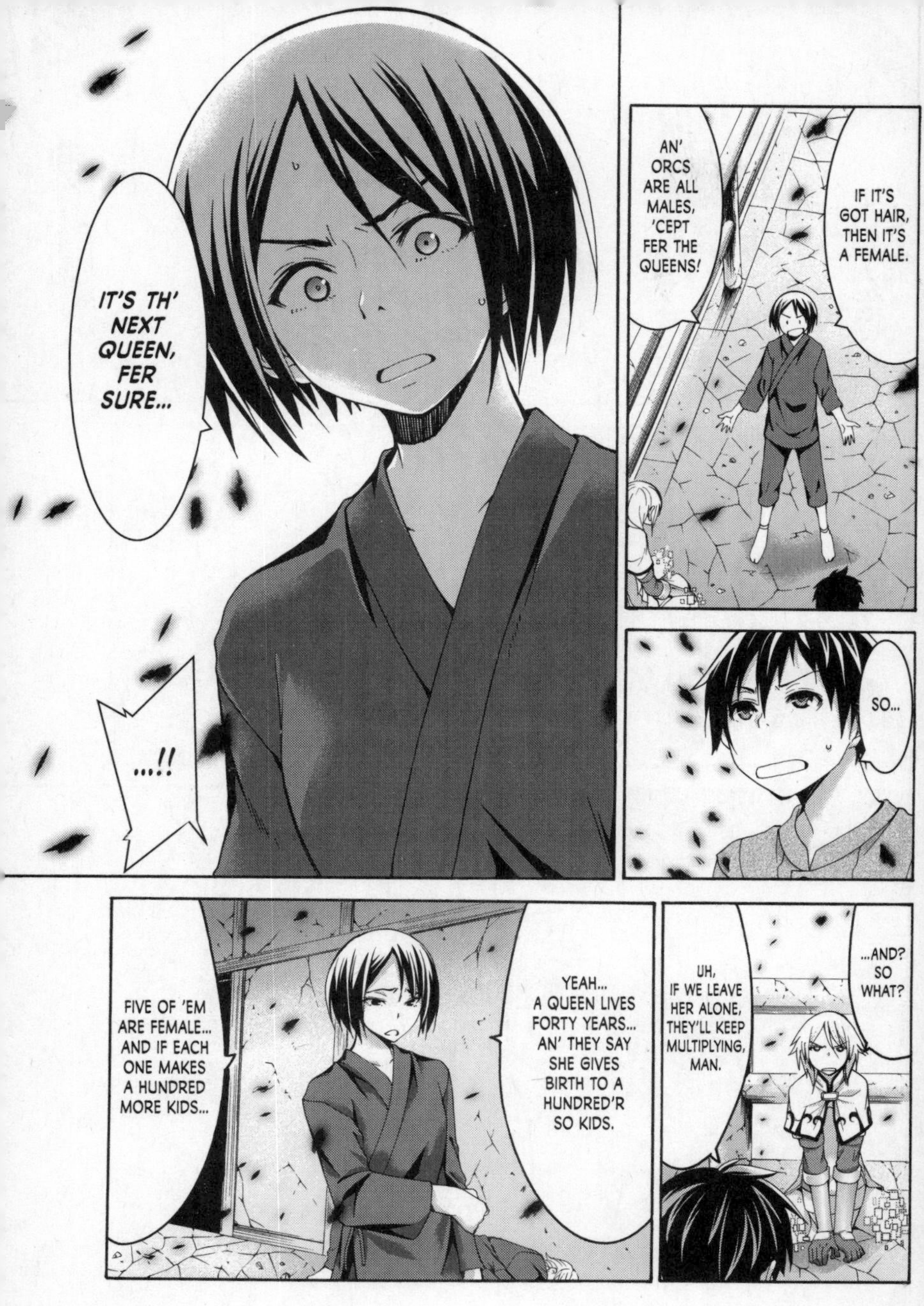
IF IT'S GOT HAIR, THEN IT'S A FEMALE.
AN' ORCS ARE ALL MALES, 'CEPT FER THE QUEENS!
SO...
IT'S TH' NEXT QUEEN, FER SURE...
...!!
...AND? SO WHAT?
UH, IF WE LEAVE HER ALONE, THEY'LL KEEP MULTIPLYING, MAN.
YEAH... A QUEEN LIVES FORTY YEARS... AN' THEY SAY SHE GIVES BIRTH TO A HUNDRED'R SO KIDS.
FIVE OF 'EM ARE FEMALE... AND IF EACH ONE MAKES A HUNDRED MORE KIDS...

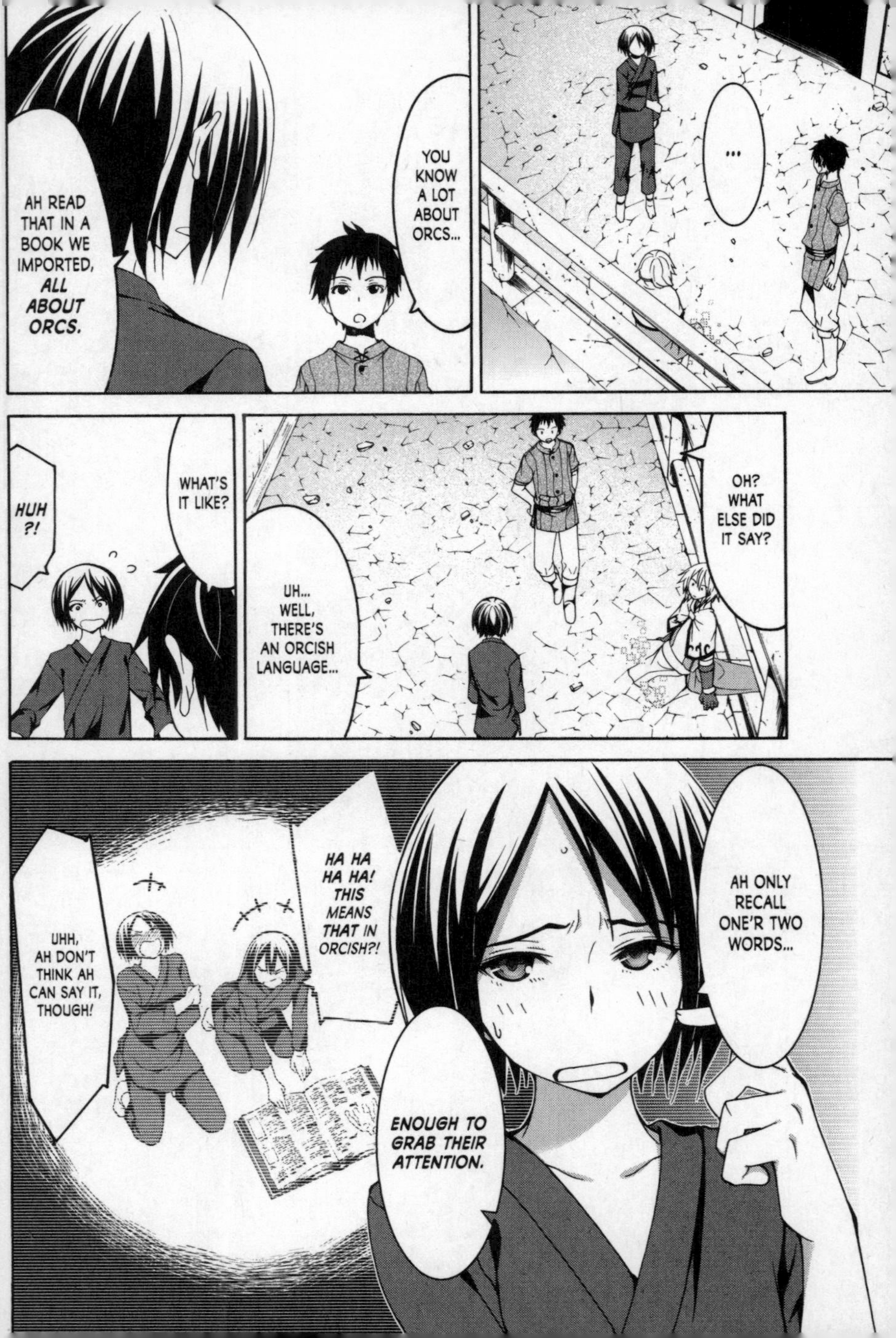
...
YOU KNOW A LOT ABOUT ORCS...
AH READ THAT IN A BOOK WE IMPORTED, ALL ABOUT ORCS.
OH? WHAT ELSE DID IT SAY?
UH... WELL, THERE'S AN ORCISH LANGUAGE...
WHAT'S IT LIKE?
HUH?!
AH ONLY RECALL ONE'R TWO WORDS...
ENOUGH TO GRAB THEIR ATTENTION.
HA HA HA HA! THIS MEANS THAT IN ORCISH?!
UHH, AH DON'T THINK AH CAN SAY IT, THOUGH!

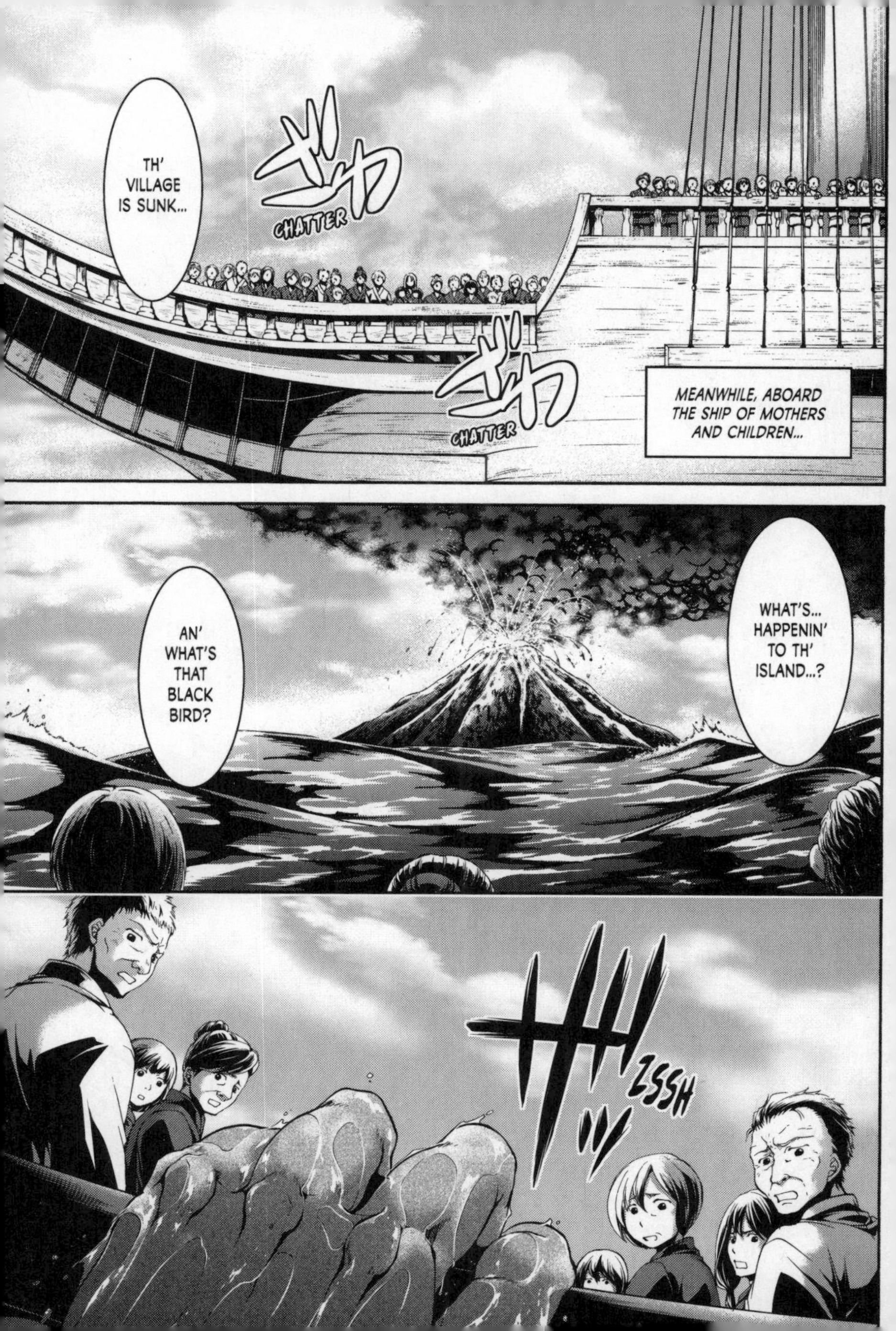
MEANWHILE, ABOARD THE SHIP OF MOTHERS AND CHILDREN...
CHATTER
CHATTER
TH' VILLAGE IS SUNK...
WHAT'S... HAPPENIN' TO TH' ISLAND...?
AN' WHAT'S THAT BLACK BIRD?
ZSSH

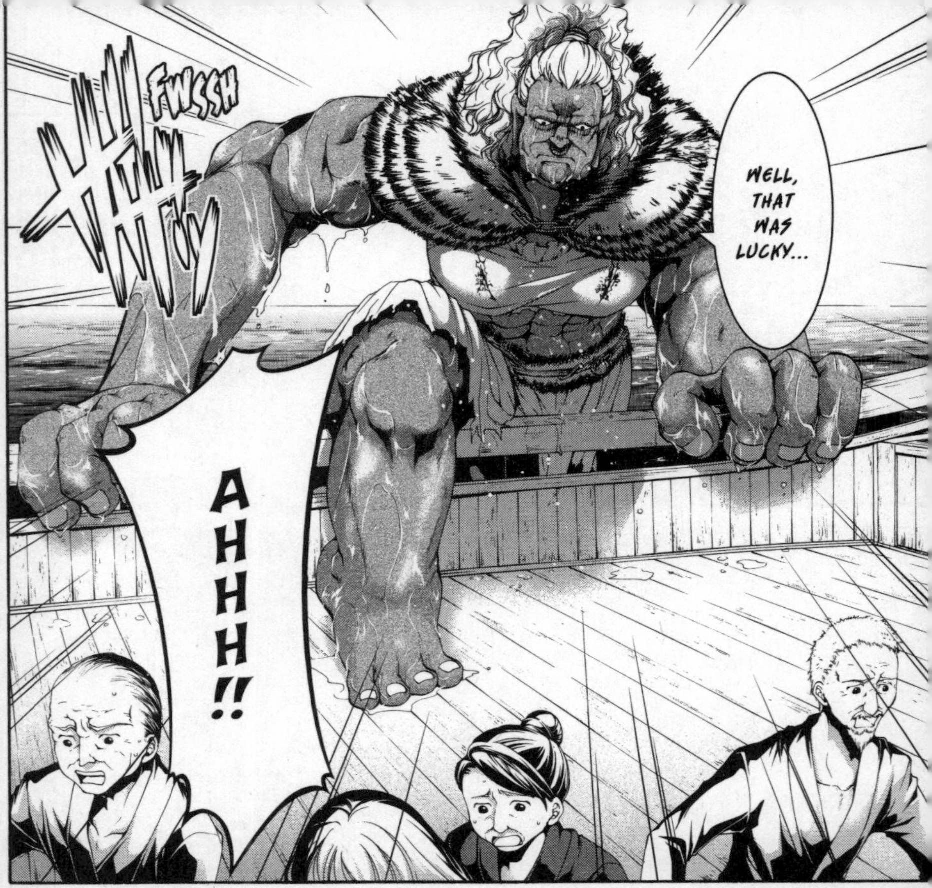
WELL, THAT WAS LUCKY...
FWSSH
AHHHH!!
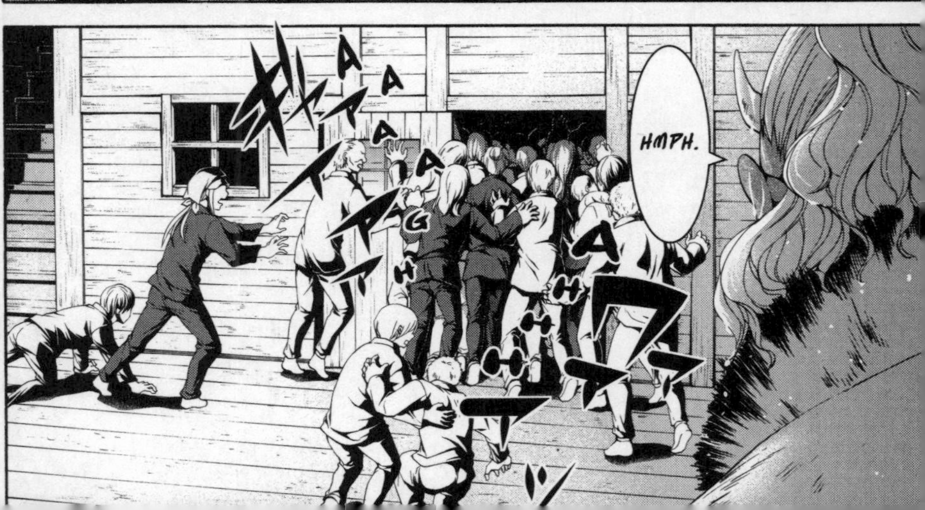
HMPH.

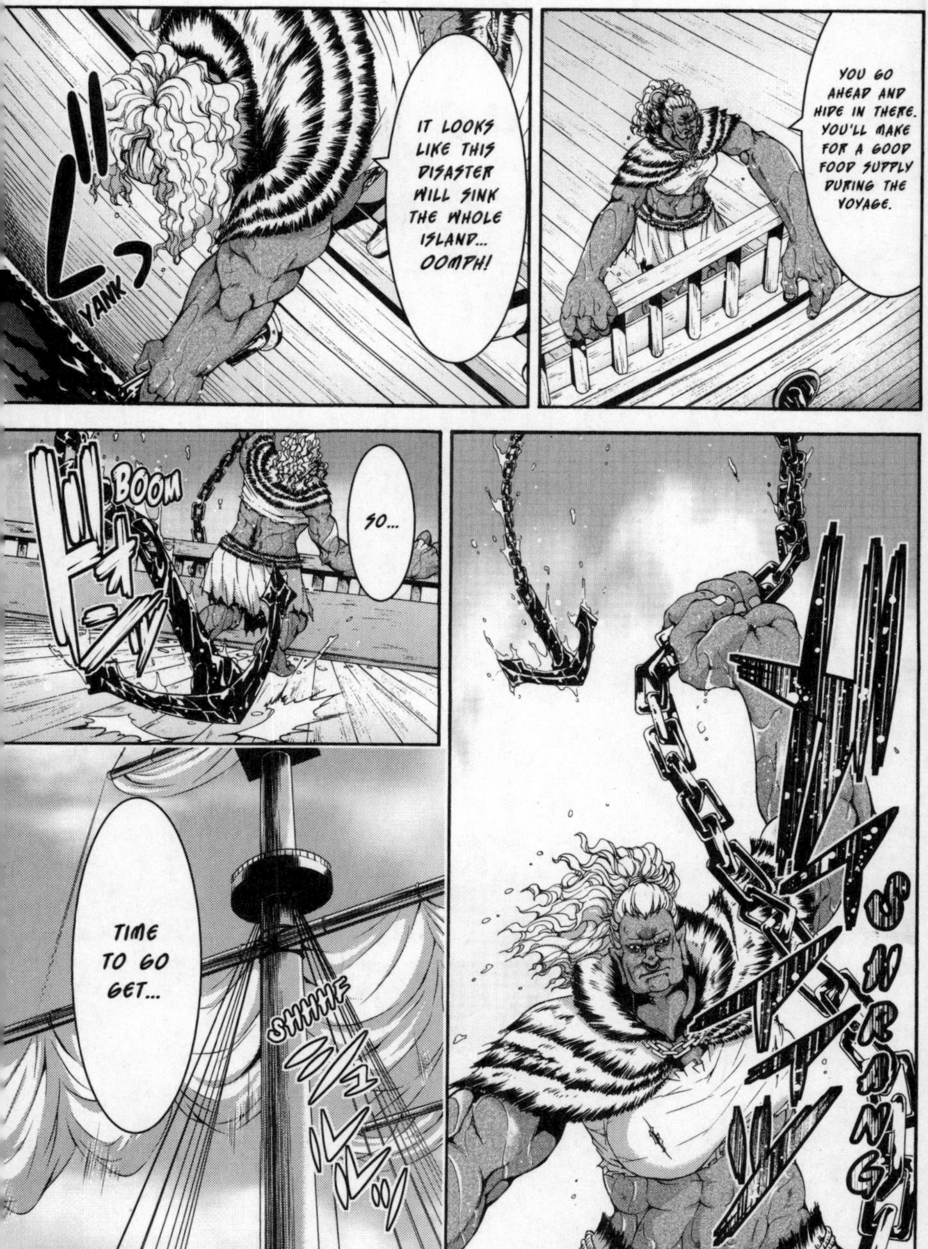
YOU GO AHEAD AND HIDE IN THERE. YOU'LL MAKE FOR A GOOD FOOD SUPPLY DURING THE VOYAGE.
IT LOOKS LIKE THIS DISASTER WILL SINK THE WHOLE ISLAND... OOMPH!
YANK
SHRANG
BOOM
SO...
TIME TO GO GET...
SHHHF

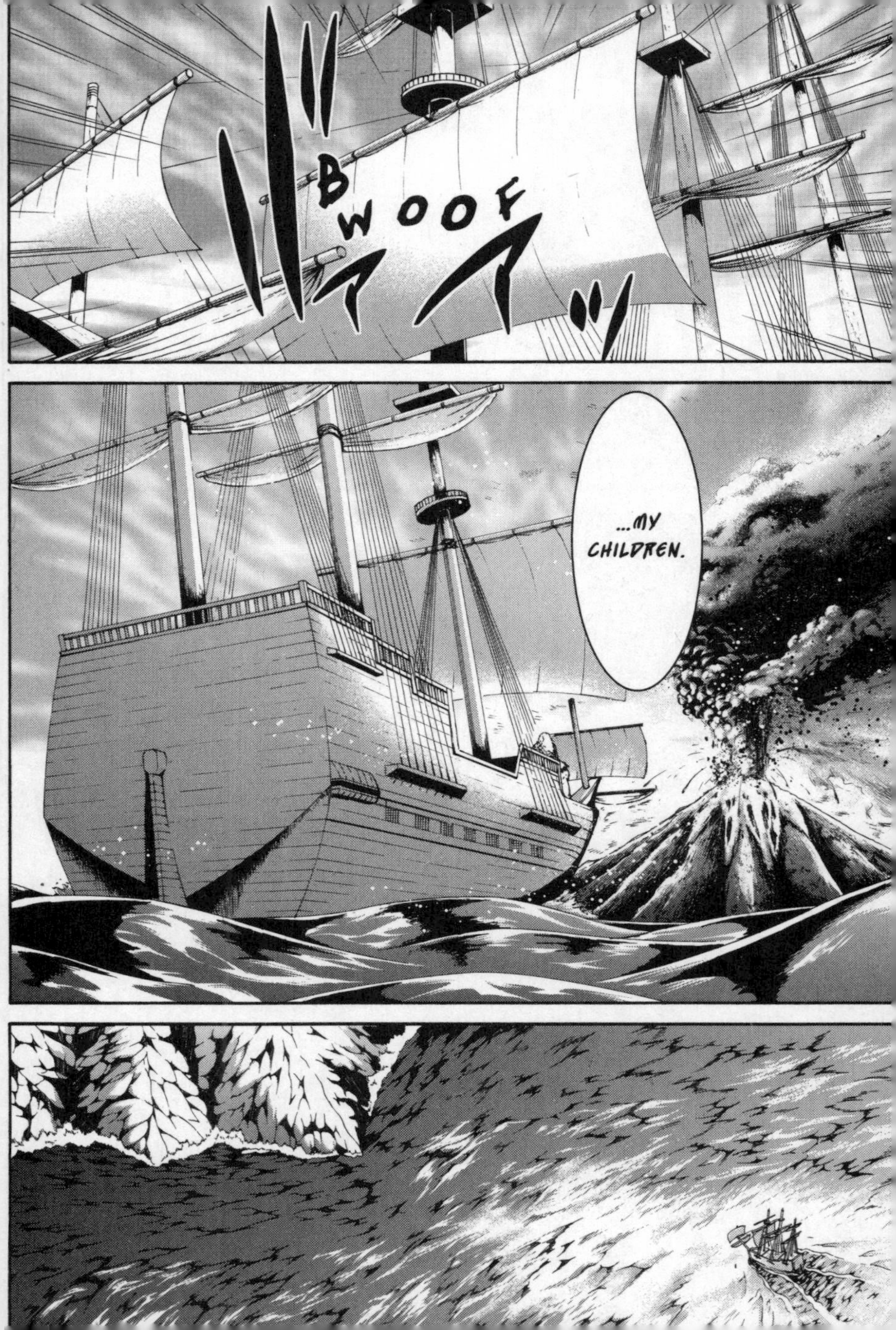
BWOOF
...MY CHILDREN.

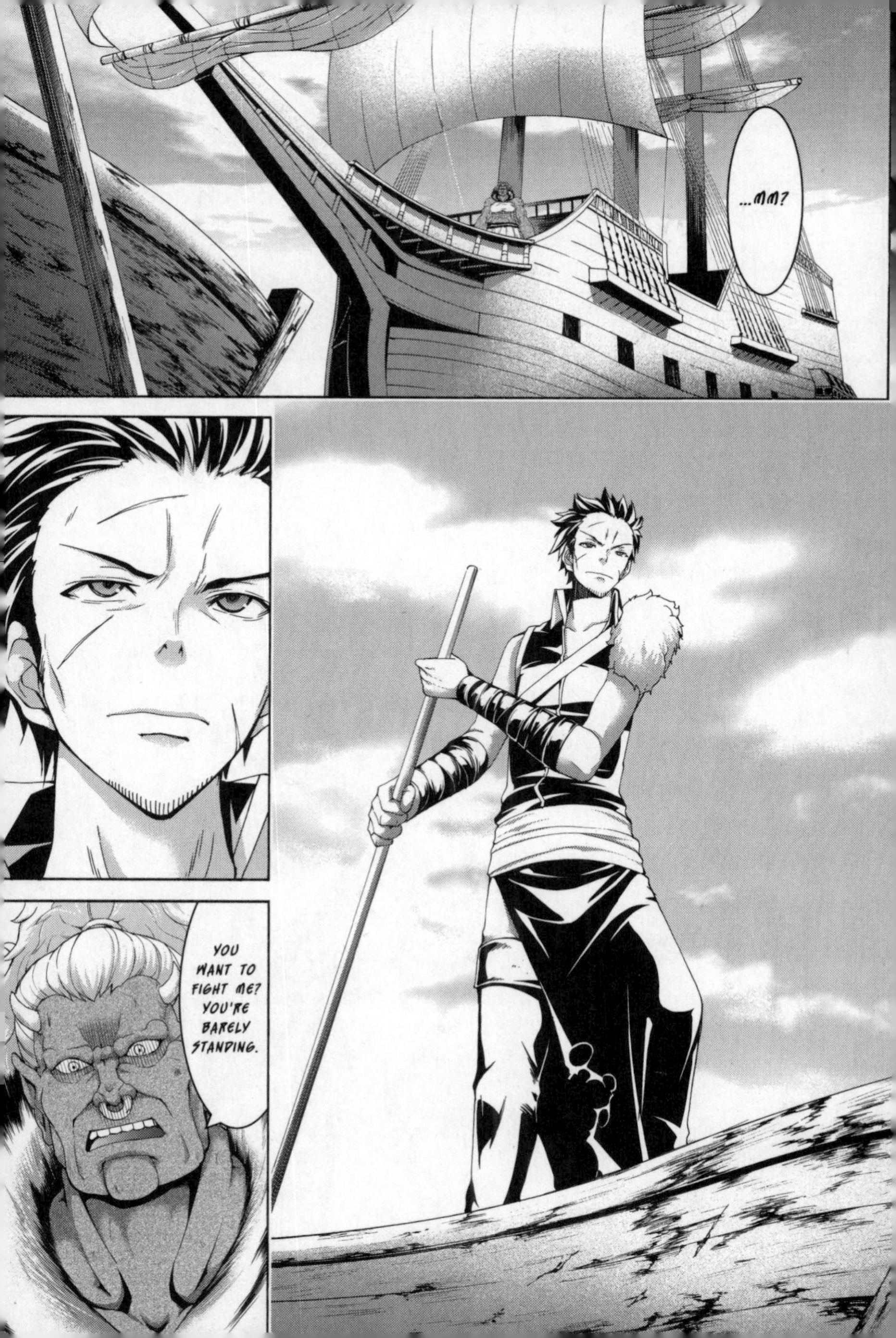
...MM?
YOU WANT TO FIGHT ME? YOU'RE BARELY STANDING.

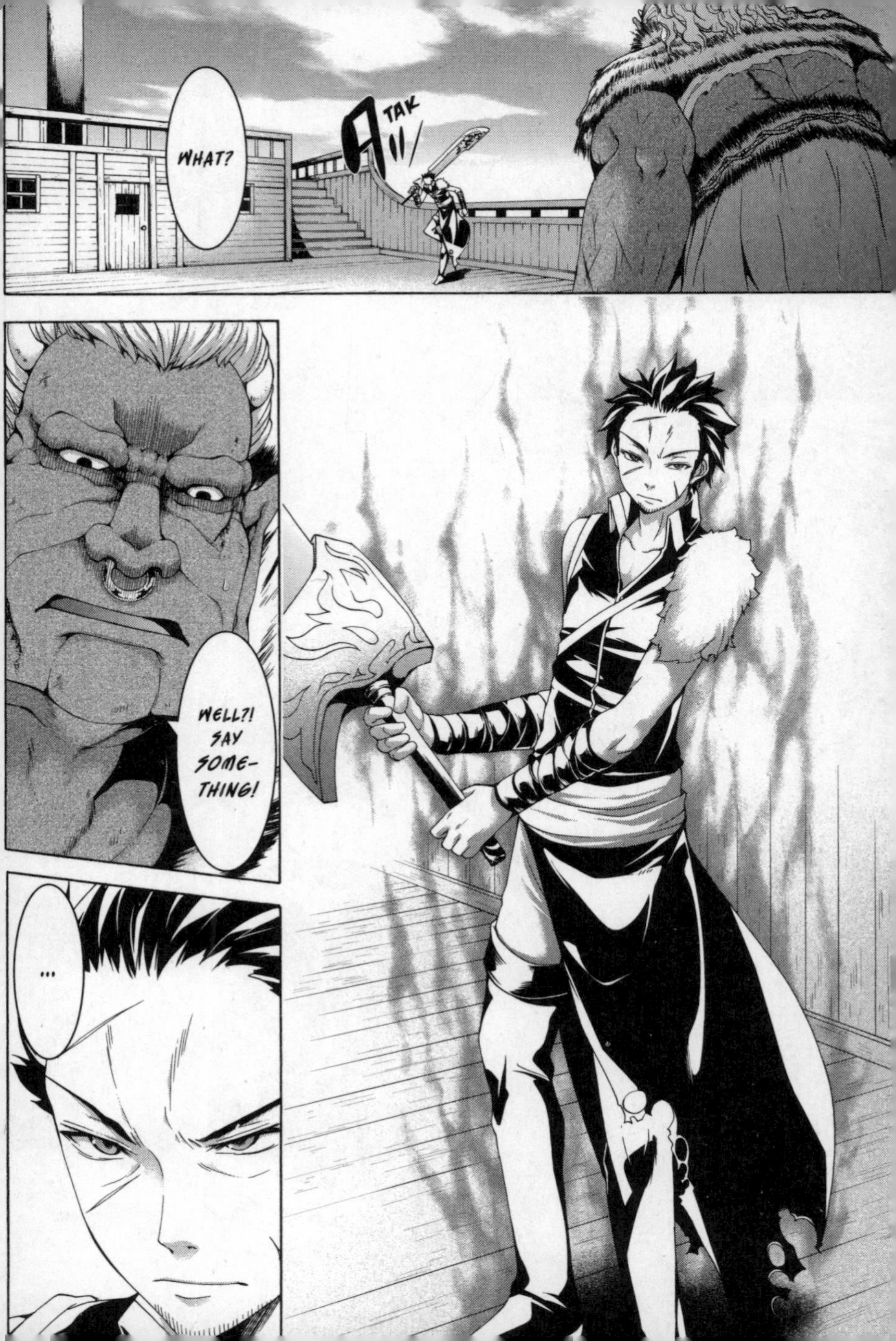
TAK
WHAT?
WELL?! SAY SOME-THING!
...

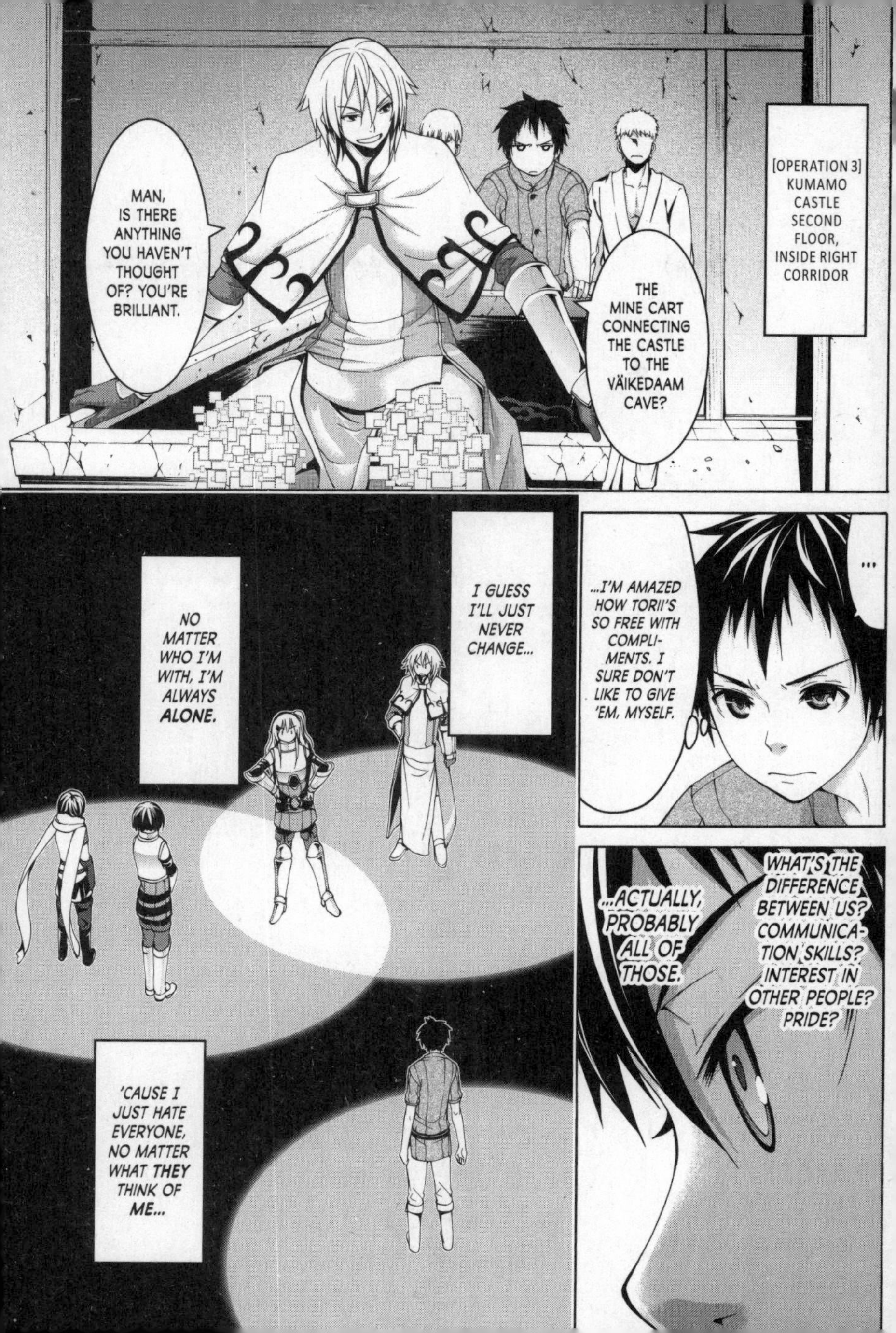
[OPERATION 3] KUMAMO CASTLE SECOND FLOOR, INSIDE RIGHT CORRIDOR
THE MINE CART CONNECTING THE CASTLE TO THE VÄIKEDAAM CAVE?
MAN, IS THERE ANYTHING YOU HAVEN'T THOUGHT OF? YOU'RE BRILLIANT.
...
...I'M AMAZED HOW TORII'S SO FREE WITH COMPLI-MENTS. I SURE DON'T LIKE TO GIVE 'EM, MYSELF.
WHAT'S THE DIFFERENCE BETWEEN US? COMMUNICA-TION SKILLS? INTEREST IN OTHER PEOPLE? PRIDE?
...ACTUALLY, PROBABLY ALL OF THOSE.
I GUESS I'LL JUST NEVER CHANGE...
NO MATTER WHO I'M WITH, I'M ALWAYS ALONE.
'CAUSE I JUST HATE EVERYONE, NO MATTER WHAT THEY THINK OF ME...

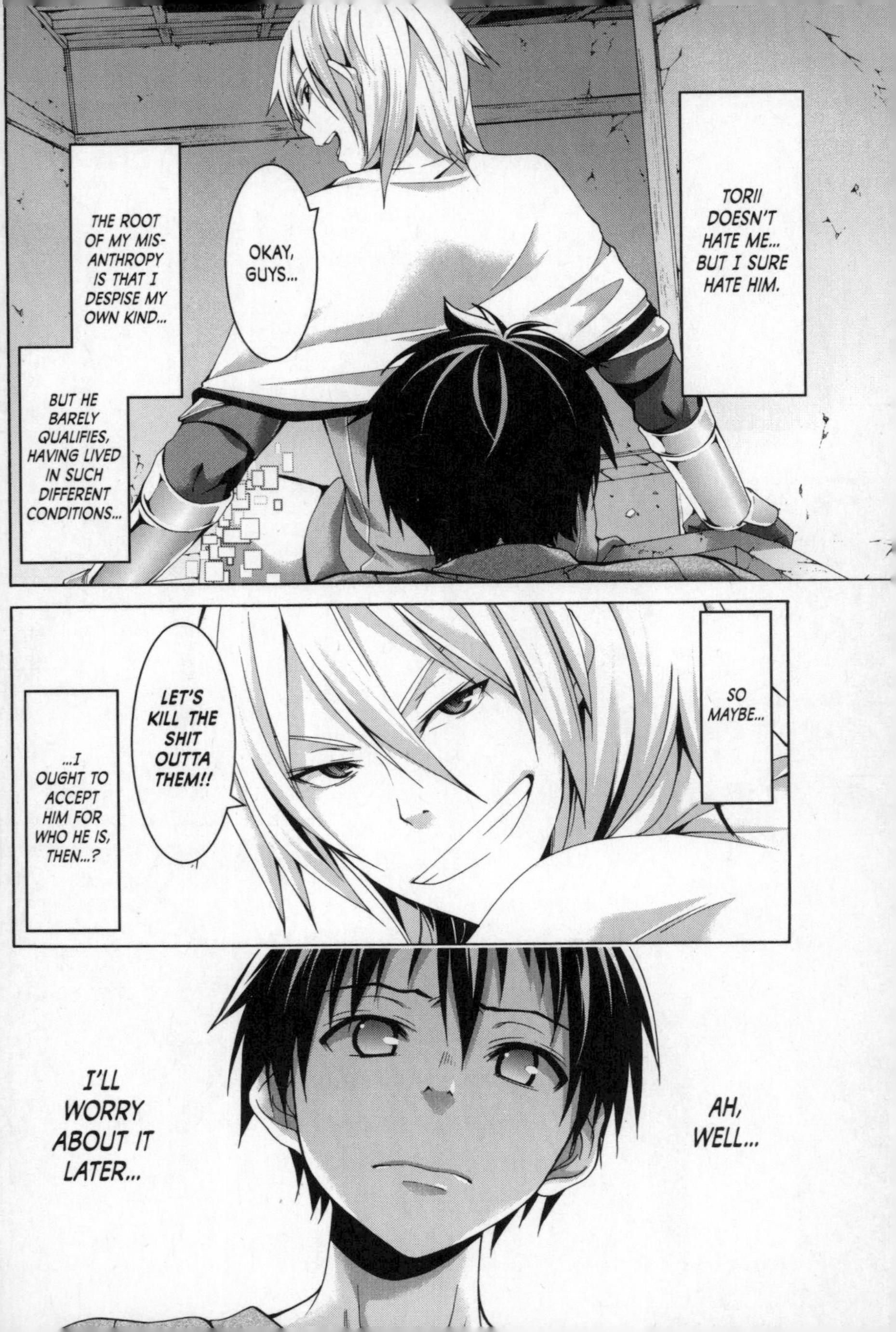
TORII DOESN'T HATE ME... BUT I SURE HATE HIM.
OKAY, GUYS...
THE ROOT OF MY MIS-ANTHROPY IS THAT I DESPISE MY OWN KIND...
BUT HE BARELY QUALIFIES, HAVING LIVED IN SUCH DIFFERENT CONDITIONS...
SO MAYBE...
LET'S KILL THE SHIT OUTTA THEM!!
...I OUGHT TO ACCEPT HIM FOR WHO HE IS, THEN...?
AH, WELL...
I'LL WORRY ABOUT IT LATER...

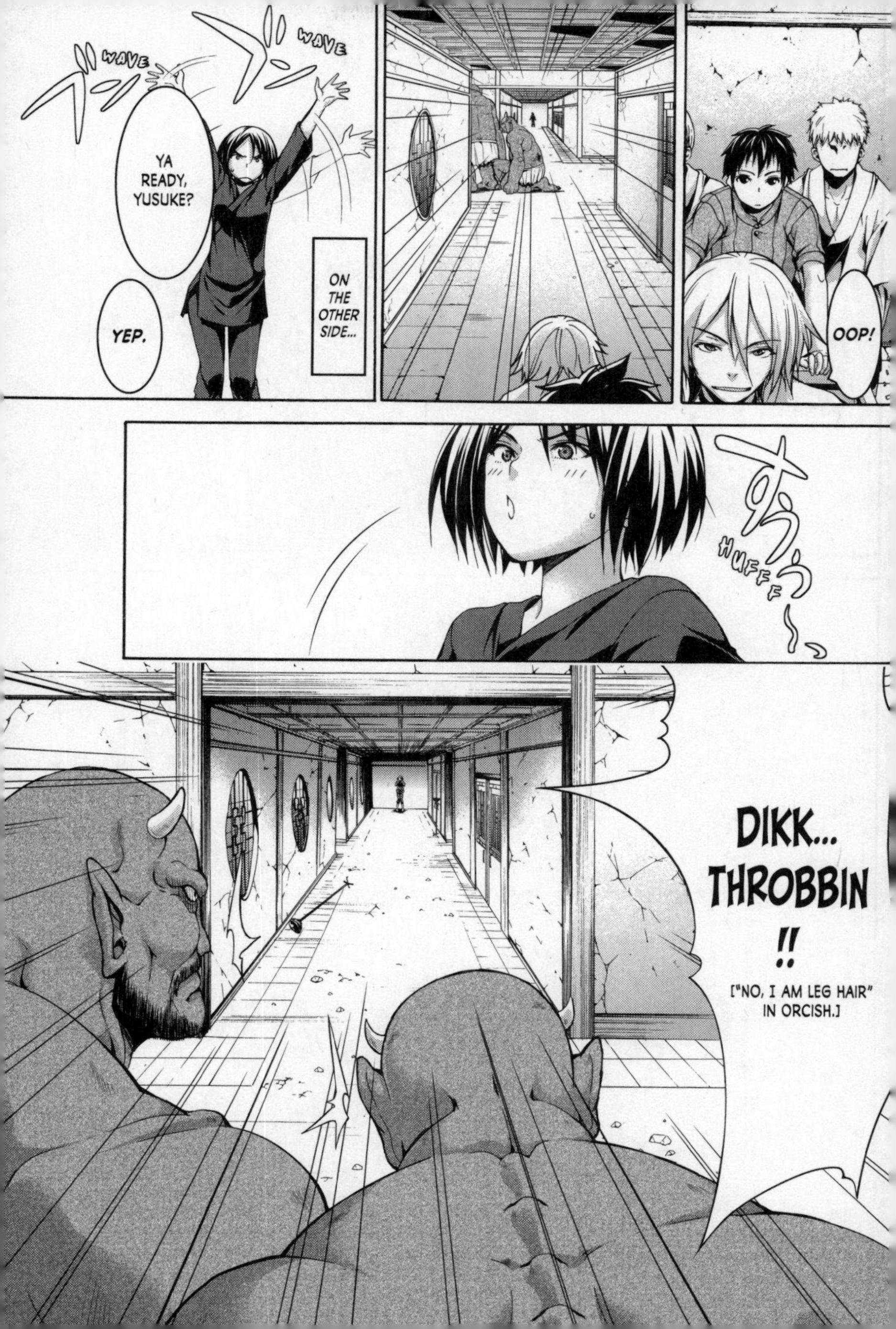
OOP!
WAVE
WAVE
ON THE OTHER SIDE...
YA READY, YUSUKE?
YEP.
HUFFF
DIKK... THROBBIN!!
["NO, I AM LEG HAIR" IN ORCISH.]

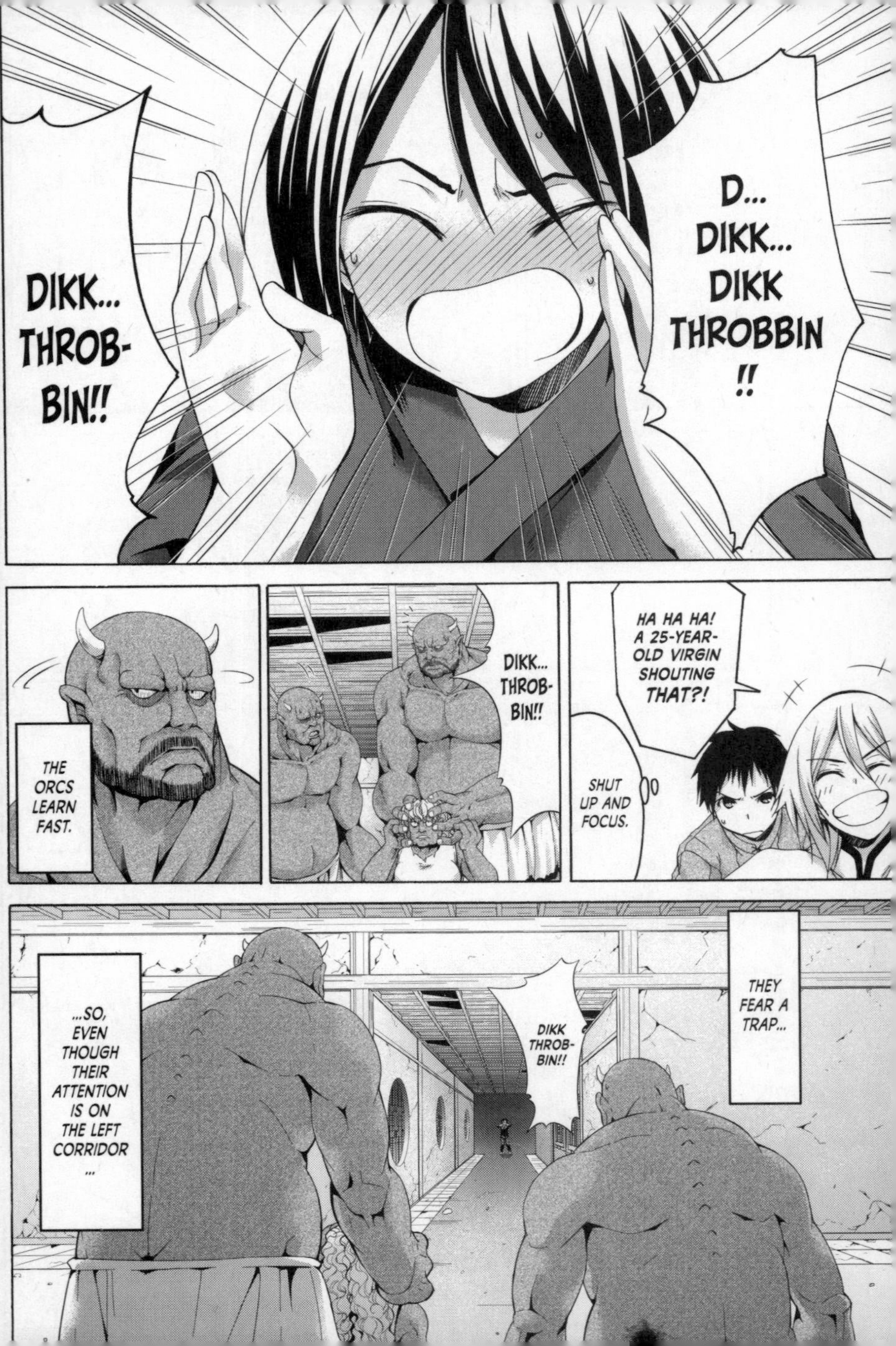
D... DIKK... DIKK THROBBIN !!
DIKK... THROB-BIN!!
HA HA HA! A 25-YEAR-OLD VIRGIN SHOUTING THAT?!
SHUT UP AND FOCUS.
DIKK... THROB-BIN!!
THE ORCS LEARN FAST.
THEY FEAR A TRAP...
DIKK THROB-BIN!!
...SO, EVEN THOUGH THEIR ATTENTION IS ON THE LEFT CORRIDOR ...

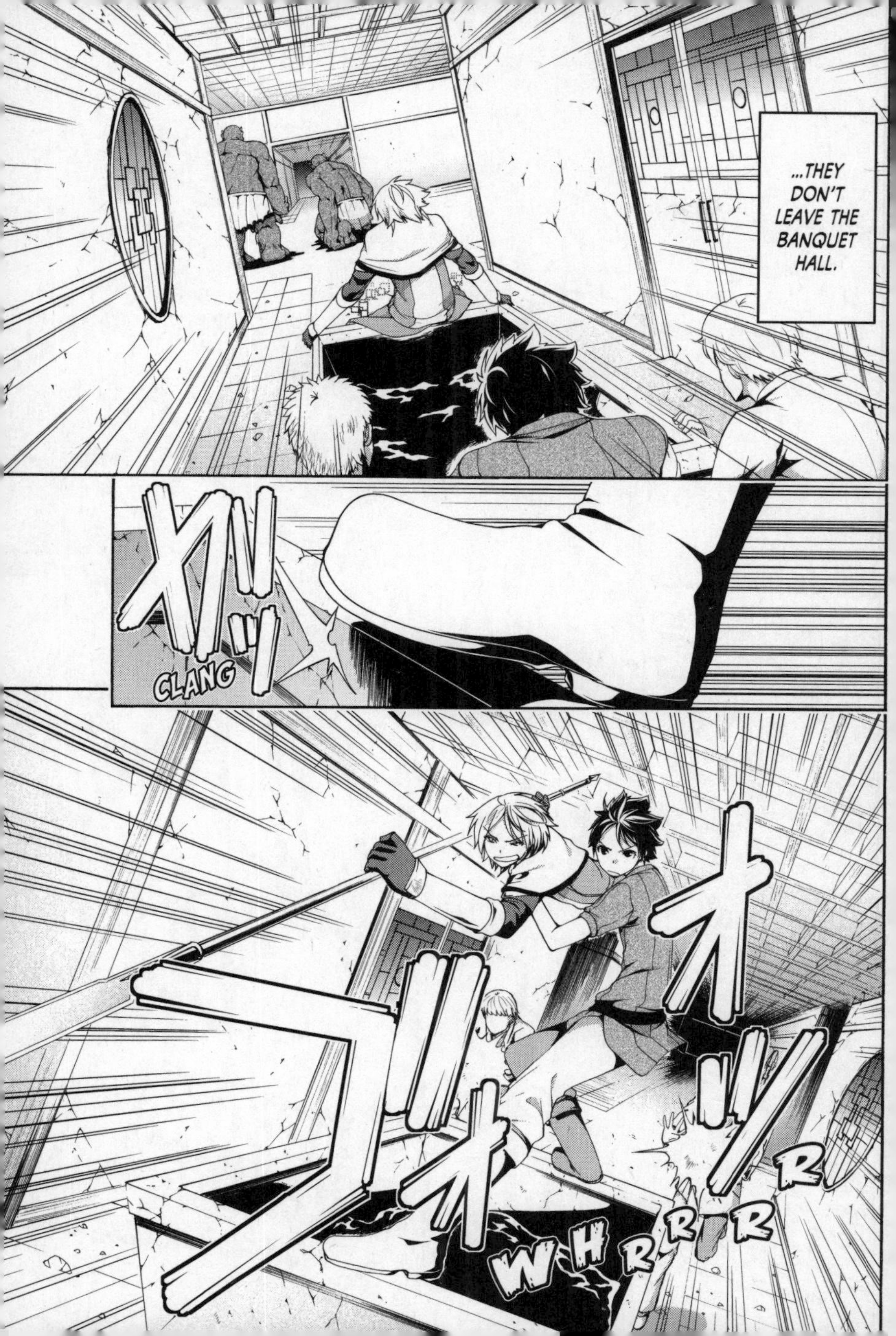
...THEY DON'T LEAVE THE BANQUET HALL.
CLANG
WHRRRR

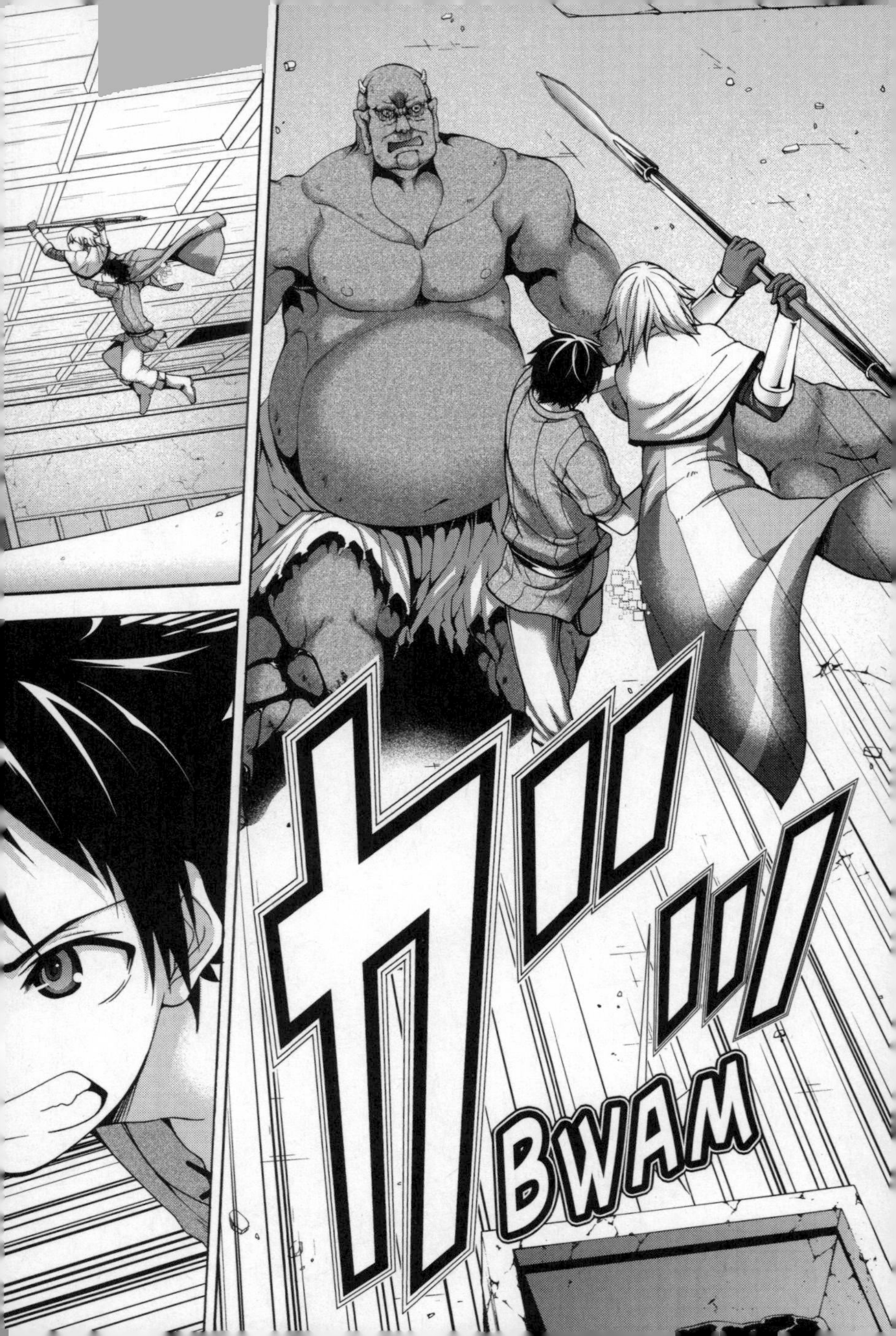
BWAM

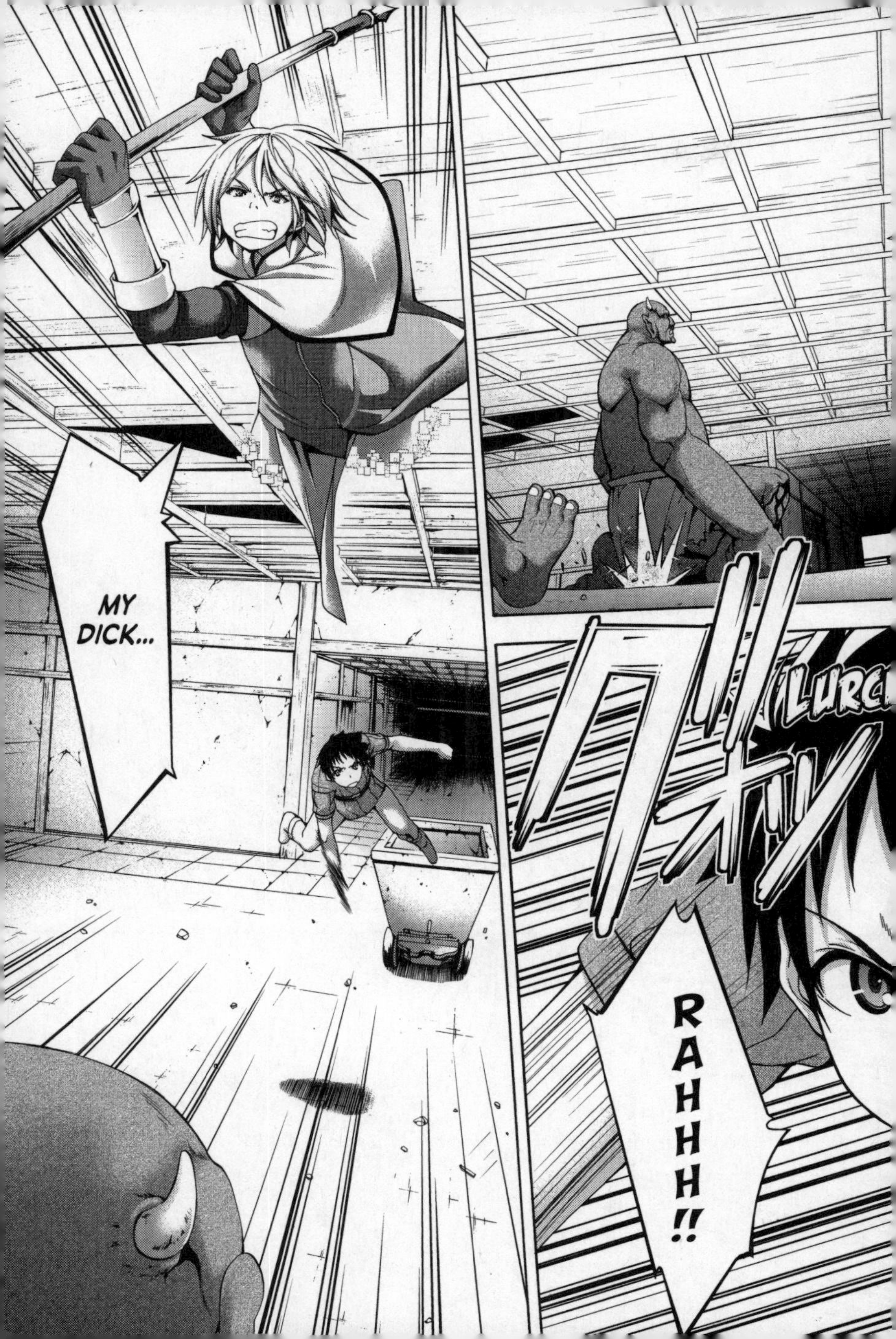
LURC
RAHHH!!
MY DICK...

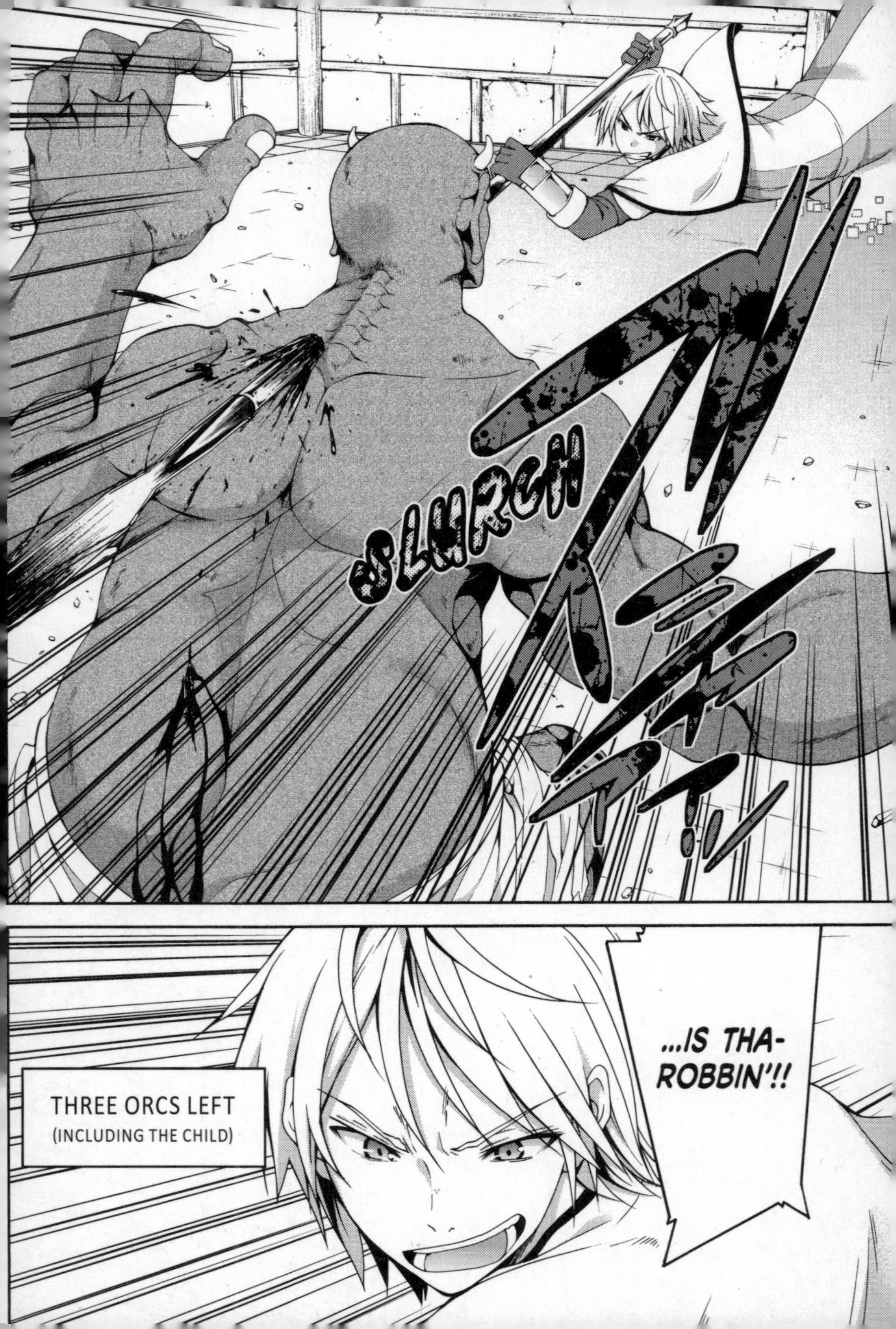
SLURCH
...IS THA-
ROBBIN'!!
THREE ORCS LEFT
(INCLUDING THE CHILD)

I'M STANDING ON A MILLION LIVES

I'M STANDING ON A MILLION LIVES.

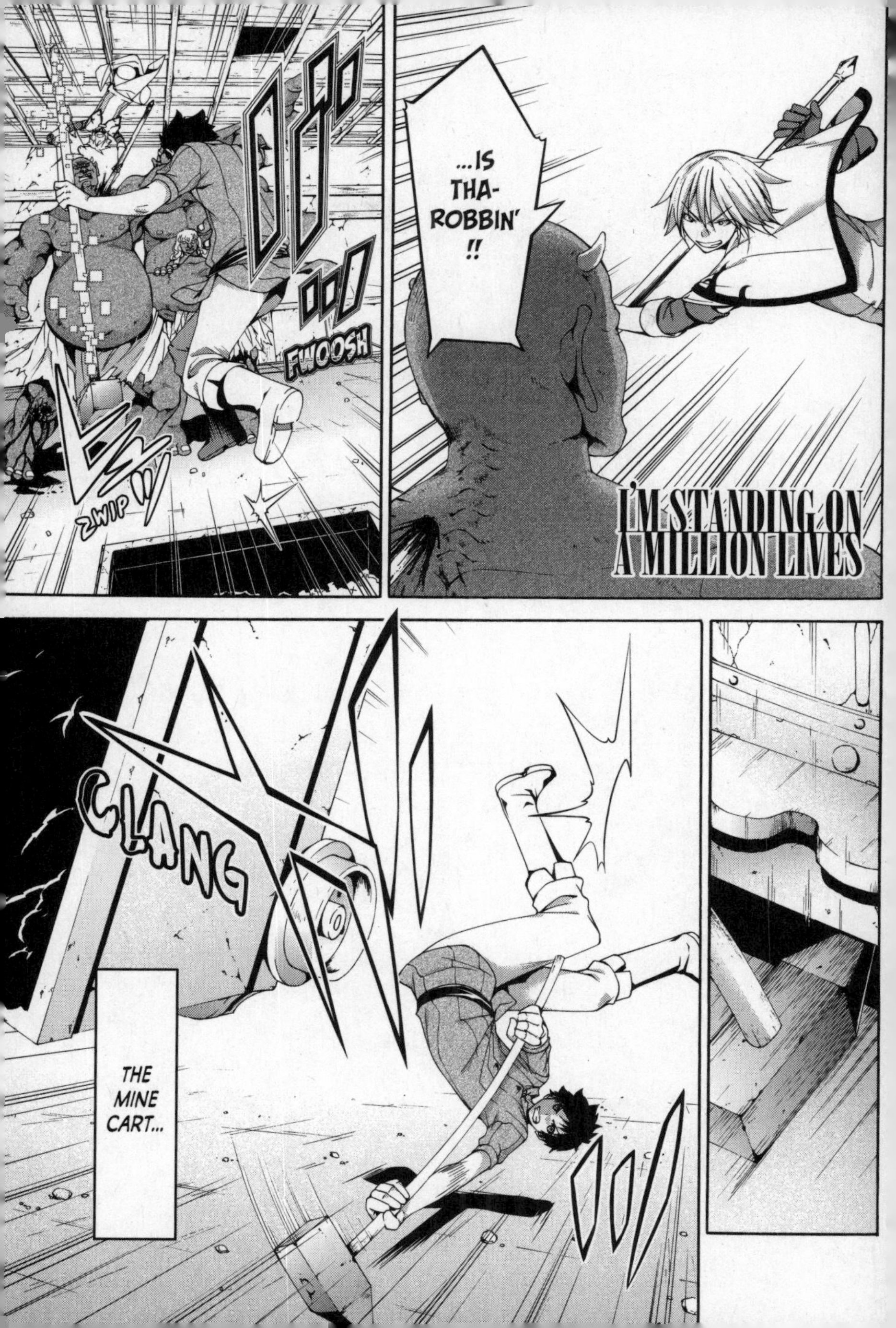
...IS THA-ROBBIN' !!
I'M STANDING ON A MILLION LIVES
FWOOSH
ZWIP !!
CLANG
THE MINE CART...

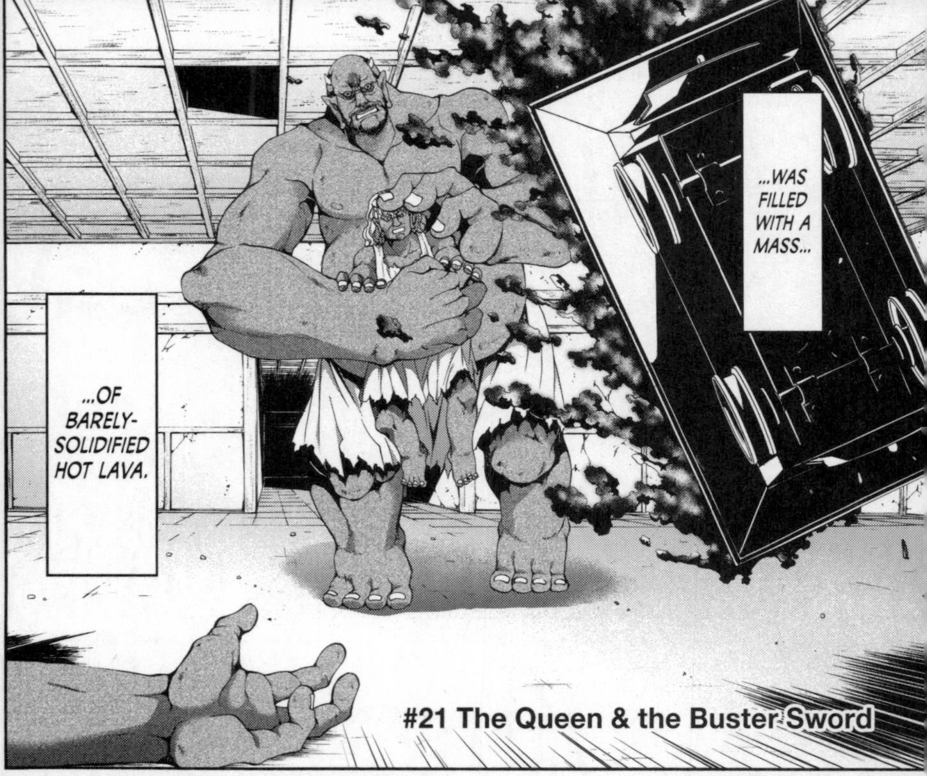
...WAS FILLED WITH A MASS...
...OF BARELY-SOLIDIFIED HOT LAVA.
#21 The Queen & the Buster Sword

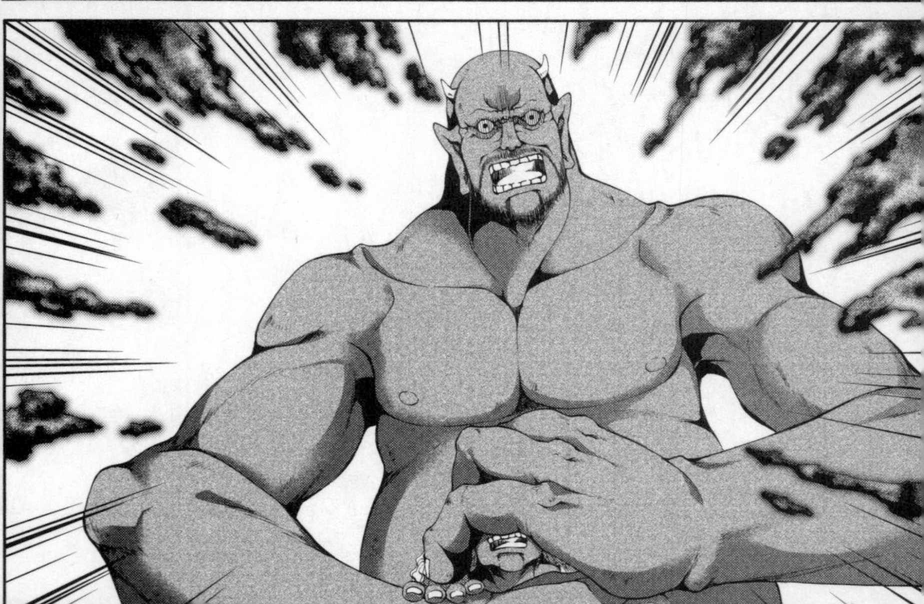

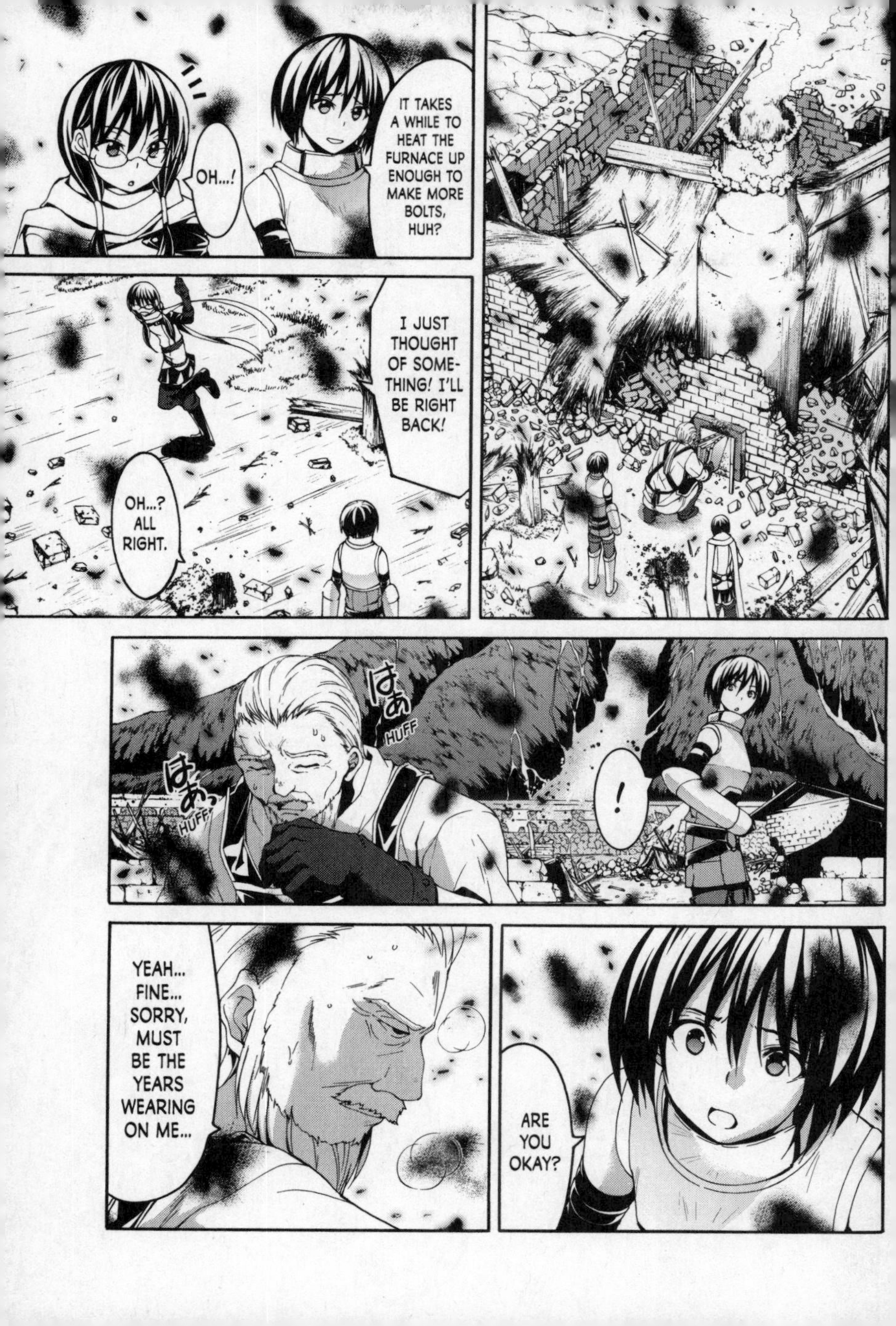
IT TAKES A WHILE TO HEAT THE FURNACE UP ENOUGH TO MAKE MORE BOLTS, HUH?
OH...!
I JUST THOUGHT OF SOME-THING! I'LL BE RIGHT BACK!
OH...? ALL RIGHT.
はぁ HUFF
はぁ HUFF
!
ARE YOU OKAY?
YEAH... FINE... SORRY, MUST BE THE YEARS WEARING ON ME...

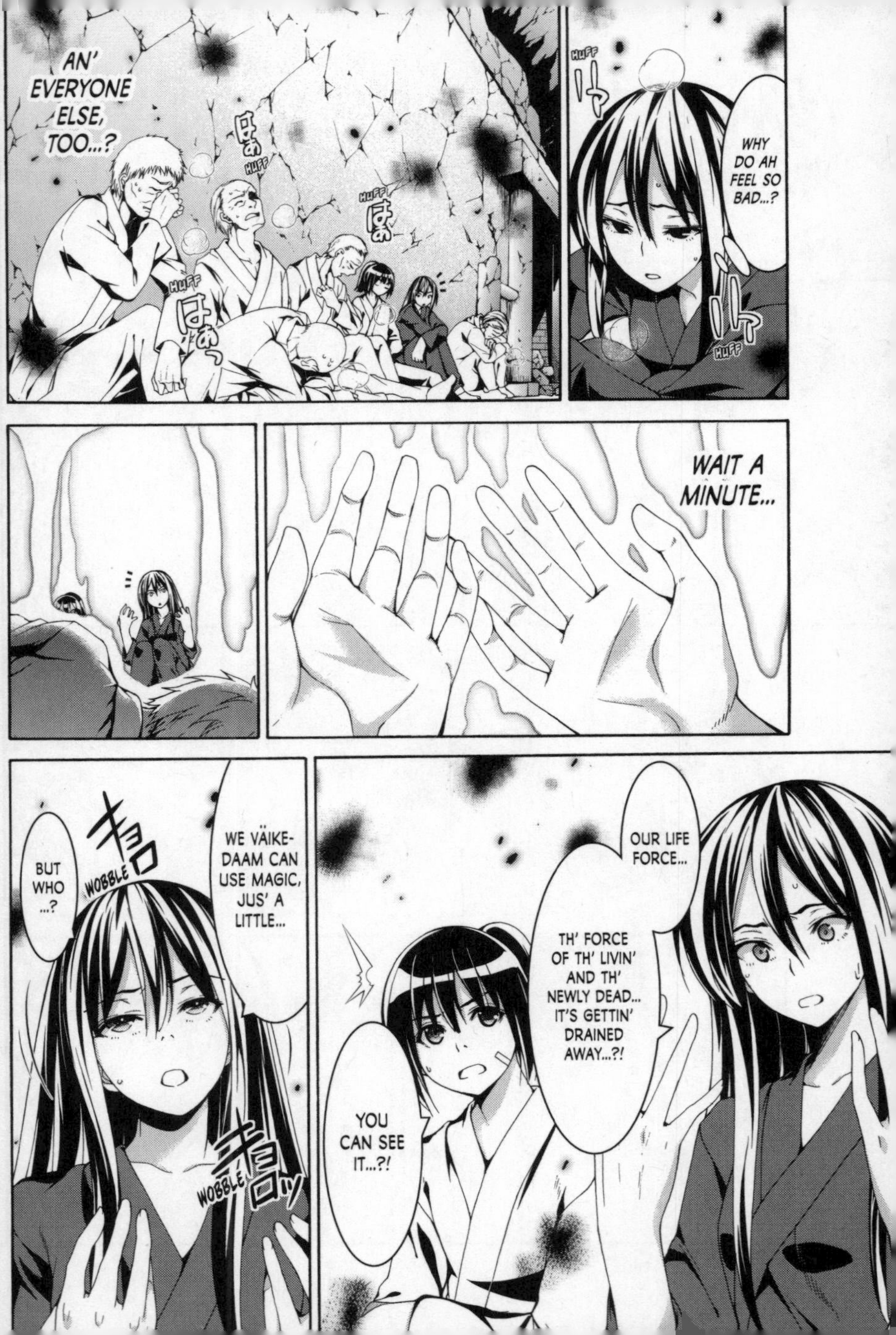
HUFF
WHY DO AH FEEL SO BAD...?
HUFF
AN' EVERYONE ELSE, TOO...?
HUFF
HUFF
HUFF
WAIT A MINUTE...
OUR LIFE FORCE...
TH' FORCE OF TH' LIVIN' AND TH' NEWLY DEAD... IT'S GETTIN' DRAINED AWAY...?!
YOU CAN SEE IT...?!
WE VÄIKE-DAAM CAN USE MAGIC, JUS' A LITTLE...
BUT WHO ...?
WOBBLE
WOBBLE

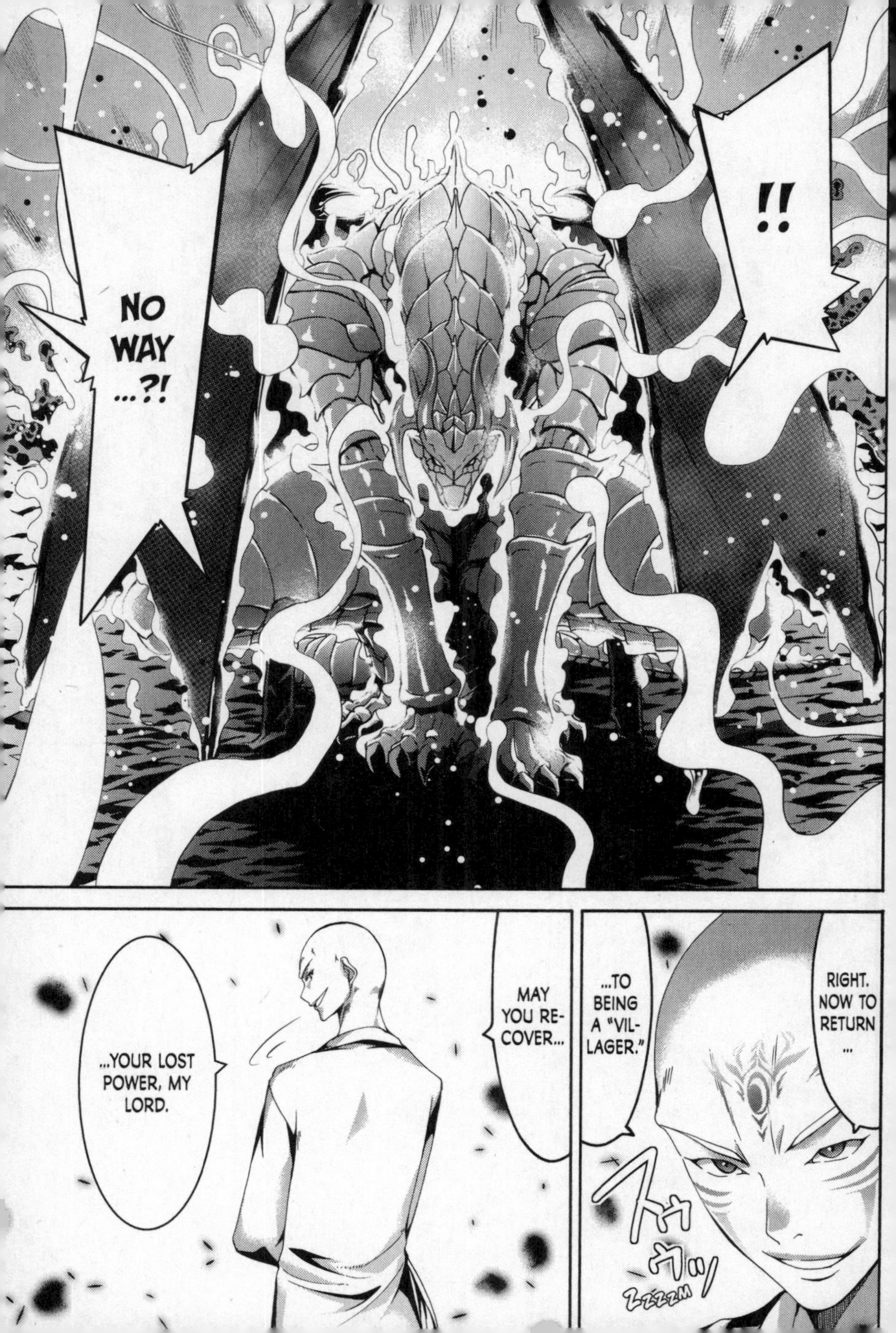
!!
NO WAY ...?!
RIGHT. NOW TO RETURN ...
...TO BEING A "VILLAGER."
ZZZZM
MAY YOU RE-COVER...
...YOUR LOST POWER, MY LORD.

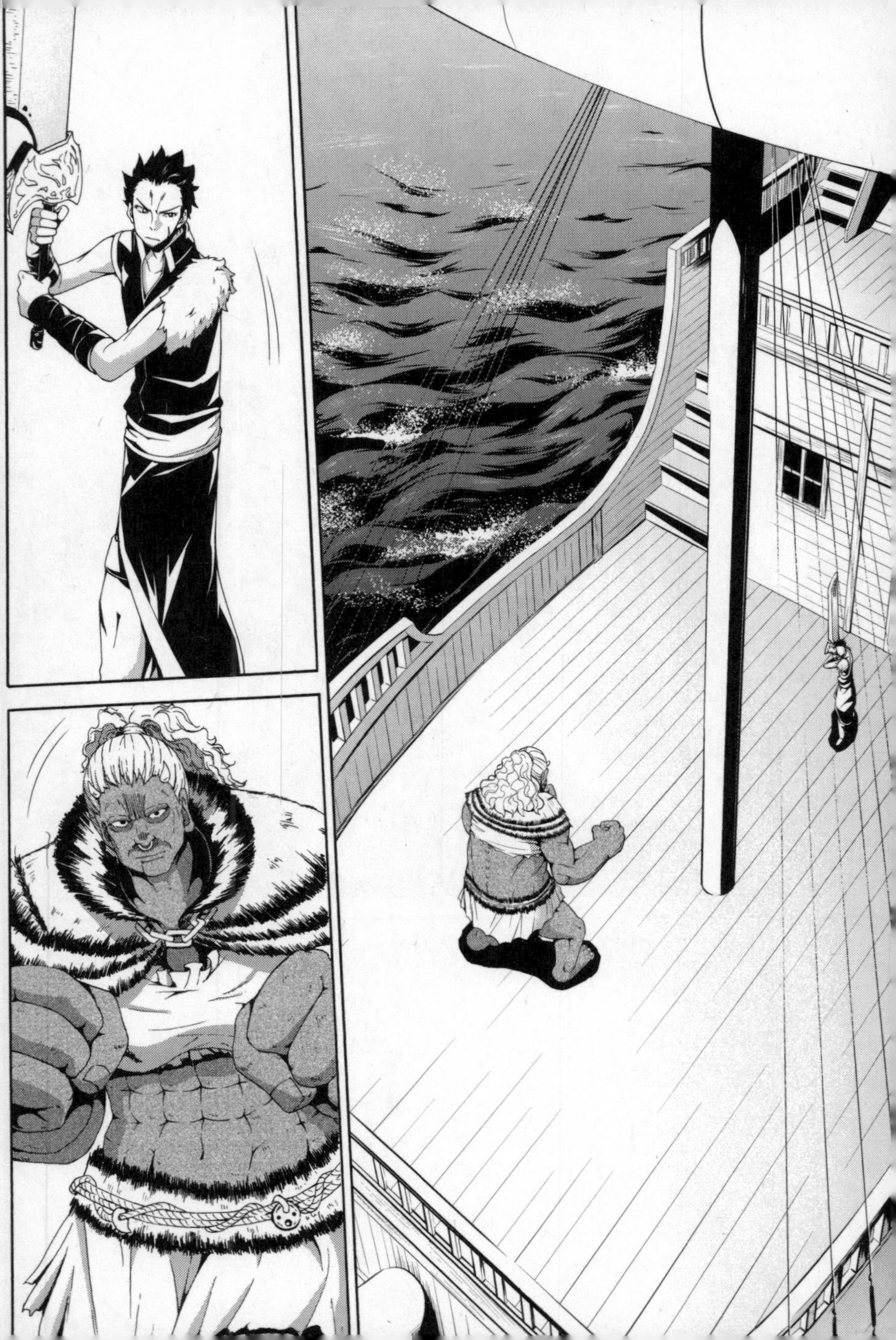

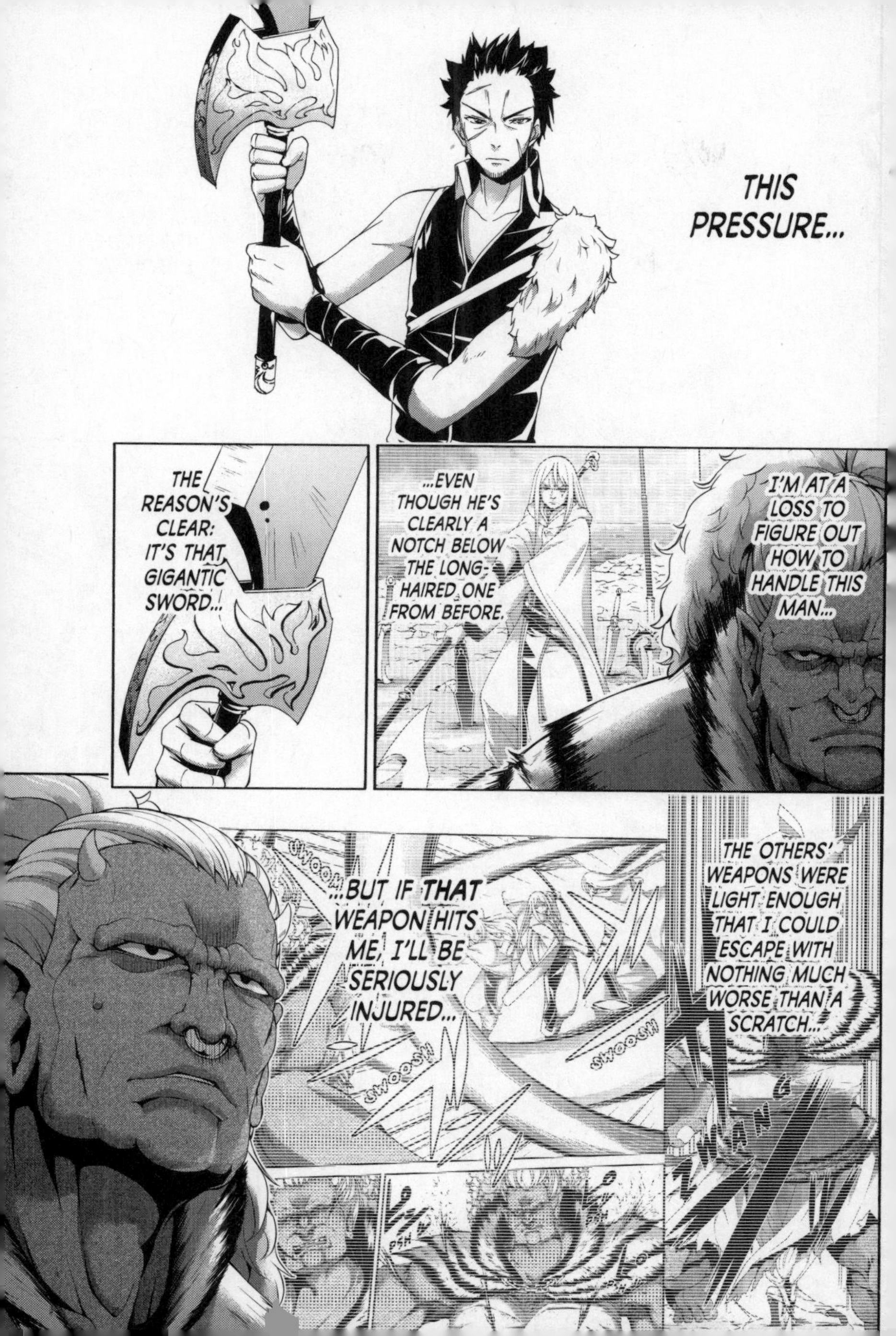
THIS PRESSURE...
I'M AT A LOSS TO FIGURE OUT HOW TO HANDLE THIS MAN...
...EVEN THOUGH HE'S CLEARLY A NOTCH BELOW THE LONG-HAIRED ONE FROM BEFORE.
THE REASON'S CLEAR: IT'S THAT GIGANTIC SWORD...
THE OTHERS' WEAPONS WERE LIGHT ENOUGH THAT I COULD ESCAPE WITH NOTHING MUCH WORSE THAN A SCRATCH...
...BUT IF THAT WEAPON HITS ME, I'LL BE SERIOUSLY INJURED...

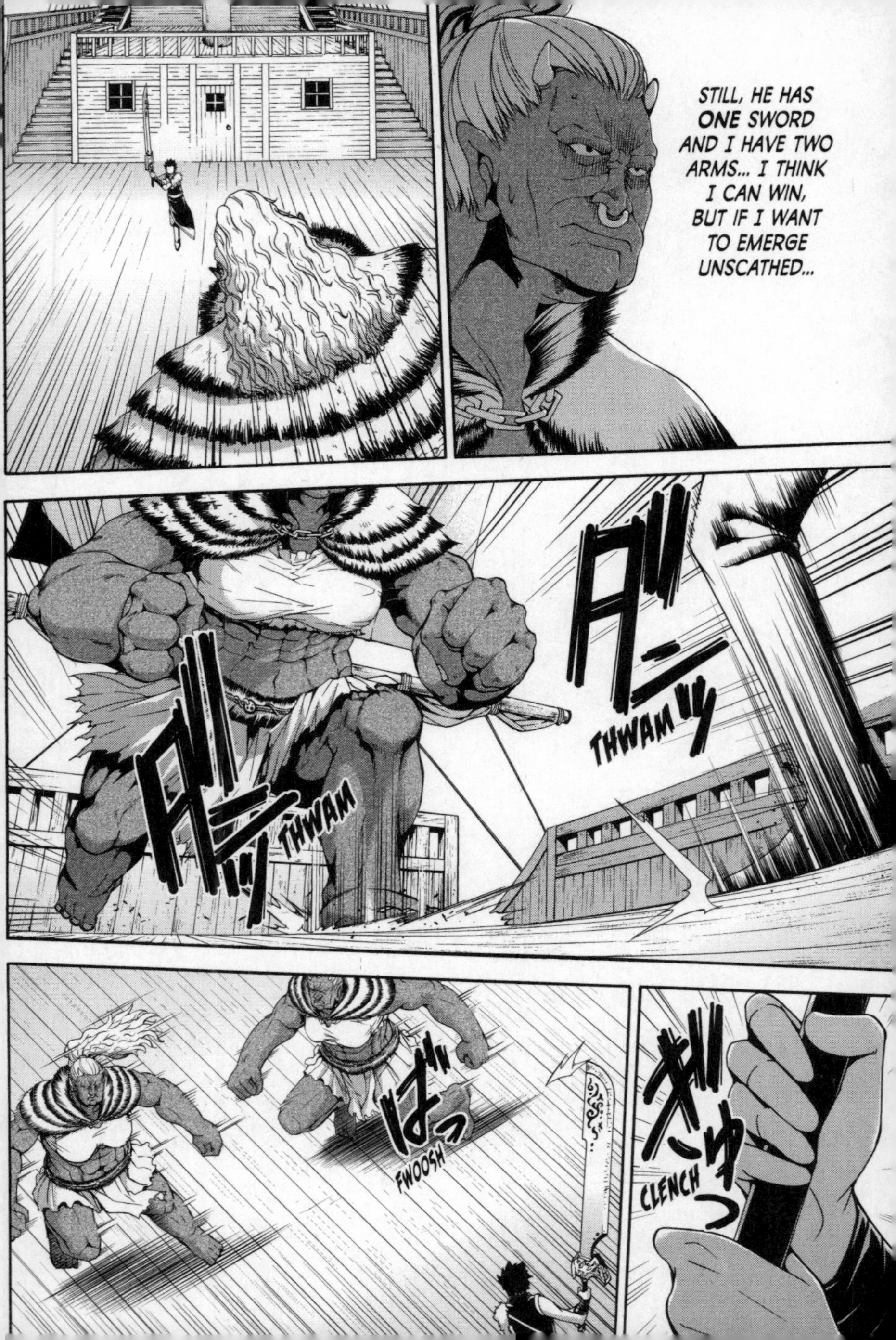
STILL, HE HAS ONE SWORD AND I HAVE TWO ARMS... I THINK I CAN WIN, BUT IF I WANT TO EMERGE UNSCATHED...
THWAM
THWAM
CLENCH
FWOOSH

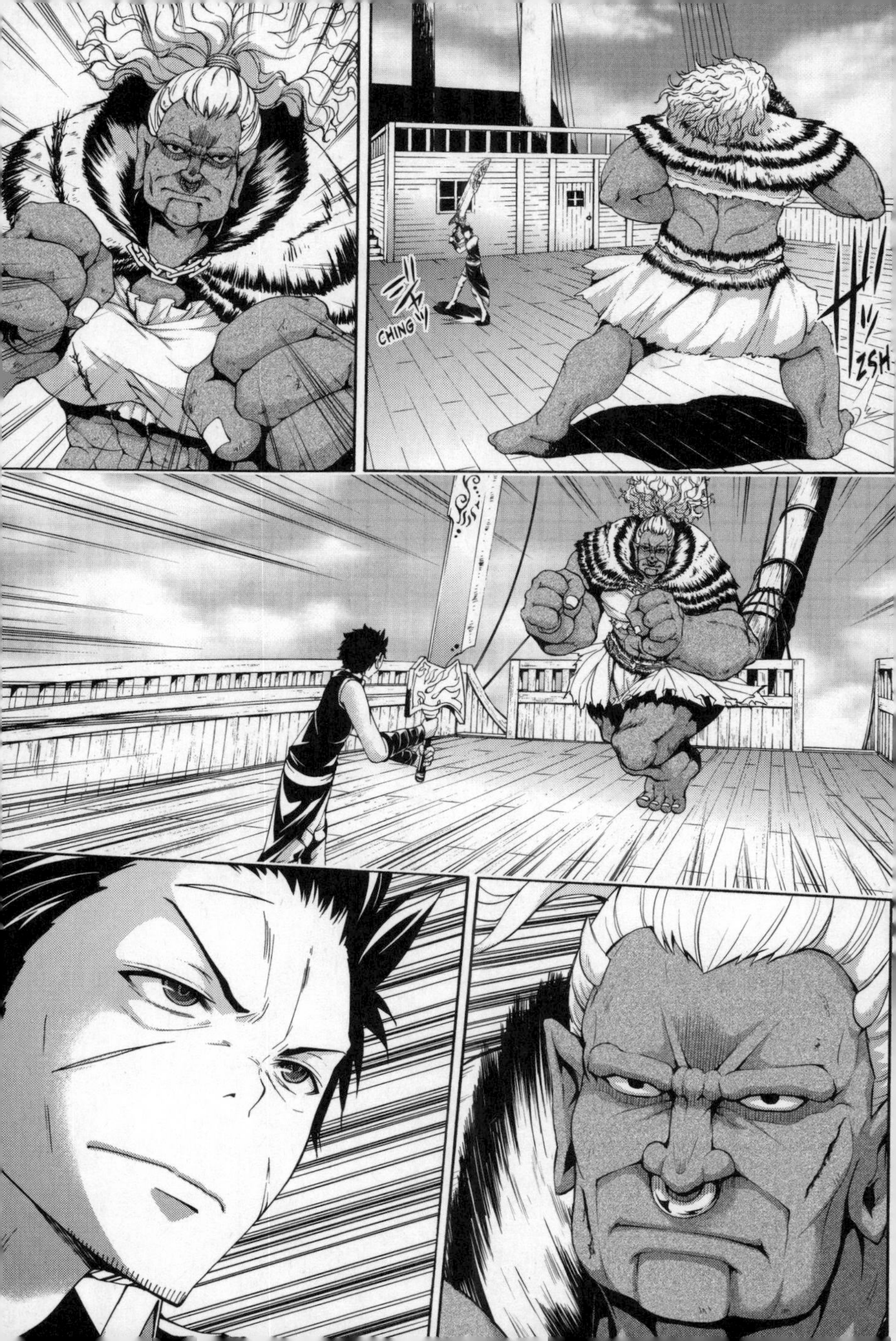
ZSH
CHING

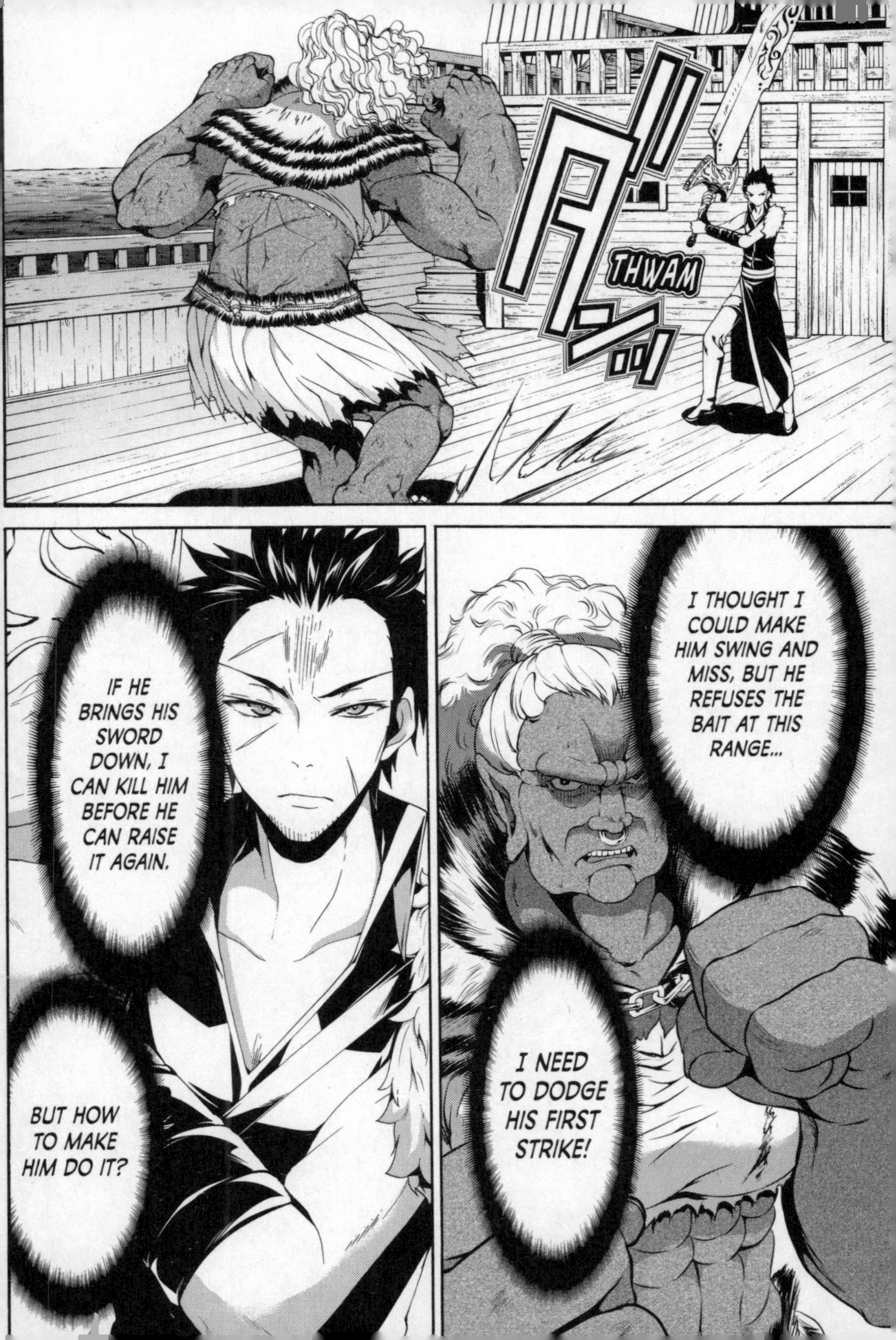
THWAM
I THOUGHT I COULD MAKE HIM SWING AND MISS, BUT HE REFUSES THE BAIT AT THIS RANGE...
I NEED TO DODGE HIS FIRST STRIKE!
IF HE BRINGS HIS SWORD DOWN, I CAN KILL HIM BEFORE HE CAN RAISE IT AGAIN.
BUT HOW TO MAKE HIM DO IT?

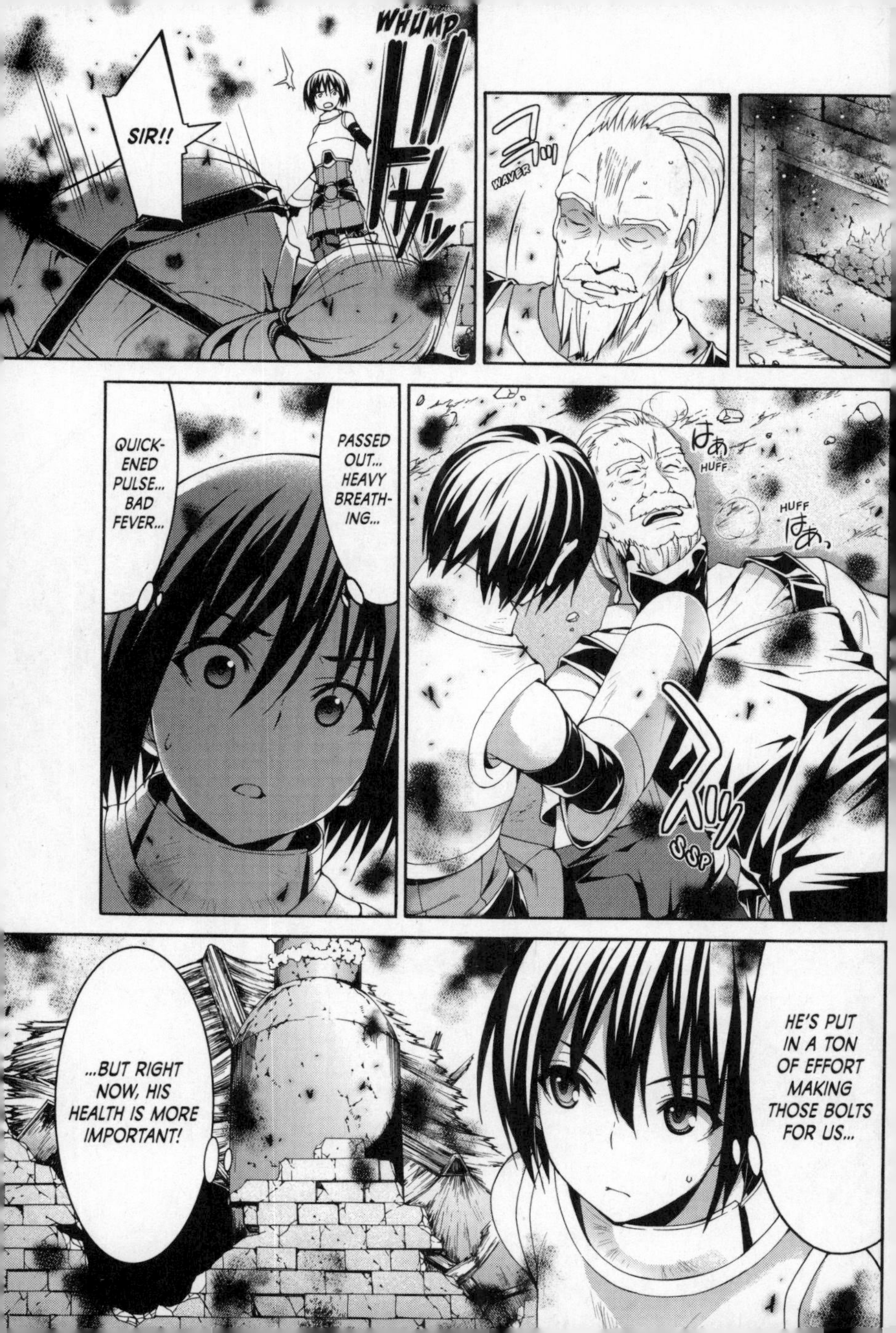
WAVER
SIR!!
WHUMP
HUFF
HUFF
SSP
PASSED OUT... HEAVY BREATH-ING...
QUICK-ENED PULSE... BAD FEVER...
HE'S PUT IN A TON OF EFFORT MAKING THOSE BOLTS FOR US...
...BUT RIGHT NOW, HIS HEALTH IS MORE IMPORTANT!

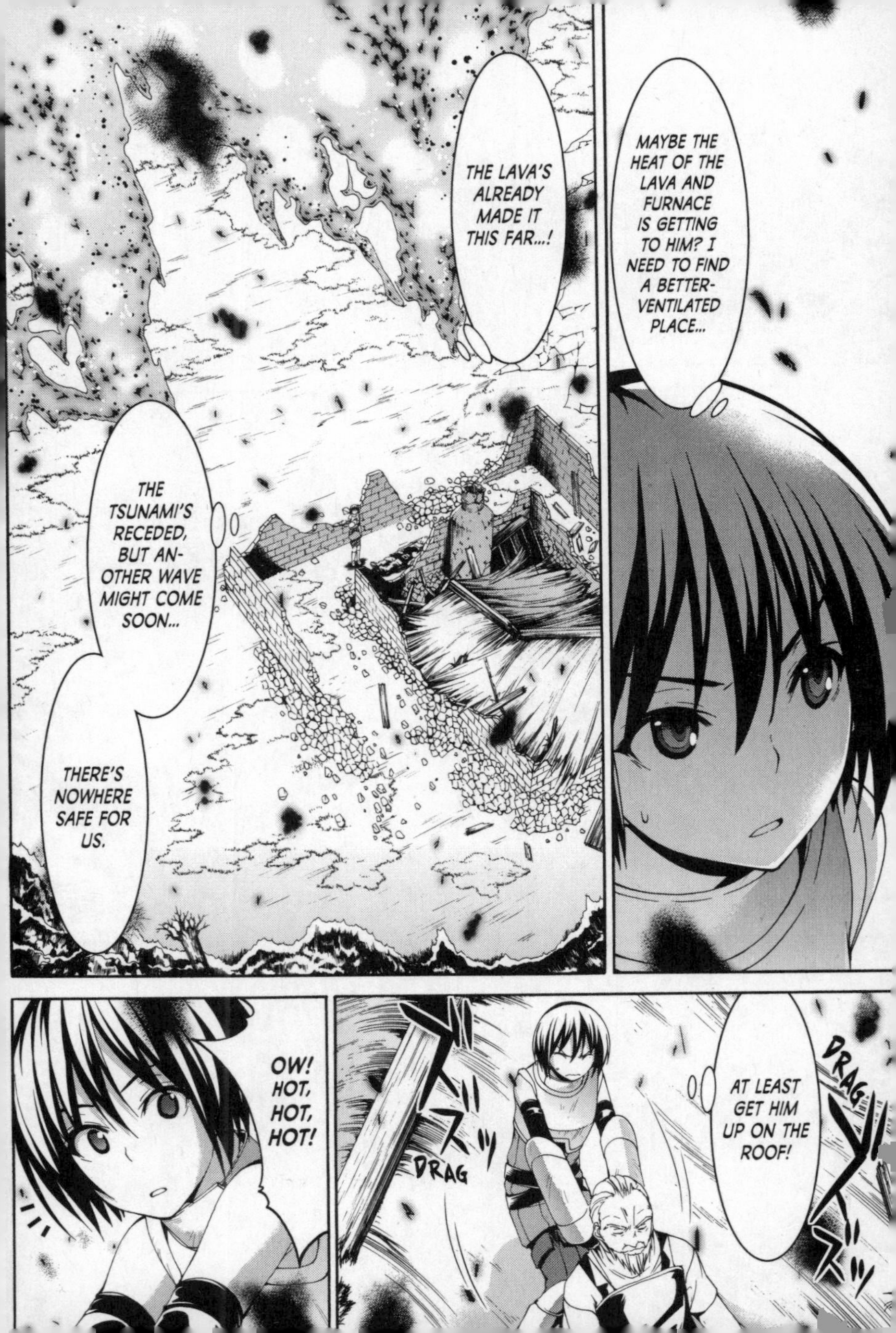
MAYBE THE HEAT OF THE LAVA AND FURNACE IS GETTING TO HIM? I NEED TO FIND A BETTER-VENTILATED PLACE...
THE LAVA'S ALREADY MADE IT THIS FAR...!
THE TSUNAMI'S RECEDED, BUT AN-OTHER WAVE MIGHT COME SOON...
THERE'S NOWHERE SAFE FOR US.
DRAG
AT LEAST GET HIM UP ON THE ROOF!
DRAG
OW! HOT, HOT, HOT!

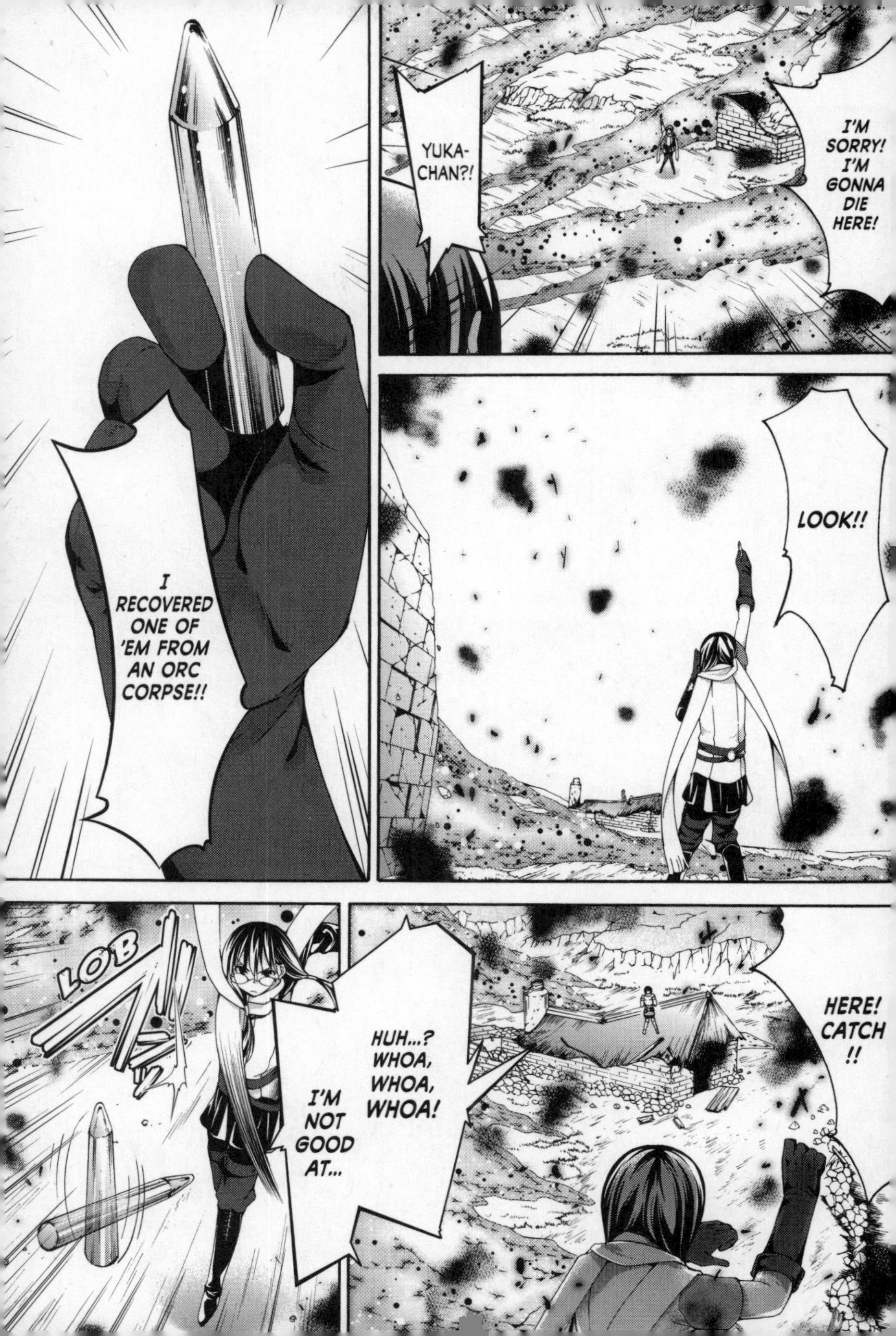
I'M SORRY! I'M GONNA DIE HERE!
YUKA-CHAN?!
LOOK!!
I RECOVERED ONE OF 'EM FROM AN ORC CORPSE!!
HERE! CATCH !!
HUH...? WHOA, WHOA, WHOA!
I'M NOT GOOD AT...
LOB

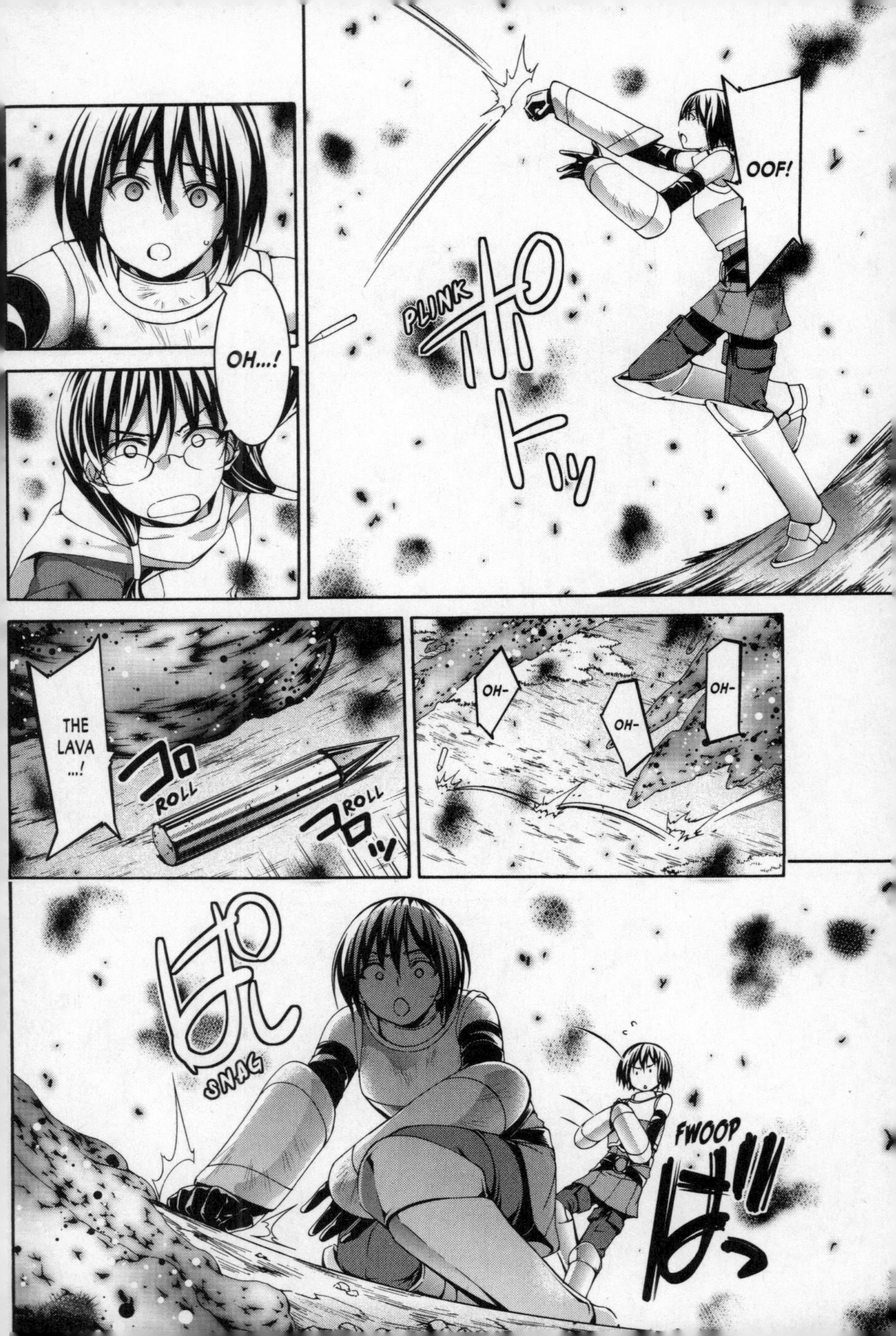
OOF!
PLINK
OH...!
OH-
OH-
OH-
THE LAVA ...!
ROLL
ROLL
FWOOP
SNAG

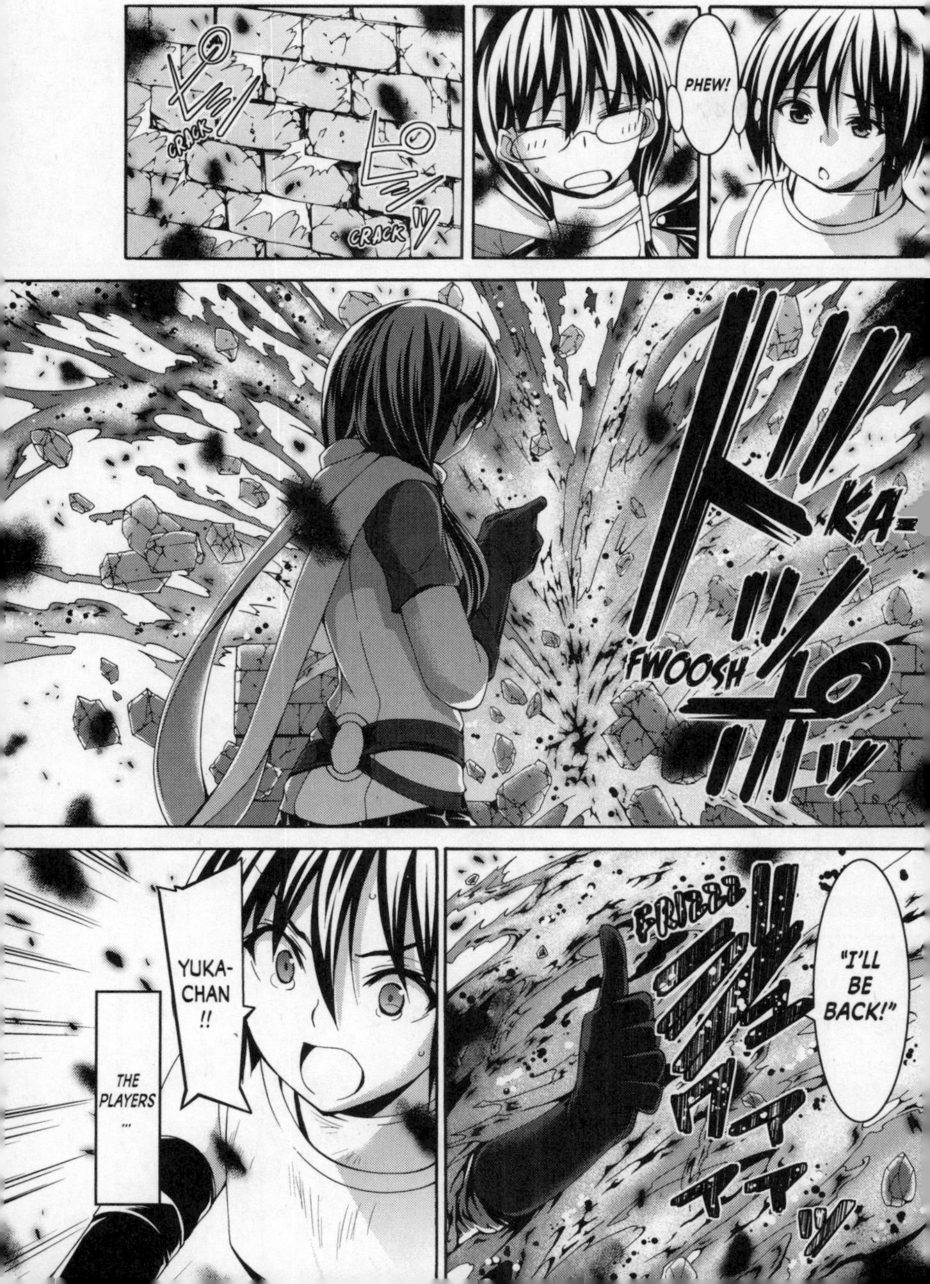
PHEW!
CRACK
CRACK
KA-
FWOOSH
"I'LL BE BACK!"
FRIZZZ
YUKA-CHAN!!
THE PLAYERS...

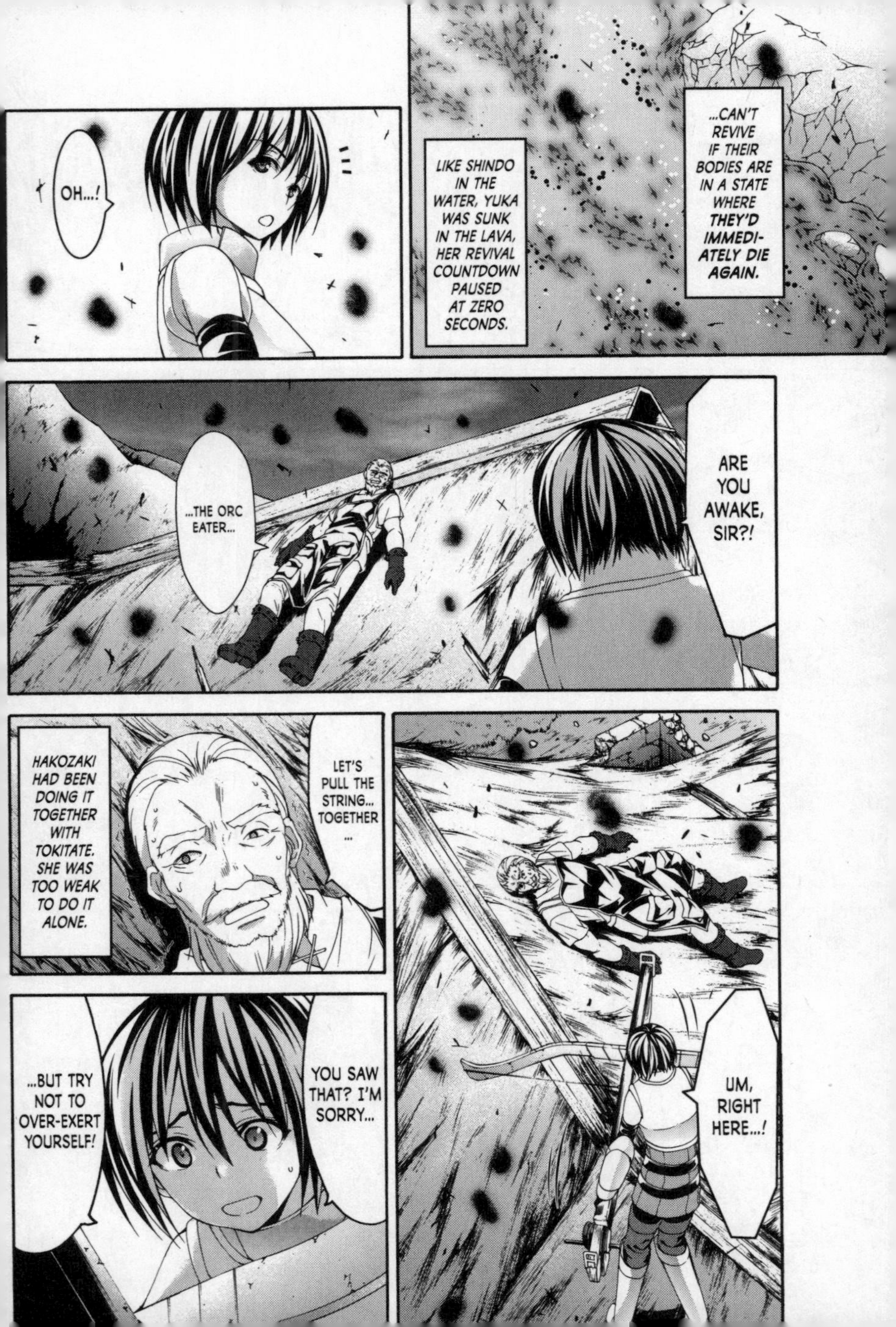
...CAN'T REVIVE IF THEIR BODIES ARE IN A STATE WHERE THEY'D IMMEDIATELY DIE AGAIN.
LIKE SHINDO IN THE WATER, YUKA WAS SUNK IN THE LAVA, HER REVIVAL COUNTDOWN PAUSED AT ZERO SECONDS.
OH...!
ARE YOU AWAKE, SIR?!
...THE ORC EATER...
UM, RIGHT HERE...!
LET'S PULL THE STRING... TOGETHER...
HAKOZAKI HAD BEEN DOING IT TOGETHER WITH TOKITATE. SHE WAS TOO WEAK TO DO IT ALONE.
YOU SAW THAT? I'M SORRY...
...BUT TRY NOT TO OVER-EXERT YOURSELF!

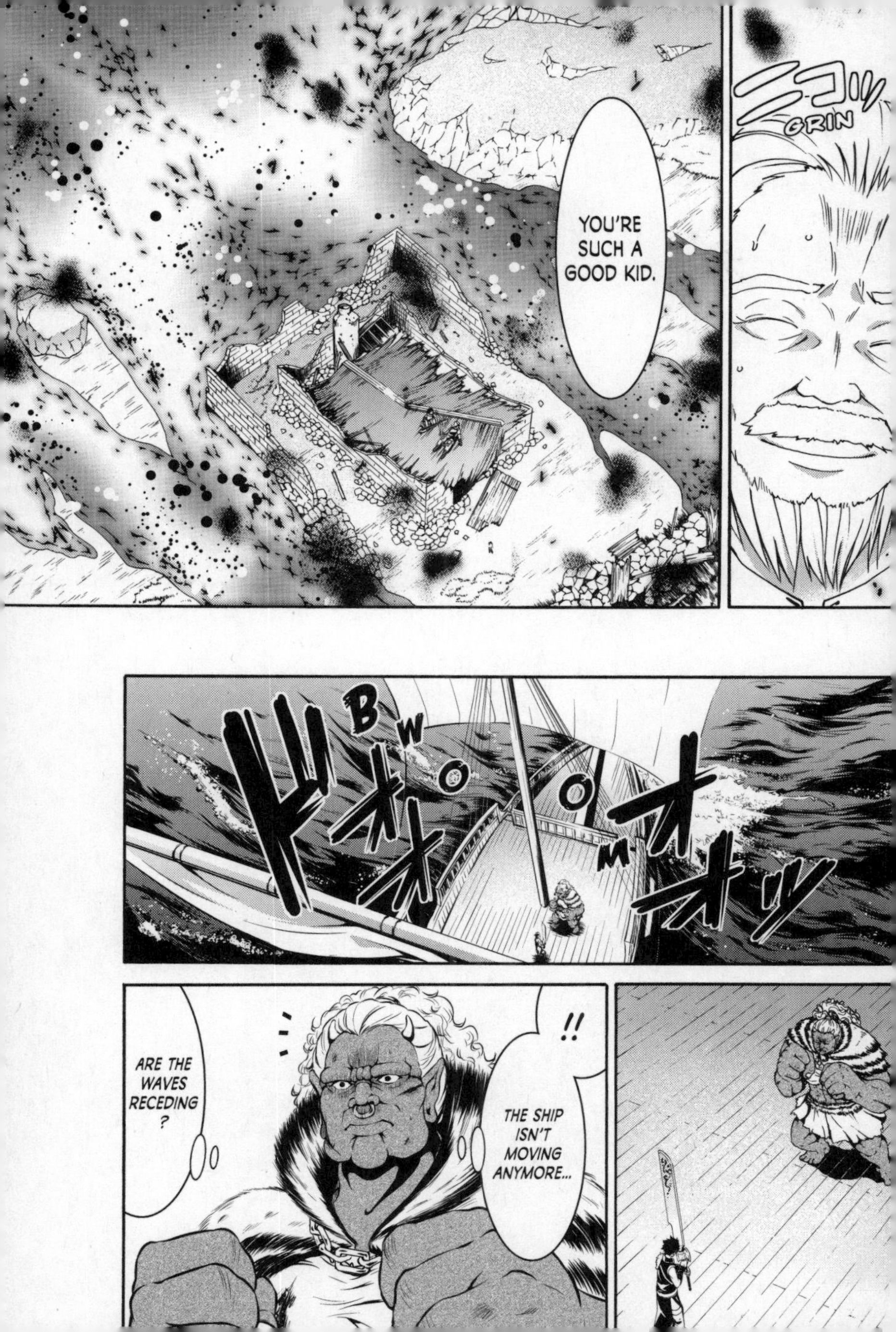
GRIN
YOU'RE SUCH A GOOD KID.
BWOOM
!!
THE SHIP ISN'T MOVING ANYMORE...
ARE THE WAVES RECEDING?

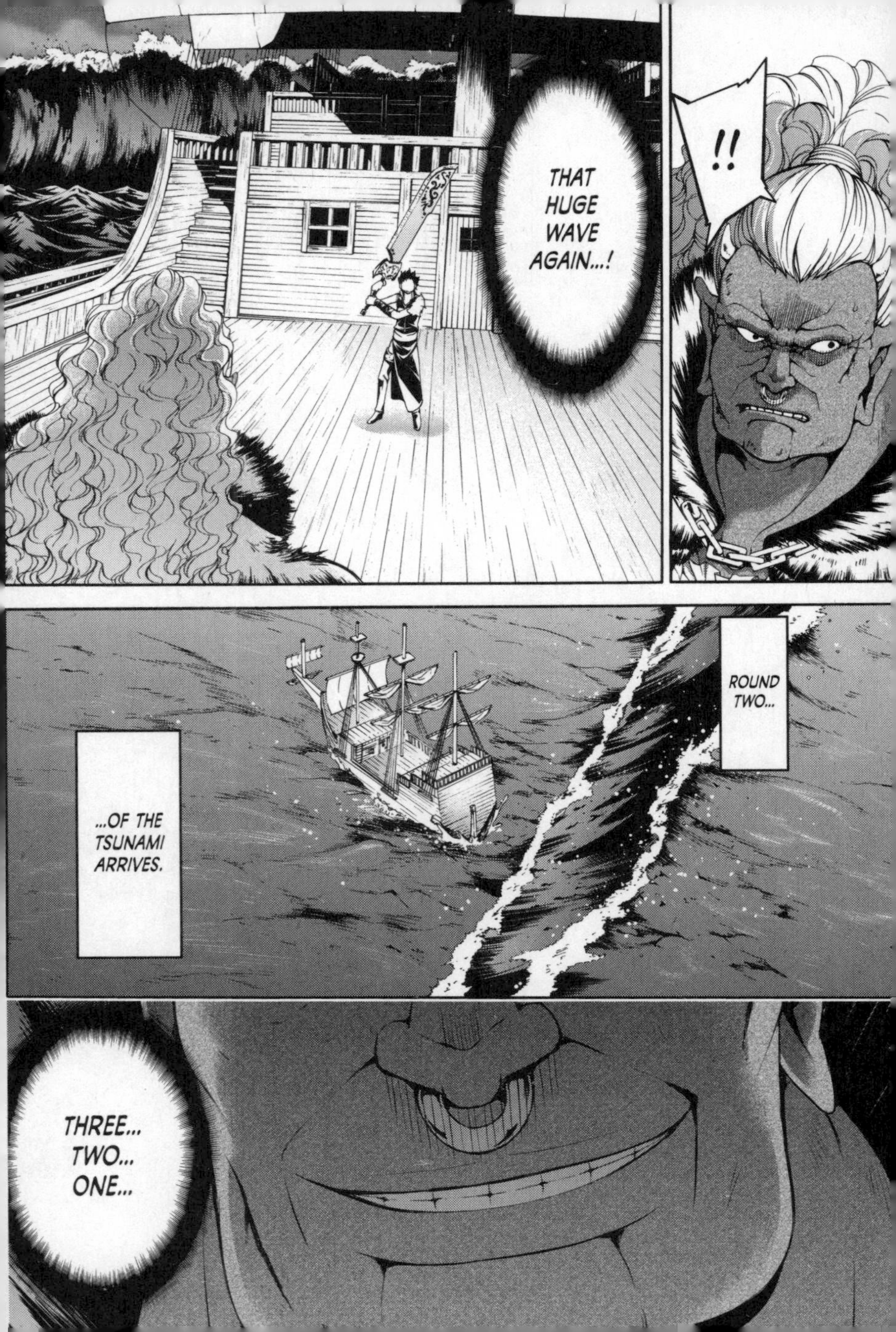
!!
THAT HUGE WAVE AGAIN...!
ROUND TWO...
...OF THE TSUNAMI ARRIVES.
THREE... TWO... ONE...

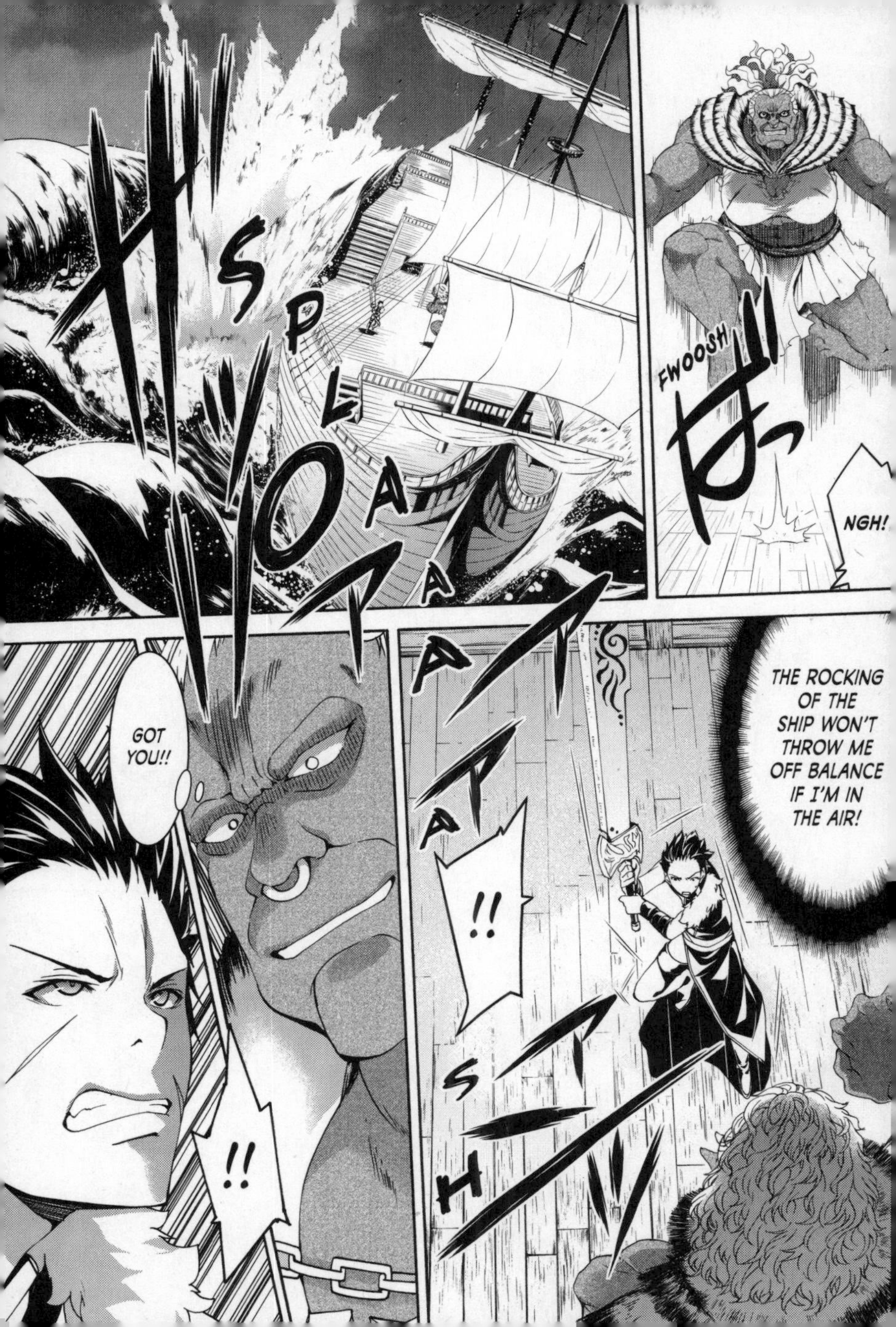
FWOOSH
NGH!
SPLAAAASH
THE ROCKING OF THE SHIP WON'T THROW ME OFF BALANCE IF I'M IN THE AIR!
!!
GOT YOU!!
!!

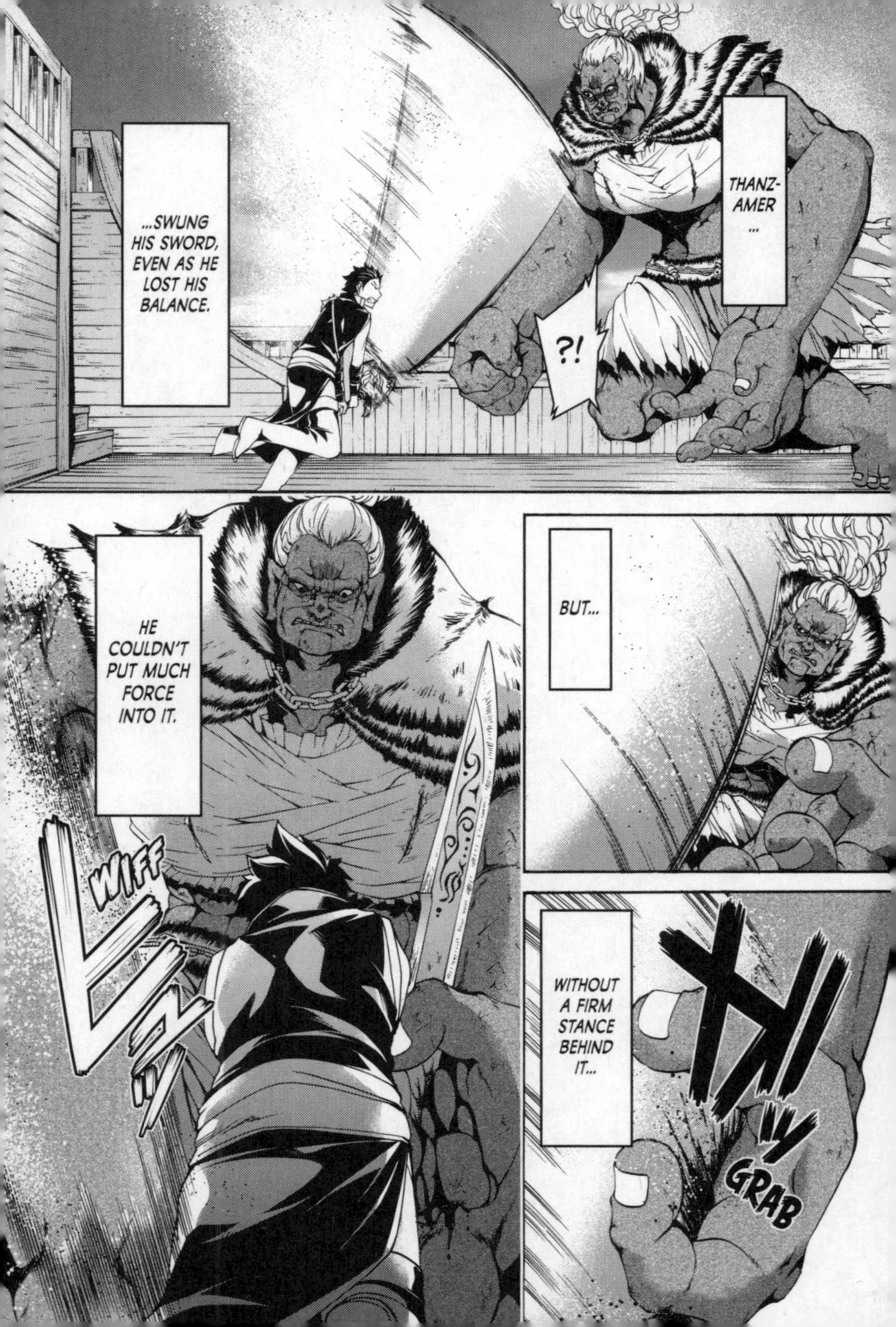
THANZ-AMER ...
?!
...SWUNG HIS SWORD, EVEN AS HE LOST HIS BALANCE.
BUT...
WITHOUT A FIRM STANCE BEHIND IT...
GRAB
HE COULDN'T PUT MUCH FORCE INTO IT.
WIFF

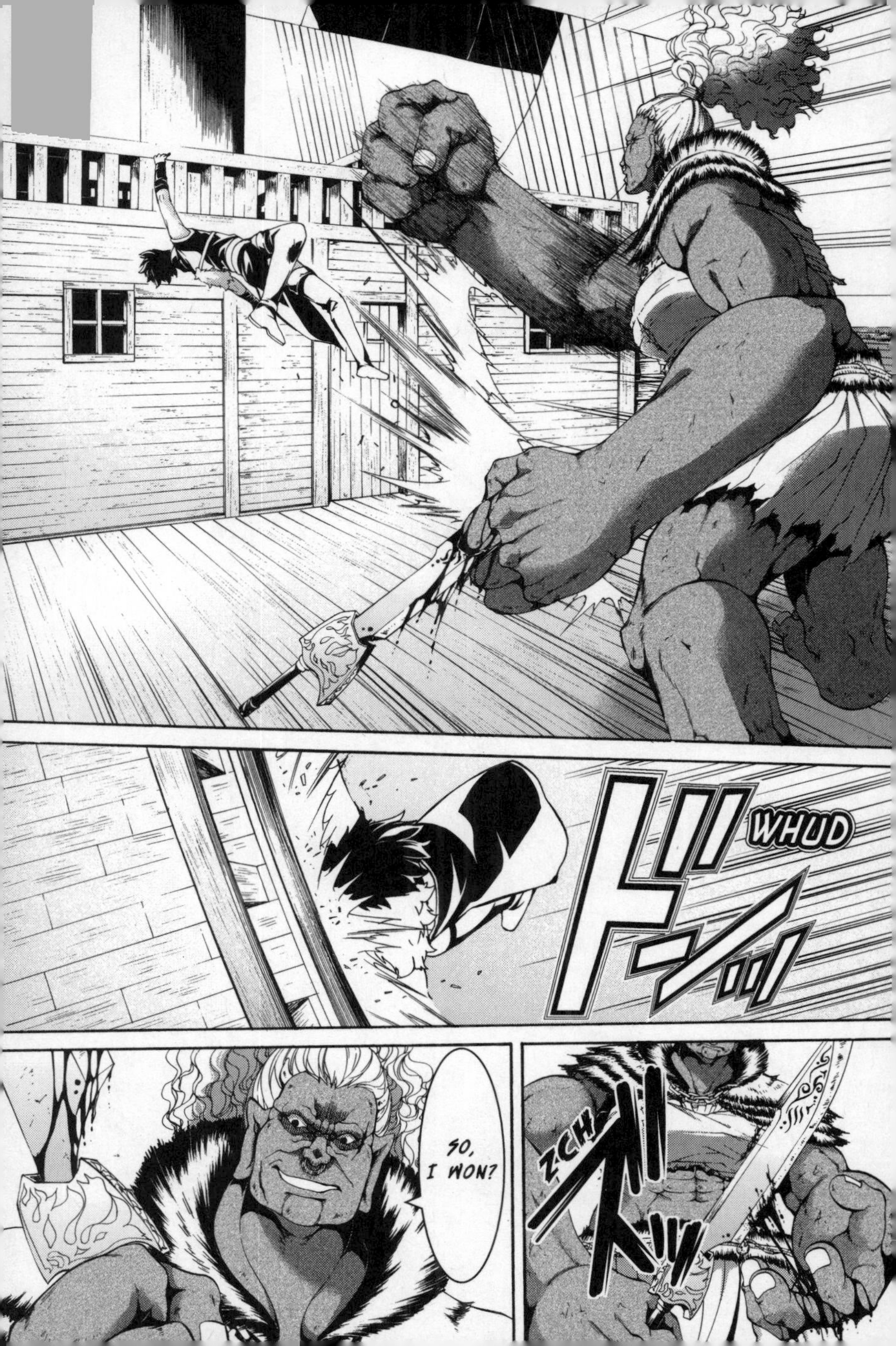
WHUD
ZCH
SO, I WON?

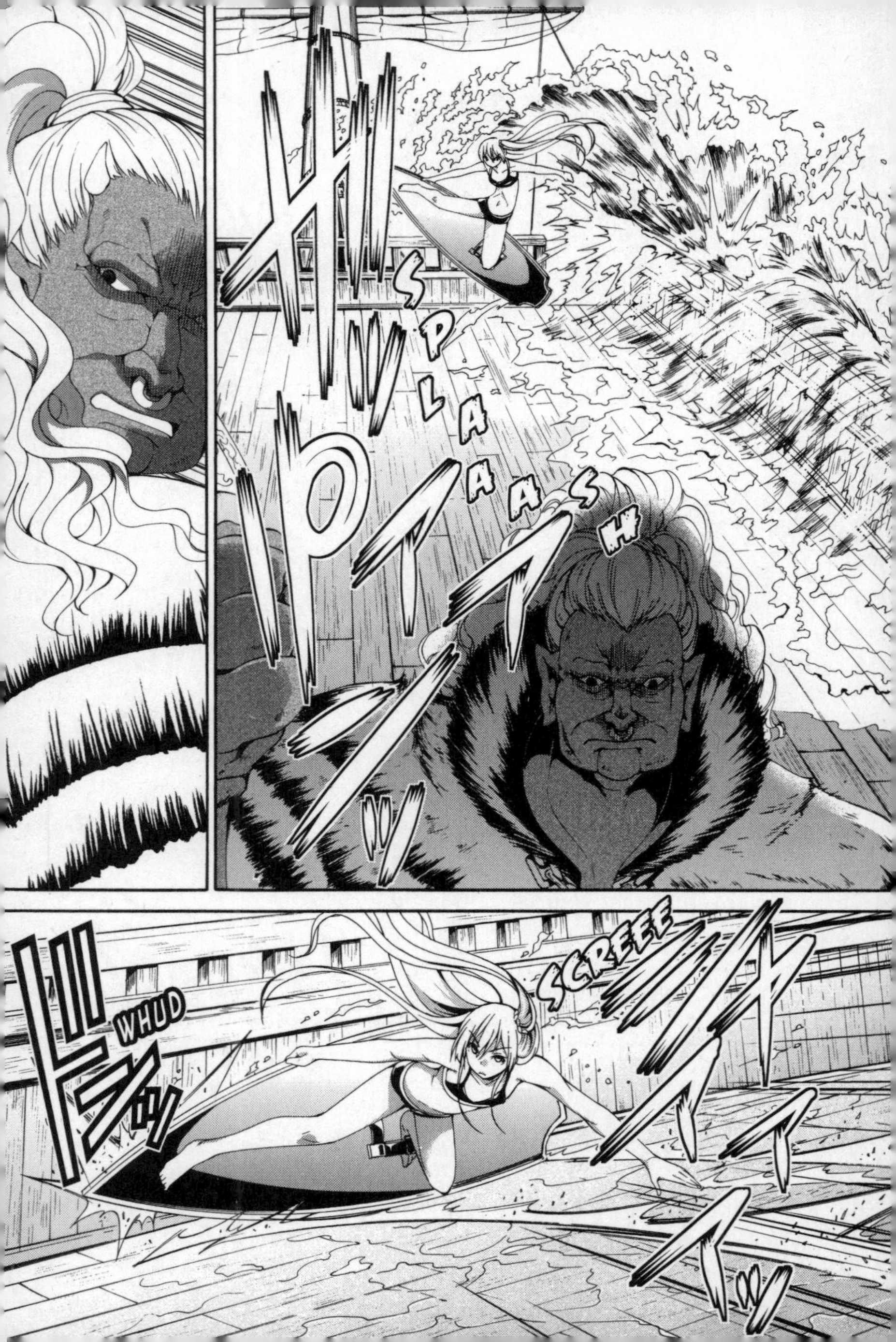
SPLAASH
SCREEE
WHUD

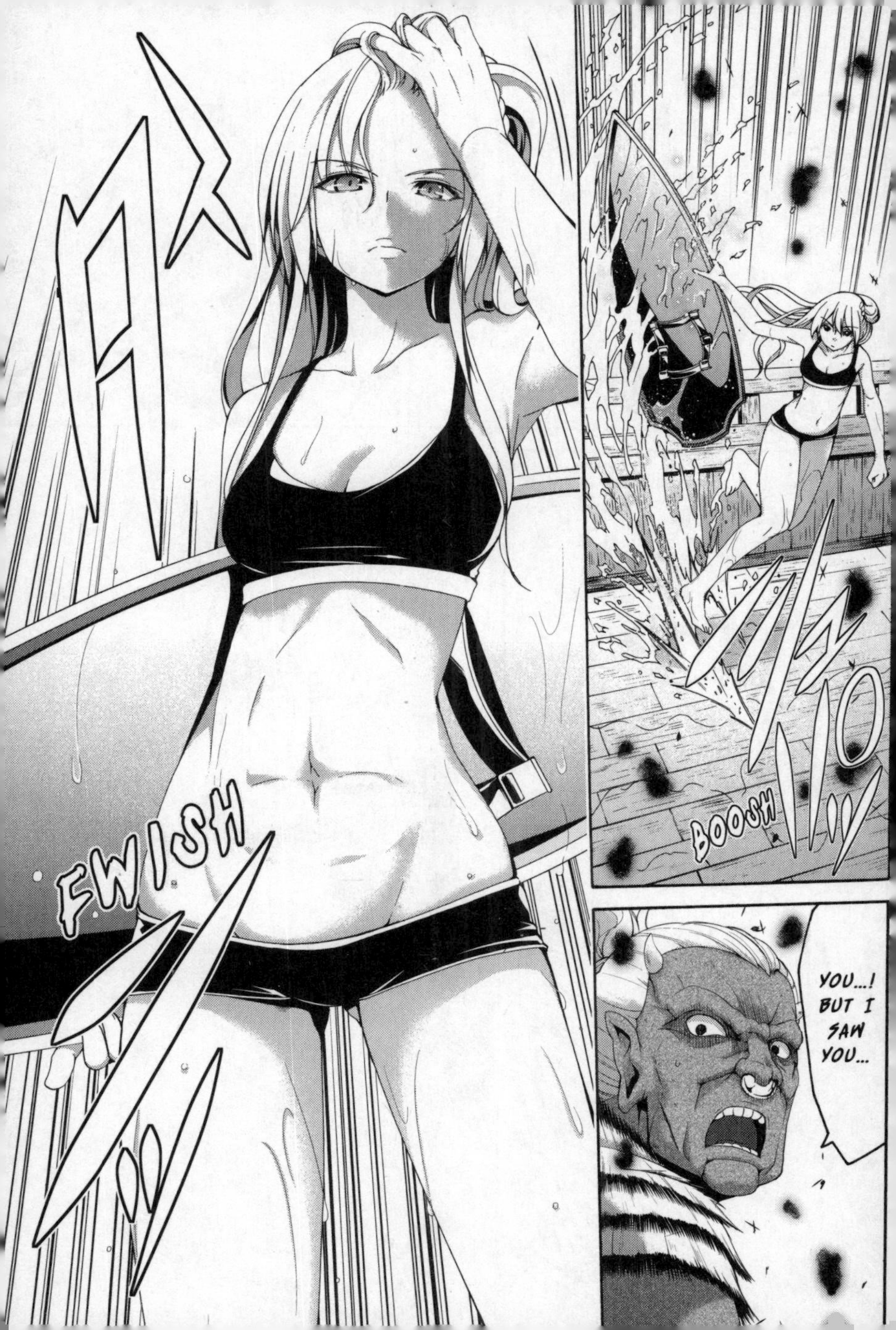
BOOSH
YOU...! BUT I SAW YOU...
FWISH

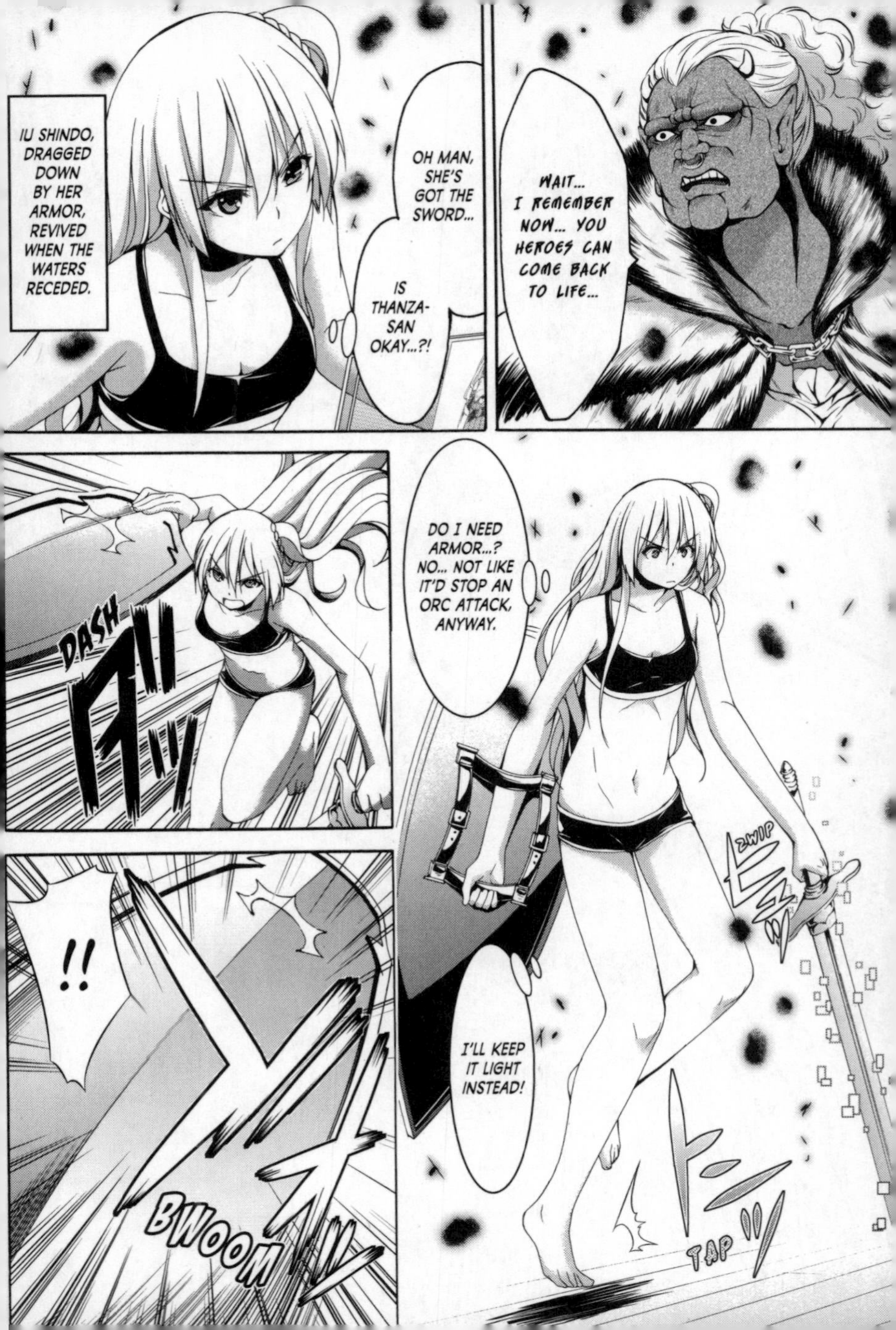
WAIT... I REMEMBER NOW... YOU HEROES CAN COME BACK TO LIFE...
OH MAN, SHE'S GOT THE SWORD...
IS THANZA-SAN OKAY...?!
IU SHINDO, DRAGGED DOWN BY HER ARMOR, REVIVED WHEN THE WATERS RECEDED.
DO I NEED ARMOR...? NO... NOT LIKE IT'D STOP AN ORC ATTACK, ANYWAY.
ZWIP
I'LL KEEP IT LIGHT INSTEAD!
TAP
DASH
!!
BWOOM

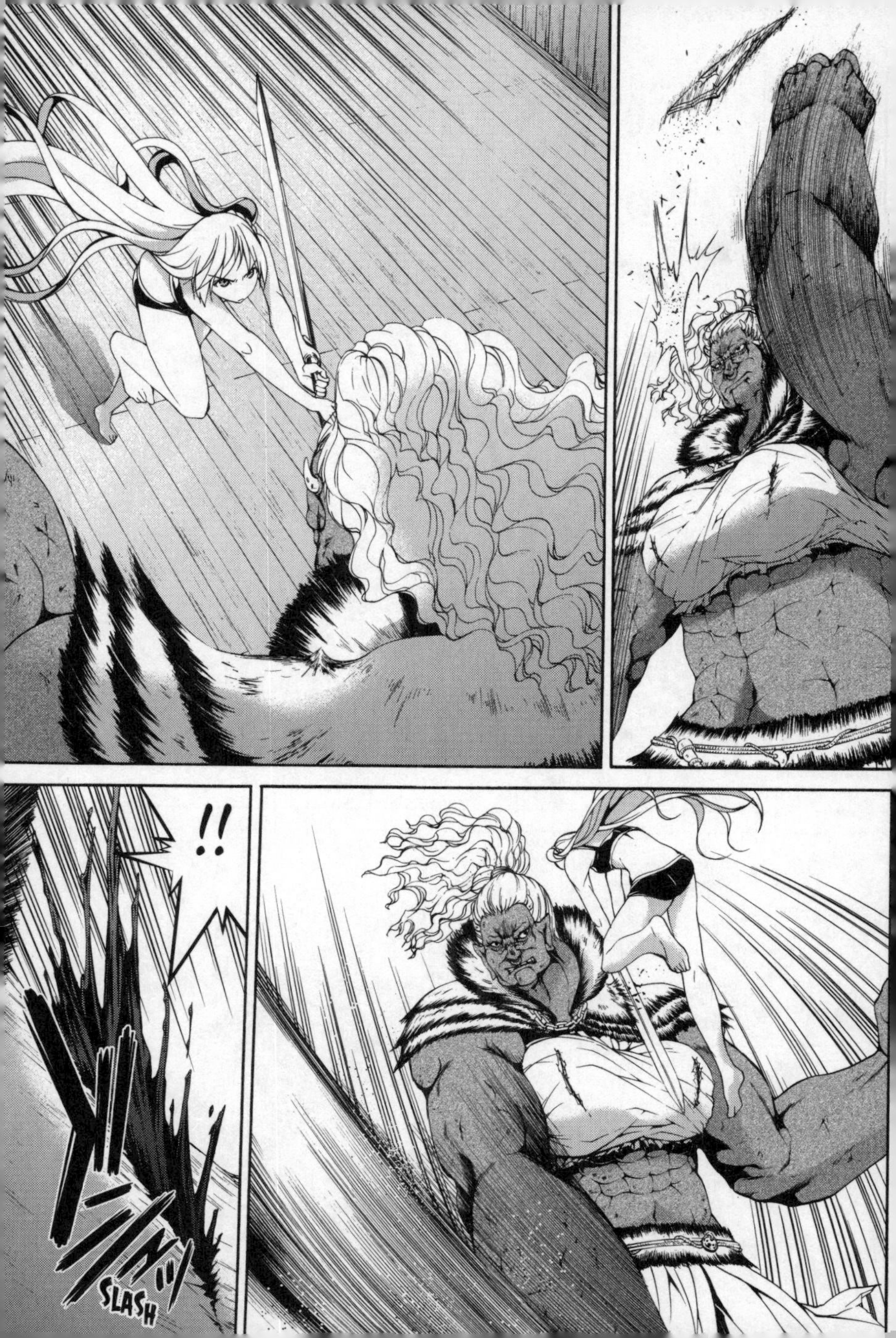
!!
SLASH

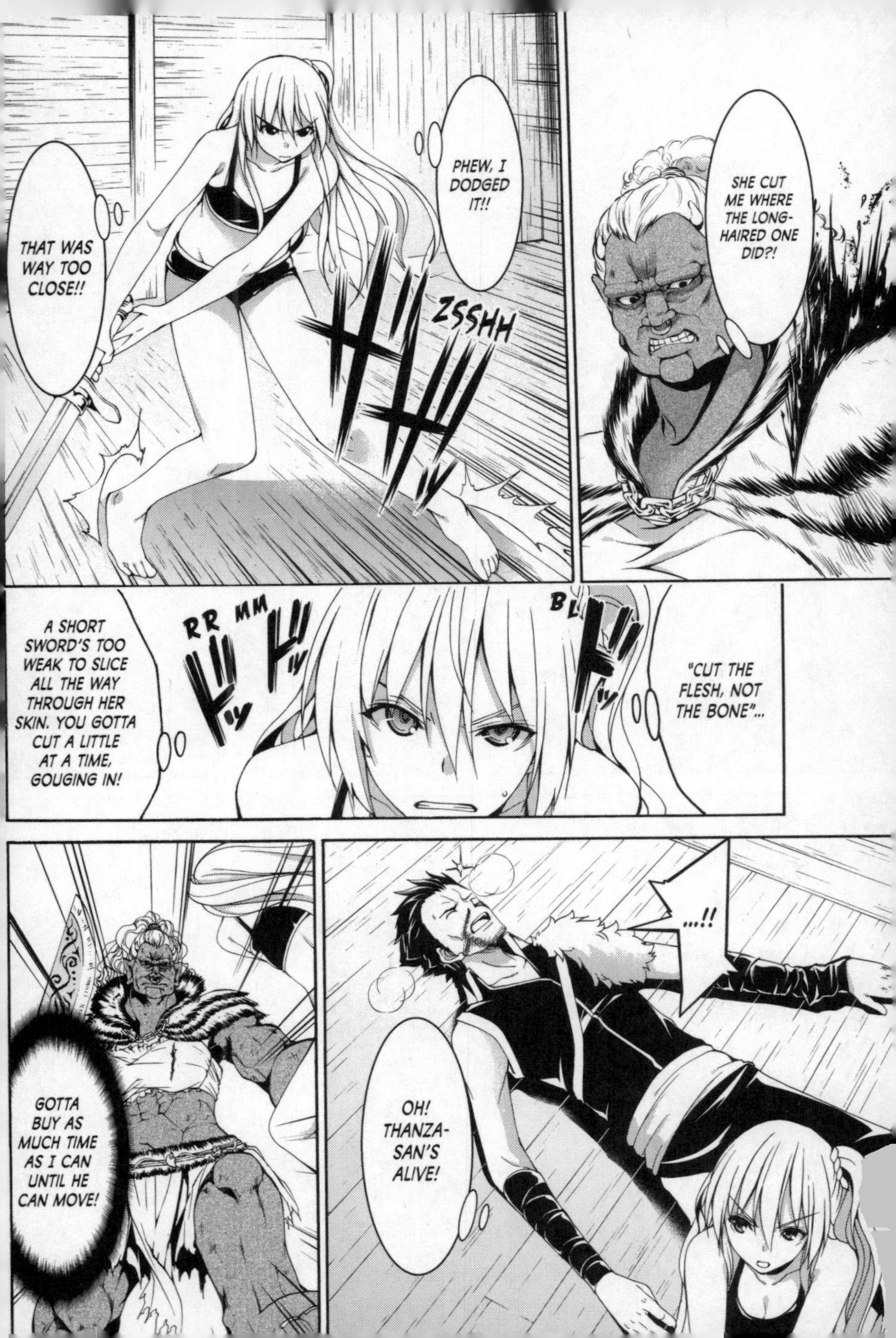
SHE CUT ME WHERE THE LONG-HAIRED ONE DID?!
PHEW, I DODGED IT!!
ZSSHH
THAT WAS WAY TOO CLOSE!!
BL
"CUT THE FLESH, NOT THE BONE"...
RR MM
A SHORT SWORD'S TOO WEAK TO SLICE ALL THE WAY THROUGH HER SKIN. YOU GOTTA CUT A LITTLE AT A TIME, GOUGING IN!
...!!
OH! THANZA-SAN'S ALIVE!
GOTTA BUY AS MUCH TIME AS I CAN UNTIL HE CAN MOVE!

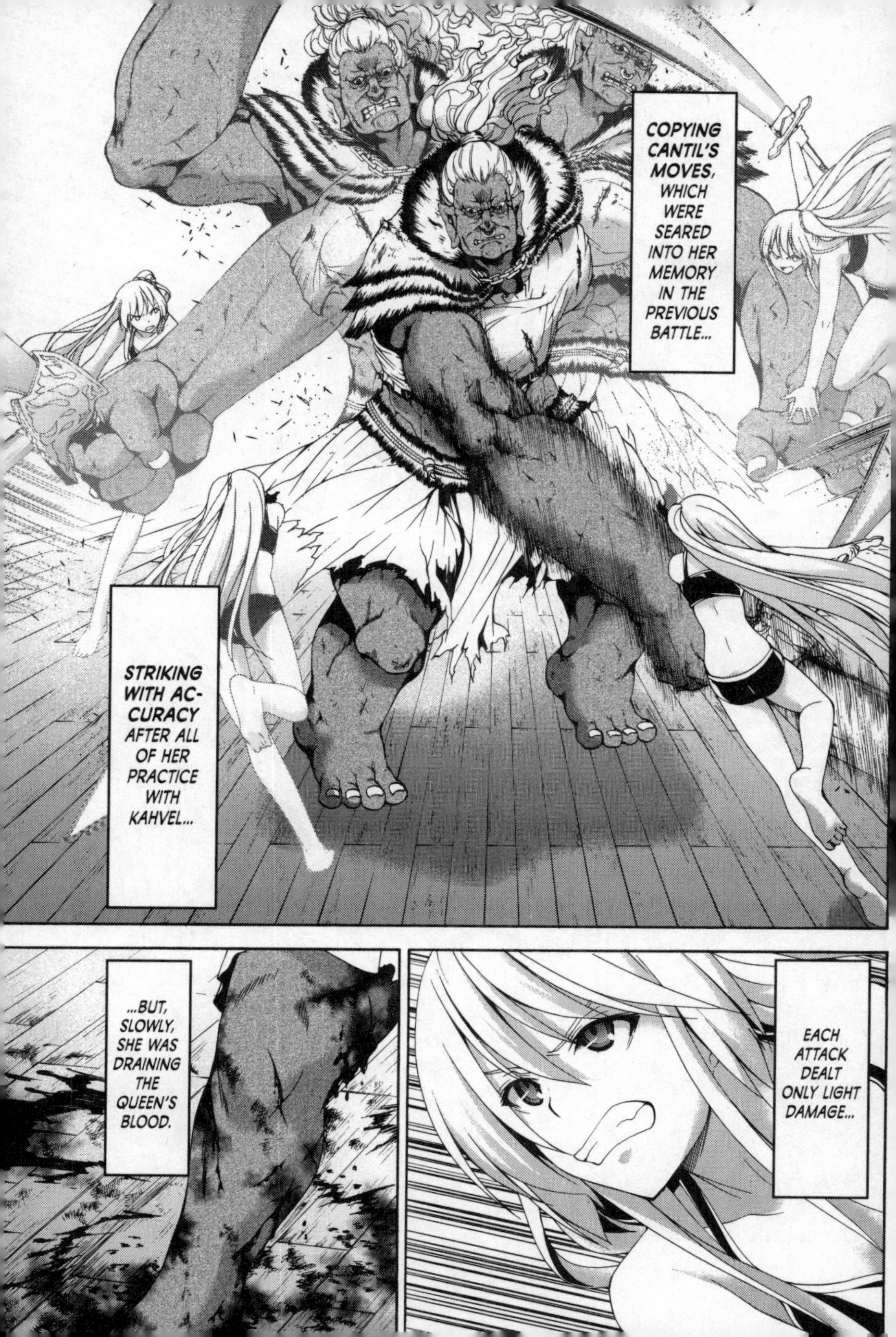
COPYING CANTIL'S MOVES, WHICH WERE SEARED INTO HER MEMORY IN THE PREVIOUS BATTLE...
STRIKING WITH AC-CURACY AFTER ALL OF HER PRACTICE WITH KAHVEL...
EACH ATTACK DEALT ONLY LIGHT DAMAGE...
...BUT, SLOWLY, SHE WAS DRAINING THE QUEEN'S BLOOD.

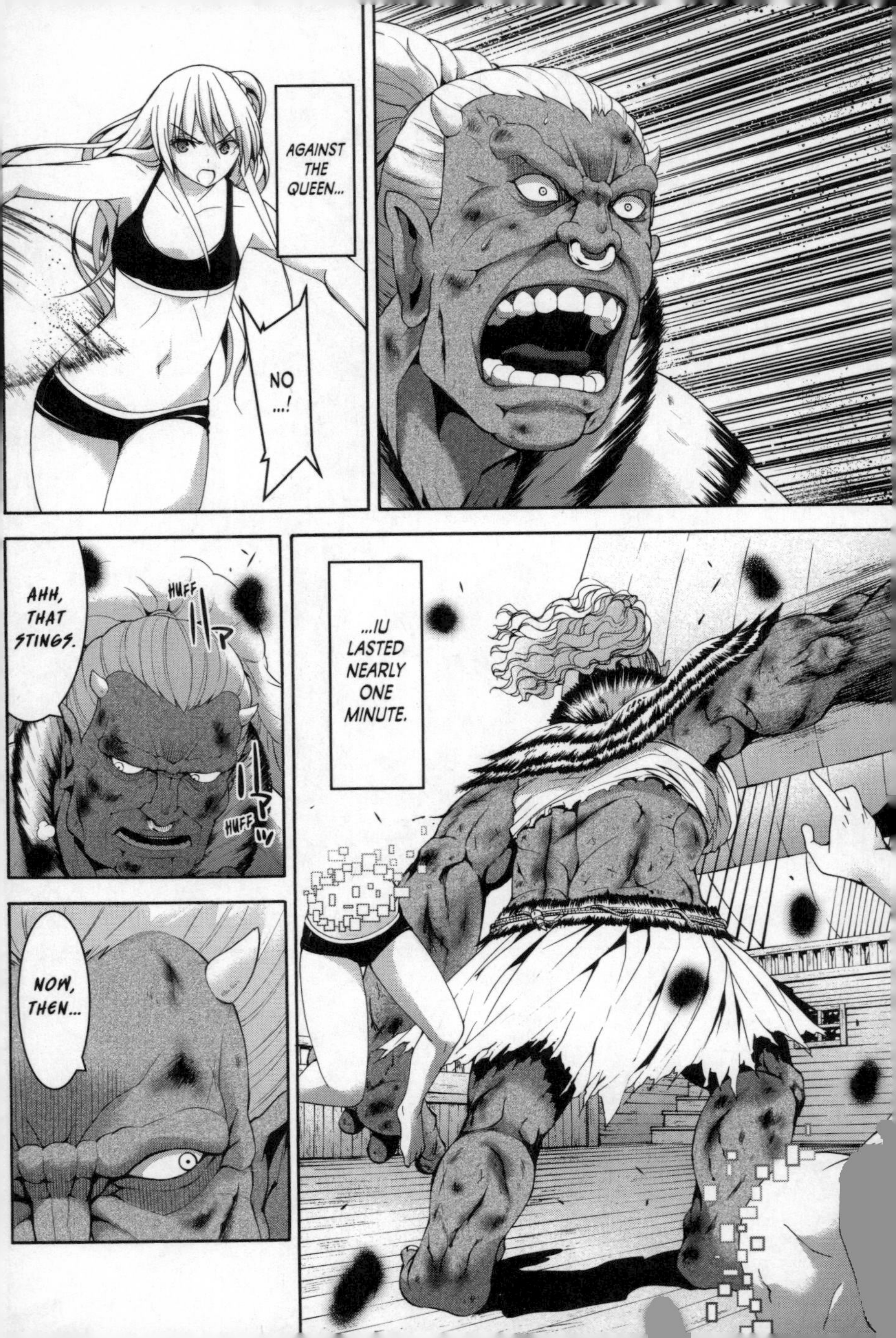
AGAINST THE QUEEN...
NO ...!
...IU LASTED NEARLY ONE MINUTE.
AHH, THAT STINGS.
HUFF
HUFF
NOW, THEN...

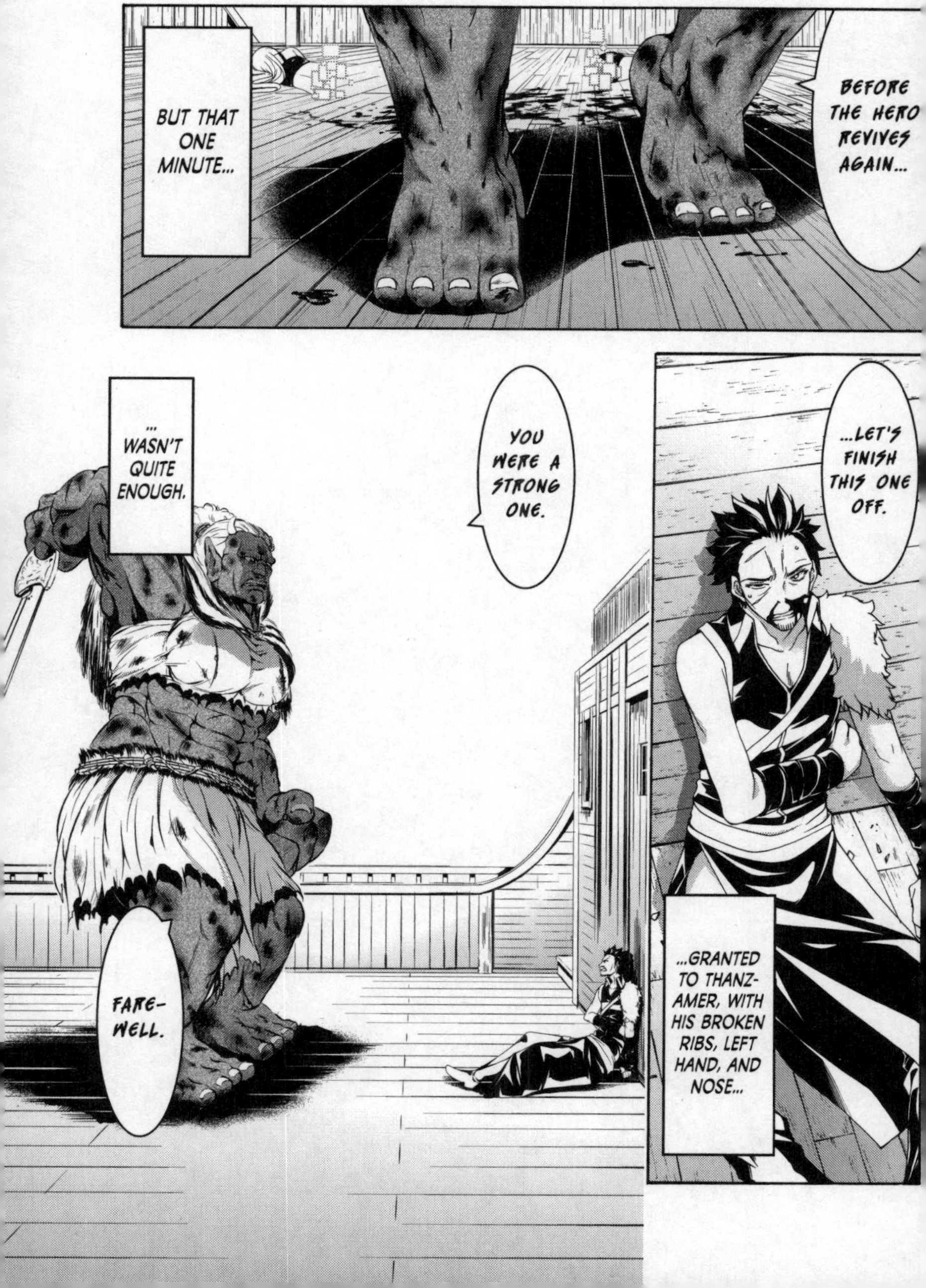
BEFORE THE HERO REVIVES AGAIN...
BUT THAT ONE MINUTE...
...LET'S FINISH THIS ONE OFF.
...GRANTED TO THANZ-AMER, WITH HIS BROKEN RIBS, LEFT HAND, AND NOSE...
YOU WERE A STRONG ONE.
...WASN'T QUITE ENOUGH.
FARE-WELL.

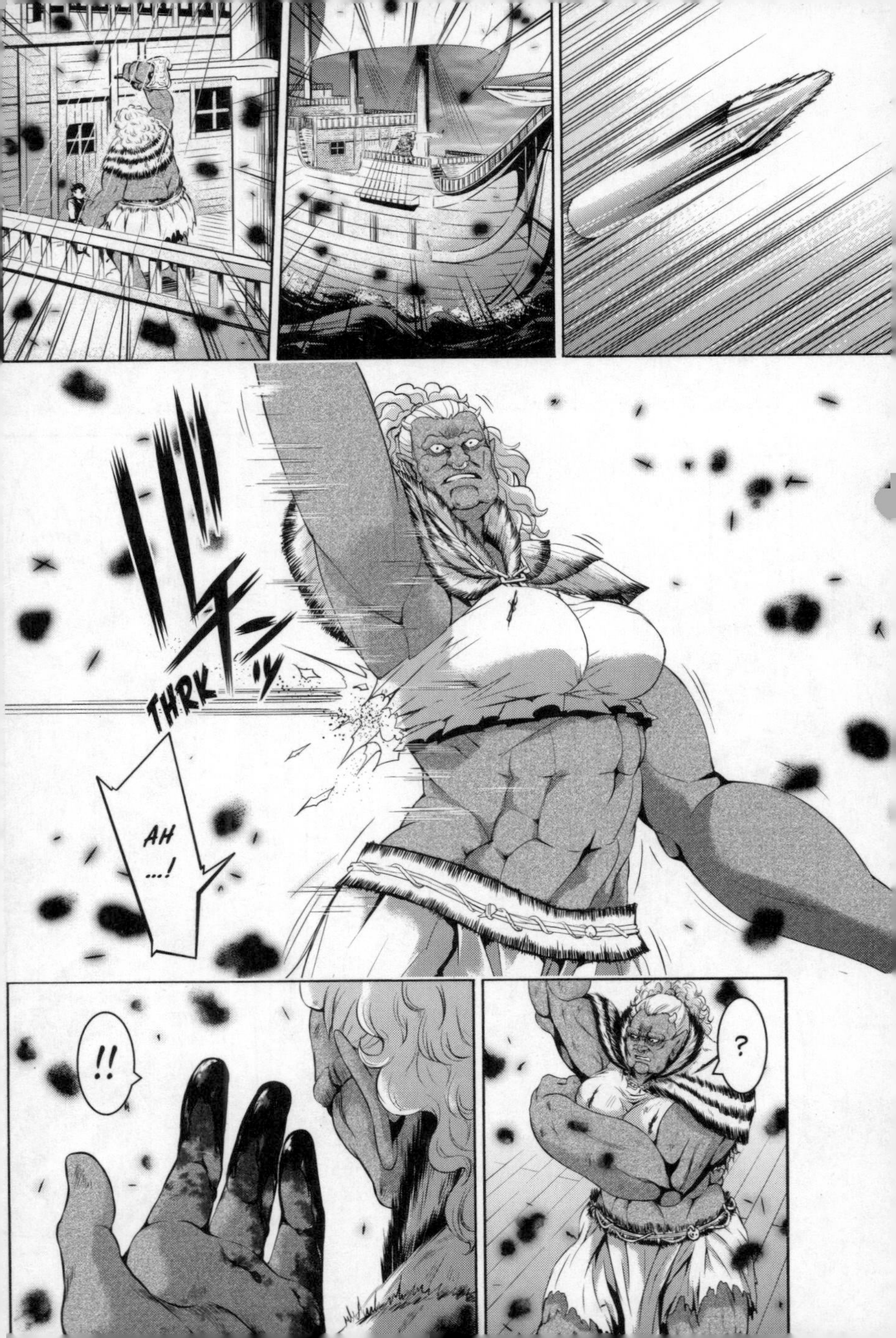
THRK
AH ...!
?
!!

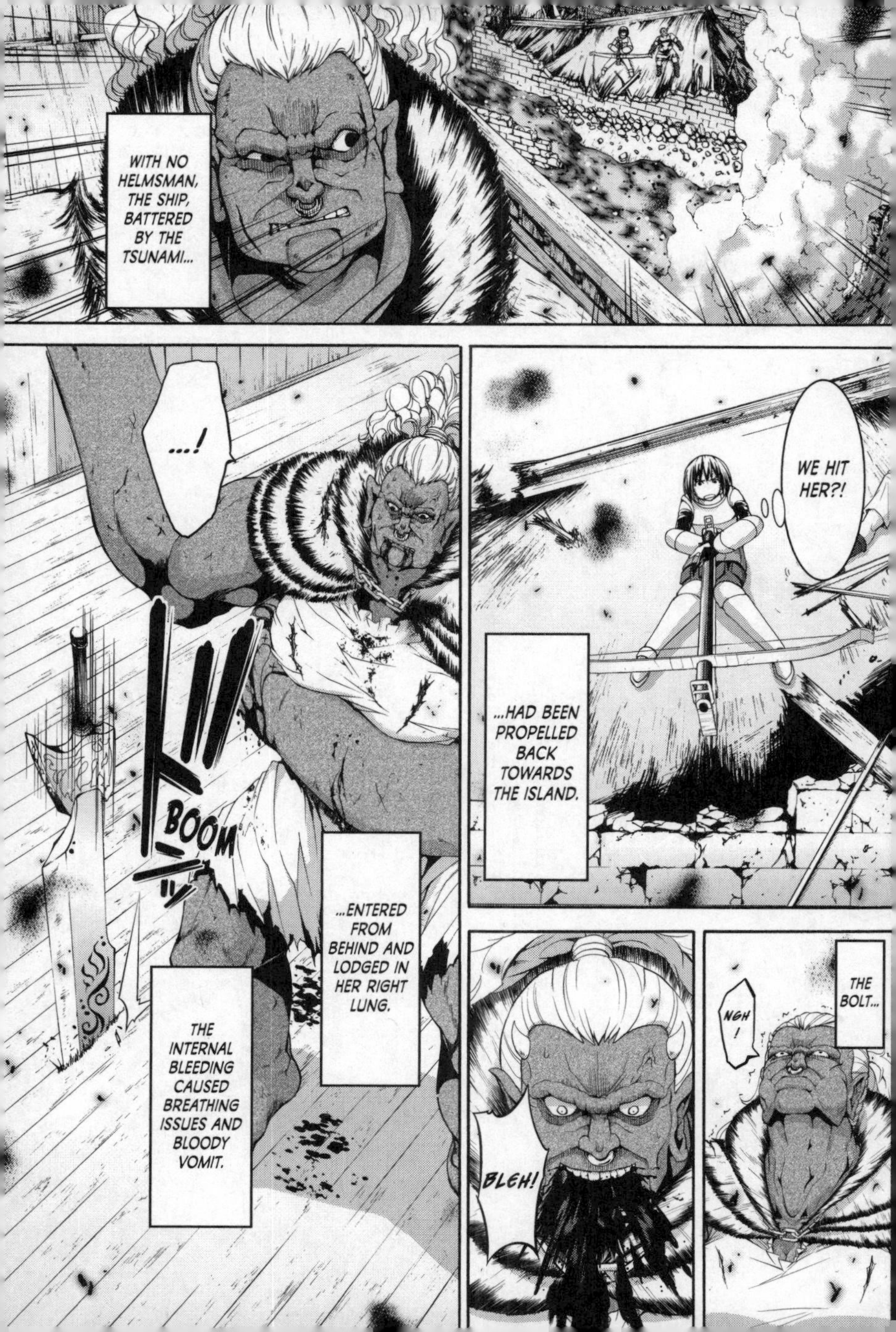
WITH NO HELMSMAN, THE SHIP, BATTERED BY THE TSUNAMI...
WE HIT HER?!
...HAD BEEN PROPELLED BACK TOWARDS THE ISLAND.
THE BOLT...
NGH!
BLEH!
...!
BOOM
...ENTERED FROM BEHIND AND LODGED IN HER RIGHT LUNG.
THE INTERNAL BLEEDING CAUSED BREATHING ISSUES AND BLOODY VOMIT.

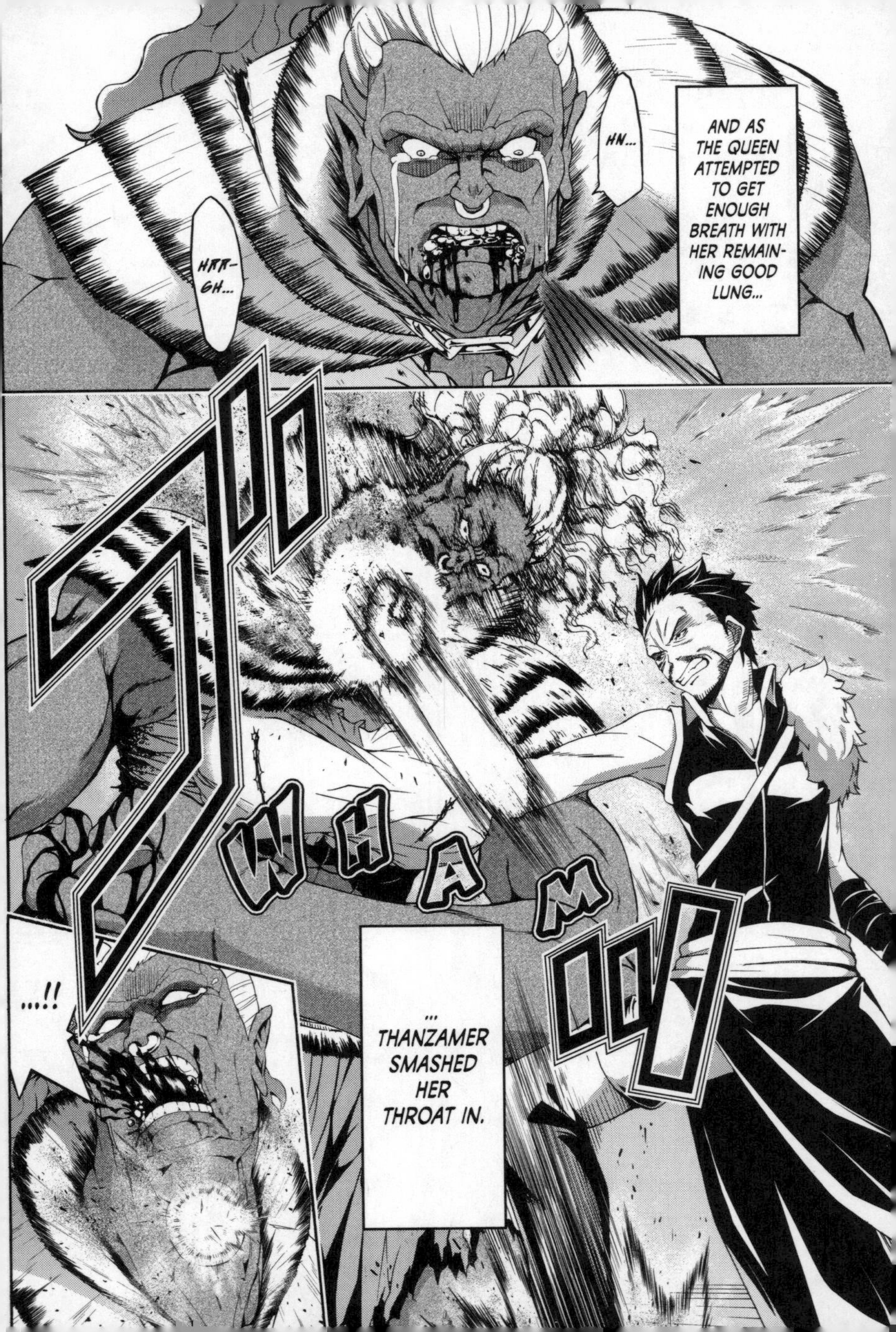
AND AS THE QUEEN ATTEMPTED TO GET ENOUGH BREATH WITH HER REMAINING GOOD LUNG...
HN...
HRR-GH...
WHAM
... THANZAMER SMASHED HER THROAT IN.
...!!

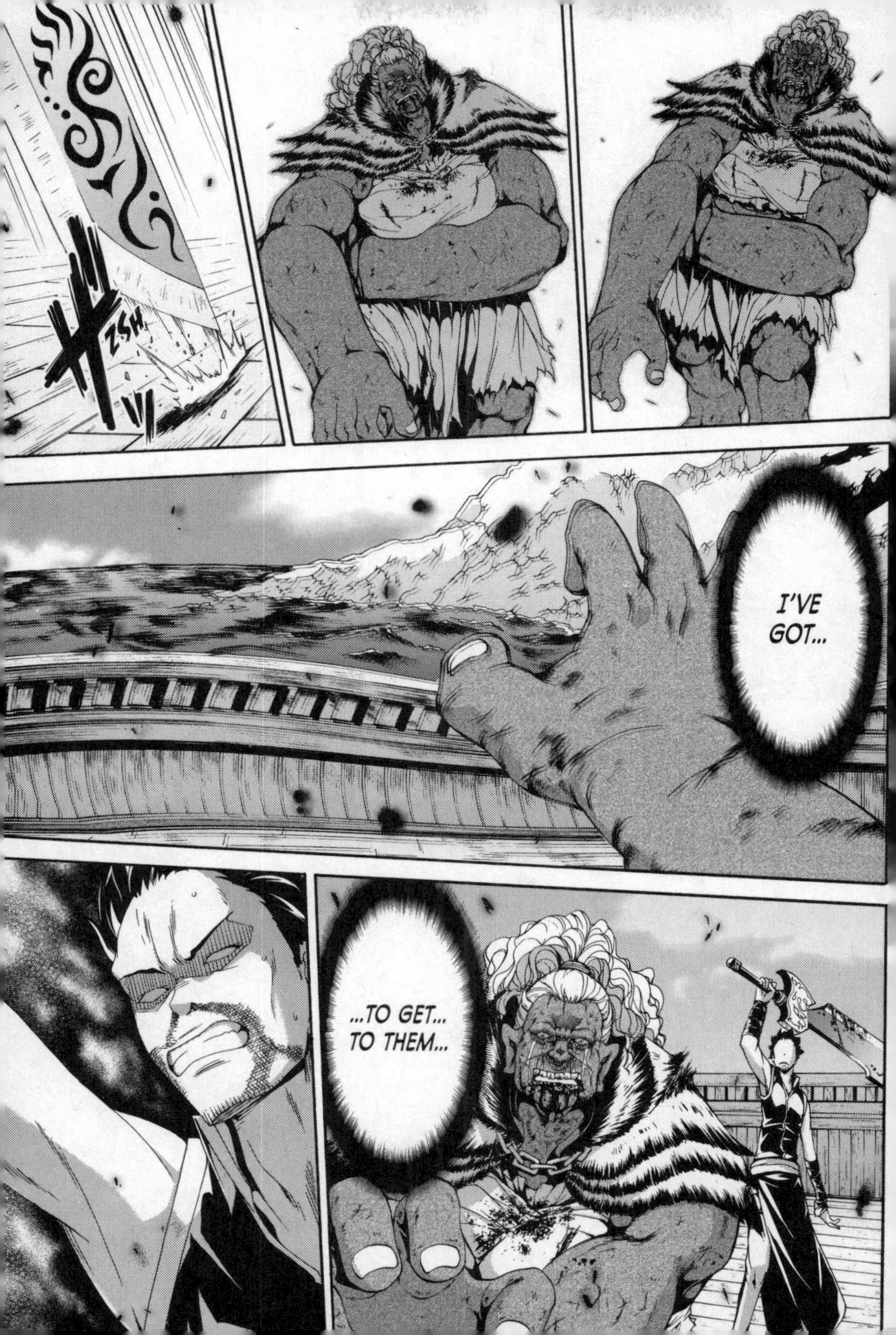
ZSH
I'VE GOT...
...TO GET... TO THEM...

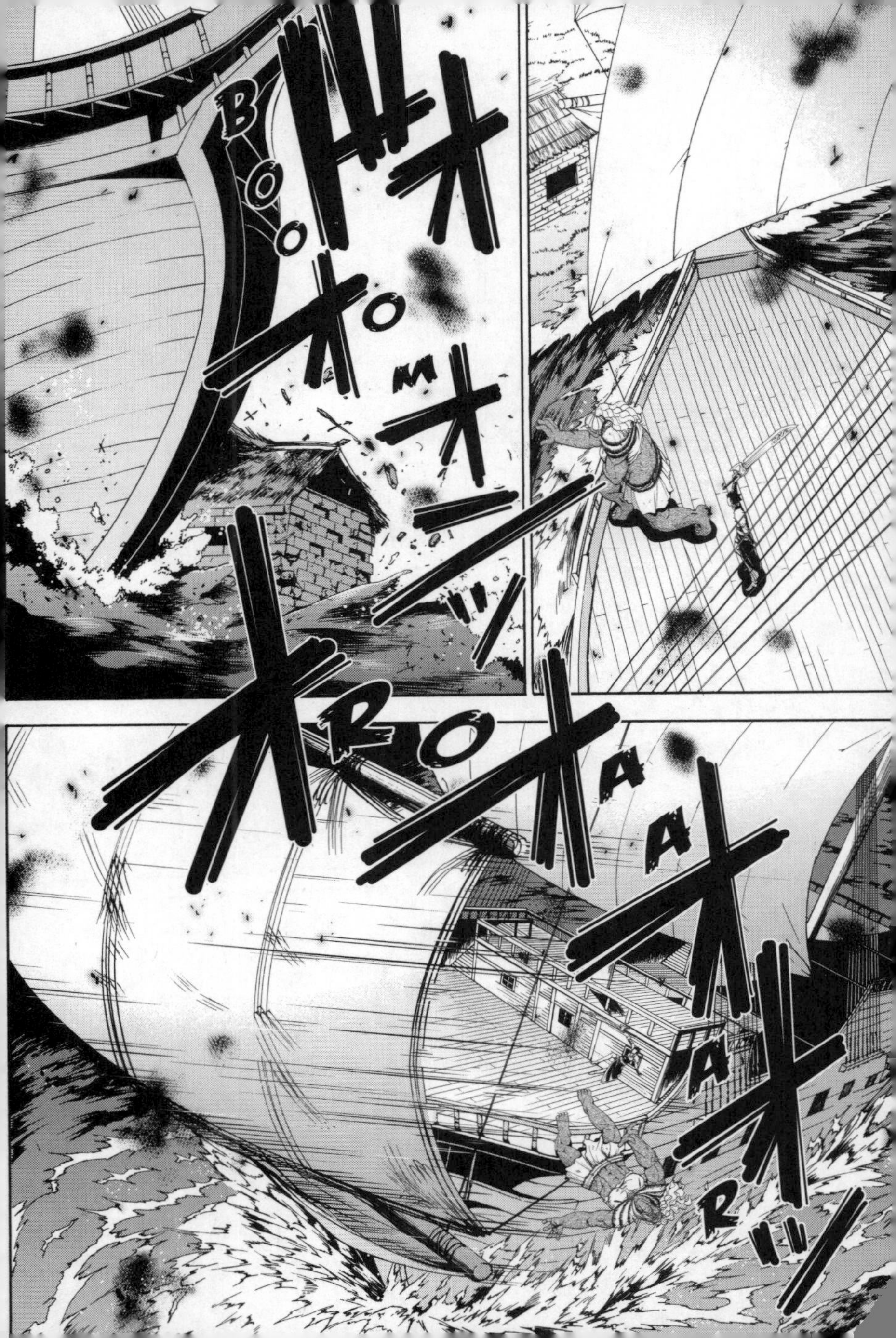
BOOOM
ROAAAR

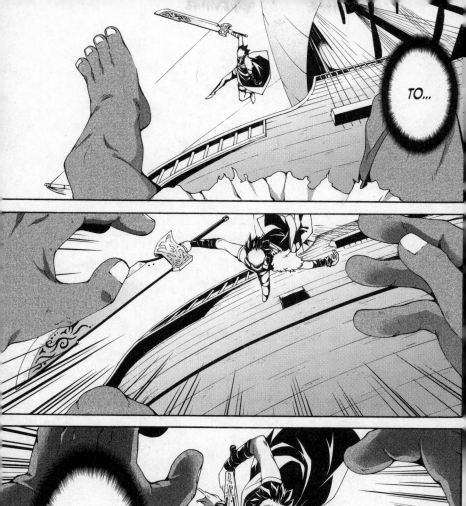

TO...

...MY
CHILDREN...

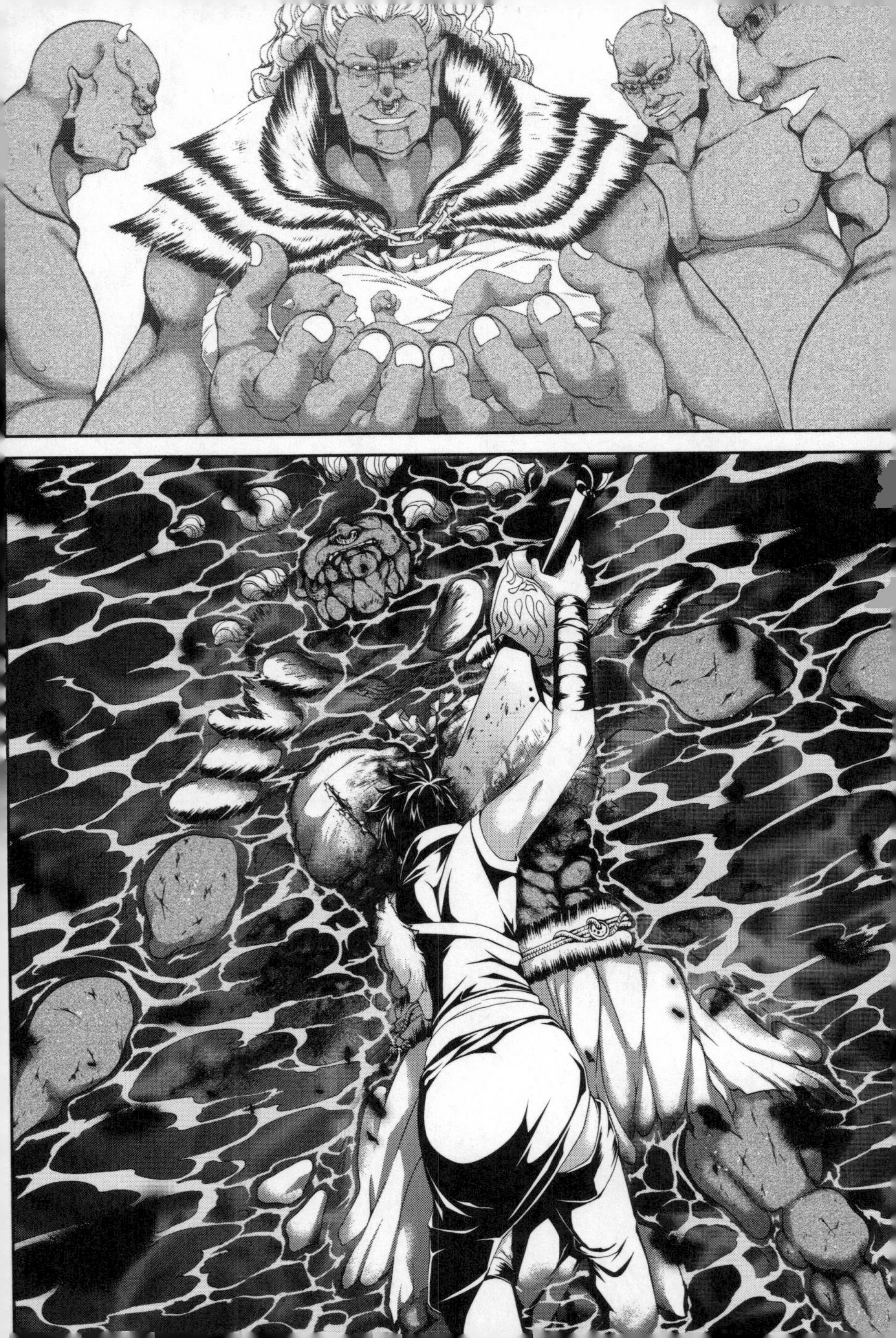

#22 Amid the Volcanic Gas...

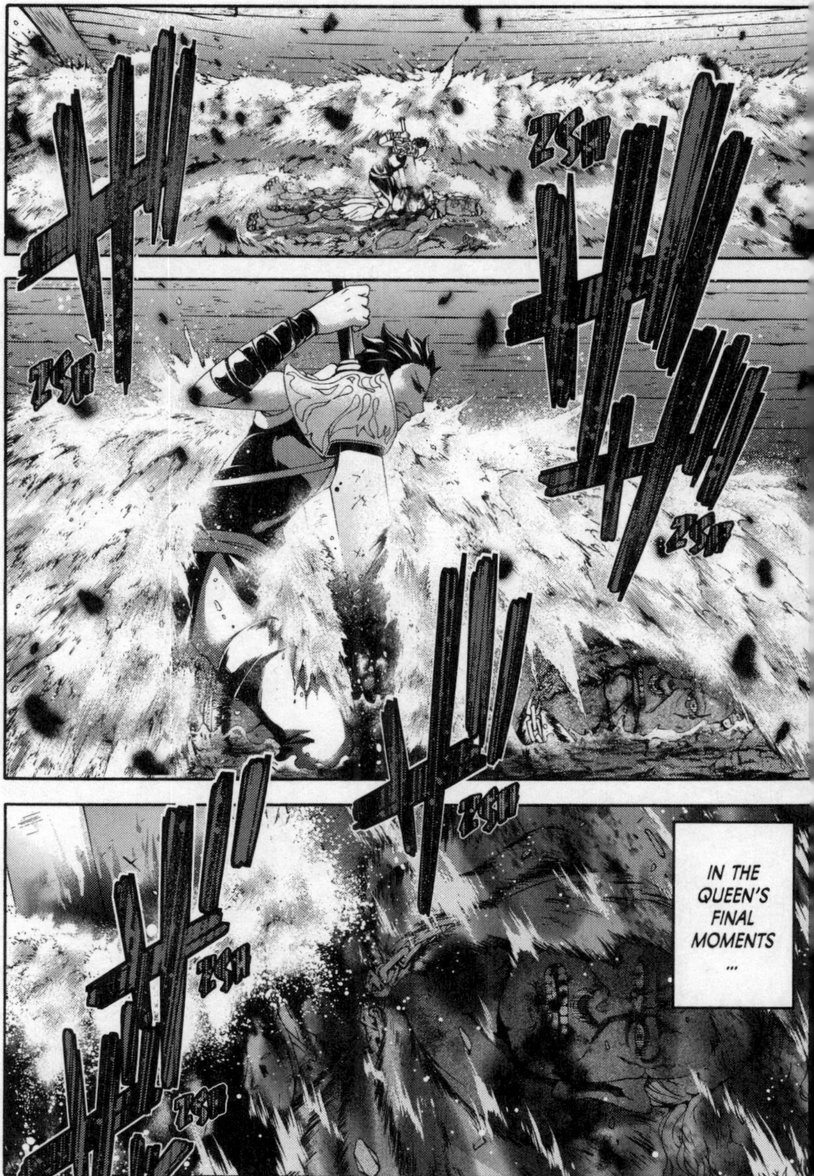
ZSH
IN THE QUEEN'S FINAL MOMENTS ...

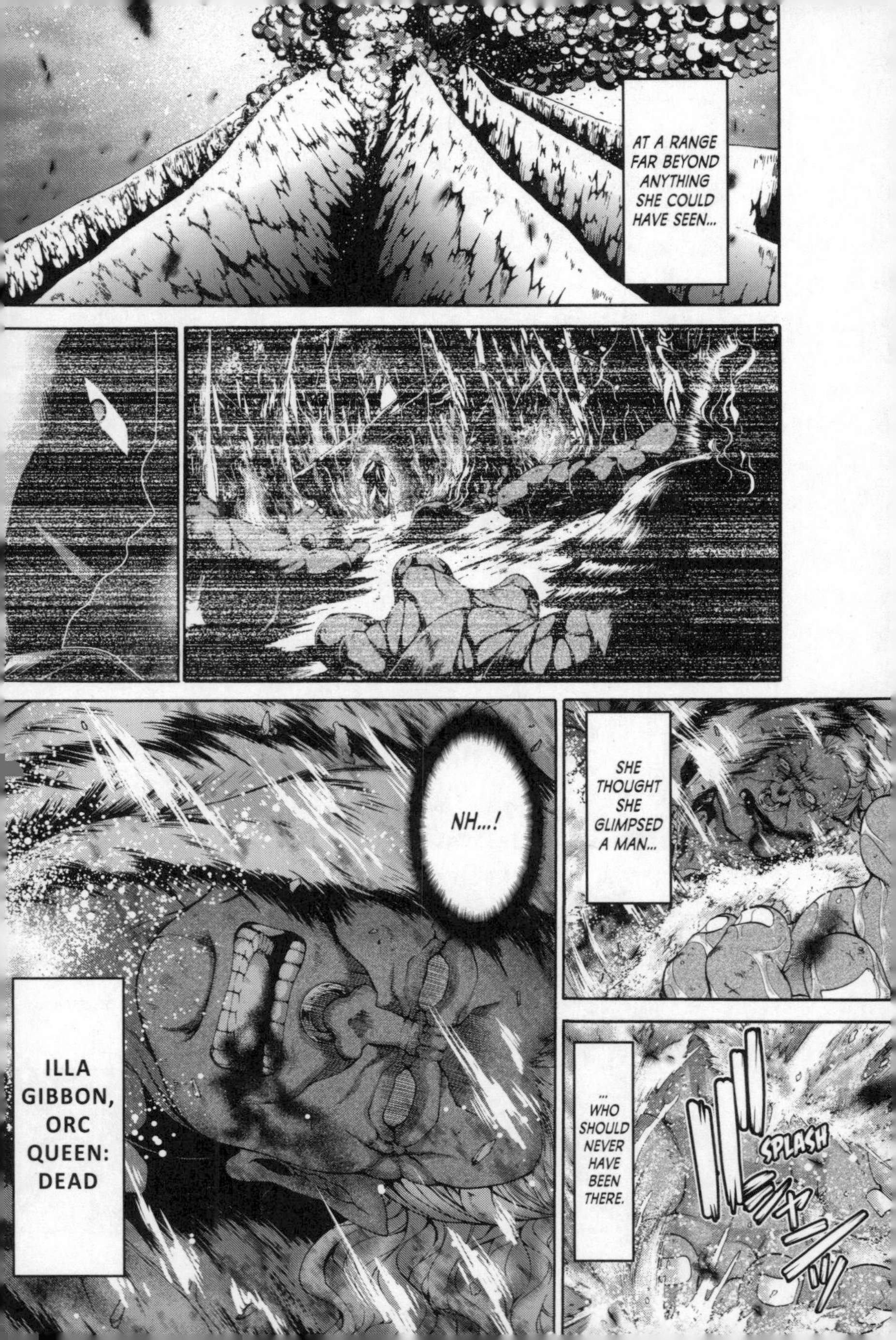
AT A RANGE FAR BEYOND ANYTHING SHE COULD HAVE SEEN...
SHE THOUGHT SHE GLIMPSED A MAN...
...WHO SHOULD NEVER HAVE BEEN THERE.
SPLASH
NH...!
ILLA GIBBON, ORC QUEEN: DEAD

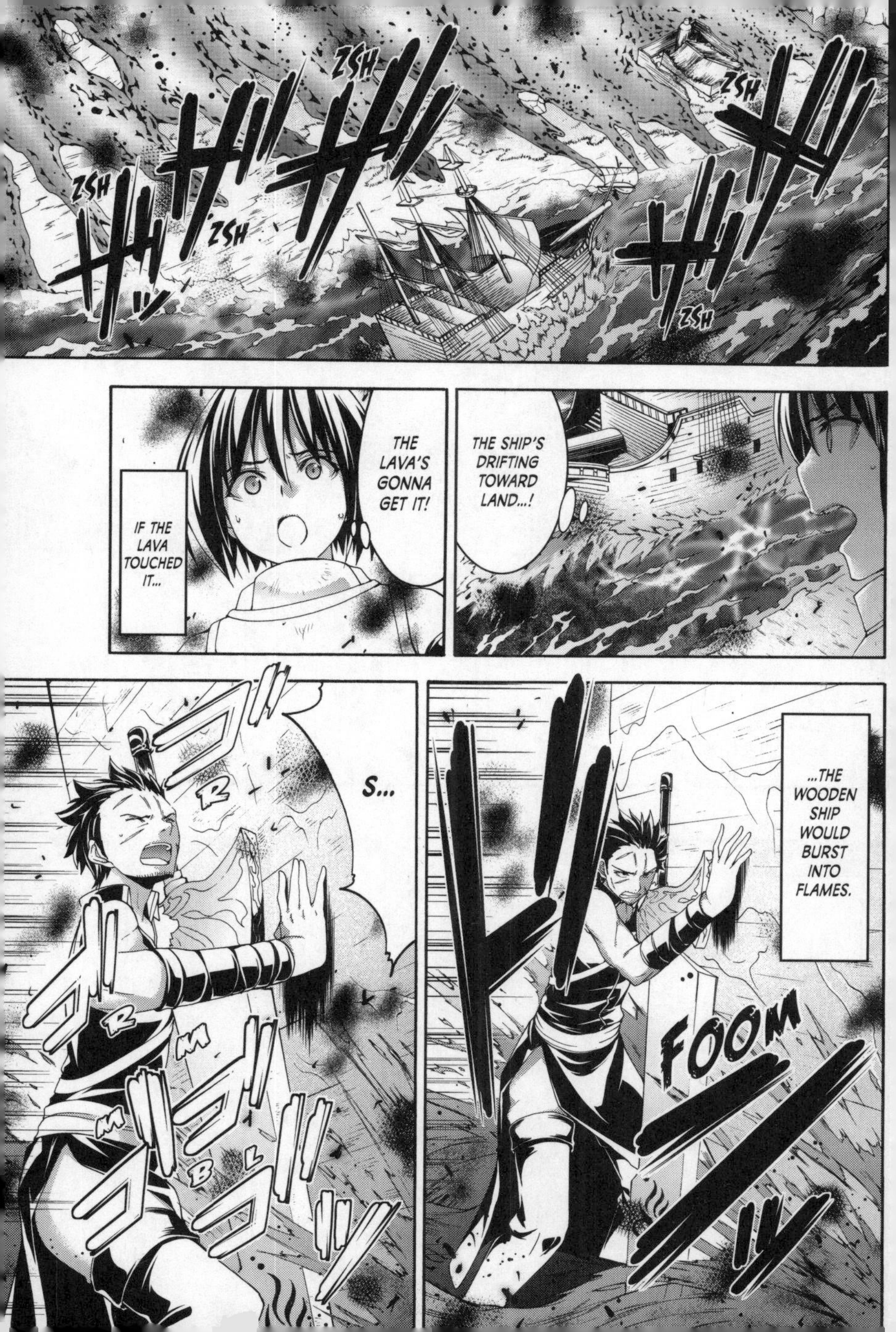
ZSH
ZSH
ZSH
ZSH
ZSH
THE SHIP'S DRIFTING TOWARD LAND...!
THE LAVA'S GONNA GET IT!
IF THE LAVA TOUCHED IT...
...THE WOODEN SHIP WOULD BURST INTO FLAMES.
FOOM
S...

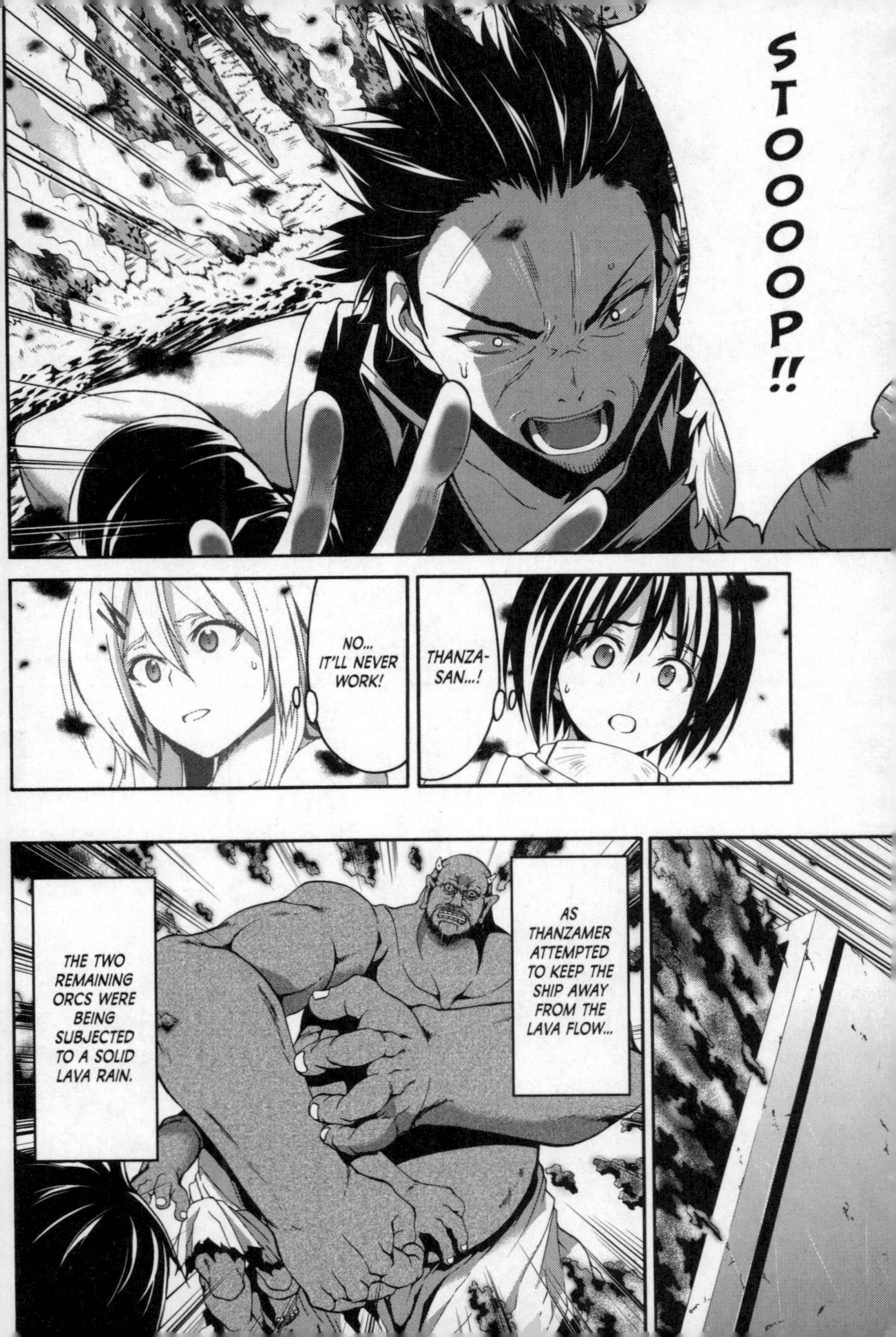
STOOOOP!!
THANZA-SAN...!
NO... IT'LL NEVER WORK!
AS THANZAMER ATTEMPTED TO KEEP THE SHIP AWAY FROM THE LAVA FLOW...
THE TWO REMAINING ORCS WERE BEING SUBJECTED TO A SOLID LAVA RAIN.

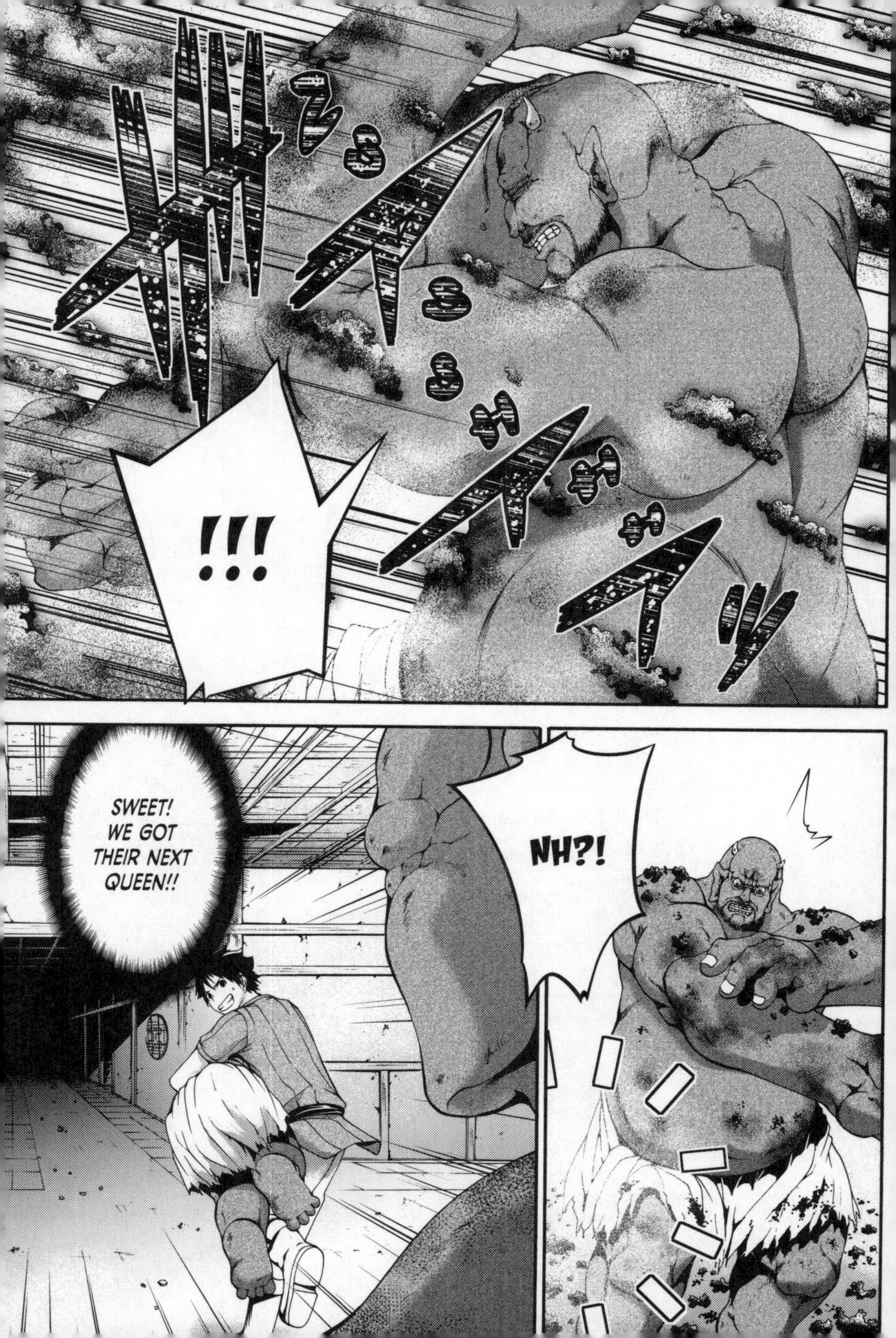
!!!
NH?!
SWEET! WE GOT THEIR NEXT QUEEN!!

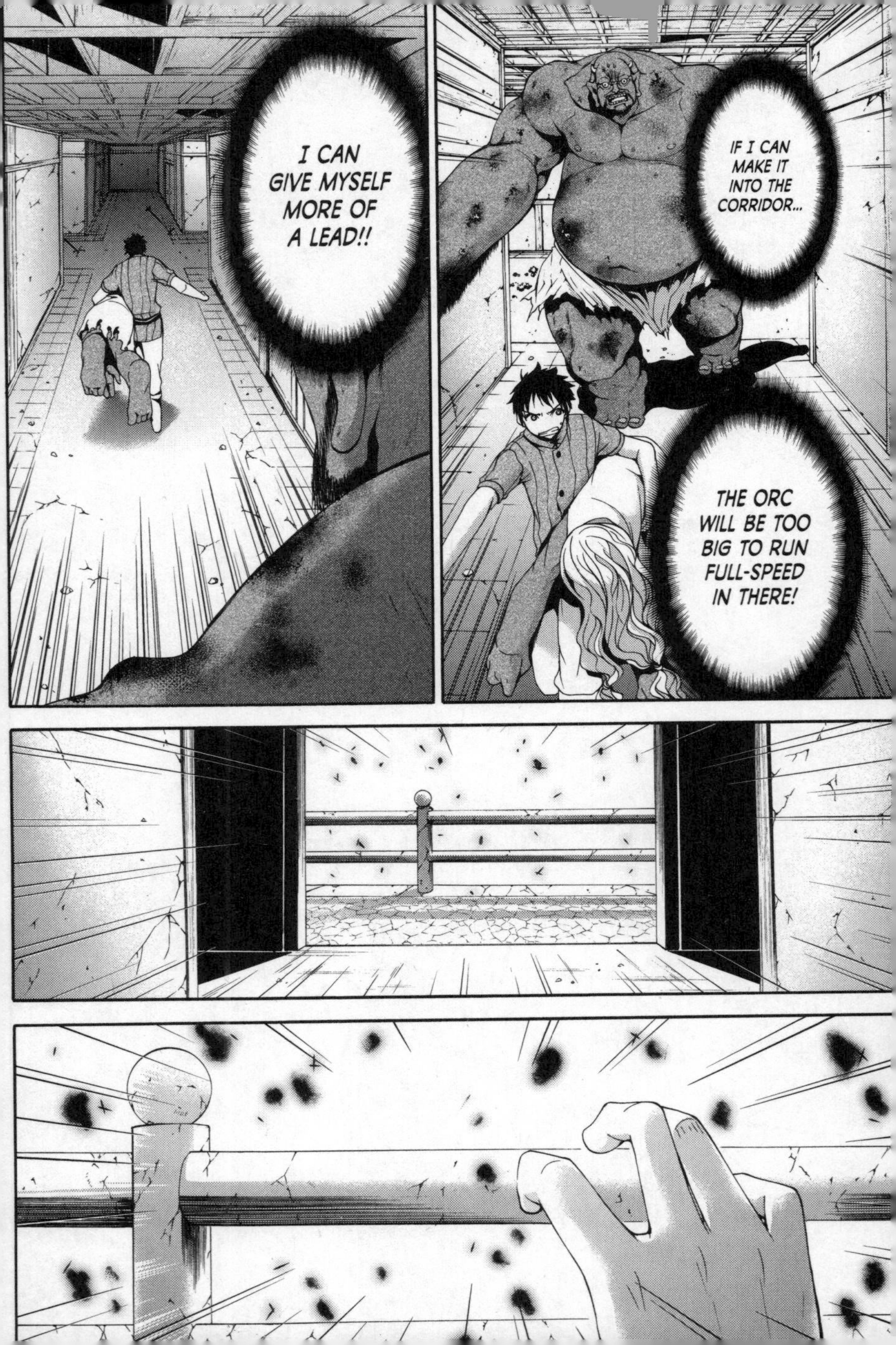
IF I CAN MAKE IT INTO THE CORRIDOR...
THE ORC WILL BE TOO BIG TO RUN FULL-SPEED IN THERE!
I CAN GIVE MYSELF MORE OF A LEAD!!

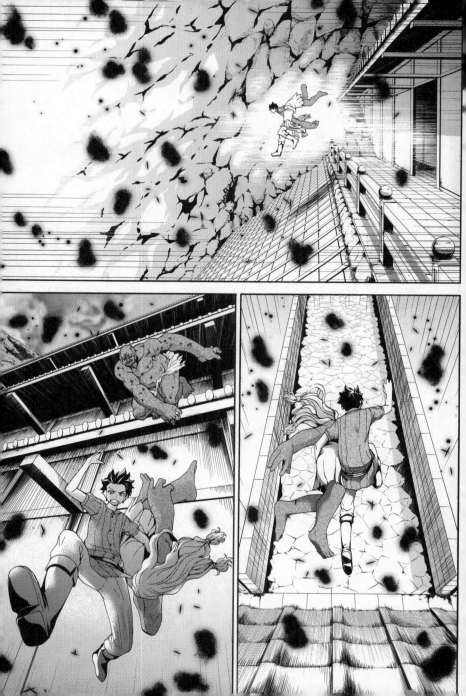

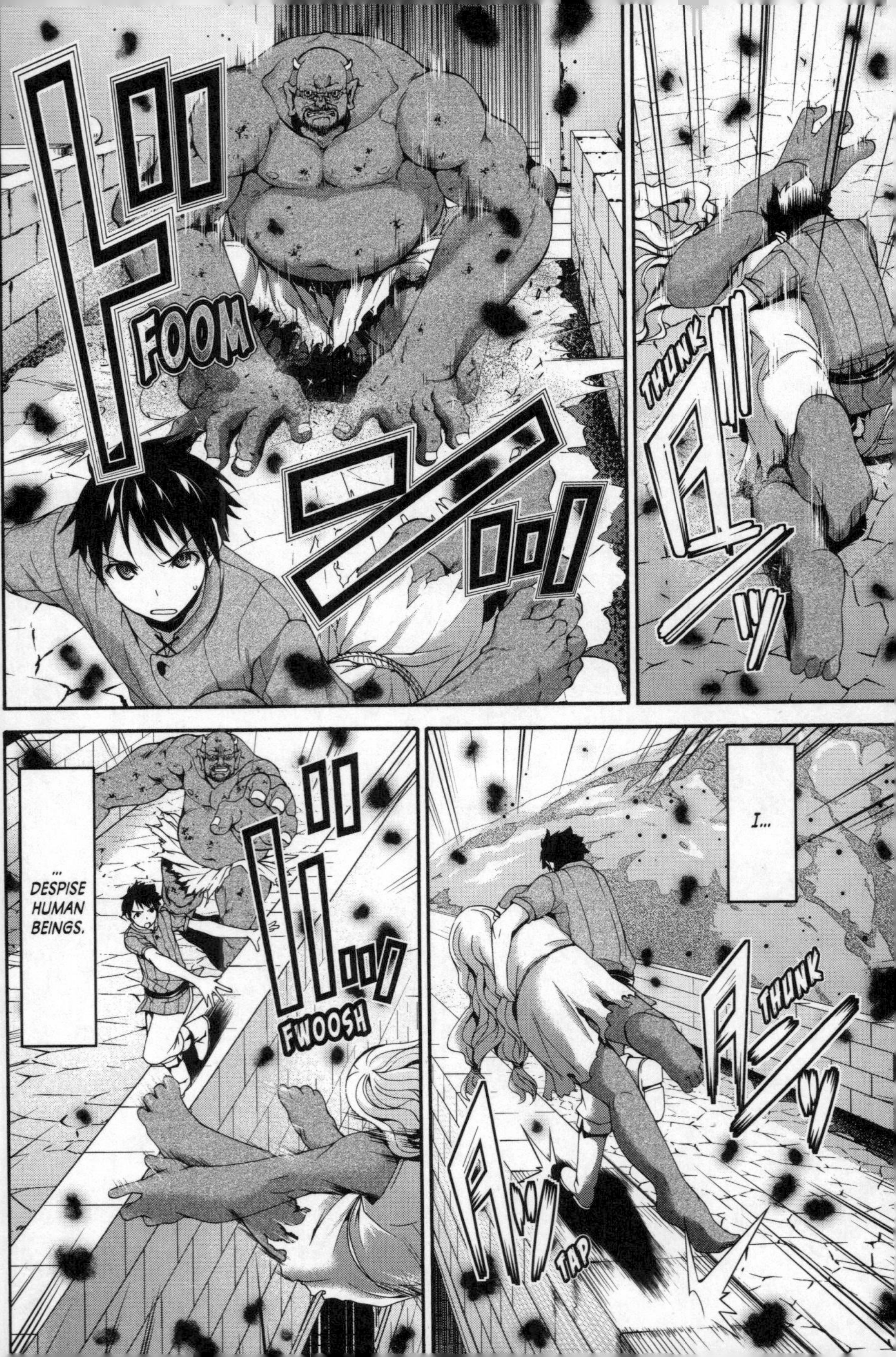
THUNK
FOOM
I...
THUNK
TAP
... DESPISE HUMAN BEINGS.
FWOOSH

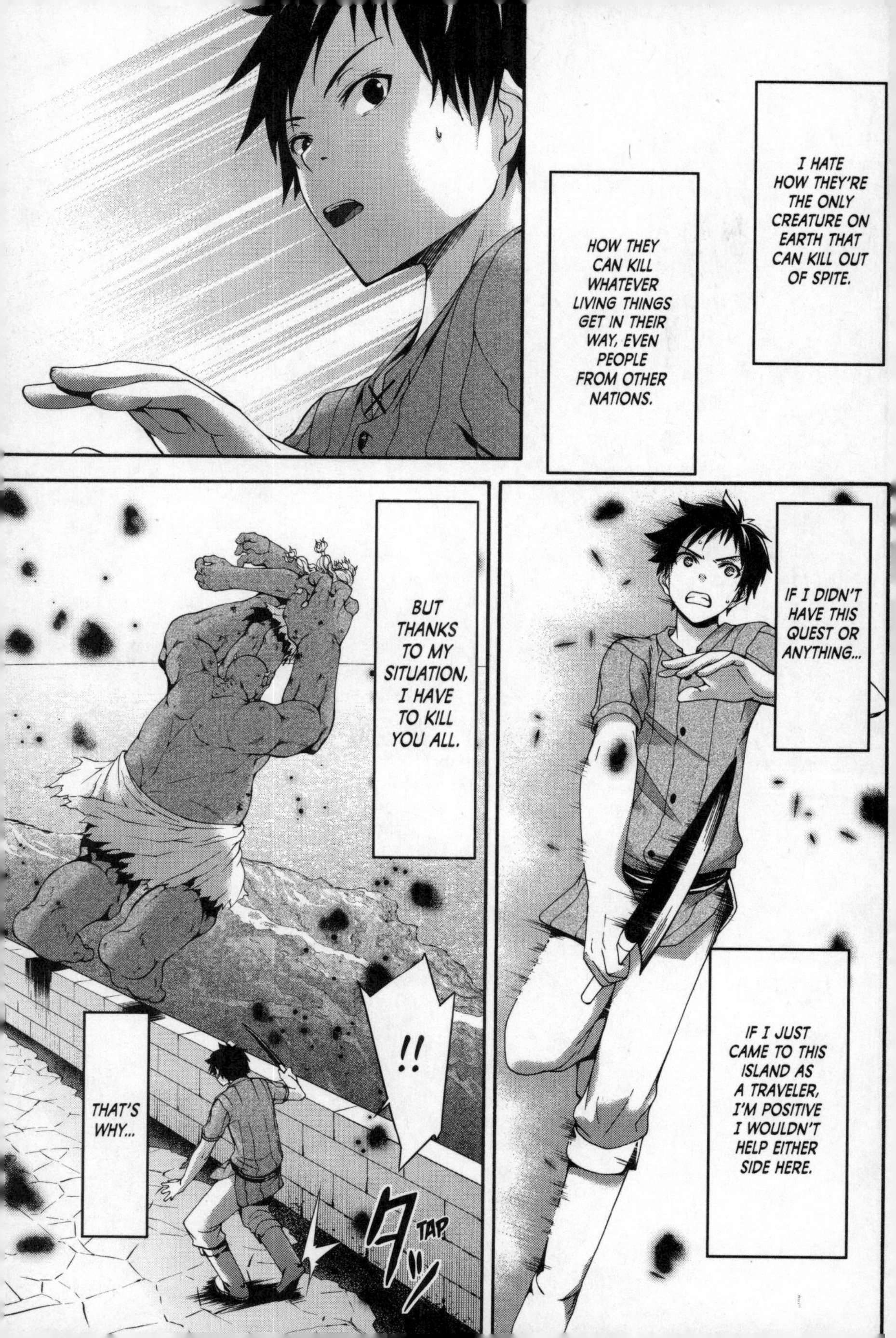
I HATE HOW THEY'RE THE ONLY CREATURE ON EARTH THAT CAN KILL OUT OF SPITE.
HOW THEY CAN KILL WHATEVER LIVING THINGS GET IN THEIR WAY, EVEN PEOPLE FROM OTHER NATIONS.
IF I DIDN'T HAVE THIS QUEST OR ANYTHING...
IF I JUST CAME TO THIS ISLAND AS A TRAVELER, I'M POSITIVE I WOULDN'T HELP EITHER SIDE HERE.
BUT THANKS TO MY SITUATION, I HAVE TO KILL YOU ALL.
!!
THAT'S WHY...
TAP

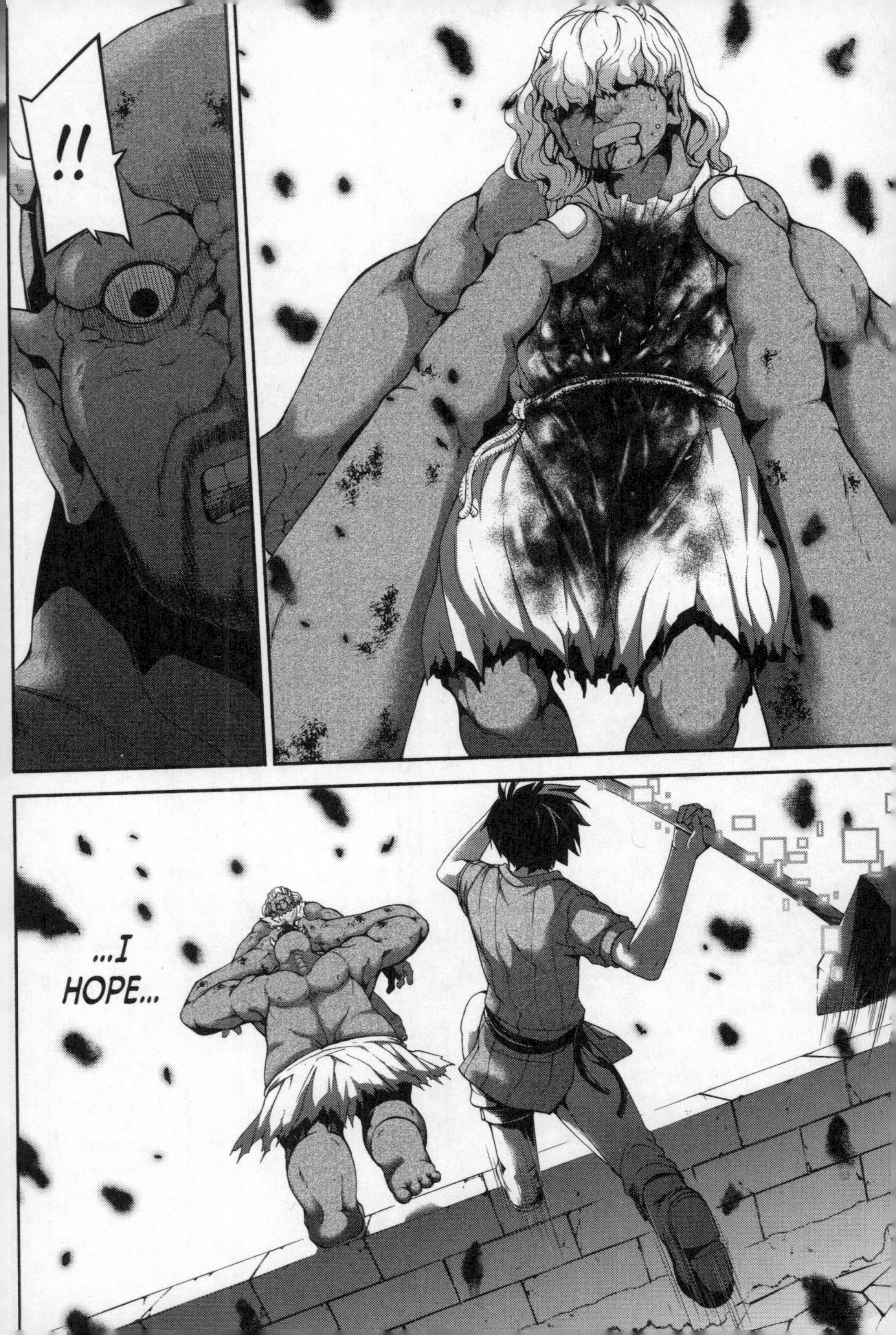
!!
...I HOPE...

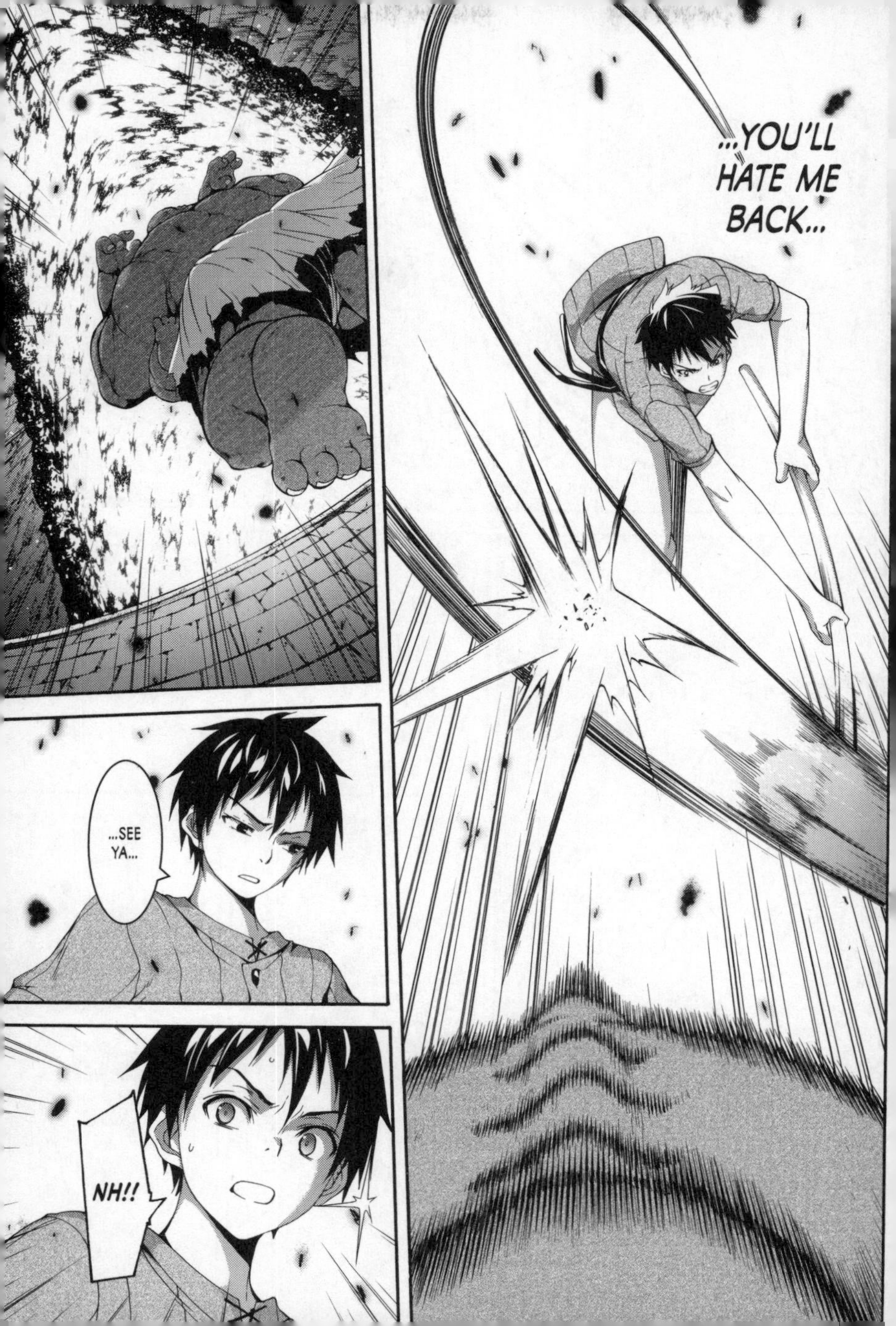
...YOU'LL HATE ME BACK...
...SEE YA...
NH!!

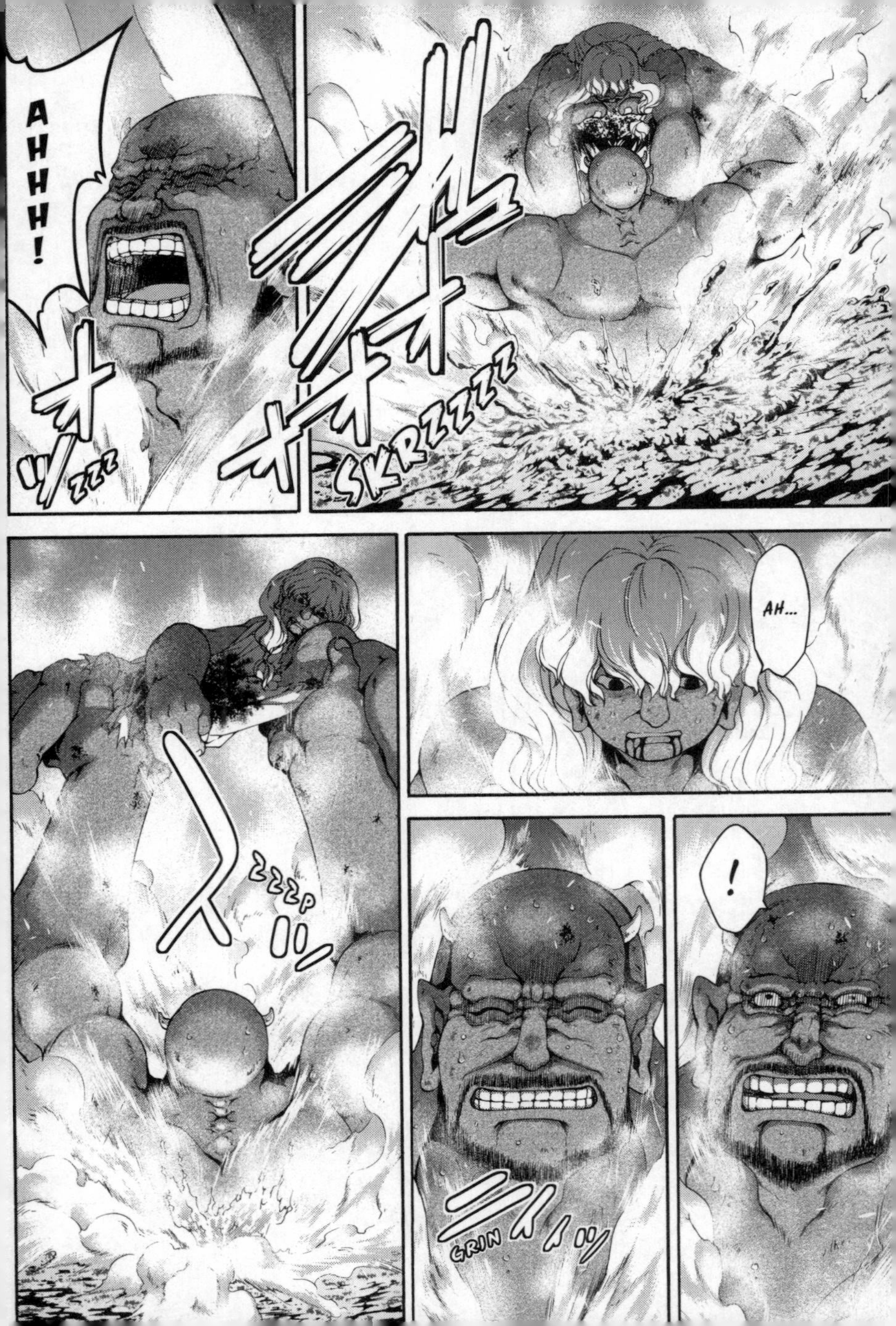
SKRZZZZ
AHHHH!
ZZZ
AH...
!
GRIN
ZZZP

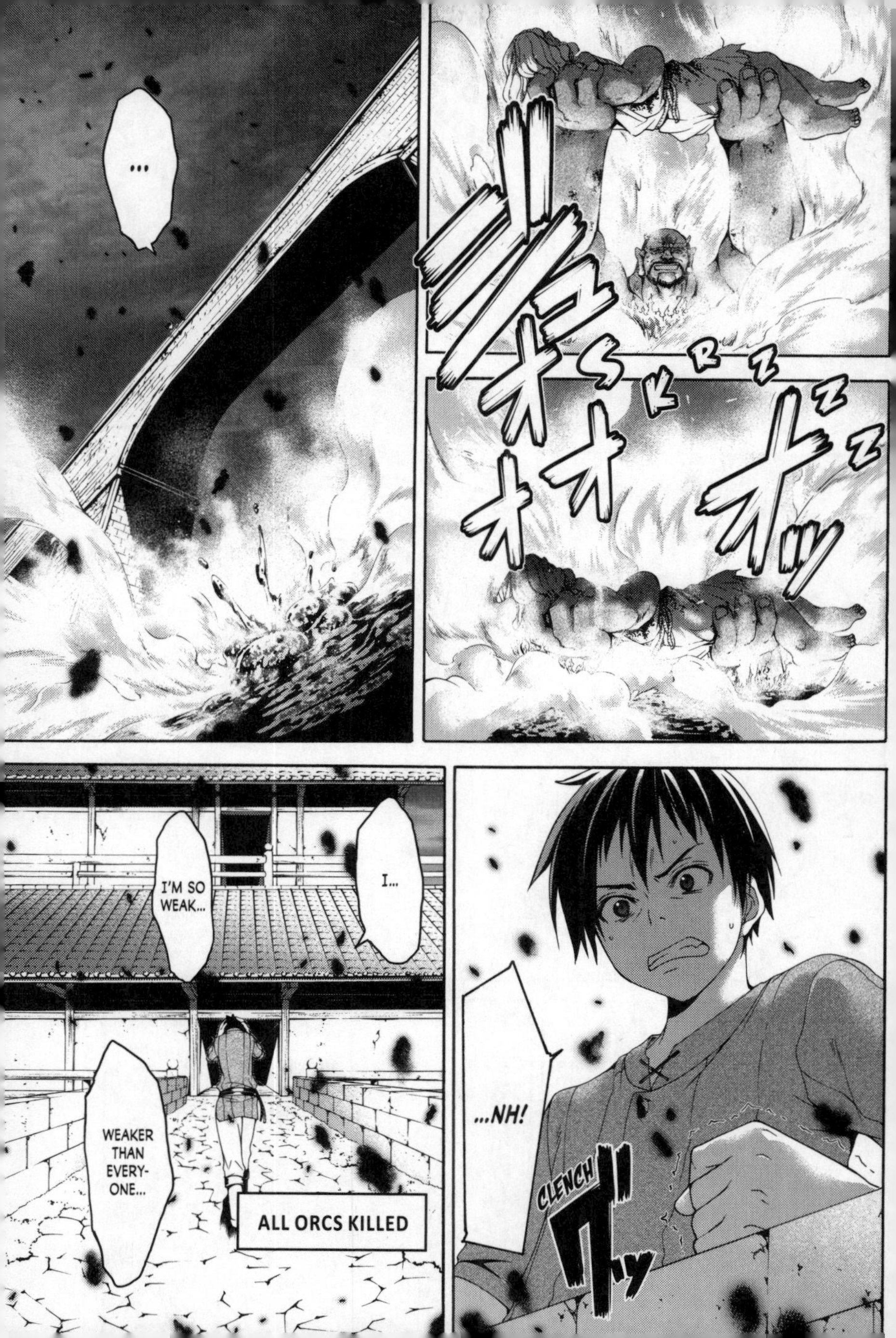
SKRZZZZ
...
...NH!
CLENCH
I...
I'M SO WEAK...
WEAKER THAN EVERYONE...
ALL ORCS KILLED

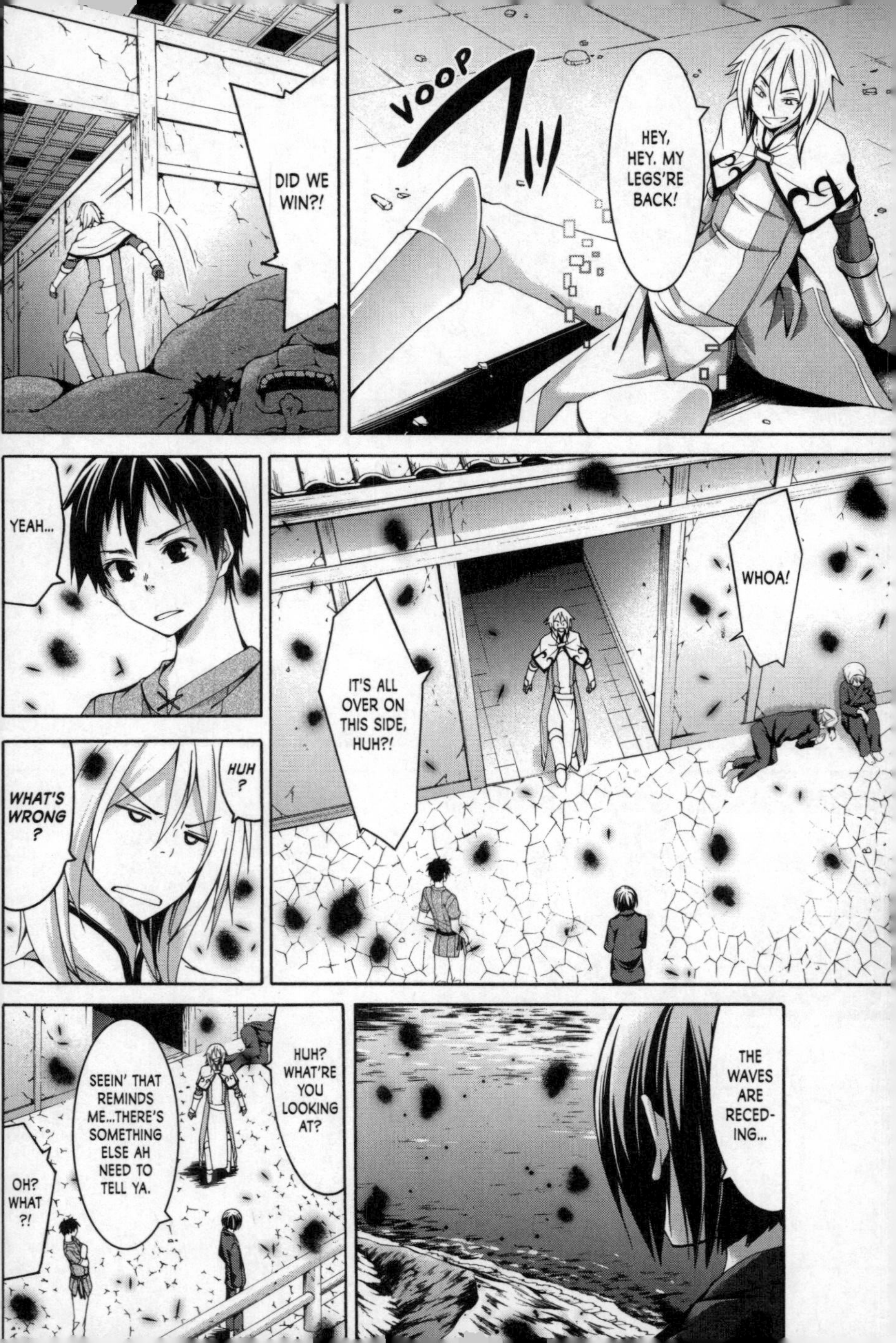
VOOP
HEY, HEY. MY LEGS'RE BACK!
DID WE WIN?!
WHOA!
IT'S ALL OVER ON THIS SIDE, HUH?!
YEAH...
HUH?
WHAT'S WRONG?
THE WAVES ARE RECEDING...
HUH? WHAT'RE YOU LOOKING AT?
SEEIN' THAT REMINDS ME...THERE'S SOMETHING ELSE AH NEED TO TELL YA.
OH? WHAT?!

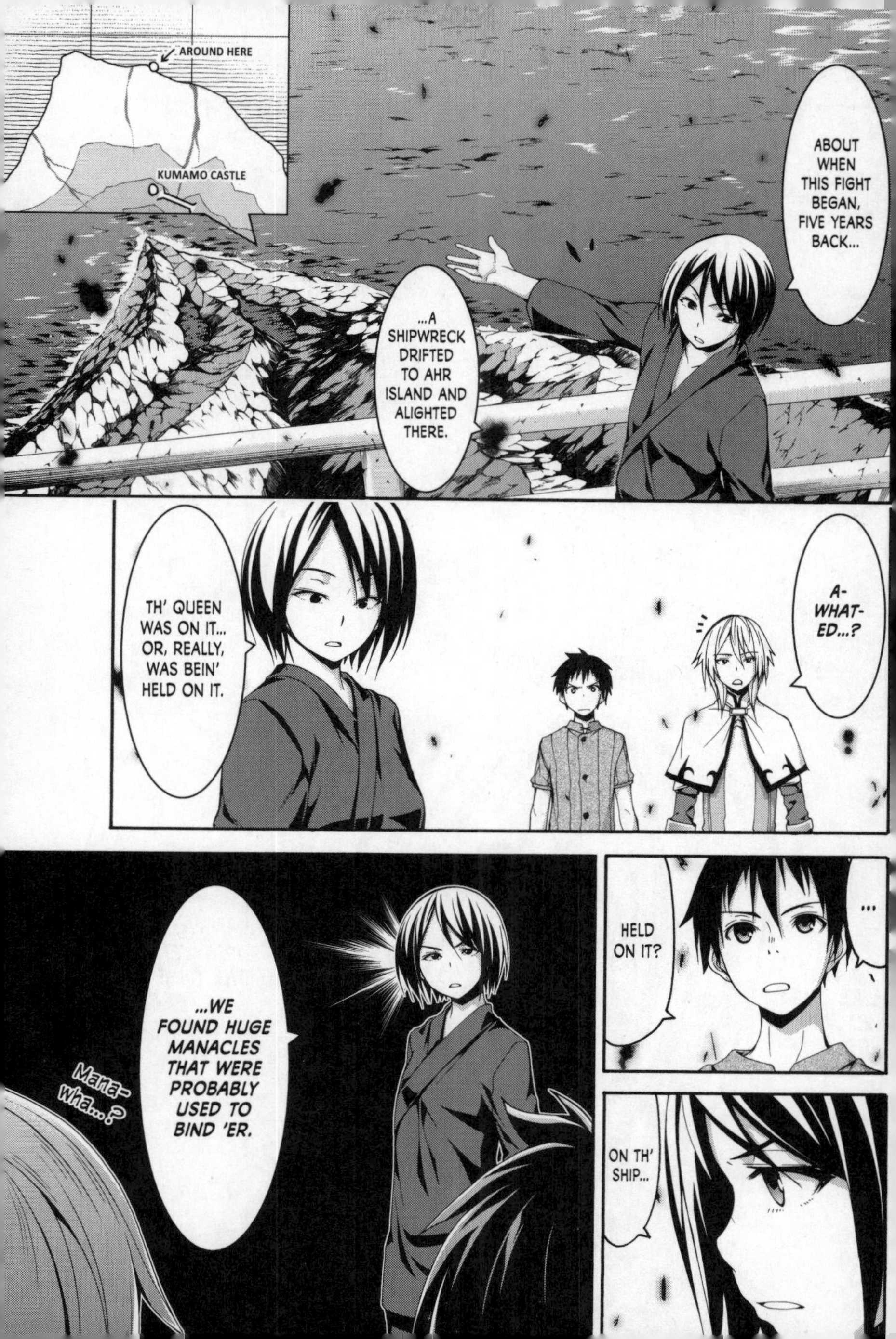
ABOUT WHEN THIS FIGHT BEGAN, FIVE YEARS BACK...
AROUND HERE
KUMAMO CASTLE
...A SHIPWRECK DRIFTED TO AHR ISLAND AND ALIGHTED THERE.
A-WHATED...?
TH' QUEEN WAS ON IT... OR, REALLY, WAS BEIN' HELD ON IT.
...
HELD ON IT?
ON TH' SHIP...
...WE FOUND HUGE MANACLES THAT WERE PROBABLY USED TO BIND 'ER.
Mana-wha...?

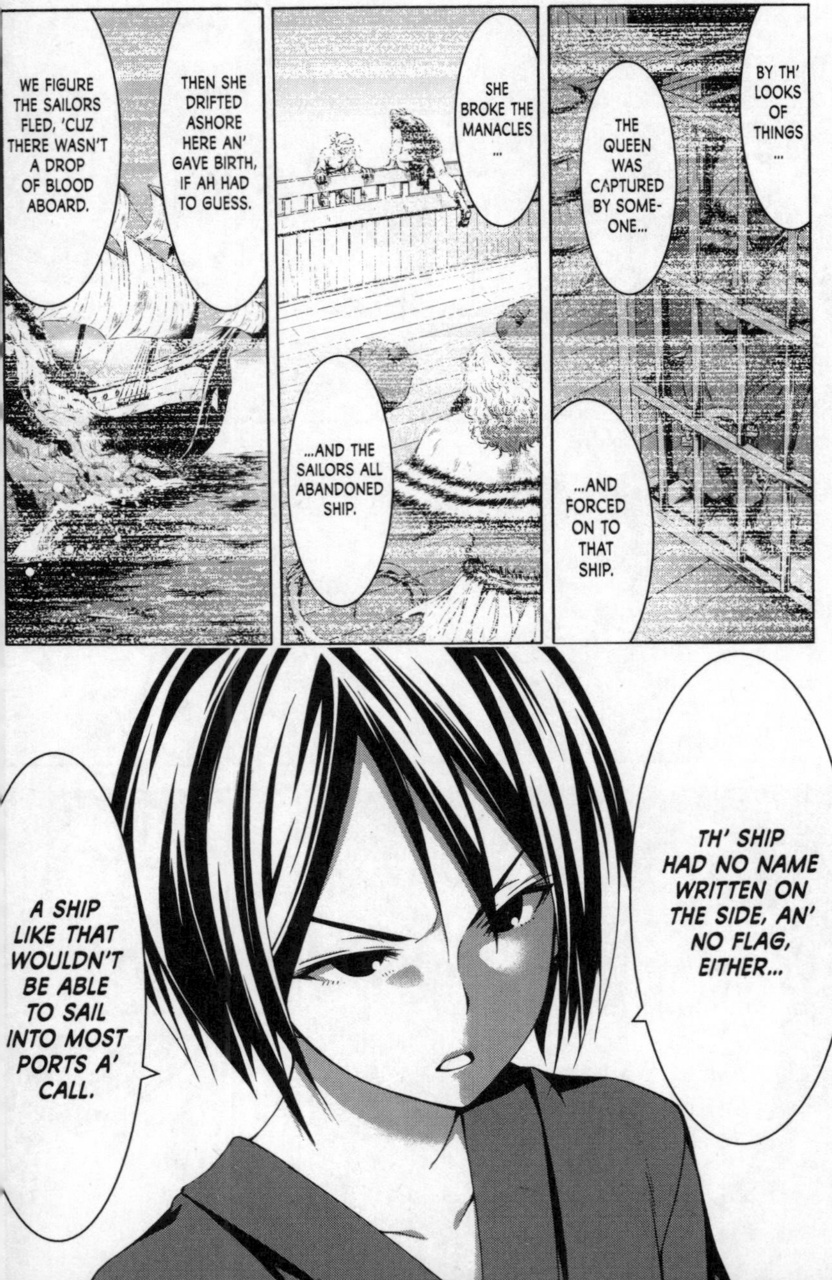
BY TH' LOOKS OF THINGS ...
THE QUEEN WAS CAPTURED BY SOME-ONE...
...AND FORCED ON TO THAT SHIP.
SHE BROKE THE MANACLES ...
...AND THE SAILORS ALL ABANDONED SHIP.
THEN SHE DRIFTED ASHORE HERE AN' GAVE BIRTH, IF AH HAD TO GUESS.
WE FIGURE THE SAILORS FLED, 'CUZ THERE WASN'T A DROP OF BLOOD ABOARD.
TH' SHIP HAD NO NAME WRITTEN ON THE SIDE, AN' NO FLAG, EITHER...
A SHIP LIKE THAT WOULDN'T BE ABLE TO SAIL INTO MOST PORTS A' CALL.

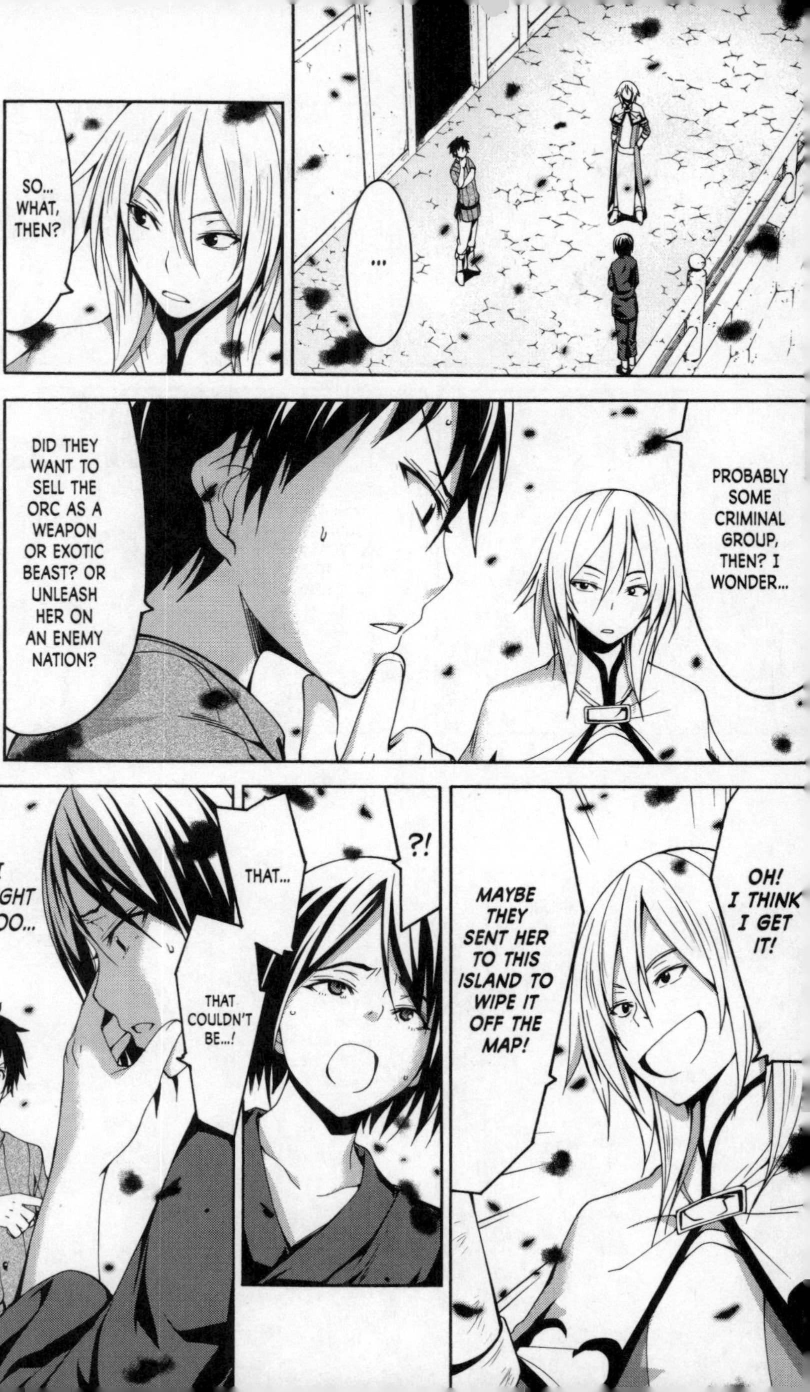
...
SO... WHAT, THEN?
PROBABLY SOME CRIMINAL GROUP, THEN? I WONDER...
DID THEY WANT TO SELL THE ORC AS A WEAPON OR EXOTIC BEAST? OR UNLEASH HER ON AN ENEMY NATION?
OH! I THINK I GET IT!
MAYBE THEY SENT HER TO THIS ISLAND TO WIPE IT OFF THE MAP!
?!
THAT...
THAT COULDN'T BE...!
...I THOUGHT SO, TOO...

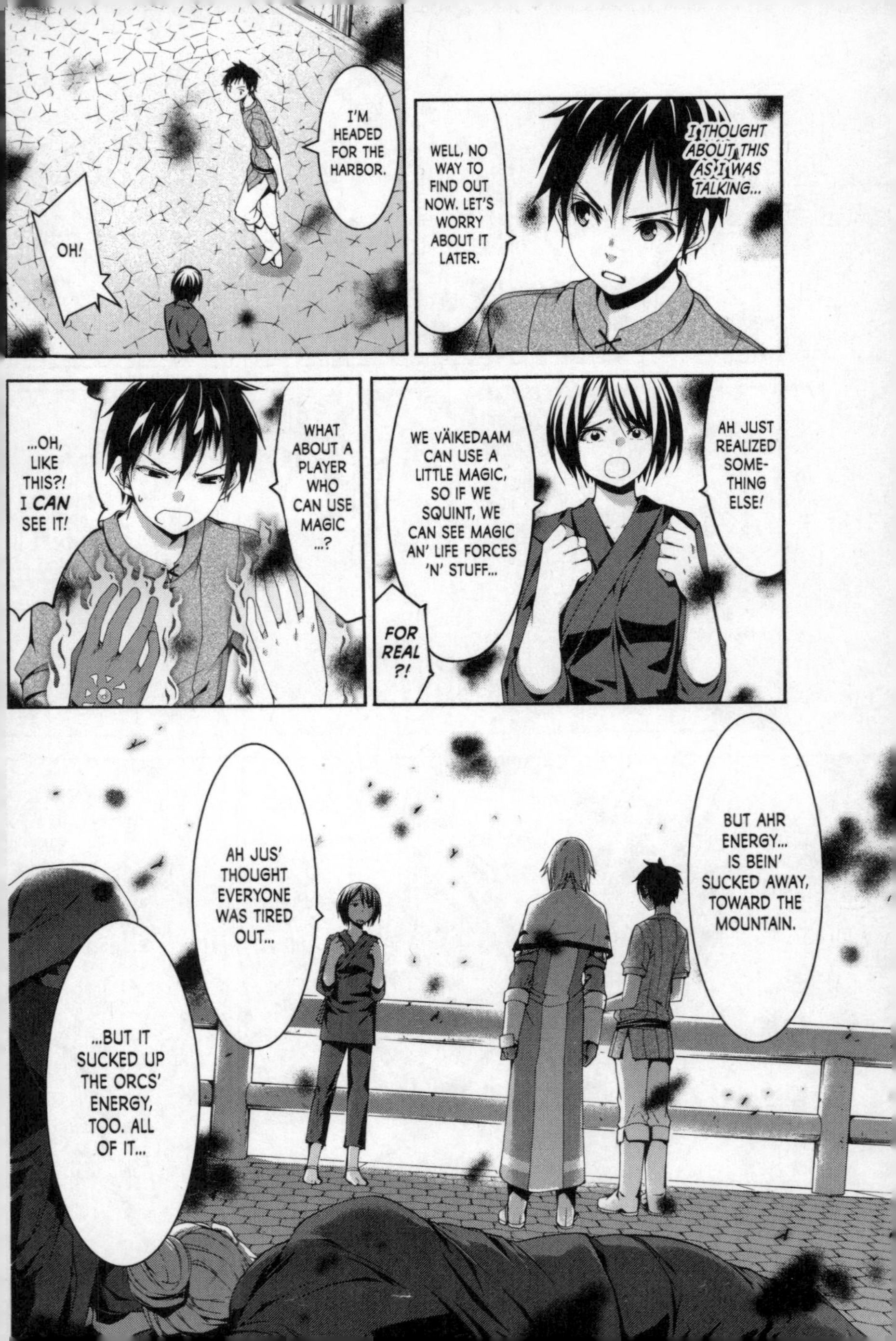
I THOUGHT ABOUT THIS AS I WAS TALKING...
WELL, NO WAY TO FIND OUT NOW. LET'S WORRY ABOUT IT LATER.
I'M HEADED FOR THE HARBOR.
OH!
AH JUST REALIZED SOME-THING ELSE!
WE VÄIKEDAAM CAN USE A LITTLE MAGIC, SO IF WE SQUINT, WE CAN SEE MAGIC AN' LIFE FORCES 'N' STUFF...
FOR REAL?!
WHAT ABOUT A PLAYER WHO CAN USE MAGIC ...?
...OH, LIKE THIS?! I CAN SEE IT!
BUT AHR ENERGY... IS BEIN' SUCKED AWAY, TOWARD THE MOUNTAIN.
AH JUS' THOUGHT EVERYONE WAS TIRED OUT...
...BUT IT SUCKED UP THE ORCS' ENERGY, TOO. ALL OF IT...

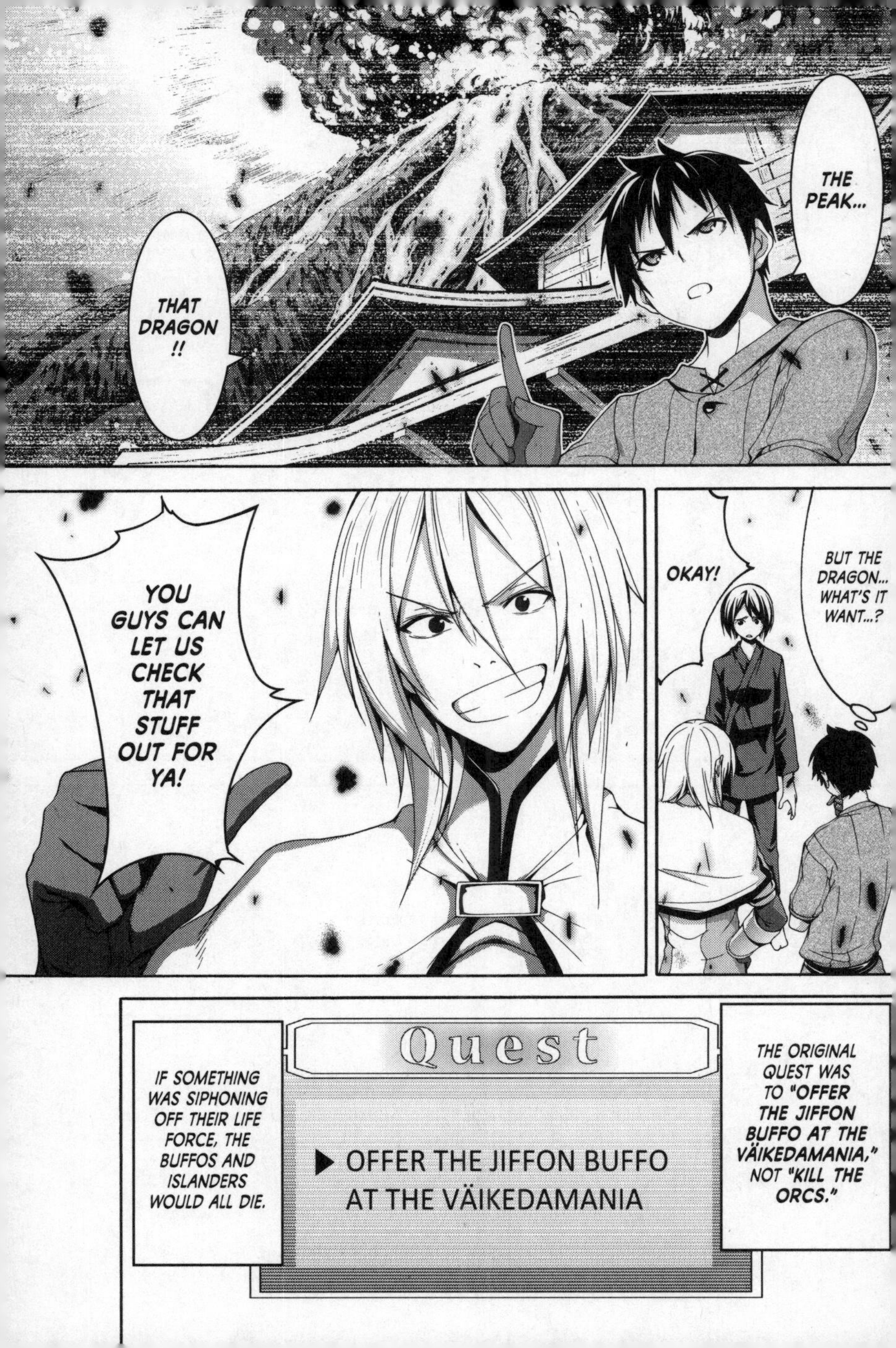
THE PEAK...
THAT DRAGON !!
BUT THE DRAGON... WHAT'S IT WANT...?
OKAY!
YOU GUYS CAN LET US CHECK THAT STUFF OUT FOR YA!
THE ORIGINAL QUEST WAS TO "OFFER THE JIFFON BUFFO AT THE VÄIKEDAMANIA," NOT "KILL THE ORCS."
Quest
▶ OFFER THE JIFFON BUFFO AT THE VÄIKEDAMANIA
IF SOMETHING WAS SIPHONING OFF THEIR LIFE FORCE, THE BUFFOS AND ISLANDERS WOULD ALL DIE.

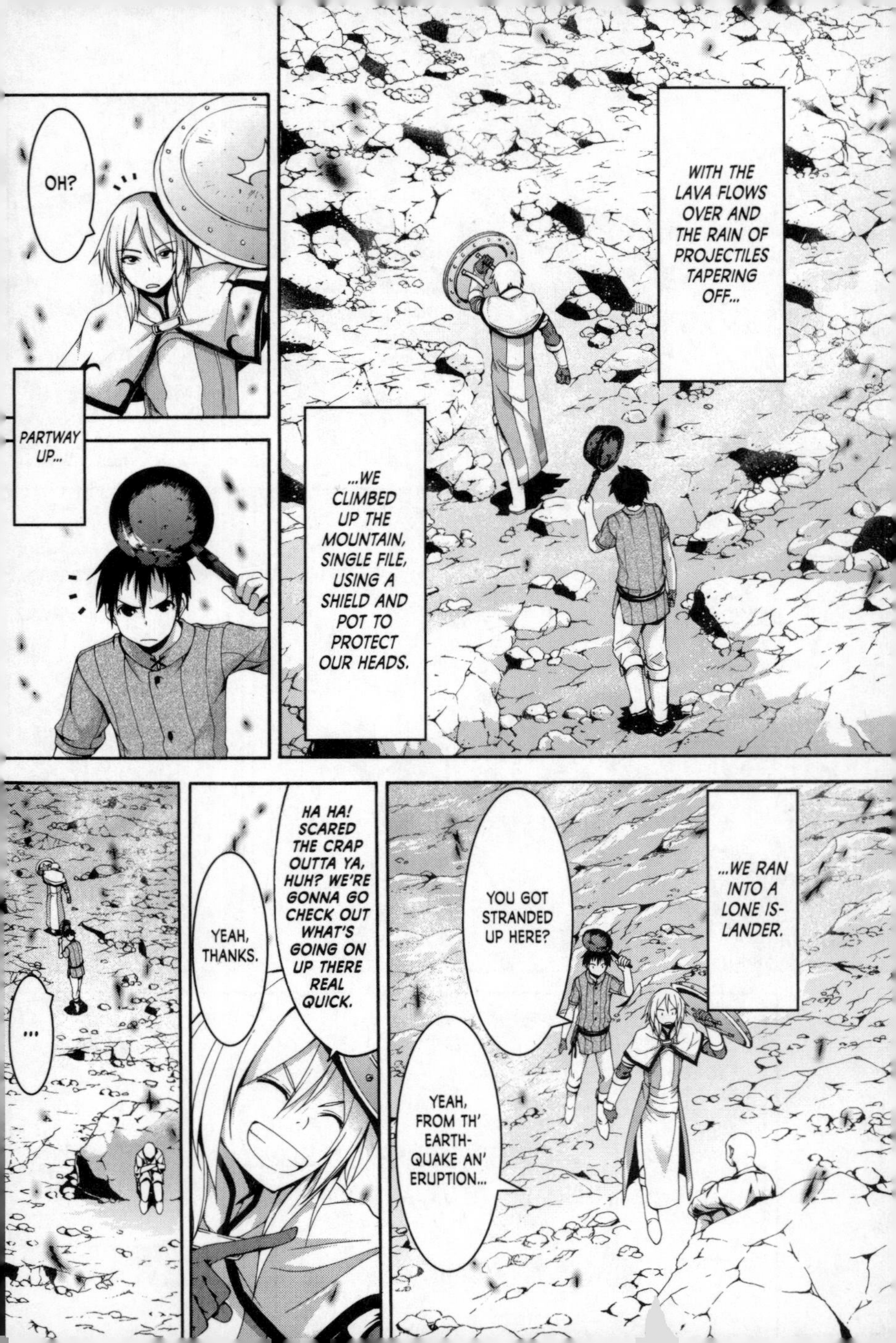
WITH THE LAVA FLOWS OVER AND THE RAIN OF PROJECTILES TAPERING OFF...
...WE CLIMBED UP THE MOUNTAIN, SINGLE FILE, USING A SHIELD AND POT TO PROTECT OUR HEADS.
OH?
PARTWAY UP...
...WE RAN INTO A LONE IS-LANDER.
YOU GOT STRANDED UP HERE?
YEAH, FROM TH' EARTH-QUAKE AN' ERUPTION...
HA HA! SCARED THE CRAP OUTTA YA, HUH? WE'RE GONNA GO CHECK OUT WHAT'S GOING ON UP THERE REAL QUICK.
YEAH, THANKS.
...

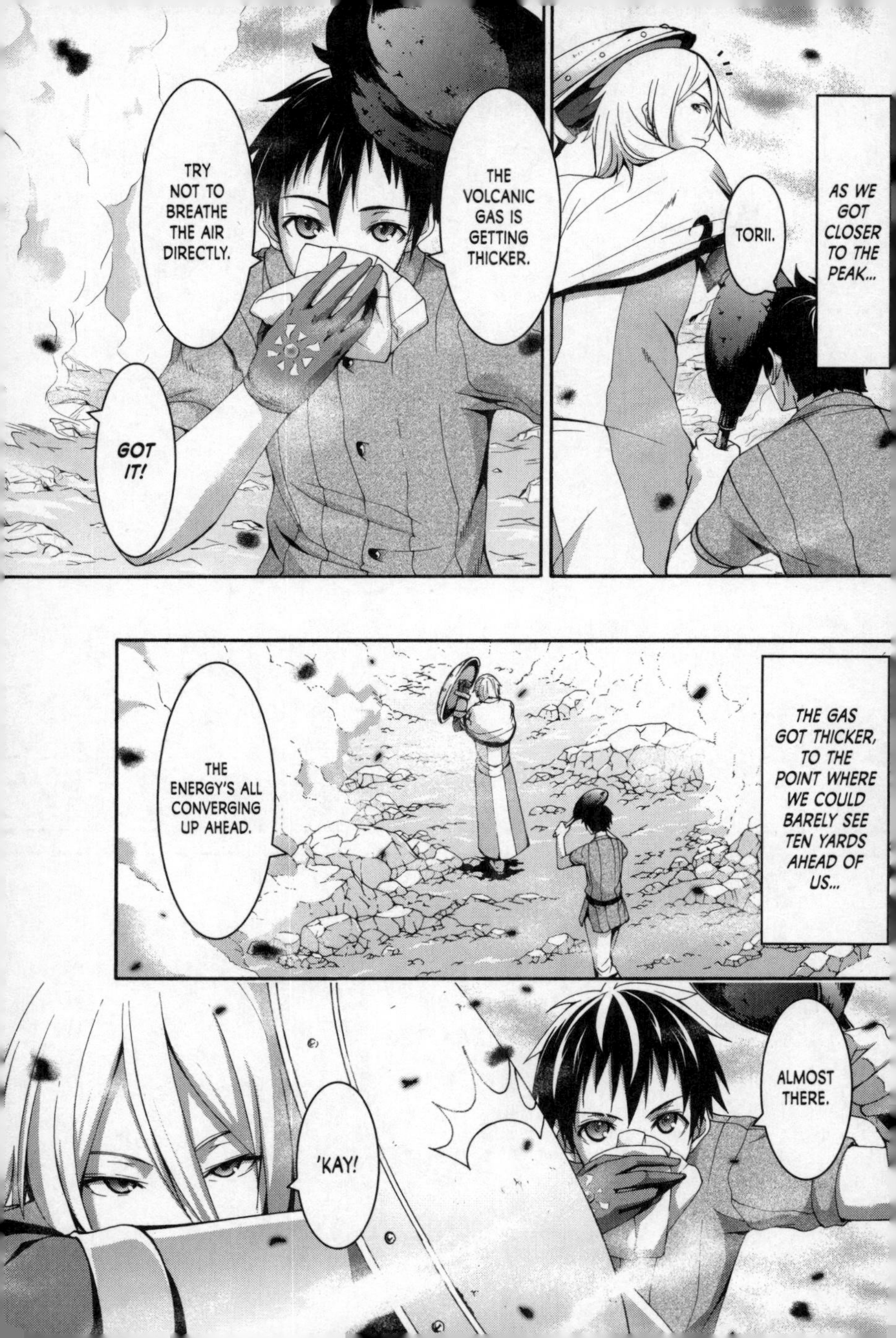
AS WE GOT CLOSER TO THE PEAK...
TORII.
THE VOLCANIC GAS IS GETTING THICKER.
TRY NOT TO BREATHE THE AIR DIRECTLY.
GOT IT!
THE GAS GOT THICKER, TO THE POINT WHERE WE COULD BARELY SEE TEN YARDS AHEAD OF US...
THE ENERGY'S ALL CONVERGING UP AHEAD.
ALMOST THERE.
'KAY!

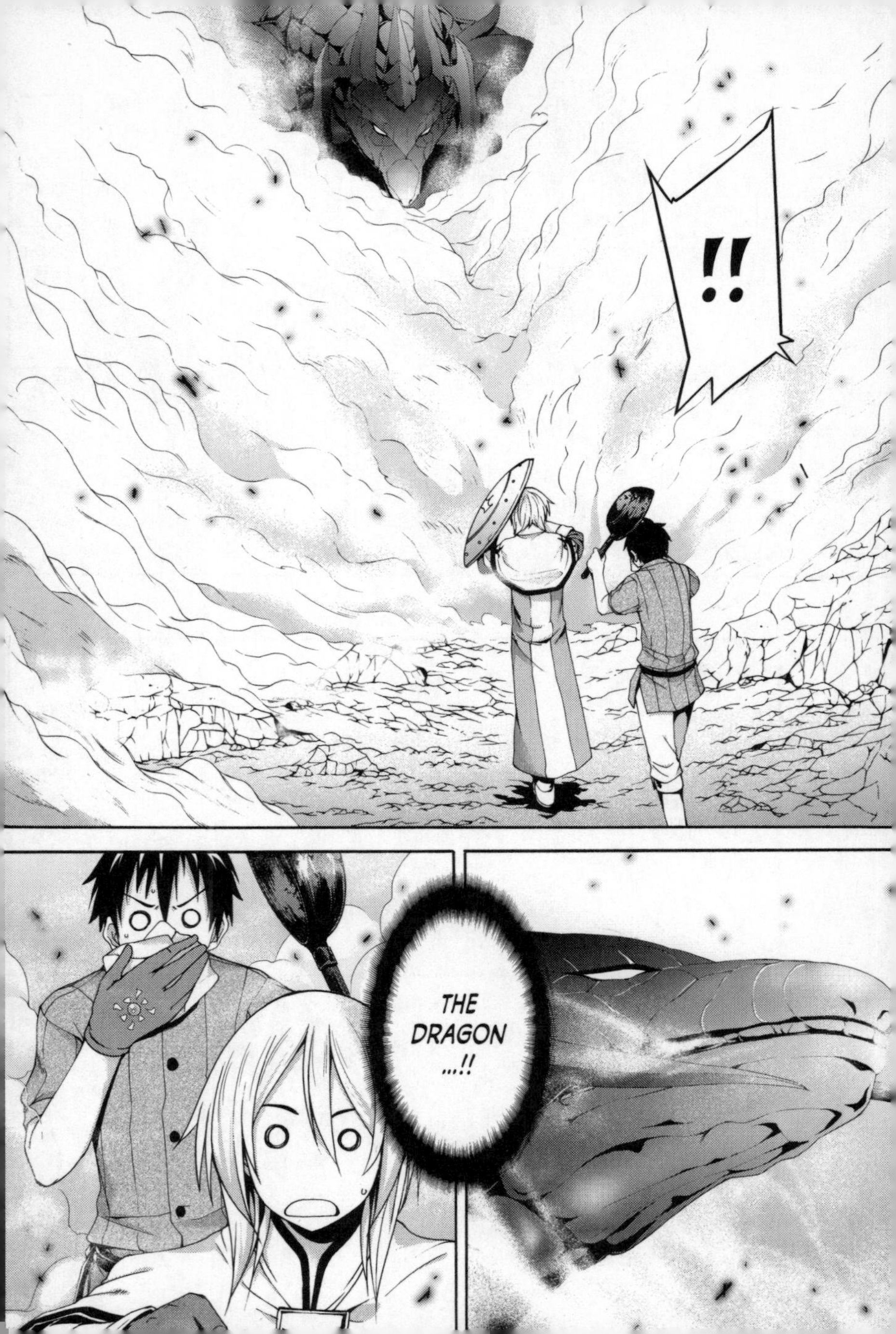
!!
THE DRAGON ...!!

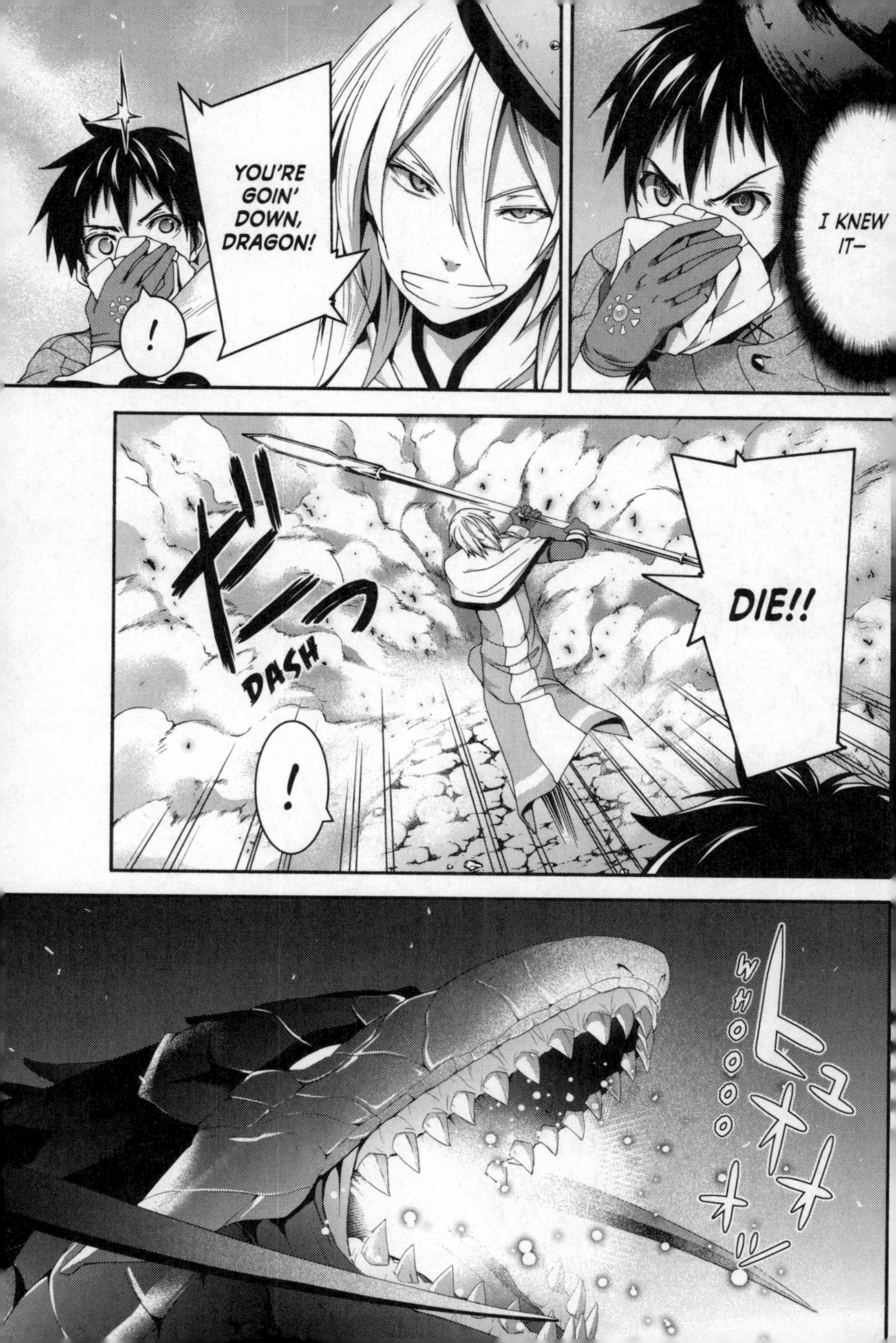
I KNEW IT—
YOU'RE GOIN' DOWN, DRAGON!
!
DIE!!
DASH
!
WHOOOOO

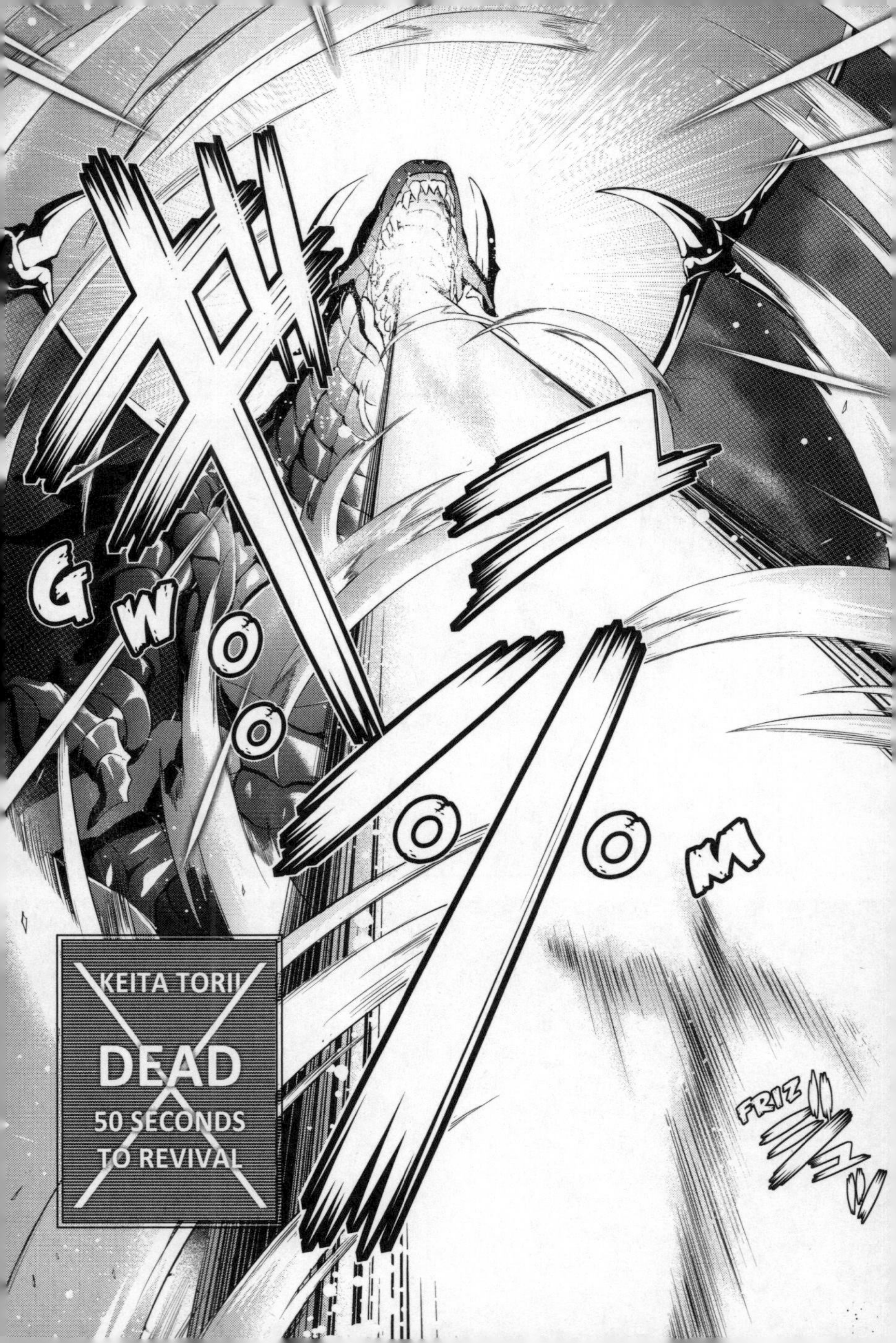
GWOOOOOM
KEITA TORII
DEAD
50 SECONDS TO REVIVAL
FRIZ

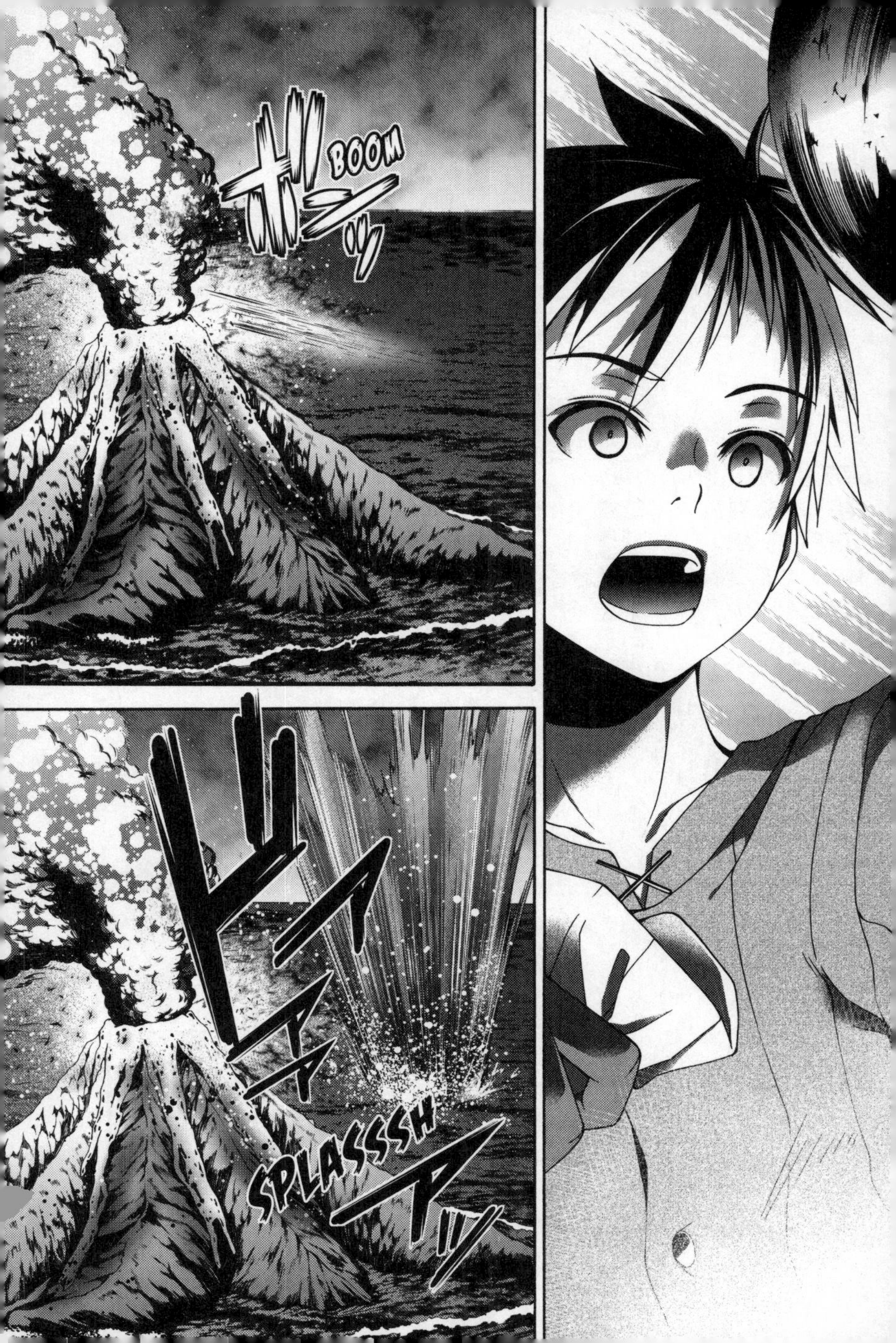
BOOM
SPLASSSH

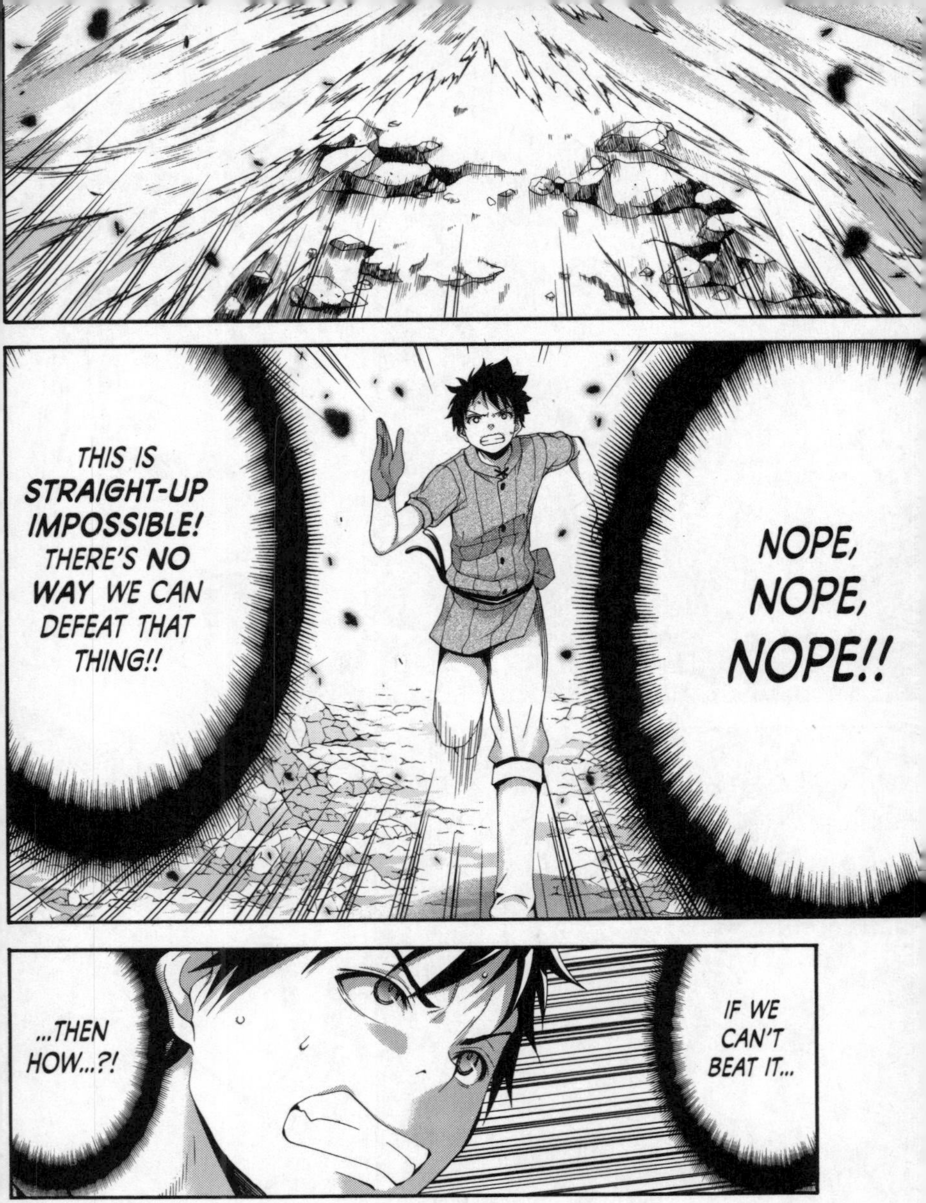
NOPE, NOPE, NOPE!!
THIS IS STRAIGHT-UP IMPOSSIBLE! THERE'S NO WAY WE CAN DEFEAT THAT THING!!
IF WE CAN'T BEAT IT...
...THEN HOW...?!

HOW CAN WE GET RID OF THIS THING WITHOUT KILLING IT?

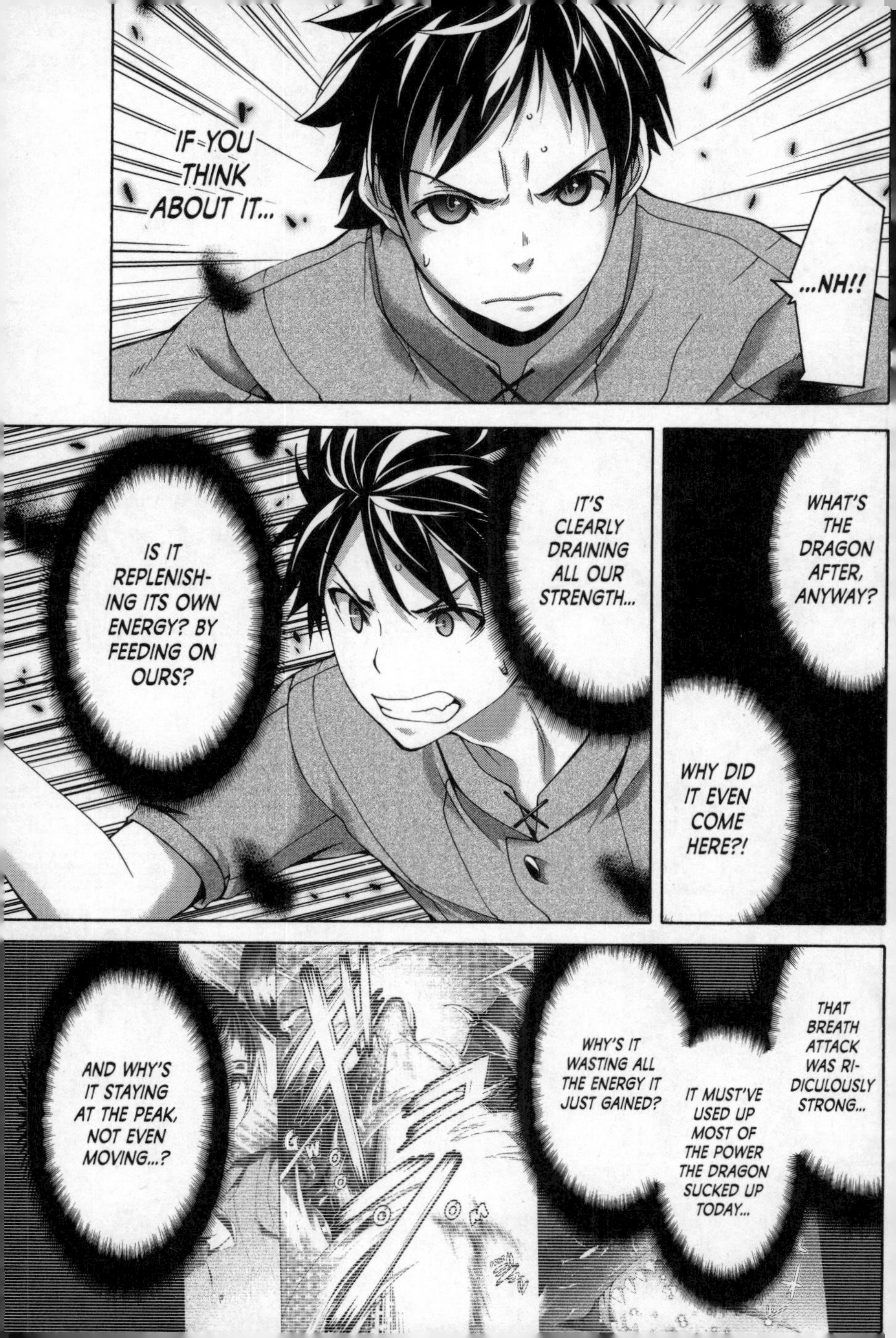
...NH!!
IF YOU THINK ABOUT IT...
WHAT'S THE DRAGON AFTER, ANYWAY?
WHY DID IT EVEN COME HERE?!
IT'S CLEARLY DRAINING ALL OUR STRENGTH...
IS IT REPLENISHING ITS OWN ENERGY? BY FEEDING ON OURS?
THAT BREATH ATTACK WAS RIDICULOUSLY STRONG...
IT MUST'VE USED UP MOST OF THE POWER THE DRAGON SUCKED UP TODAY...
WHY'S IT WASTING ALL THE ENERGY IT JUST GAINED?
AND WHY'S IT STAYING AT THE PEAK, NOT EVEN MOVING...?

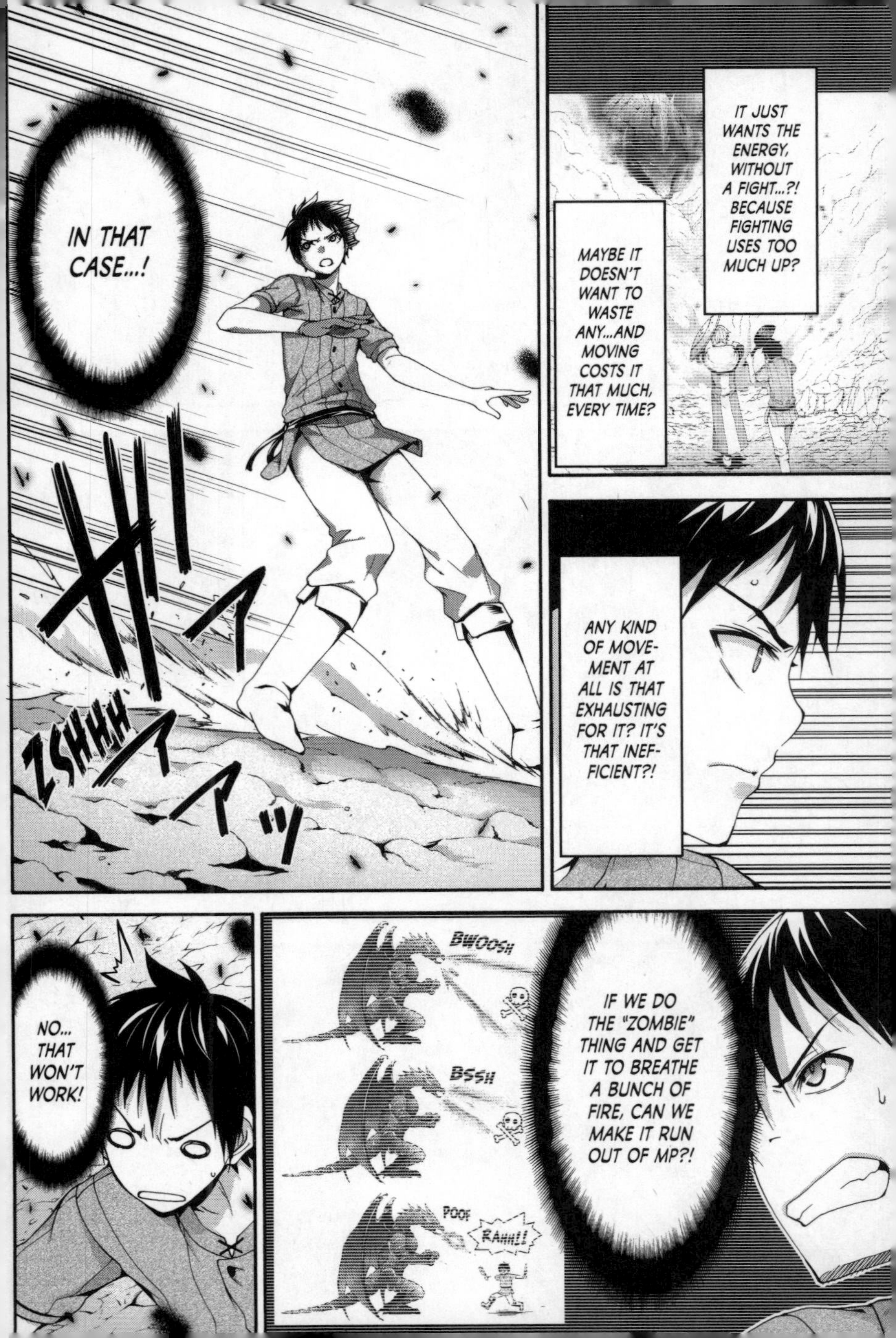
IT JUST WANTS THE ENERGY, WITHOUT A FIGHT...?! BECAUSE FIGHTING USES TOO MUCH UP?
MAYBE IT DOESN'T WANT TO WASTE ANY...AND MOVING COSTS IT THAT MUCH, EVERY TIME?
ANY KIND OF MOVE-MENT AT ALL IS THAT EXHAUSTING FOR IT? IT'S THAT INEF-FICIENT?!
IN THAT CASE...!
ZSHHH
IF WE DO THE "ZOMBIE" THING AND GET IT TO BREATHE A BUNCH OF FIRE, CAN WE MAKE IT RUN OUT OF MP?!
BWOOSH
BSSH
POOF
RAHH!!
NO... THAT WON'T WORK!

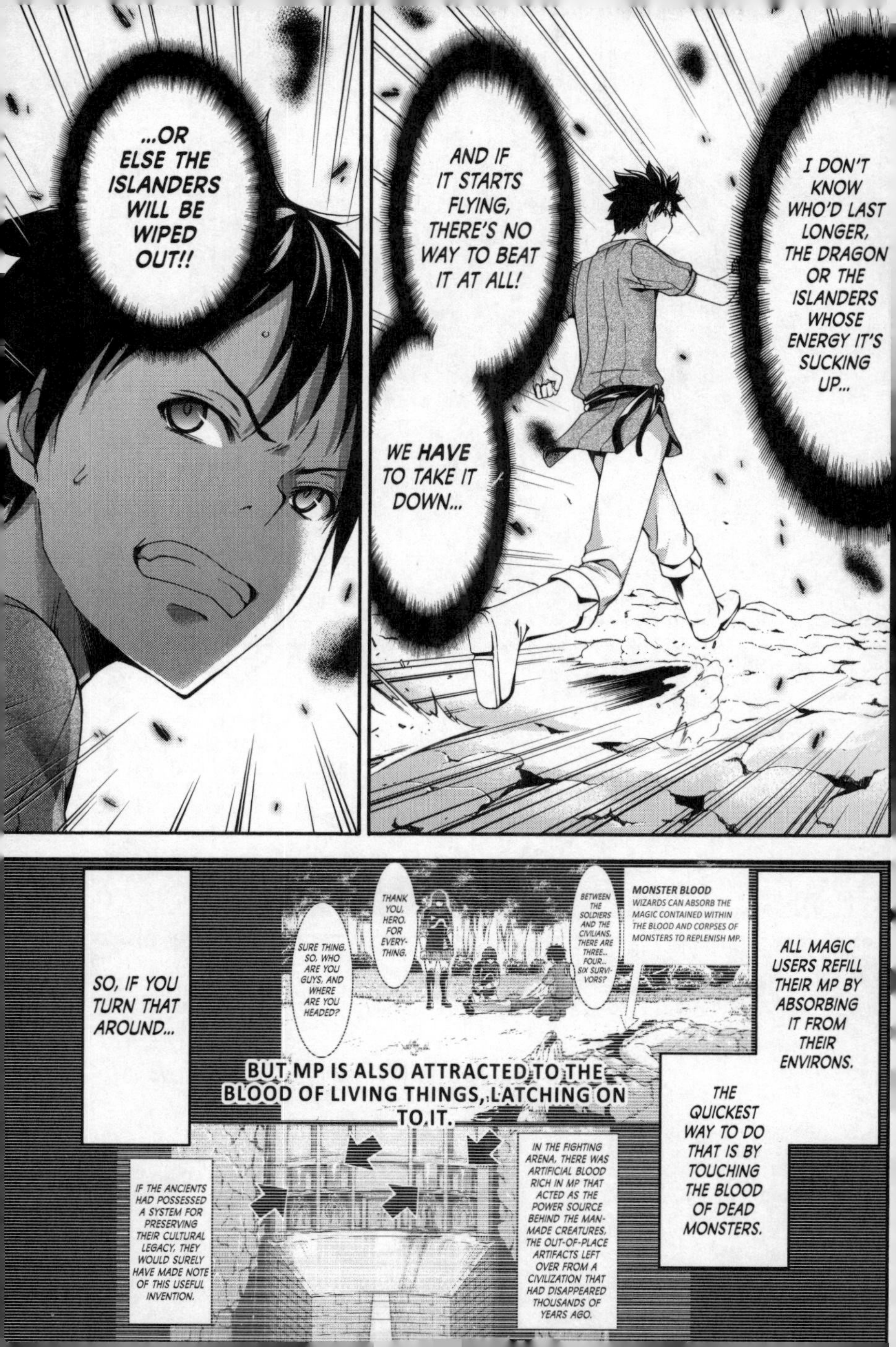
I DON'T KNOW WHO'D LAST LONGER, THE DRAGON OR THE ISLANDERS WHOSE ENERGY IT'S SUCKING UP...
AND IF IT STARTS FLYING, THERE'S NO WAY TO BEAT IT AT ALL!
WE HAVE TO TAKE IT DOWN...
...OR ELSE THE ISLANDERS WILL BE WIPED OUT!!
ALL MAGIC USERS REFILL THEIR MP BY ABSORBING IT FROM THEIR ENVIRONS.
THE QUICKEST WAY TO DO THAT IS BY TOUCHING THE BLOOD OF DEAD MONSTERS.
MONSTER BLOOD
WIZARDS CAN ABSORB THE MAGIC CONTAINED WITHIN THE BLOOD AND CORPSES OF MONSTERS TO REPLENISH MP.
BETWEEN THE SOLDIERS AND THE CIVILIANS, THERE ARE THREE... FOUR... SIX SURVIVORS?
THANK YOU, HERO. FOR EVERYTHING.
SURE THING. SO, WHO ARE YOU GUYS, AND WHERE ARE YOU HEADED?
SO, IF YOU TURN THAT AROUND...
BUT MP IS ALSO ATTRACTED TO THE BLOOD OF LIVING THINGS, LATCHING ON TO IT.
IN THE FIGHTING ARENA, THERE WAS ARTIFICIAL BLOOD RICH IN MP THAT ACTED AS THE POWER SOURCE BEHIND THE MAN-MADE CREATURES, THE OUT-OF-PLACE ARTIFACTS LEFT OVER FROM A CIVILIZATION THAT HAD DISAPPEARED THOUSANDS OF YEARS AGO.
IF THE ANCIENTS HAD POSSESSED A SYSTEM FOR PRESERVING THEIR CULTURAL LEGACY, THEY WOULD SURELY HAVE MADE NOTE OF THIS USEFUL INVENTION.

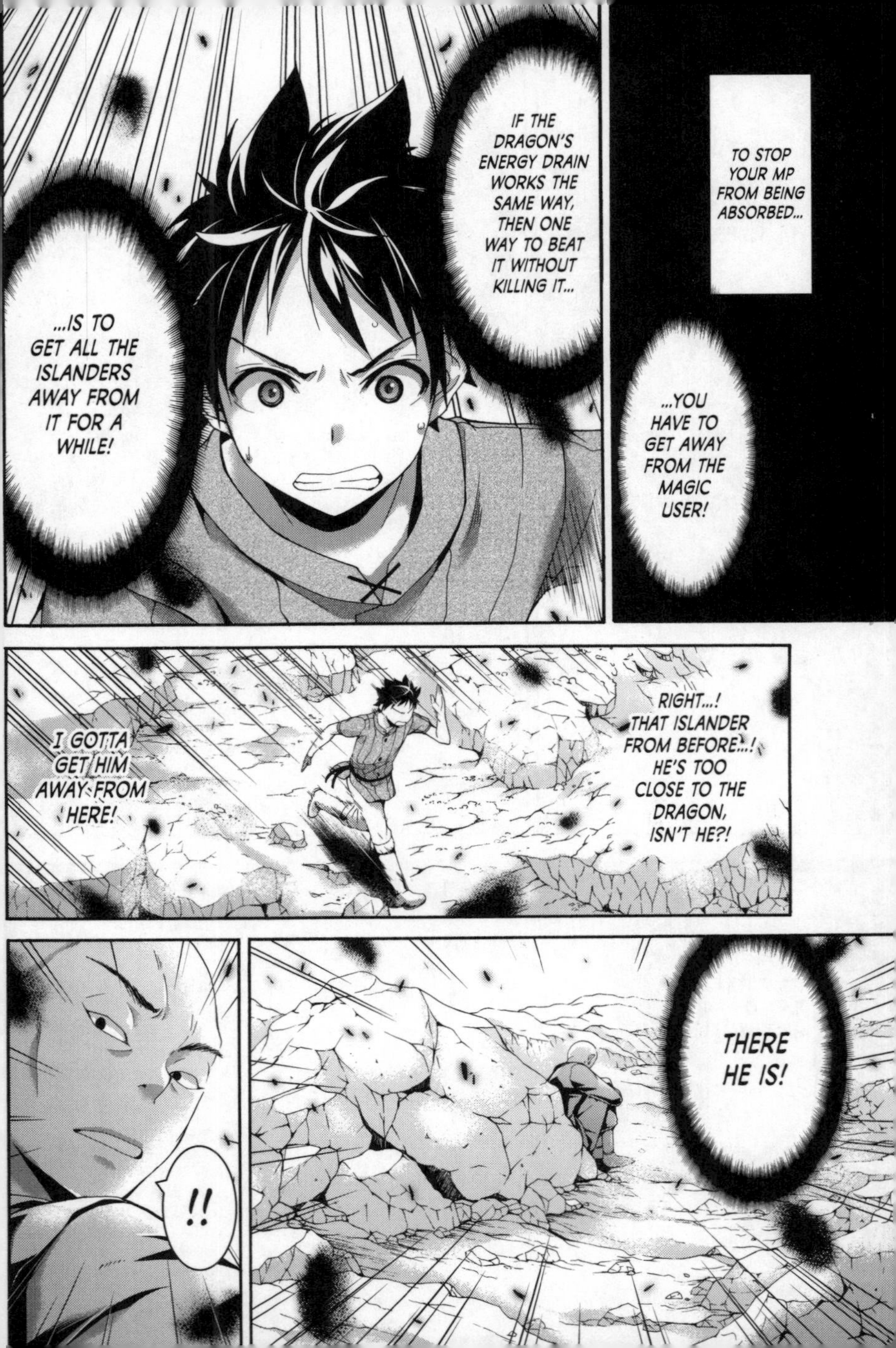
TO STOP YOUR MP FROM BEING ABSORBED...
...YOU HAVE TO GET AWAY FROM THE MAGIC USER!
IF THE DRAGON'S ENERGY DRAIN WORKS THE SAME WAY, THEN ONE WAY TO BEAT IT WITHOUT KILLING IT...
...IS TO GET ALL THE ISLANDERS AWAY FROM IT FOR A WHILE!
RIGHT...! THAT ISLANDER FROM BEFORE...! HE'S TOO CLOSE TO THE DRAGON, ISN'T HE?!
I GOTTA GET HIM AWAY FROM HERE!
THERE HE IS!
!!

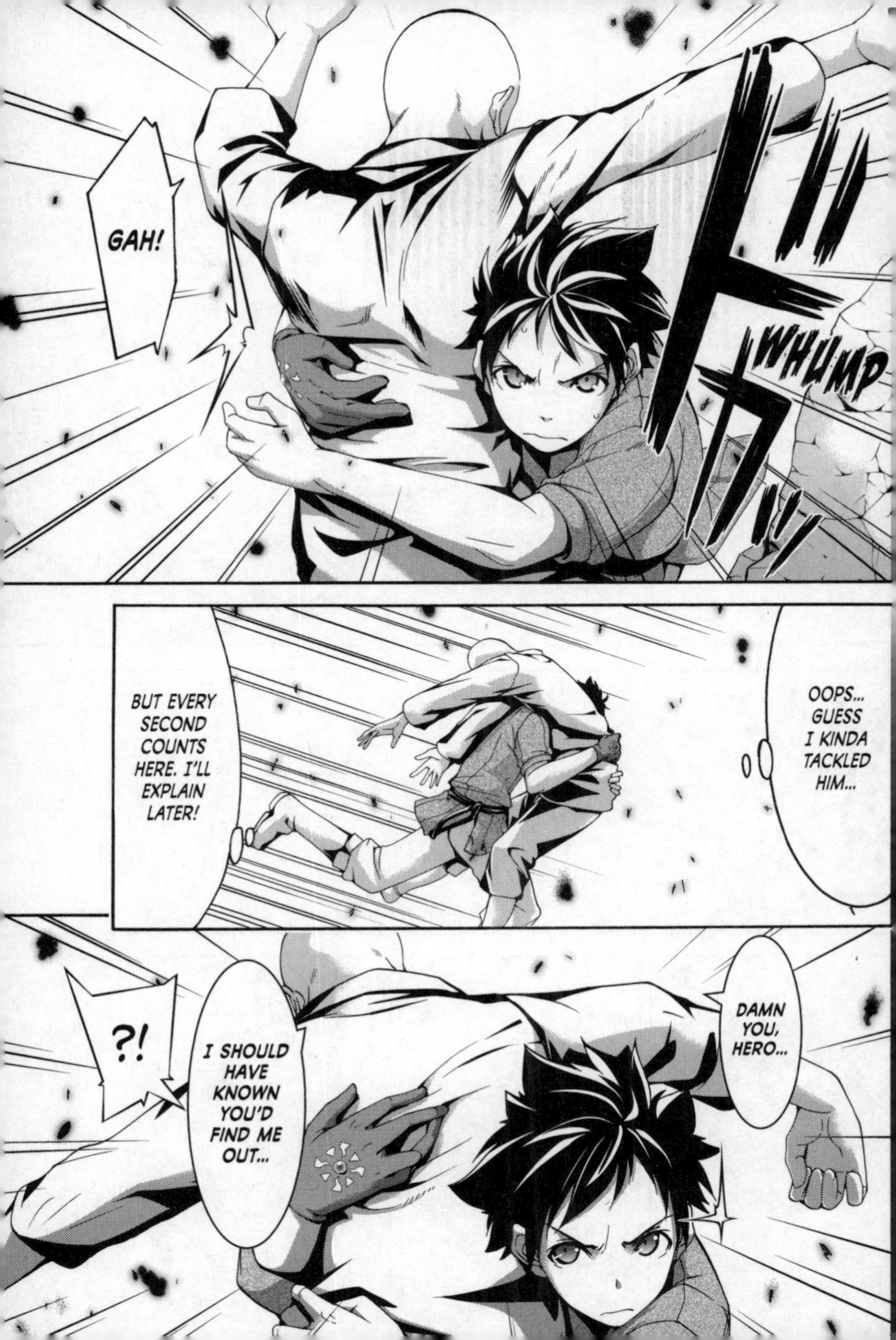
WHUMP
GAH!
OOPS... GUESS I KINDA TACKLED HIM...
BUT EVERY SECOND COUNTS HERE. I'LL EXPLAIN LATER!
DAMN YOU, HERO...
I SHOULD HAVE KNOWN YOU'D FIND ME OUT...
?!

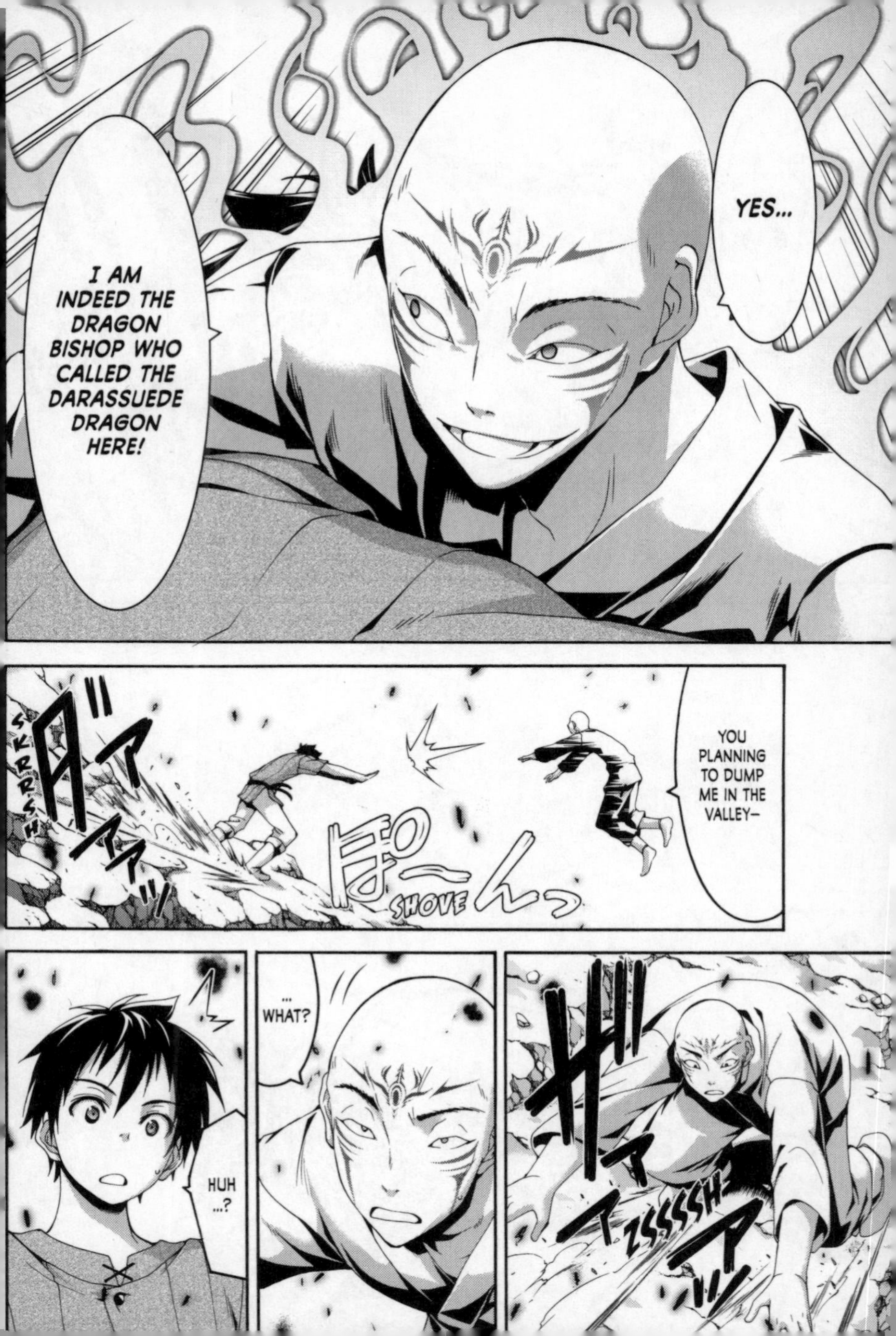
YES...
I AM INDEED THE DRAGON BISHOP WHO CALLED THE DARASSUEDE DRAGON HERE!
YOU PLANNING TO DUMP ME IN THE VALLEY—
SHOVE
SKRRRSH
ZSSSSSH
... WHAT?
HUH ...?

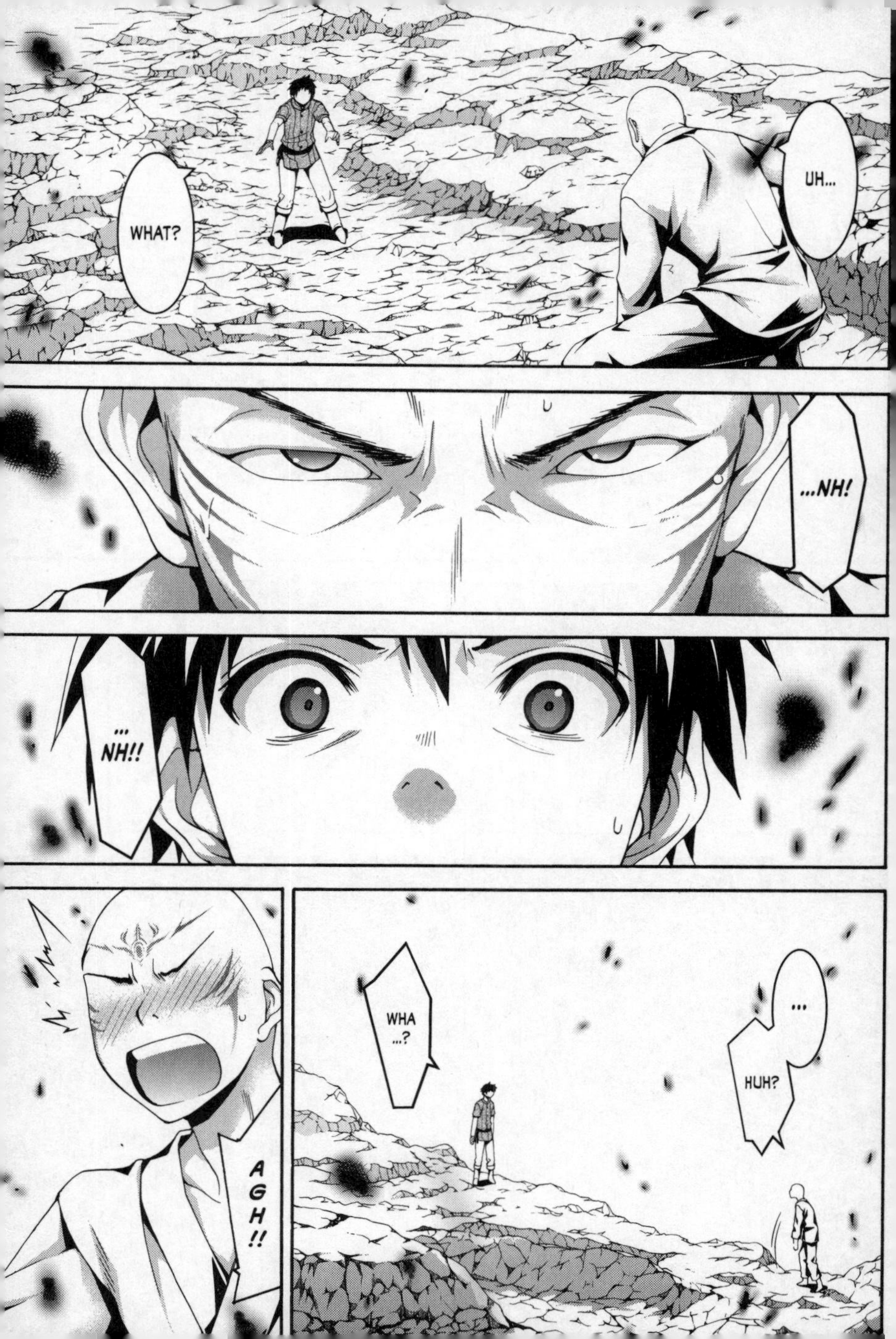
UH...
WHAT?
...NH!
... NH!!
...
HUH?
WHA ...?
AGH!!

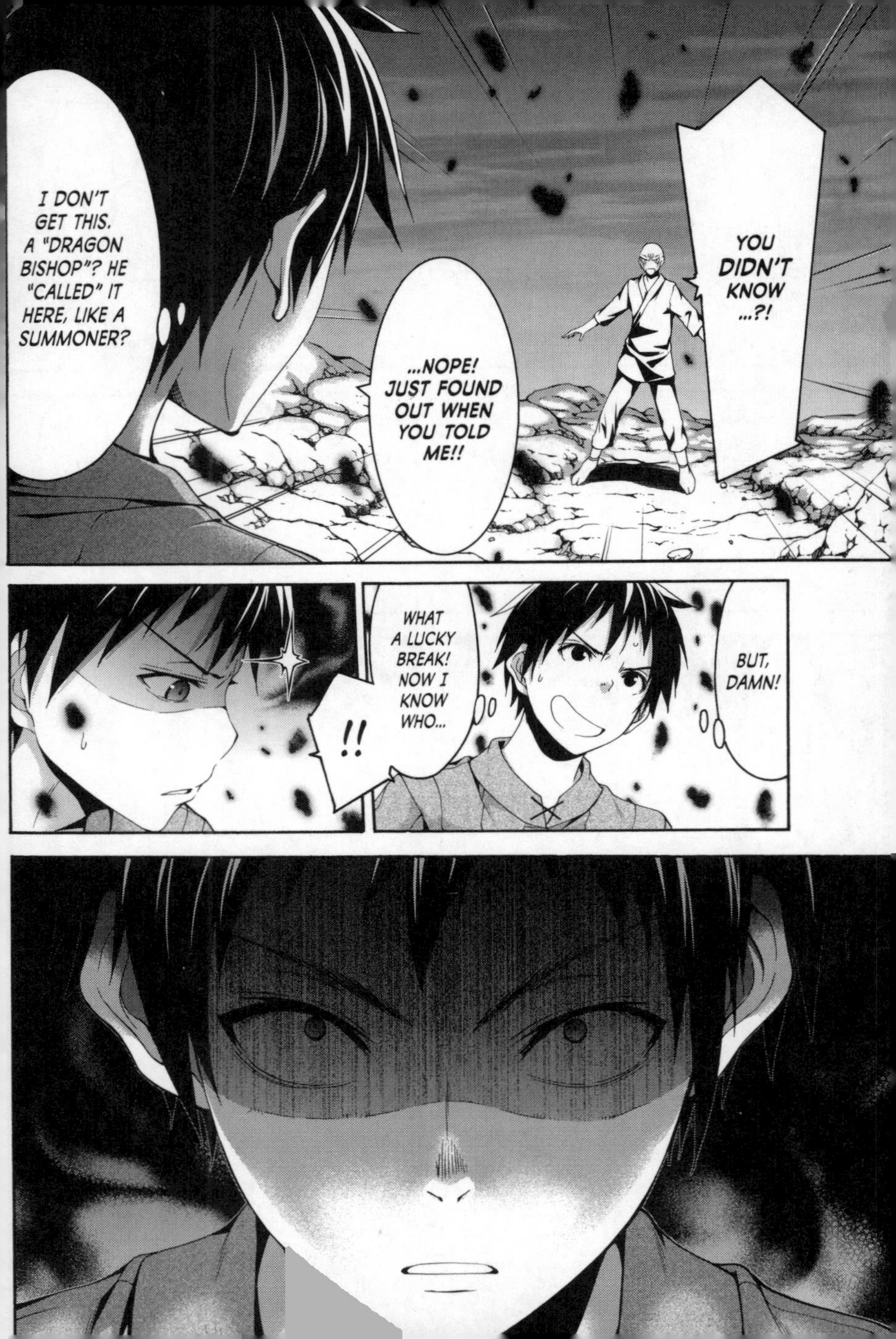
YOU DIDN'T KNOW ...?!
...NOPE! JUST FOUND OUT WHEN YOU TOLD ME!!
I DON'T GET THIS. A "DRAGON BISHOP"? HE "CALLED" IT HERE, LIKE A SUMMONER?
BUT, DAMN!
WHAT A LUCKY BREAK! NOW I KNOW WHO...
!!

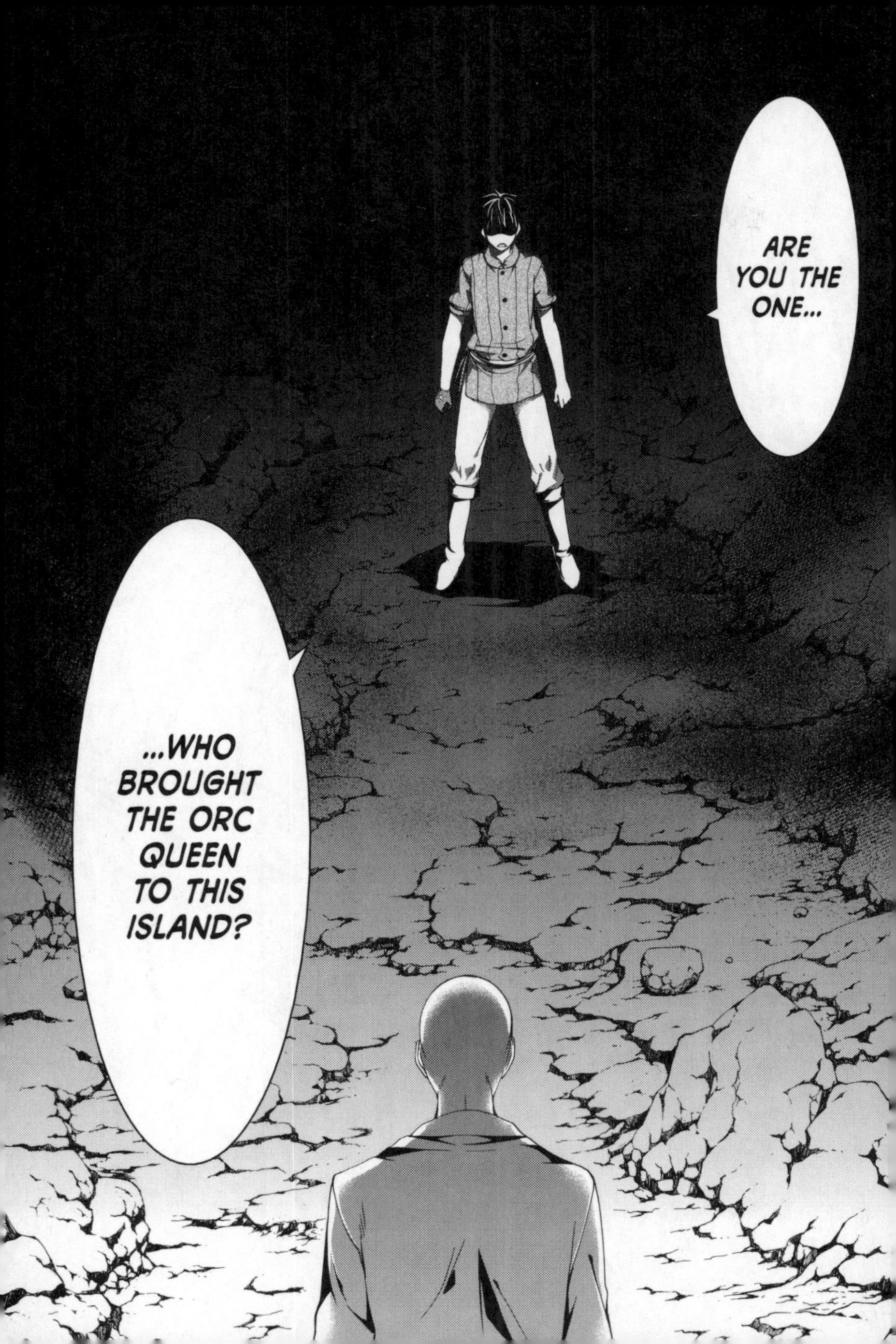
ARE YOU THE ONE...
...WHO BROUGHT THE ORC QUEEN TO THIS ISLAND?

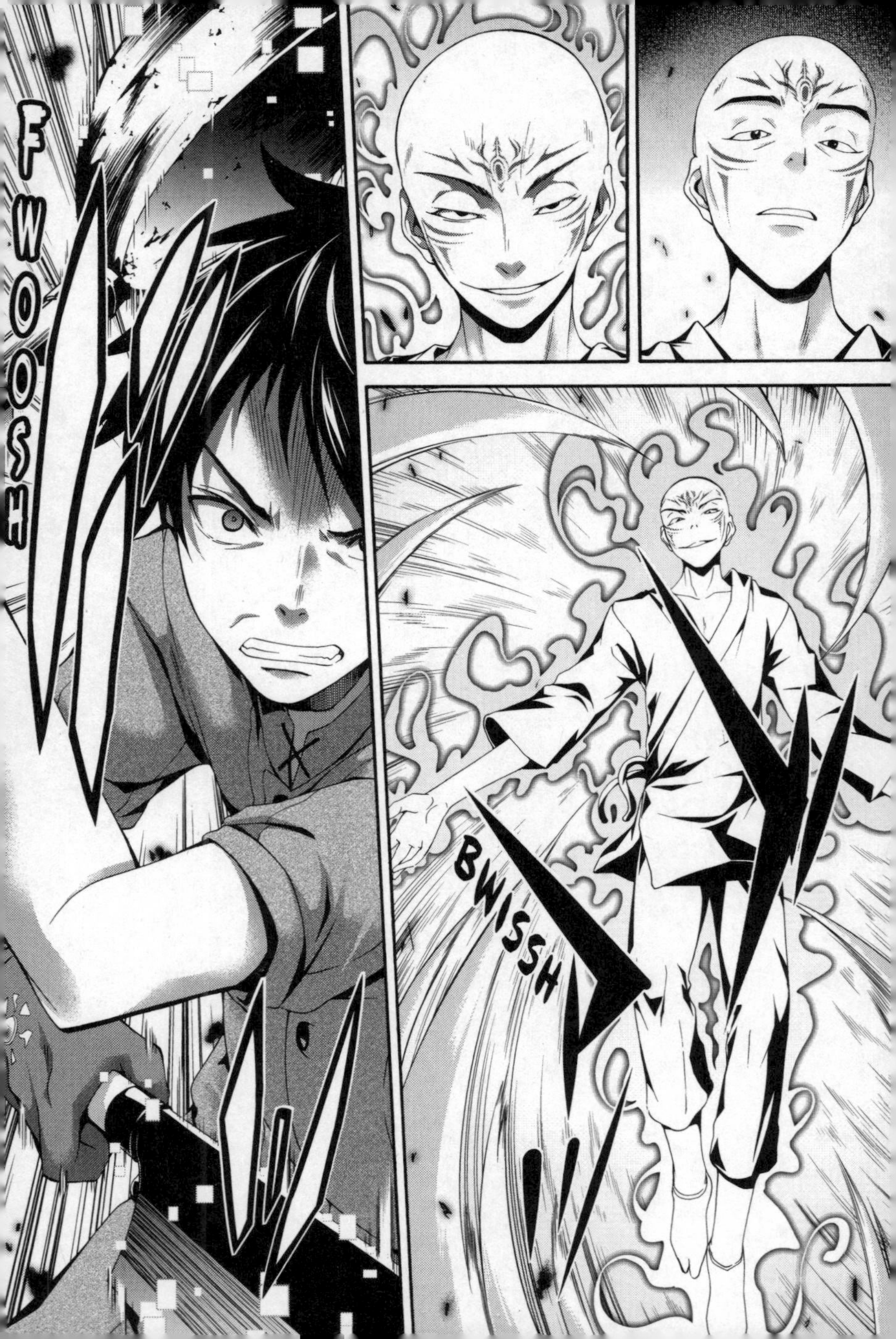
BWISSH
FWOOSH

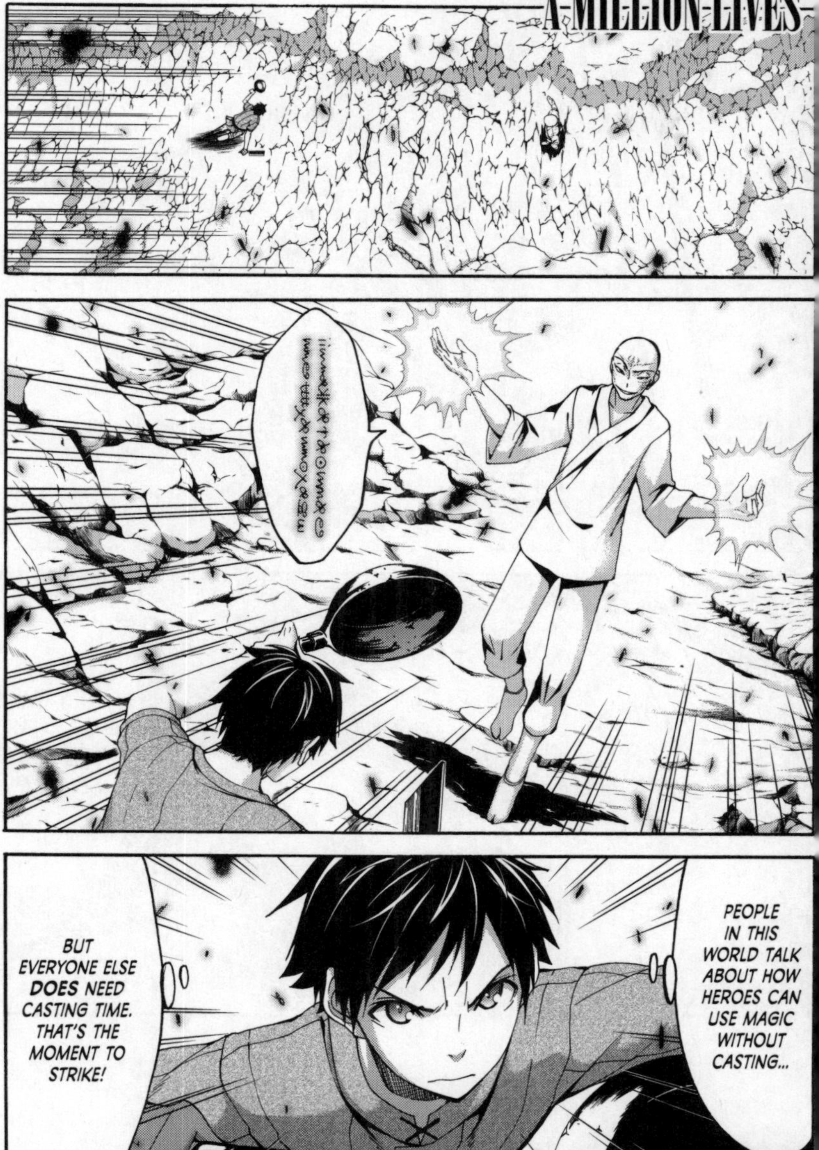
PEOPLE IN THIS WORLD TALK ABOUT HOW HEROES CAN USE MAGIC WITHOUT CASTING...
BUT EVERYONE ELSE **DOES** NEED CASTING TIME. THAT'S THE MOMENT TO STRIKE!

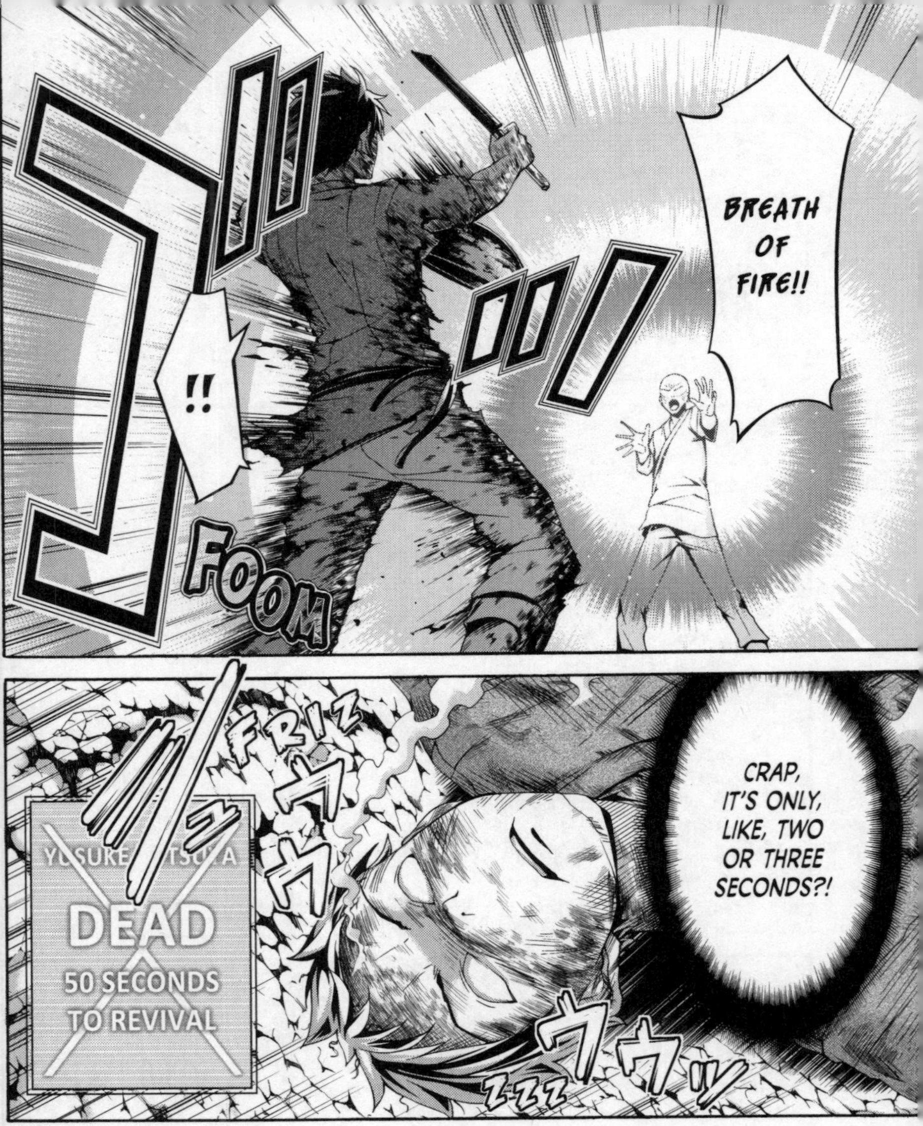
BREATH OF FIRE!!
!!
FOOM
CRAP, IT'S ONLY, LIKE, TWO OR THREE SECONDS?!
FRIZ
DEAD
50 SECONDS TO REVIVAL
ZZZ

#23 The Great Draining Hexagrams

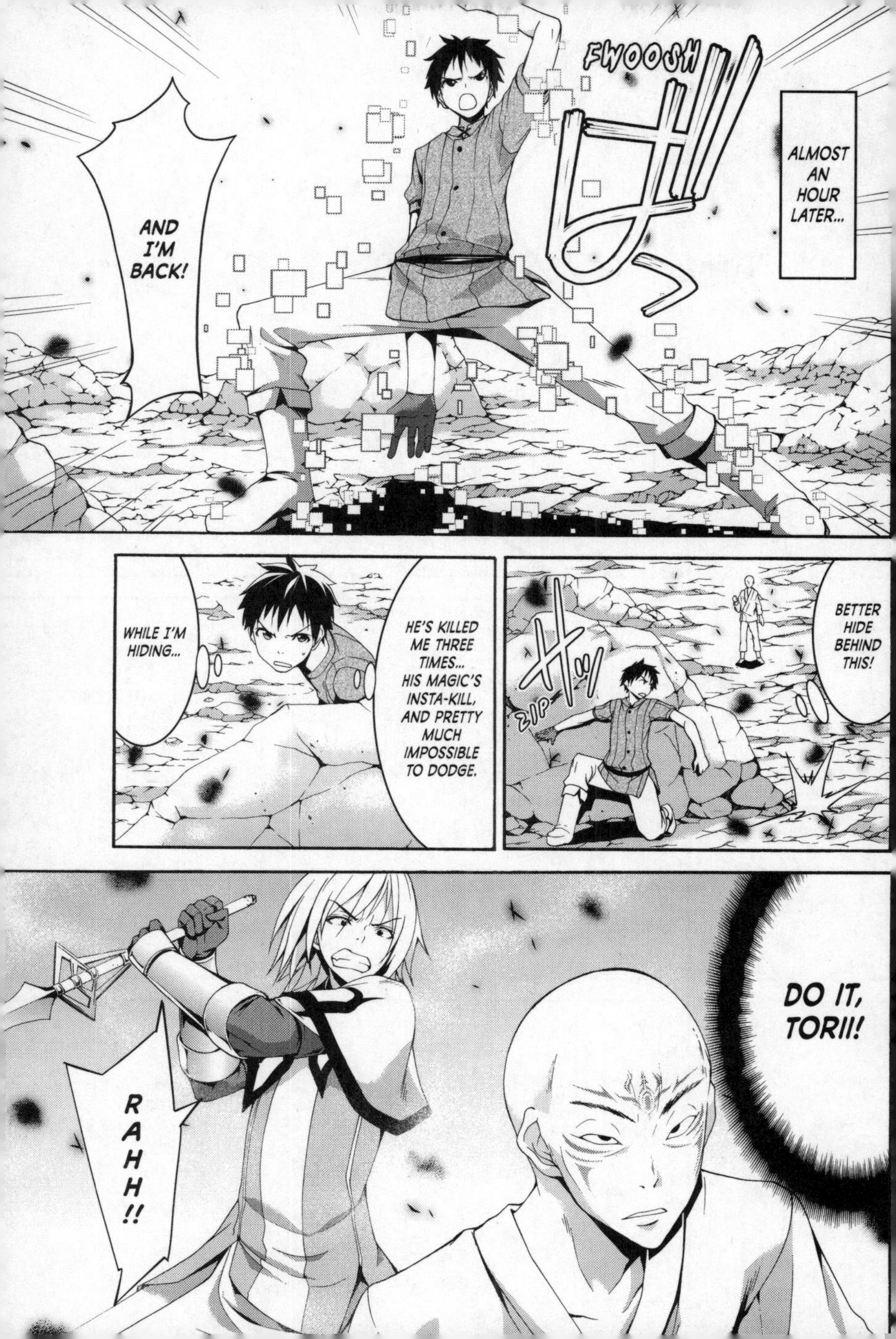
ALMOST AN HOUR LATER...
FWOOSH
AND I'M BACK!
BETTER HIDE BEHIND THIS!
ZIP
HE'S KILLED ME THREE TIMES... HIS MAGIC'S INSTA-KILL, AND PRETTY MUCH IMPOSSIBLE TO DODGE.
WHILE I'M HIDING...
DO IT, TORII!
RAHH!!

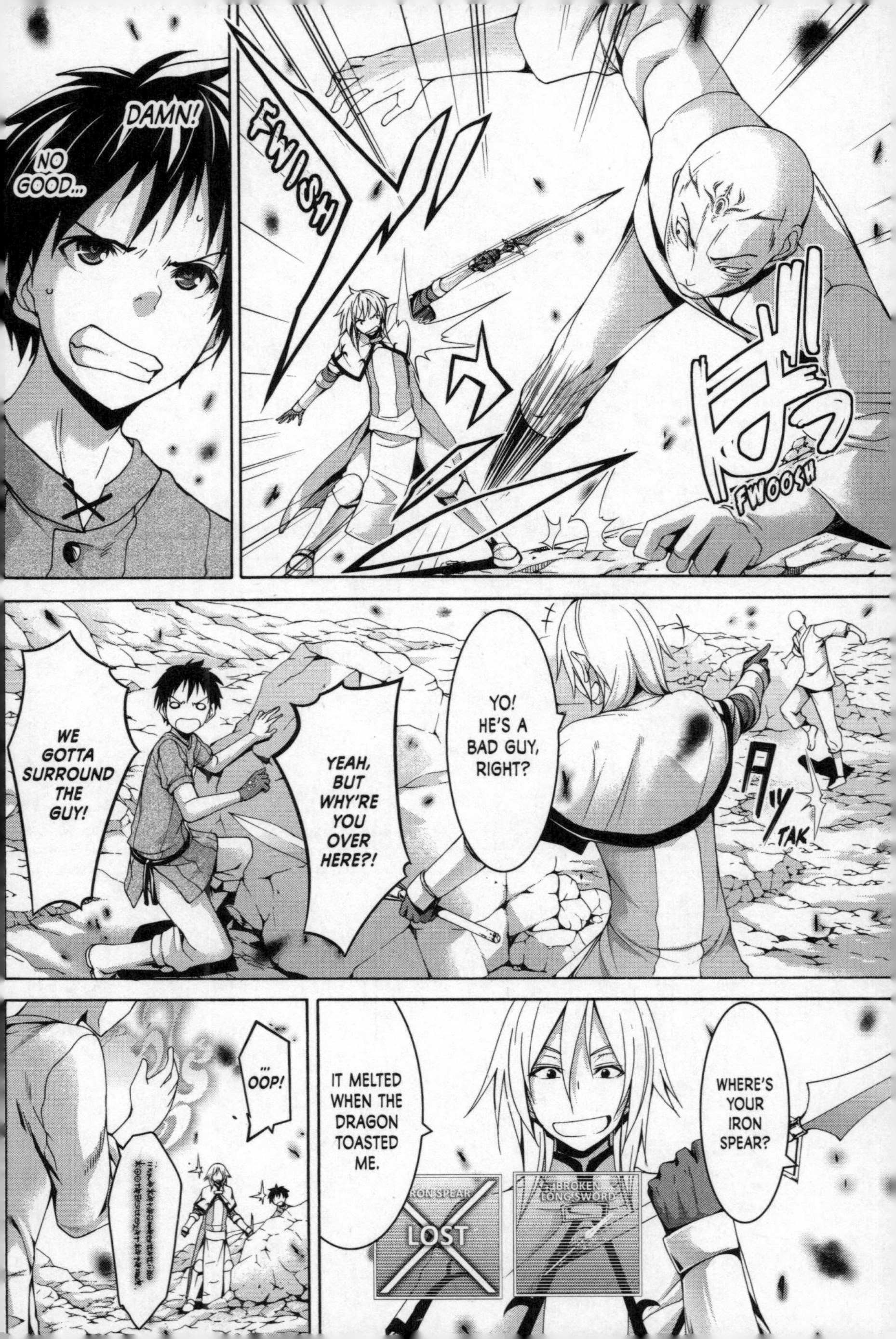
FWISH
FWOOSH
DAMN!
NO GOOD...
TAK
YO! HE'S A BAD GUY, RIGHT?
YEAH, BUT WHY'RE YOU OVER HERE?!
WE GOTTA SURROUND THE GUY!
WHERE'S YOUR IRON SPEAR?
IT MELTED WHEN THE DRAGON TOASTED ME.
BROKEN LONG SWORD
IRON SPEAR
LOST
... OOP!

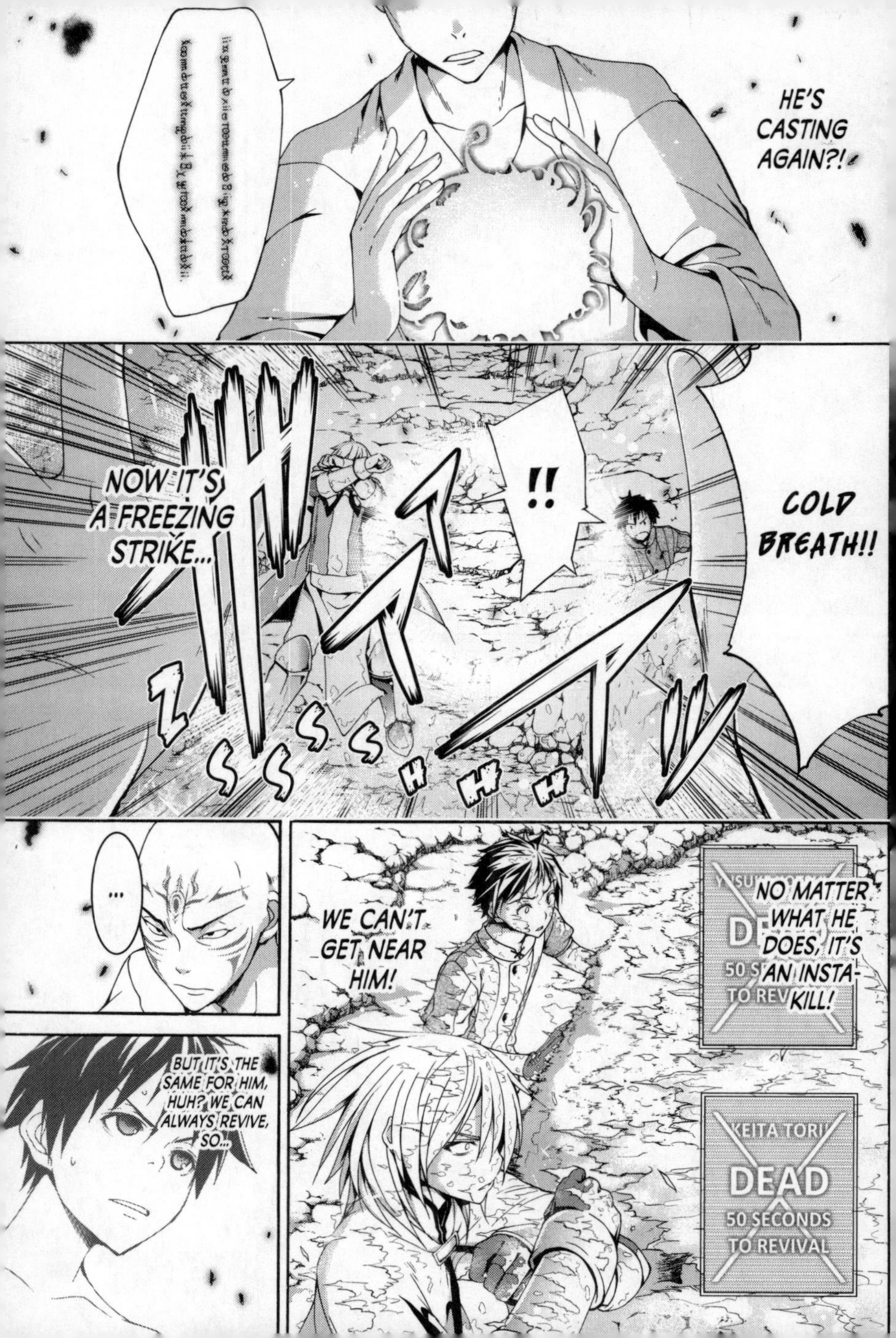
HE'S CASTING AGAIN?!
COLD BREATH!!
!!
NOW IT'S A FREEZING STRIKE...
NO MATTER WHAT HE DOES, IT'S AN INSTA-KILL!
WE CAN'T GET NEAR HIM!
KEITA TORU DEAD 50 SECONDS TO REVIVAL
...
BUT IT'S THE SAME FOR HIM, HUH? WE CAN ALWAYS REVIVE, SO...

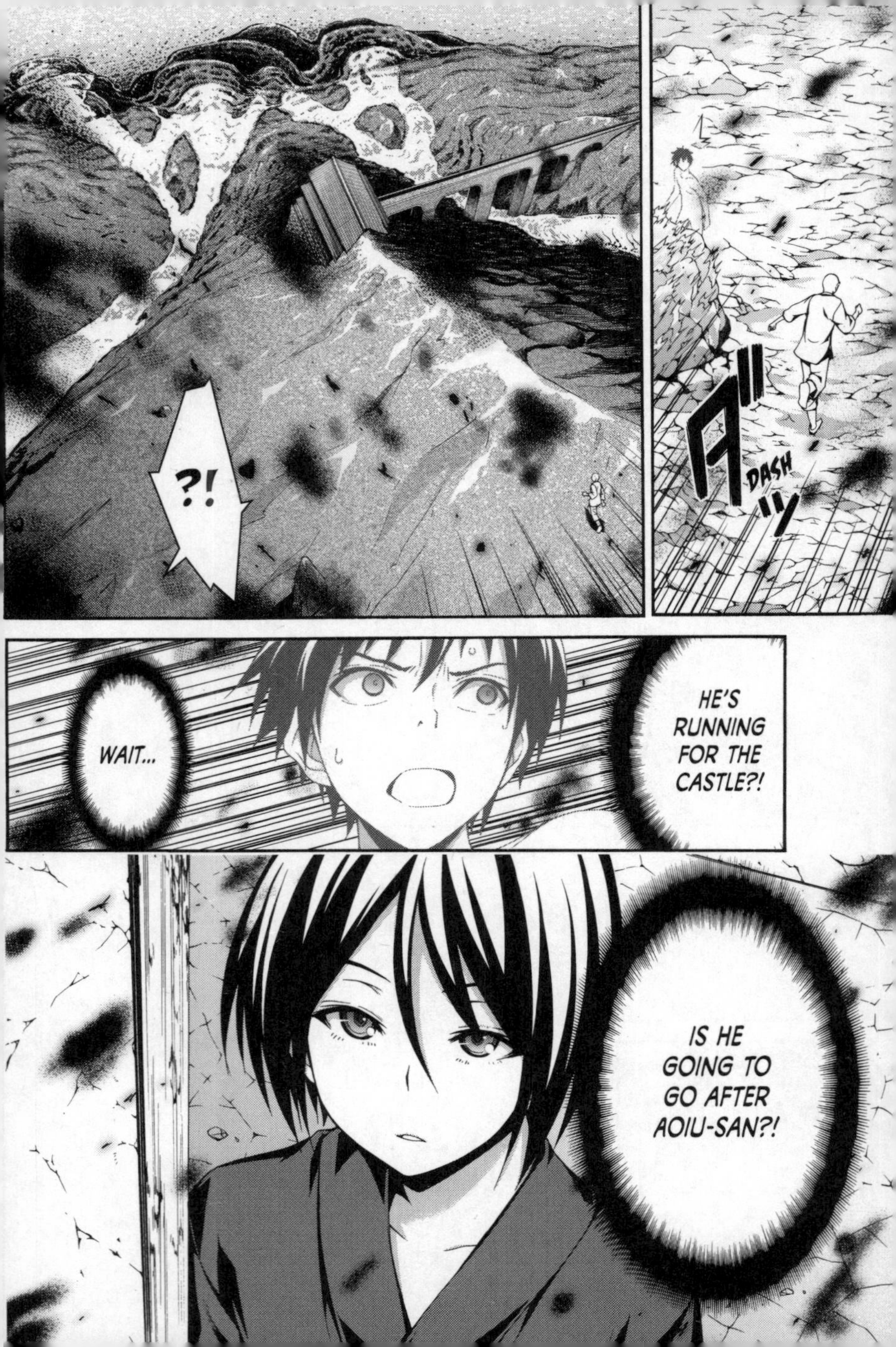

ダッ
DASH
?!
WAIT...
HE'S RUNNING FOR THE CASTLE?!
IS HE GOING TO GO AFTER AOIU-SAN?!

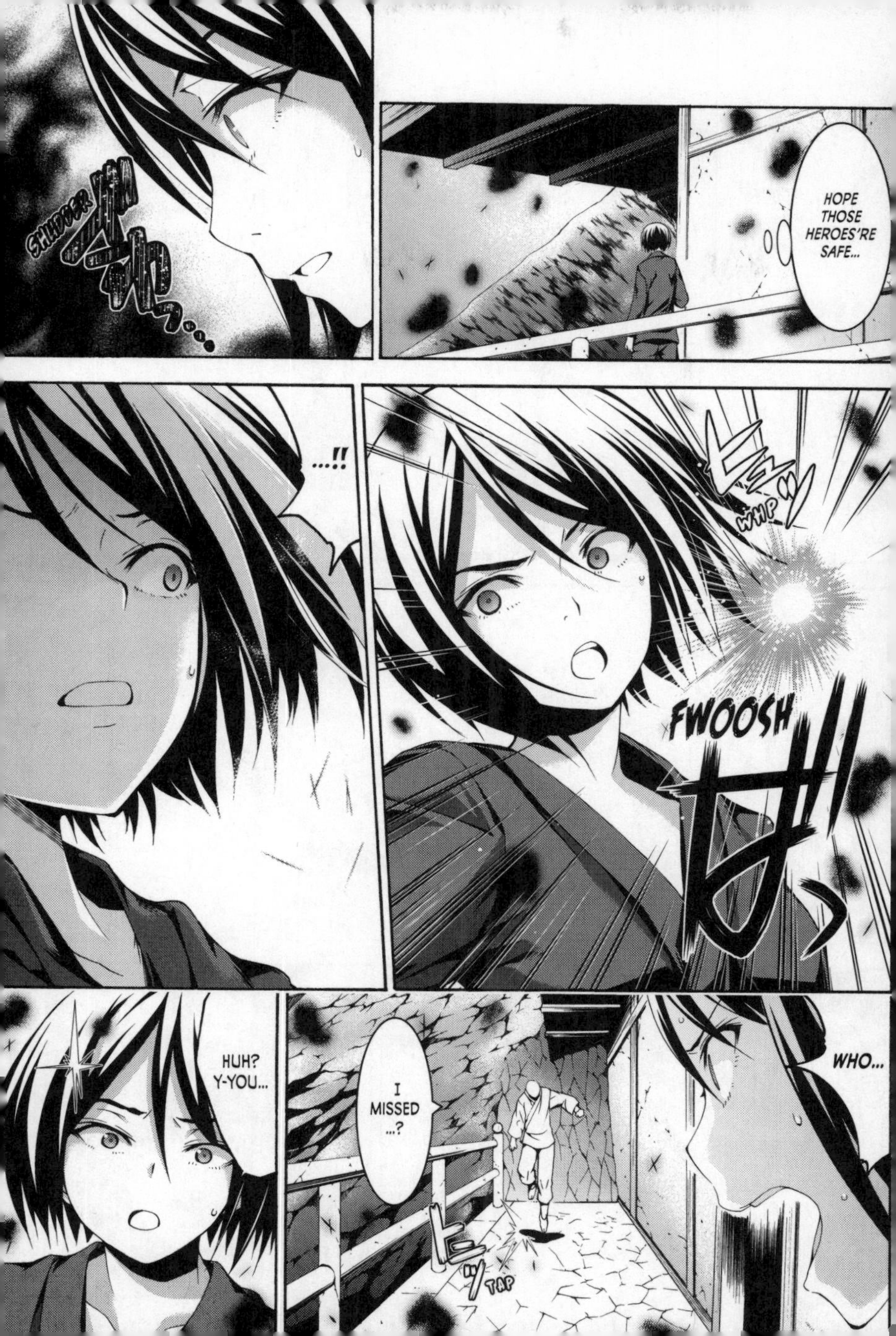
HOPE THOSE HEROES'RE SAFE...
SHUDDER
WHIP
FWOOSH
...!!
WHO...
I MISSED ...?
TAP
HUH? Y-YOU...

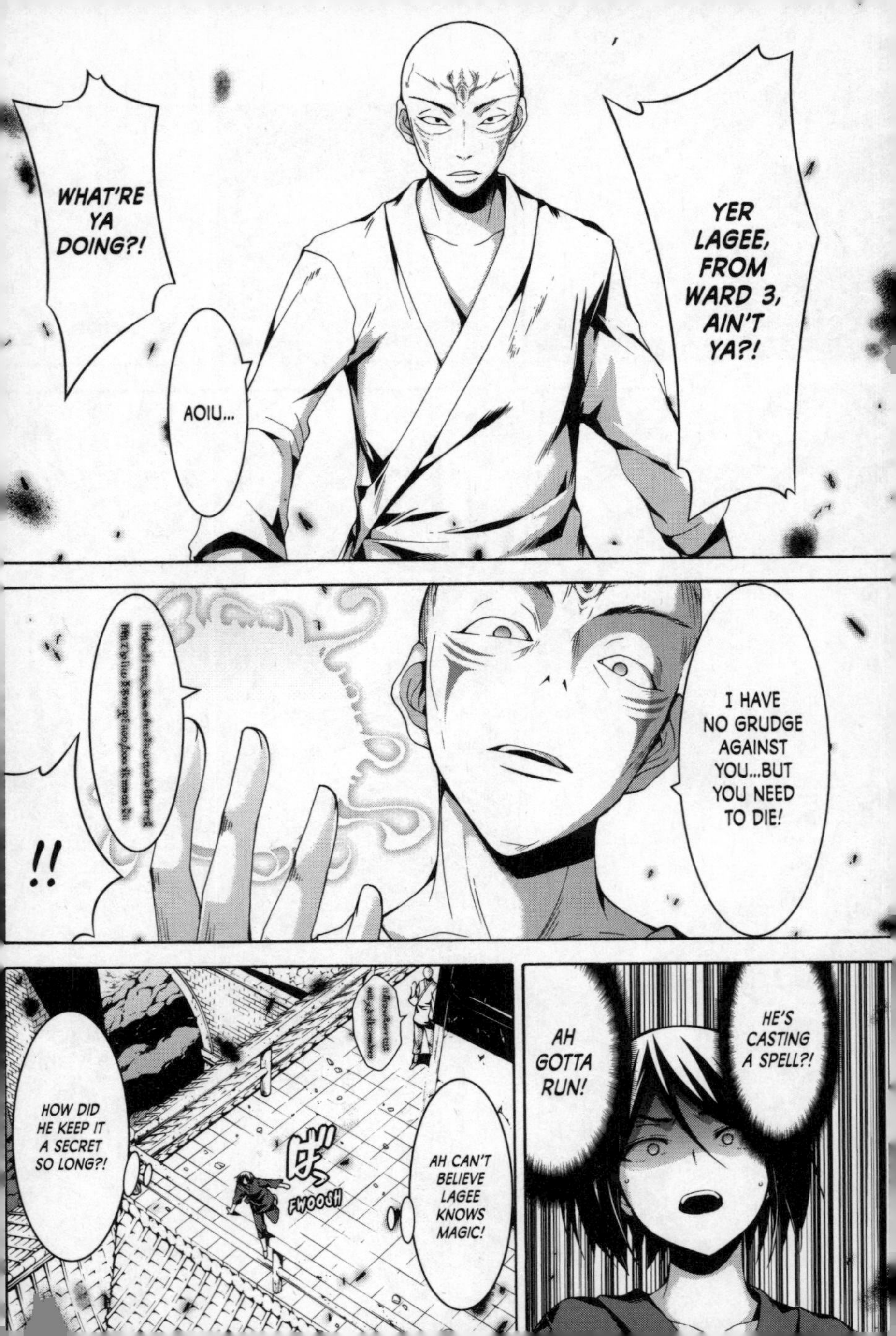
YER LAGEE, FROM WARD 3, AIN'T YA?!
WHAT'RE YA DOING?!
AOIU...
I HAVE NO GRUDGE AGAINST YOU...BUT YOU NEED TO DIE!
!!
HE'S CASTING A SPELL?!
AH GOTTA RUN!
AH CAN'T BELIEVE LAGEE KNOWS MAGIC!
ばっ
FWOOSH
HOW DID HE KEEP IT A SECRET SO LONG?!

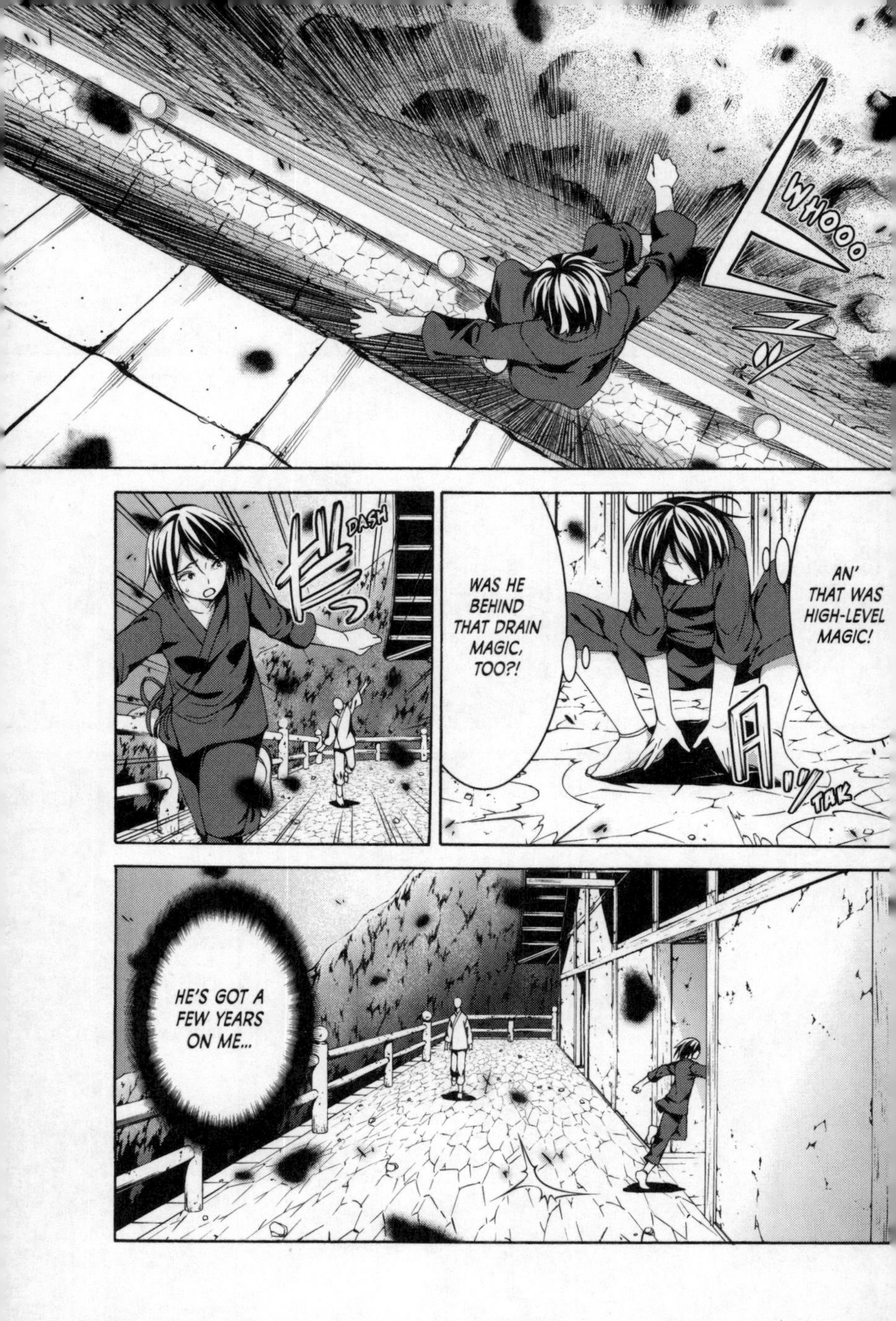
WHOOO
WAS HE BEHIND THAT DRAIN MAGIC, TOO?!
AN' THAT WAS HIGH-LEVEL MAGIC!
TAK
DASH
HE'S GOT A FEW YEARS ON ME...

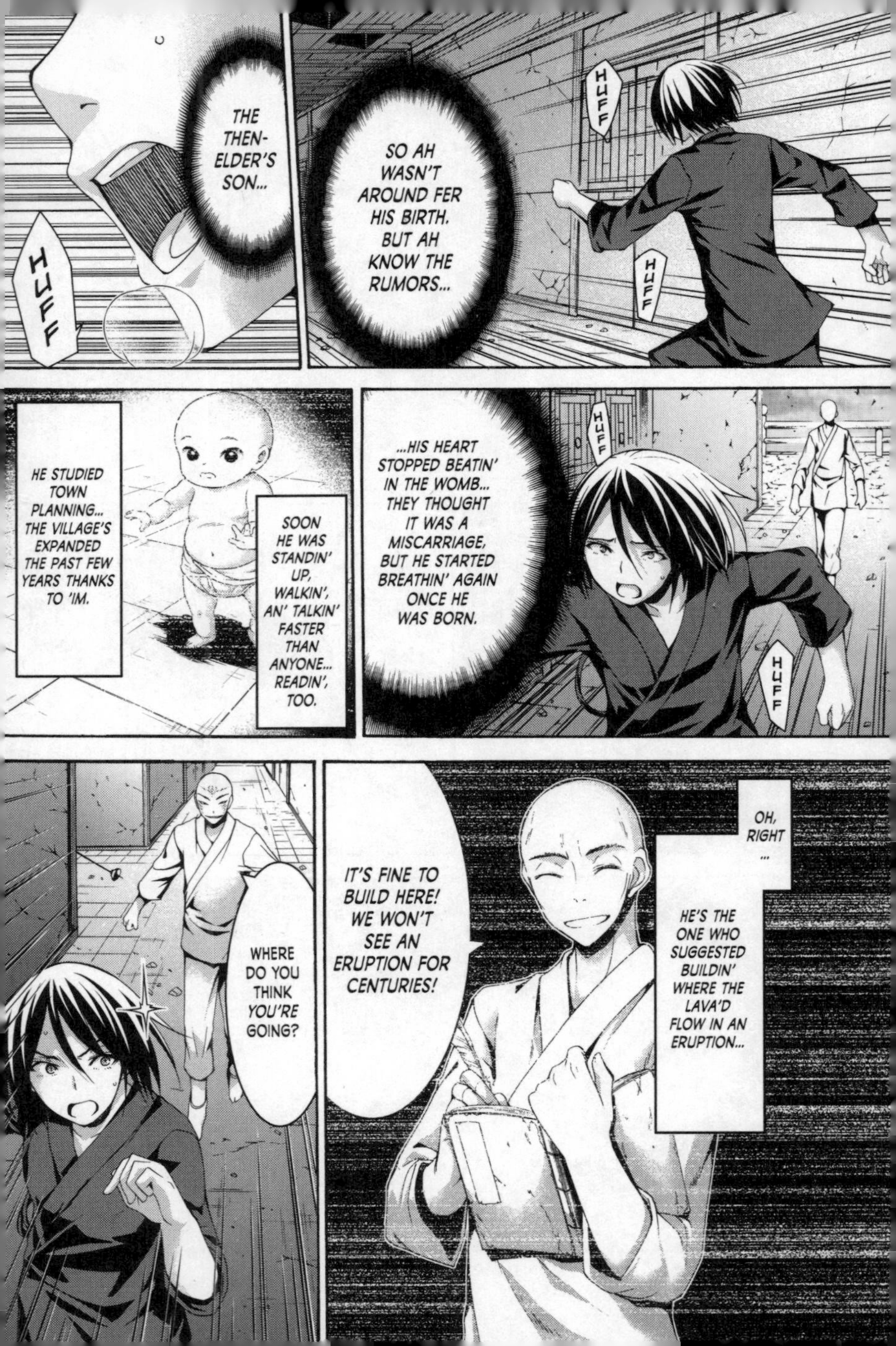
HUFF
SO AH WASN'T AROUND FER HIS BIRTH. BUT AH KNOW THE RUMORS...
HUFF
THE THEN-ELDER'S SON...
HUFF
HUFF
...HIS HEART STOPPED BEATIN' IN THE WOMB... THEY THOUGHT IT WAS A MISCARRIAGE, BUT HE STARTED BREATHIN' AGAIN ONCE HE WAS BORN.
HUFF
SOON HE WAS STANDIN' UP, WALKIN', AN' TALKIN' FASTER THAN ANYONE... READIN', TOO.
HE STUDIED TOWN PLANNING... THE VILLAGE'S EXPANDED THE PAST FEW YEARS THANKS TO 'IM.
OH, RIGHT ...
HE'S THE ONE WHO SUGGESTED BUILDIN' WHERE THE LAVA'D FLOW IN AN ERUPTION...
IT'S FINE TO BUILD HERE! WE WON'T SEE AN ERUPTION FOR CENTURIES!
WHERE DO YOU THINK YOU'RE GOING?

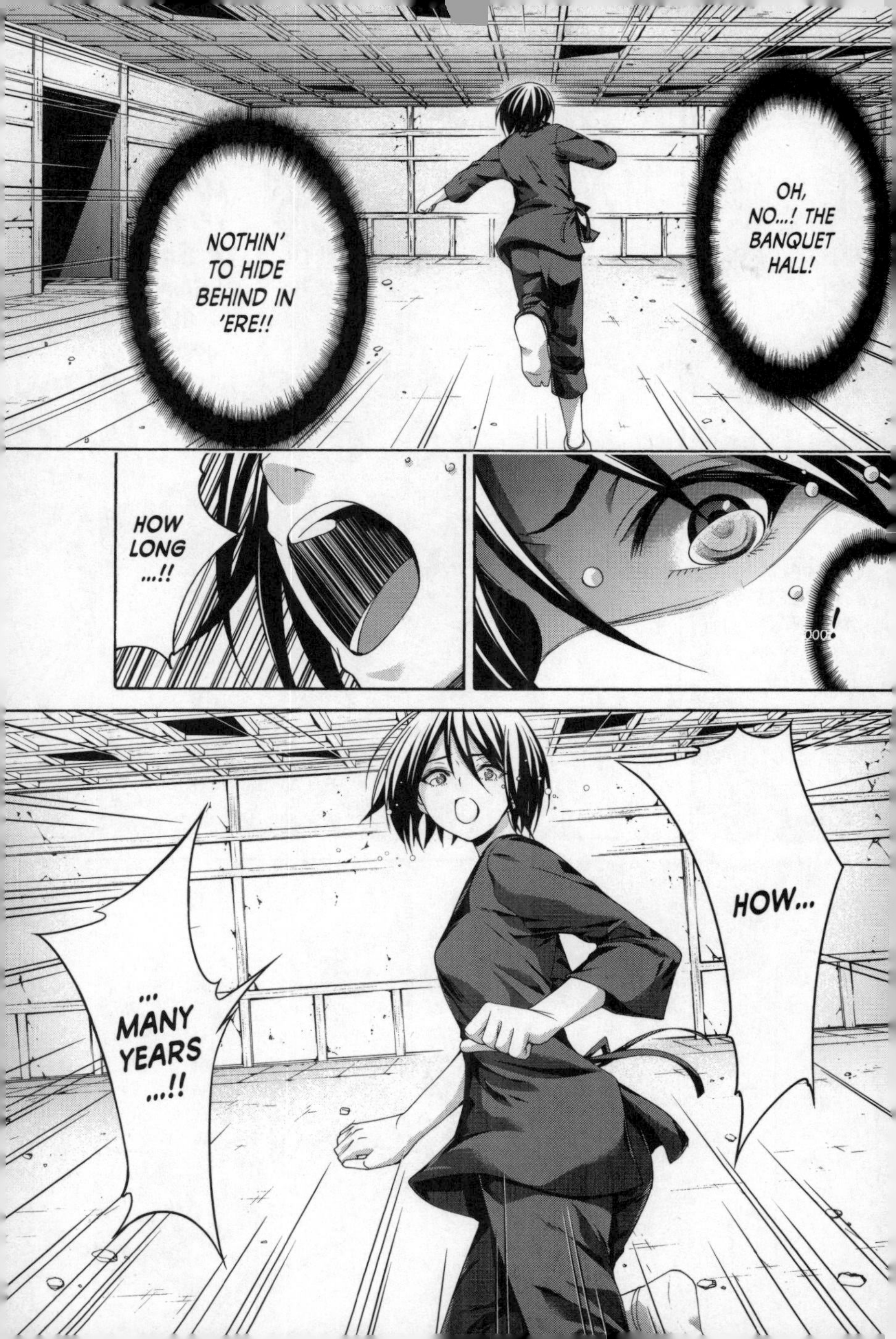
OH, NO...! THE BANQUET HALL!
NOTHIN' TO HIDE BEHIND IN 'ERE!!
!
HOW LONG ...!!
HOW...
... MANY YEARS ...!!

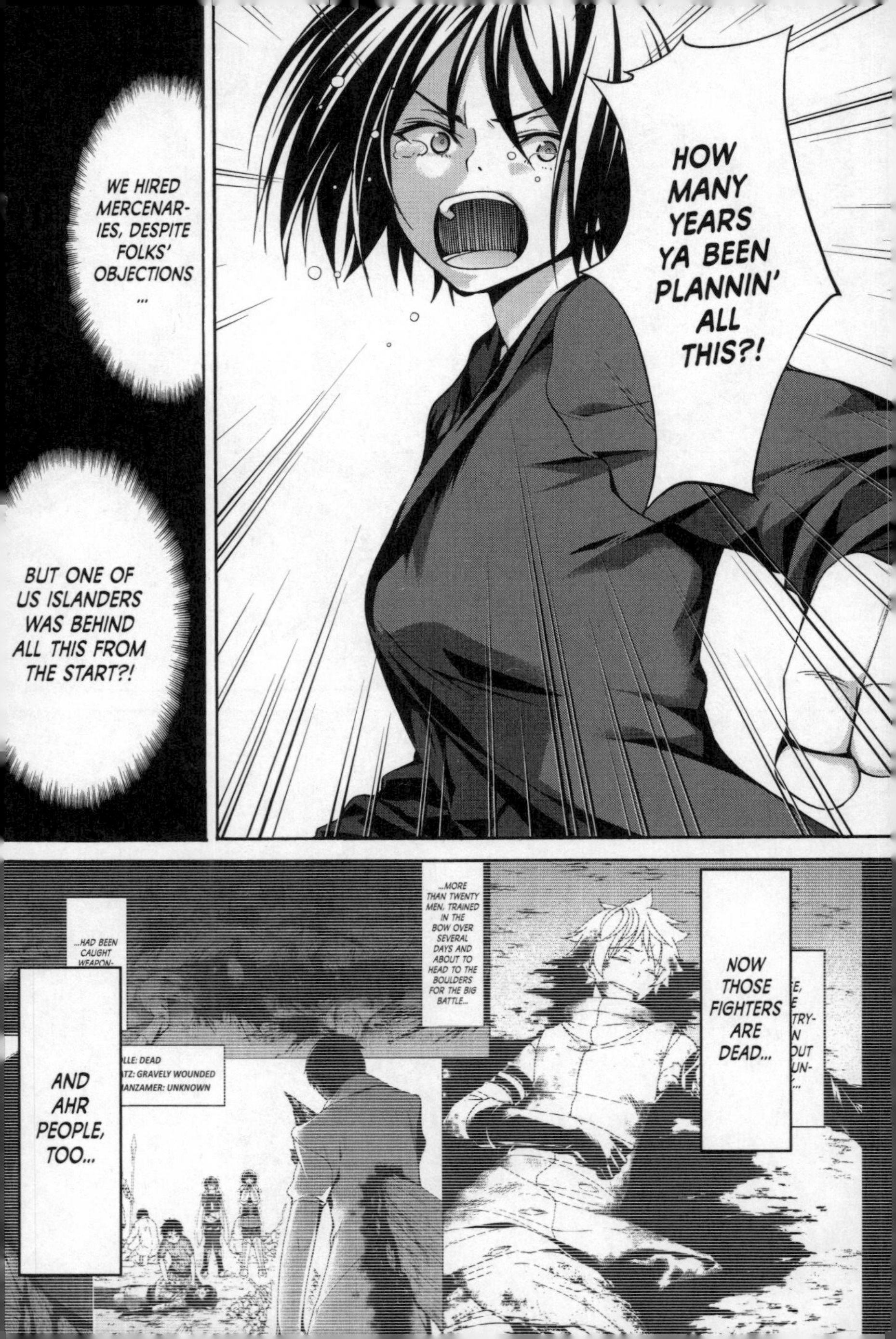
HOW MANY YEARS YA BEEN PLANNIN' ALL THIS?!
WE HIRED MERCENAR-IES, DESPITE FOLKS' OBJECTIONS ...
BUT ONE OF US ISLANDERS WAS BEHIND ALL THIS FROM THE START?!
NOW THOSE FIGHTERS ARE DEAD...
...MORE THAN TWENTY MEN, TRAINED IN THE BOW OVER SEVERAL DAYS AND ABOUT TO HEAD TO THE BOULDERS FOR THE BIG BATTLE...
...HAD BEEN CAUGHT WEAPON-
OLLE: DEAD
ATZ: GRAVELY WOUNDED
ANZAMER: UNKNOWN
AND AHR PEOPLE, TOO...

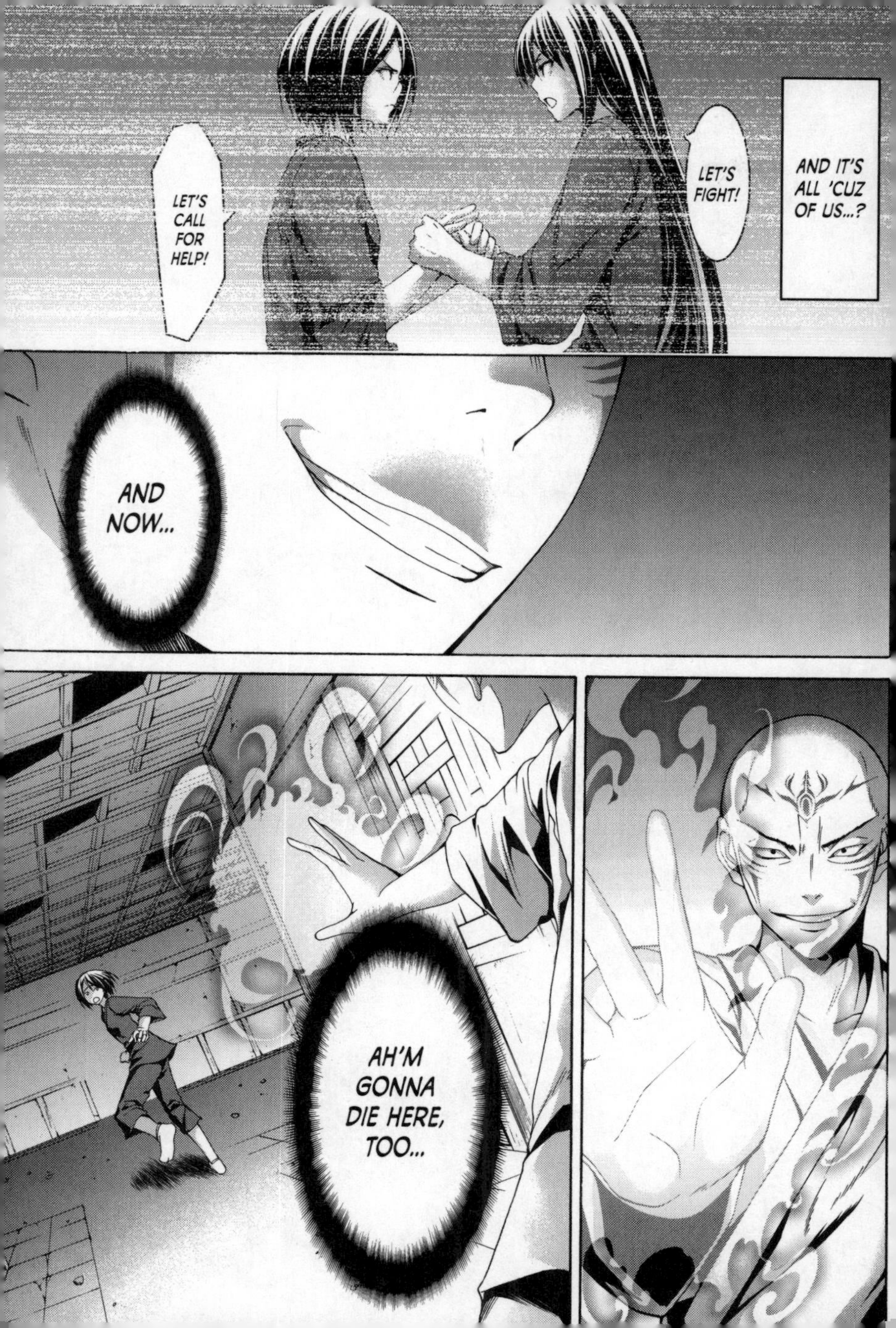
AND IT'S ALL 'CUZ OF US...?
LET'S FIGHT!
LET'S CALL FOR HELP!
AND NOW...
AH'M GONNA DIE HERE, TOO...

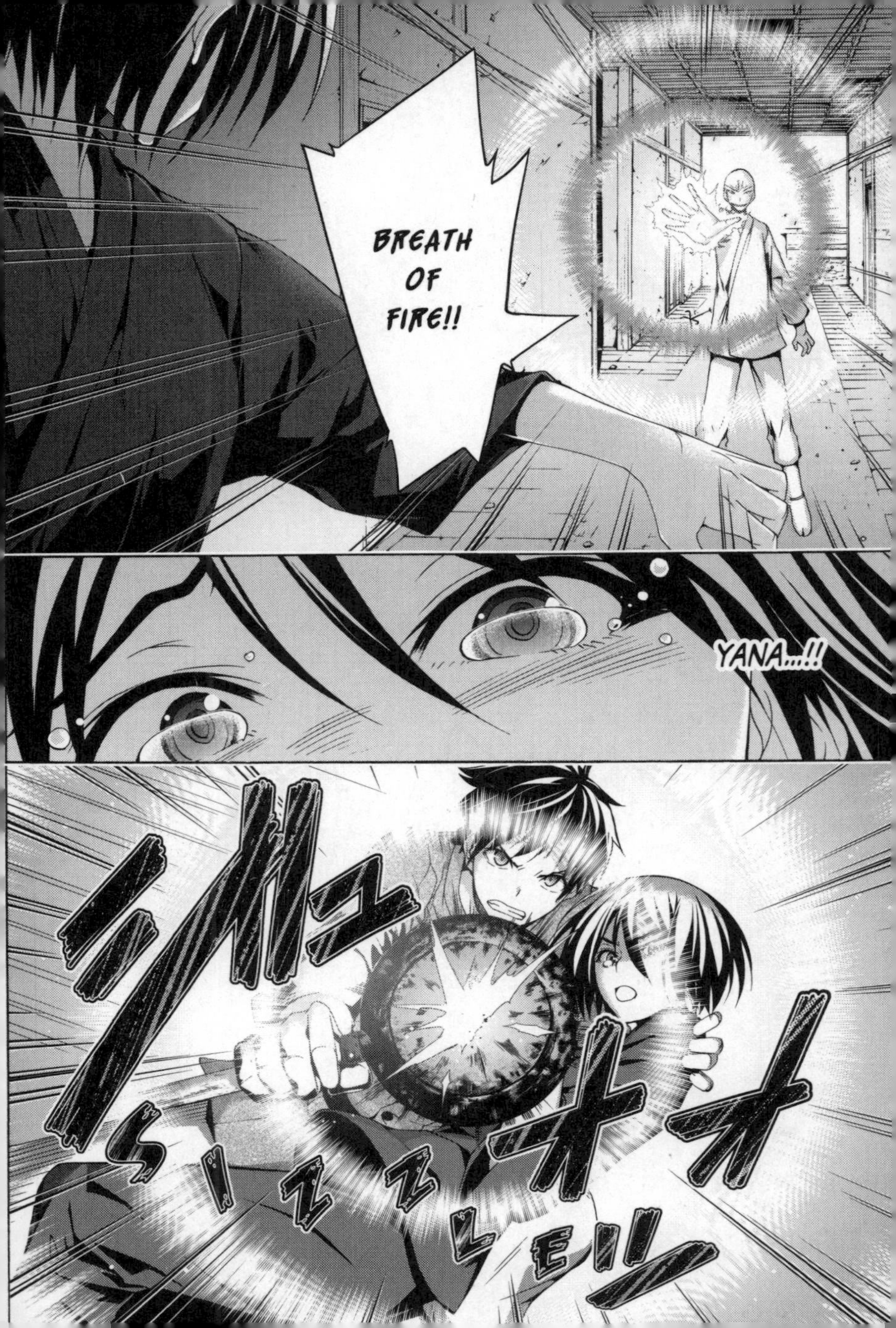
BREATH OF FIRE!!
YANA...!!
SIZZLE!!

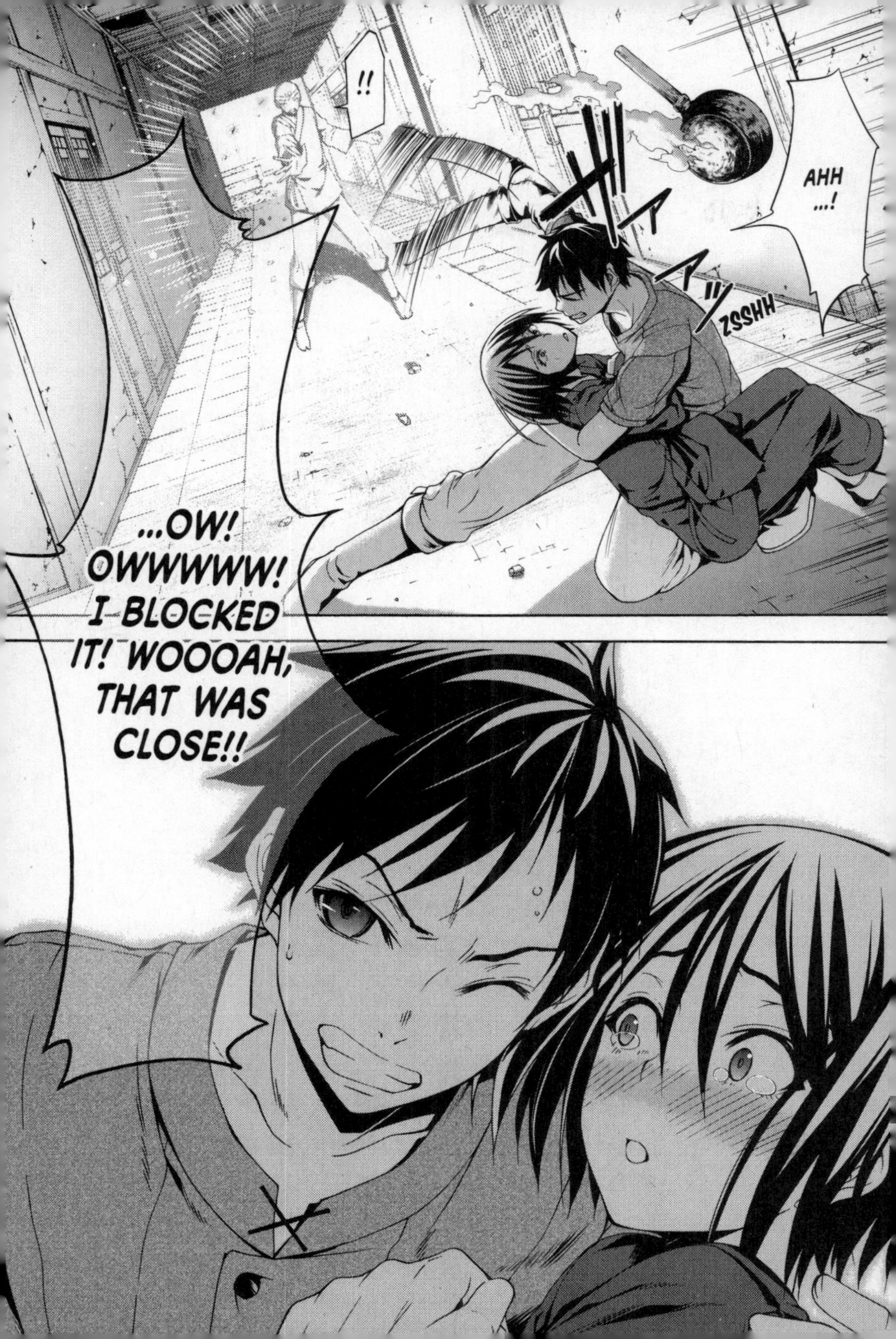
AHH ...!
ZSSHH
!!
...OW! OWWWWW! I BLOCKED IT! WOOOAH, THAT WAS CLOSE!!

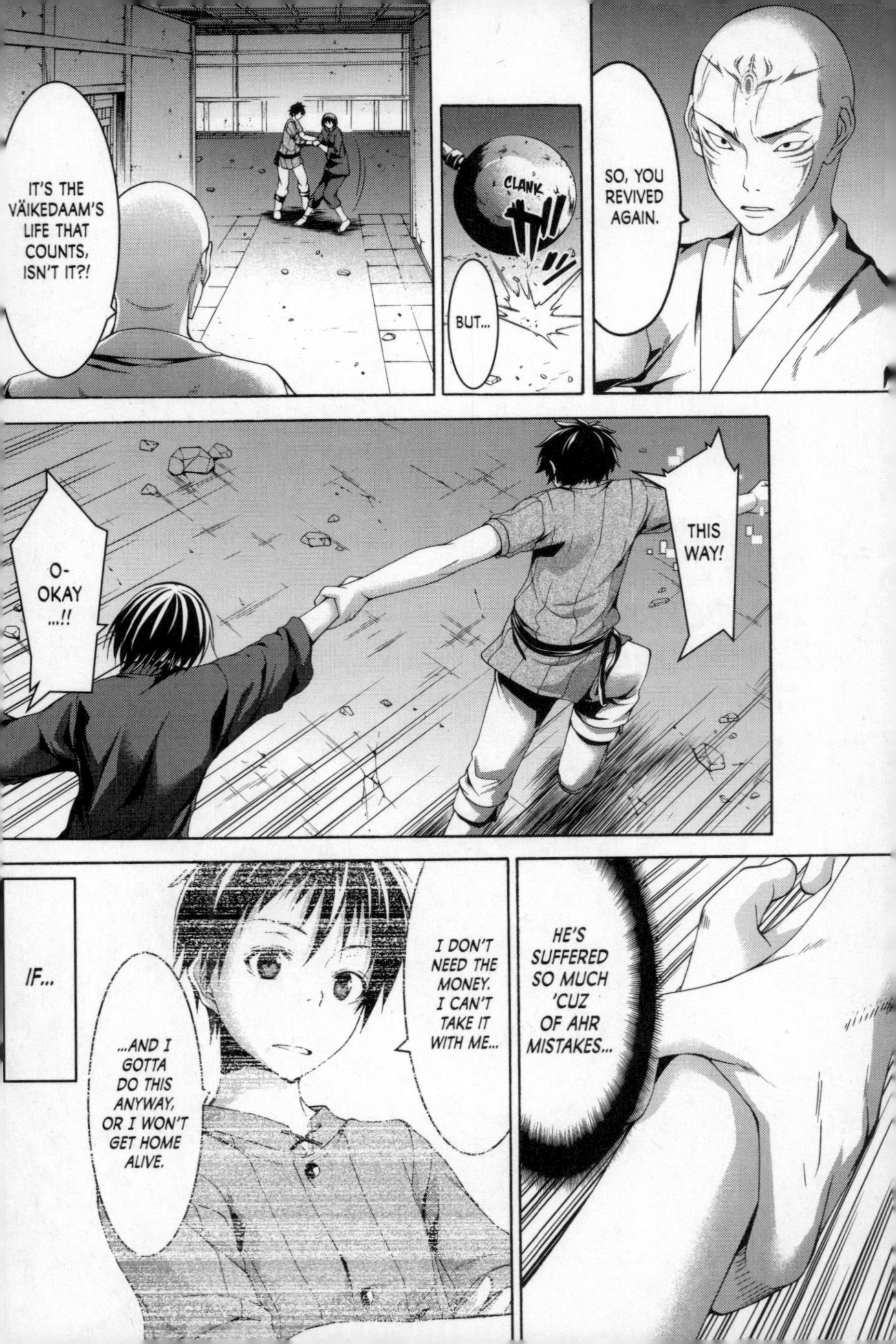
SO, YOU REVIVED AGAIN.
CLANK
BUT...
IT'S THE VÄIKEDAAM'S LIFE THAT COUNTS, ISN'T IT?!
THIS WAY!
O-OKAY ...!!
HE'S SUFFERED SO MUCH 'CUZ OF AHR MISTAKES...
I DON'T NEED THE MONEY. I CAN'T TAKE IT WITH ME...
...AND I GOTTA DO THIS ANYWAY, OR I WON'T GET HOME ALIVE.
IF...

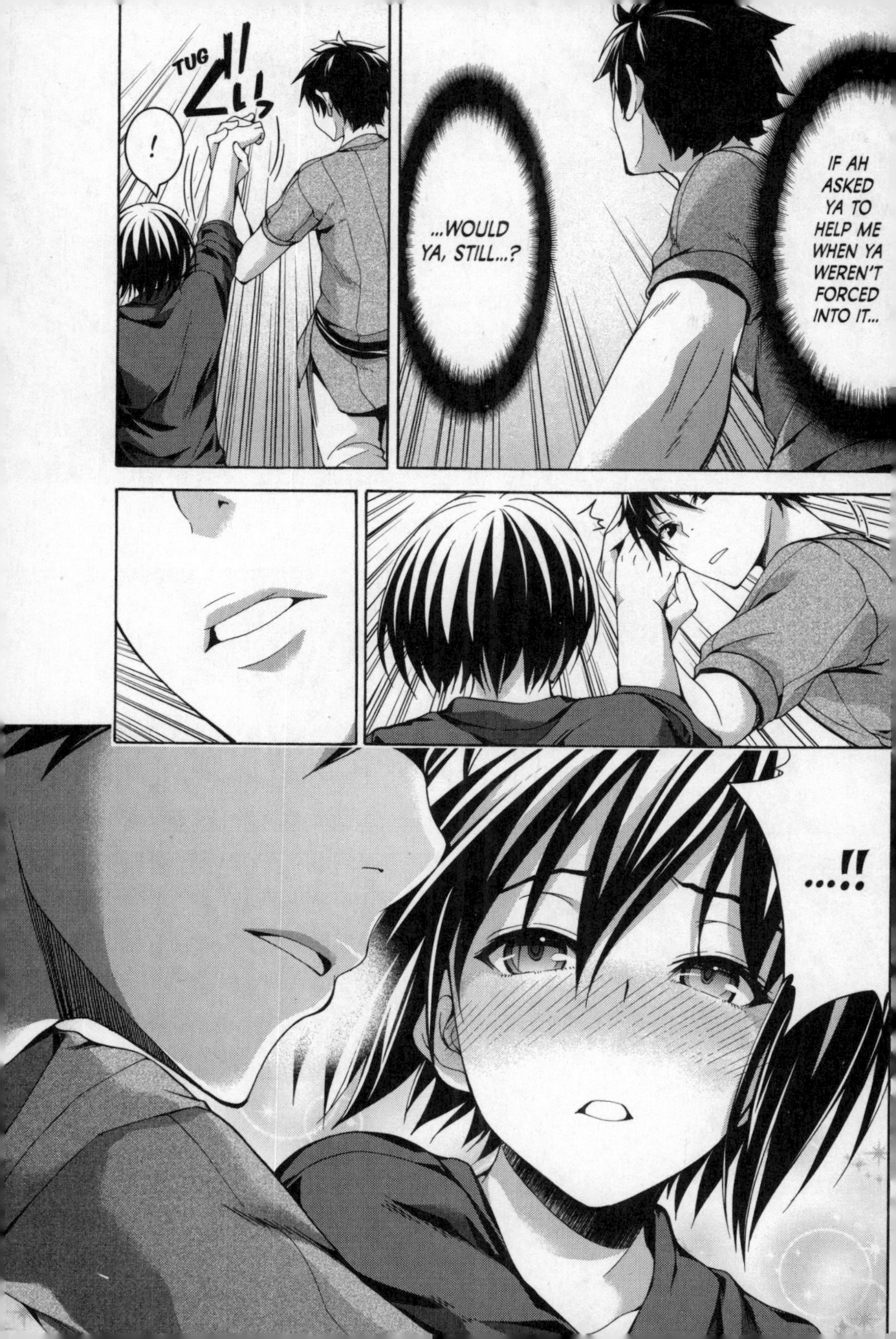
IF AH ASKED YA TO HELP ME WHEN YA WEREN'T FORCED INTO IT...
...WOULD YA, STILL...?
TUG
ぐいっ
!
...!!

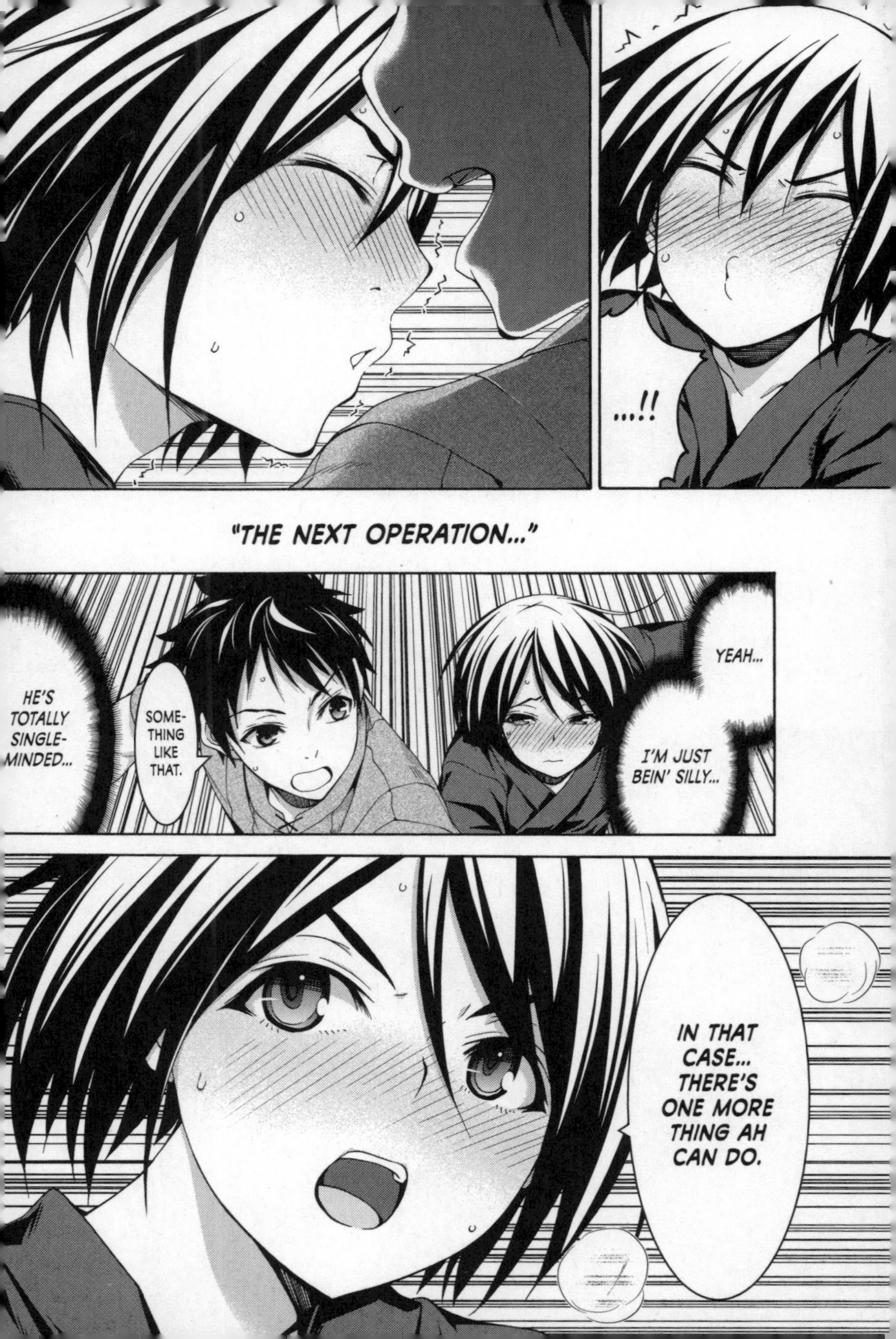
...!!
"THE NEXT OPERATION..."
YEAH...
I'M JUST BEIN' SILLY...
SOME-THING LIKE THAT.
HE'S TOTALLY SINGLE-MINDED...
IN THAT CASE... THERE'S ONE MORE THING AH CAN DO.

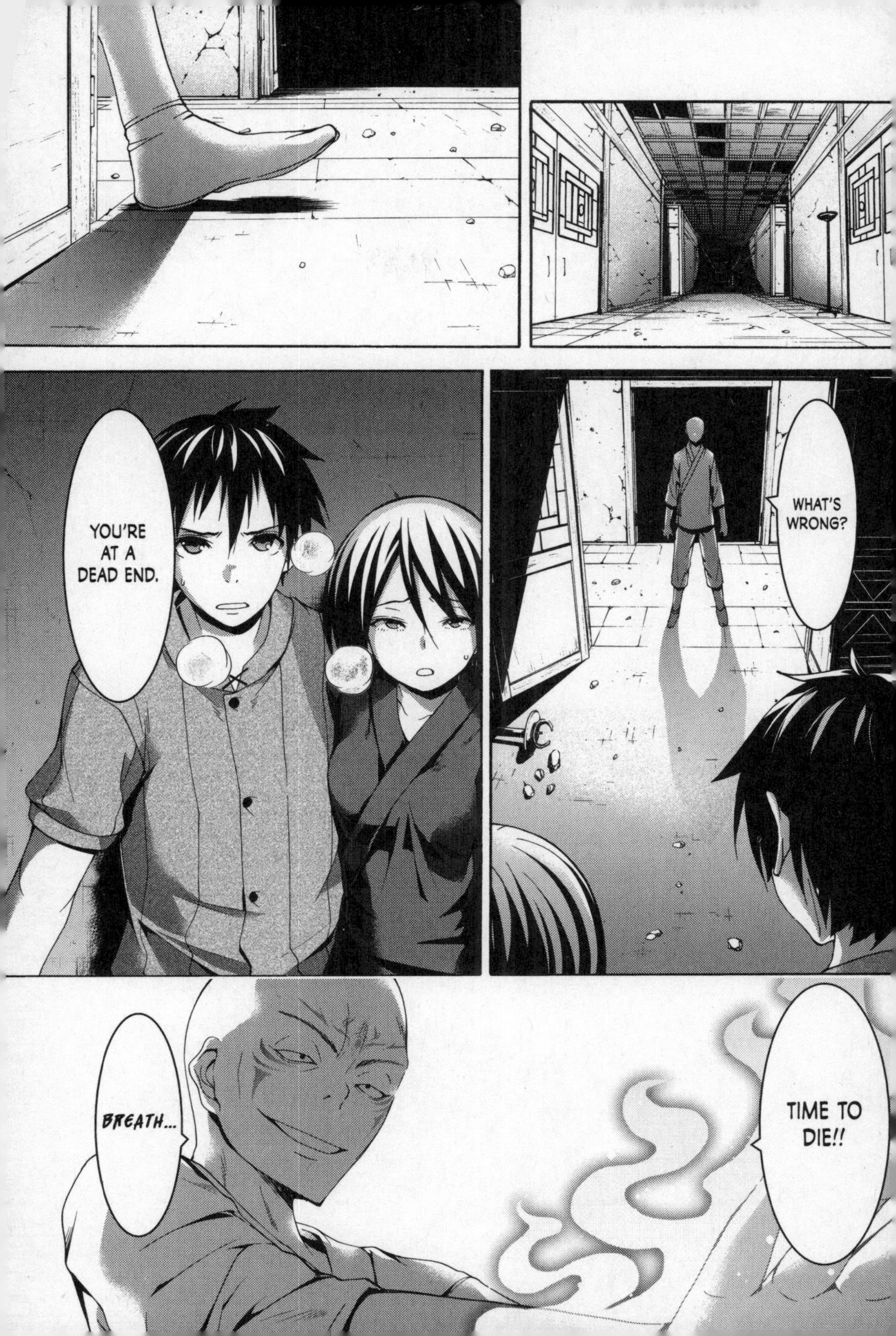
WHAT'S WRONG?
YOU'RE AT A DEAD END.
TIME TO DIE!!
BREATH...

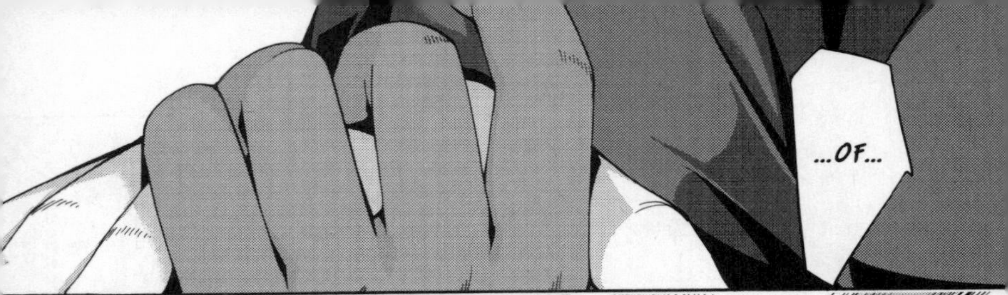
...OF...
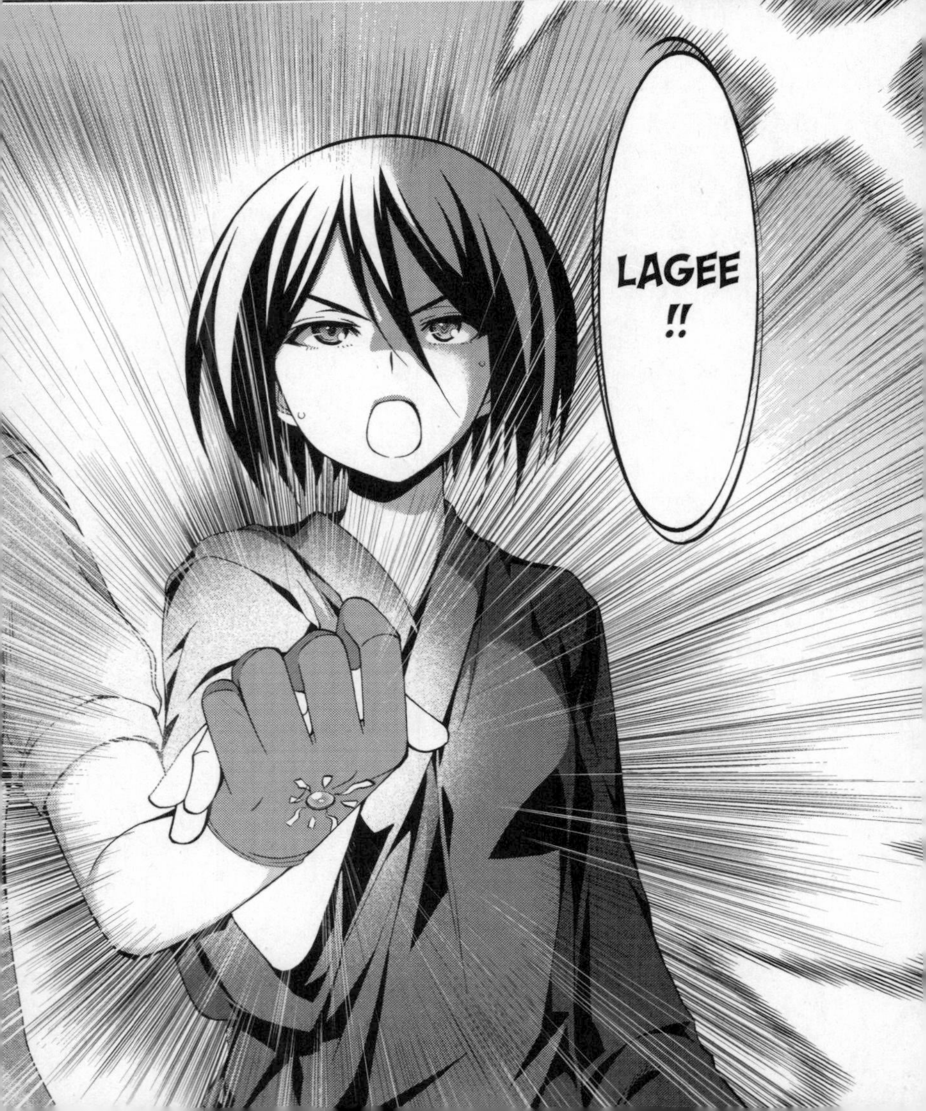
LAGEE !!

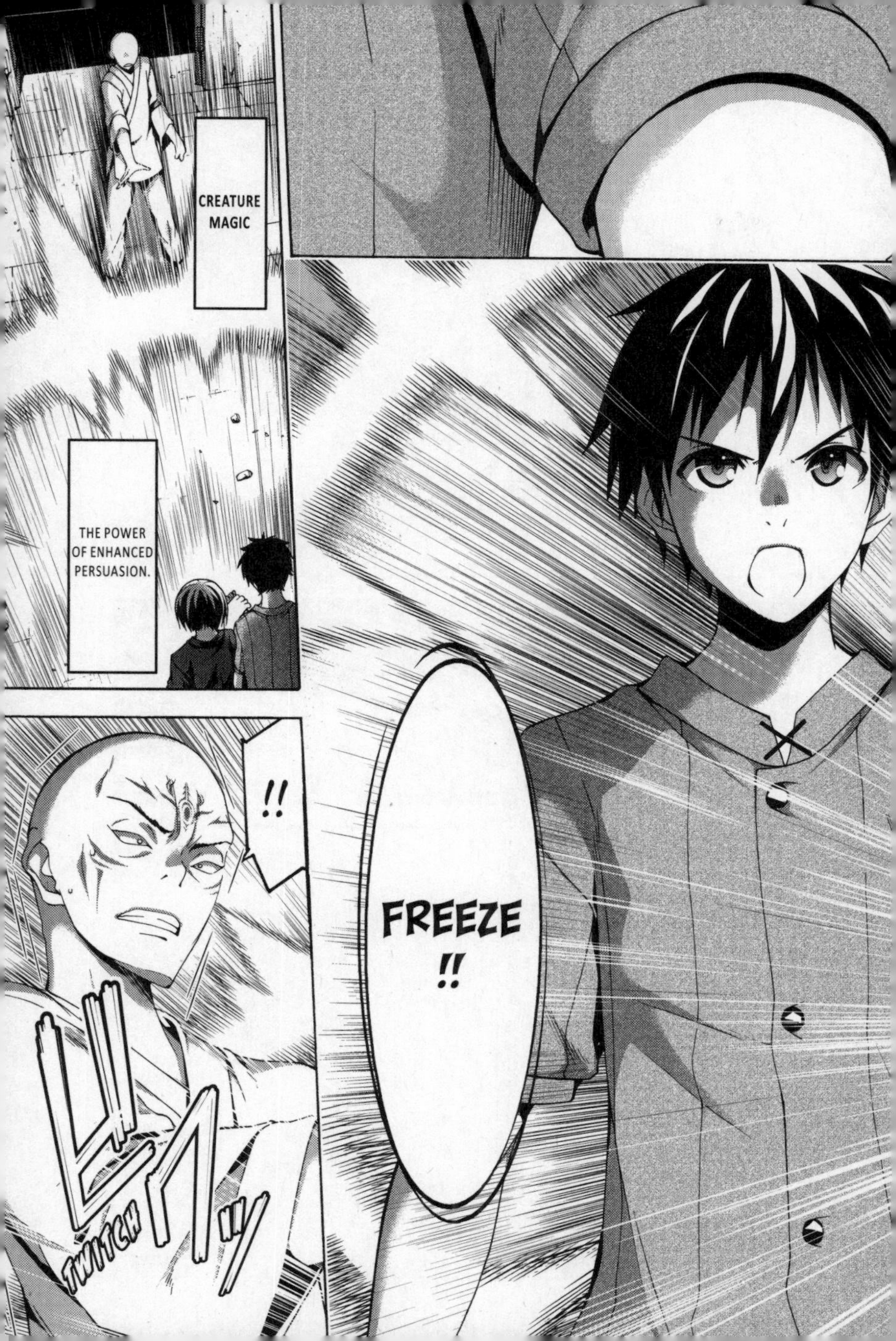
CREATURE MAGIC
THE POWER OF ENHANCED PERSUASION.
FREEZE!!
!!
TWITCH

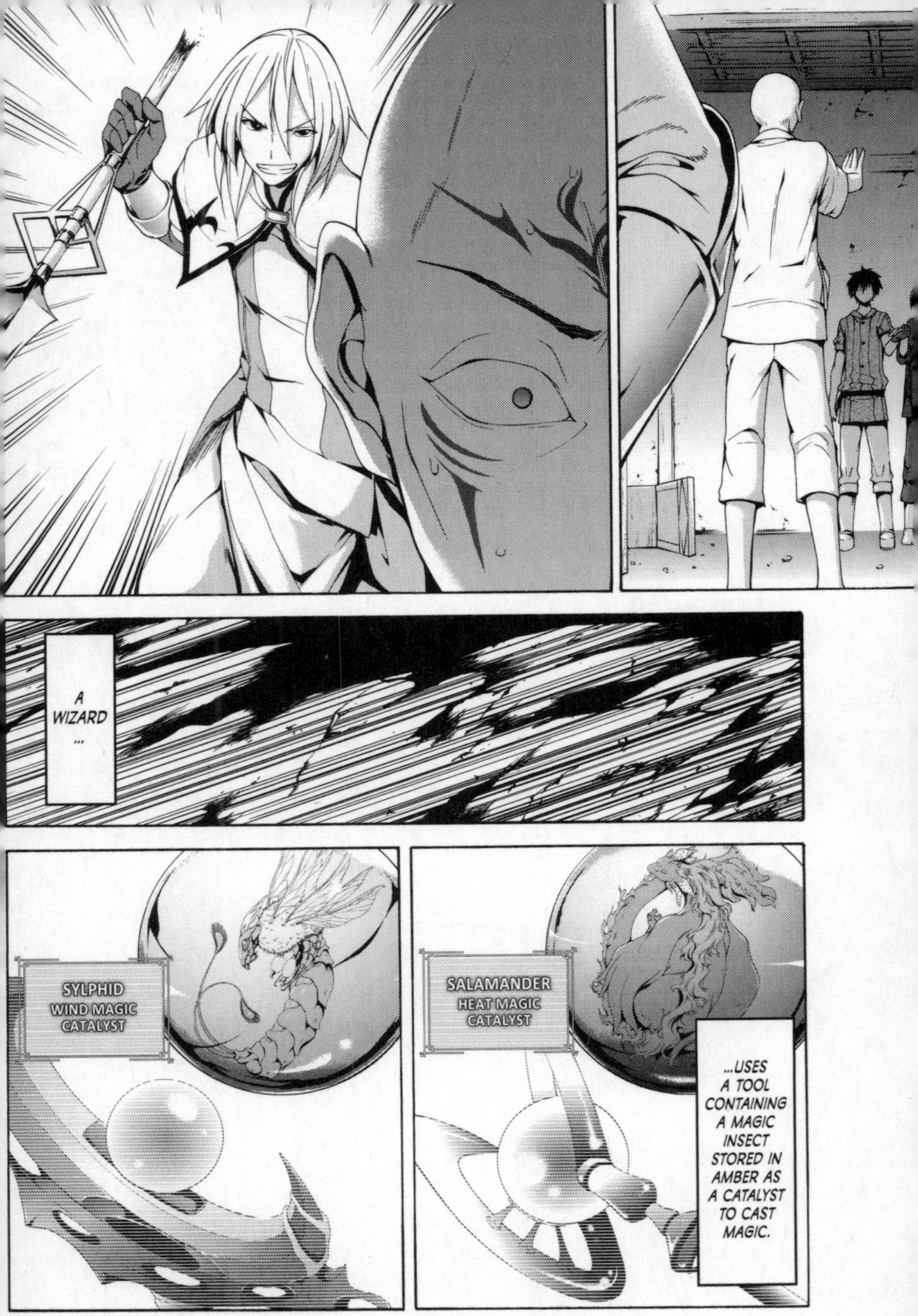
A WIZARD ...
SALAMANDER HEAT MAGIC CATALYST
...USES A TOOL CONTAINING A MAGIC INSECT STORED IN AMBER AS A CATALYST TO CAST MAGIC.
SYLPHID WIND MAGIC CATALYST

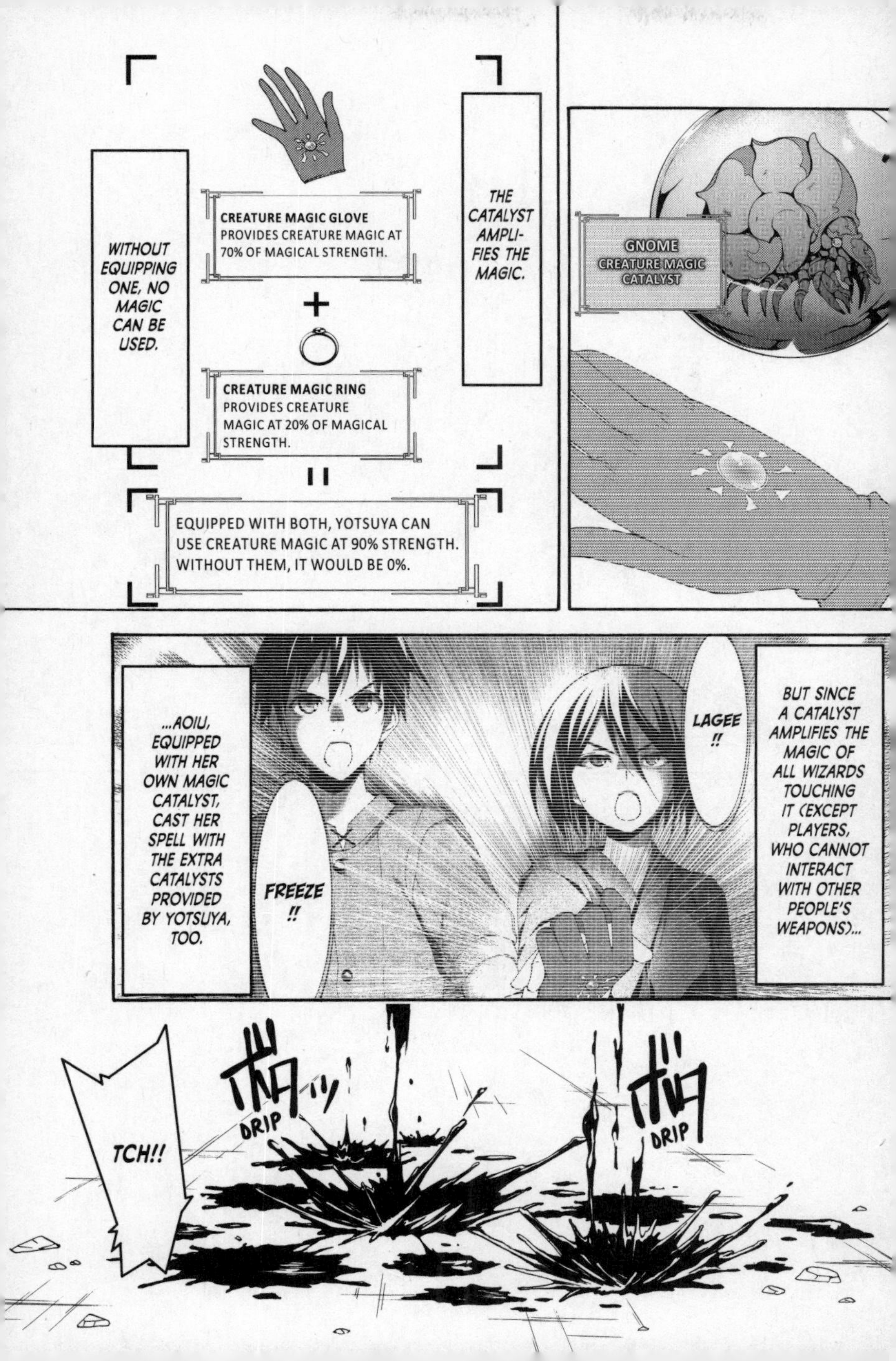
GNOME
CREATURE MAGIC CATALYST
THE CATALYST AMPLIFIES THE MAGIC.
WITHOUT EQUIPPING ONE, NO MAGIC CAN BE USED.
CREATURE MAGIC GLOVE
PROVIDES CREATURE MAGIC AT 70% OF MAGICAL STRENGTH.
+
CREATURE MAGIC RING
PROVIDES CREATURE MAGIC AT 20% OF MAGICAL STRENGTH.
=
EQUIPPED WITH BOTH, YOTSUYA CAN USE CREATURE MAGIC AT 90% STRENGTH. WITHOUT THEM, IT WOULD BE 0%.
BUT SINCE A CATALYST AMPLIFIES THE MAGIC OF ALL WIZARDS TOUCHING IT (EXCEPT PLAYERS, WHO CANNOT INTERACT WITH OTHER PEOPLE'S WEAPONS)...
LAGEE!!
FREEZE!!
...AOIU, EQUIPPED WITH HER OWN MAGIC CATALYST, CAST HER SPELL WITH THE EXTRA CATALYSTS PROVIDED BY YOTSUYA, TOO.
ボタ
DRIP
ボタッ
DRIP
TCH!!

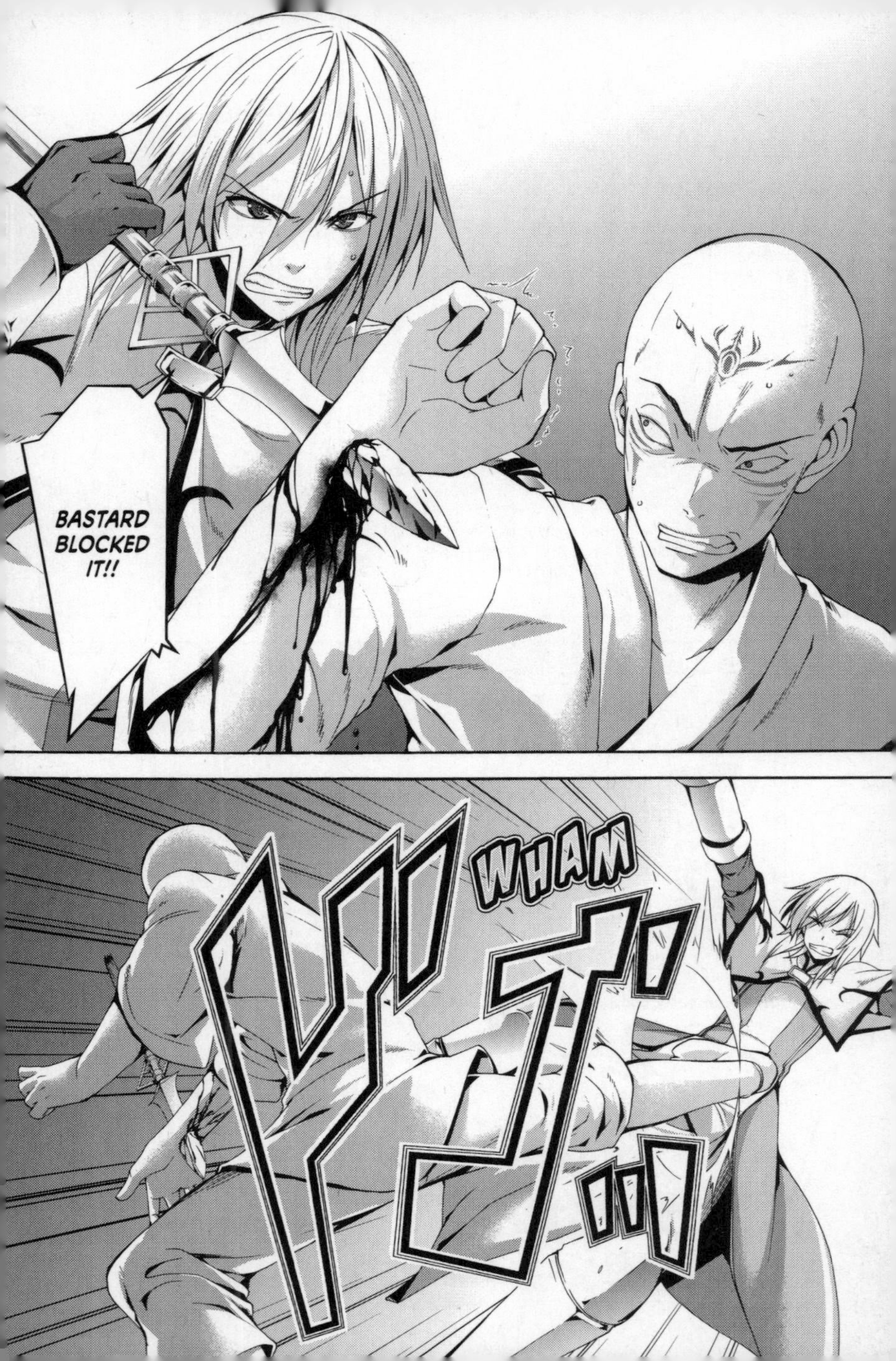
BASTARD BLOCKED IT!!
WHAM

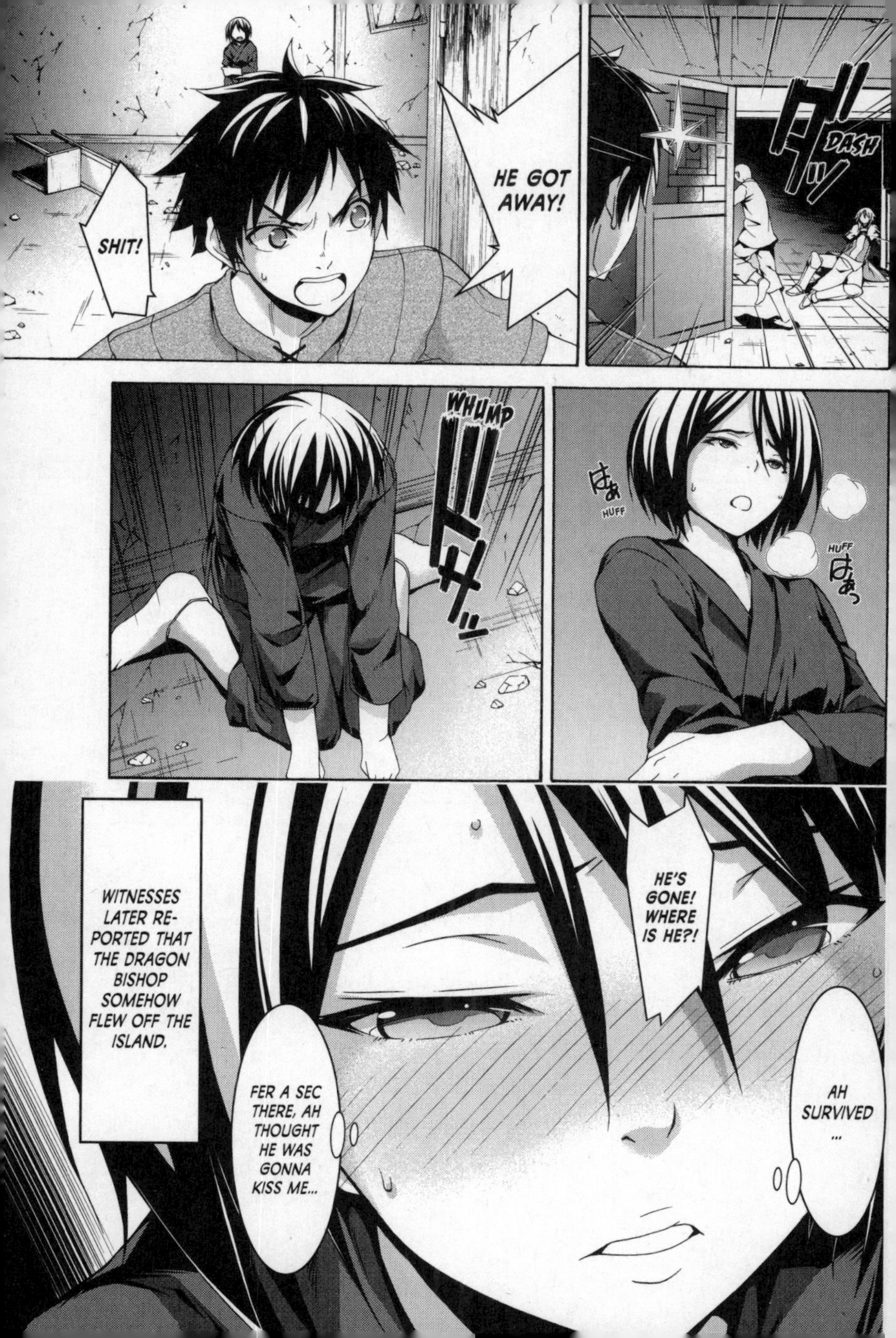
ダッ
DASH
HE GOT AWAY!
SHIT!
はぁ
HUFF
HUFF
はあっ
WHUMP
HE'S GONE! WHERE IS HE?!
AH SURVIVED ...
FER A SEC THERE, AH THOUGHT HE WAS GONNA KISS ME...
WITNESSES LATER RE-PORTED THAT THE DRAGON BISHOP SOMEHOW FLEW OFF THE ISLAND.

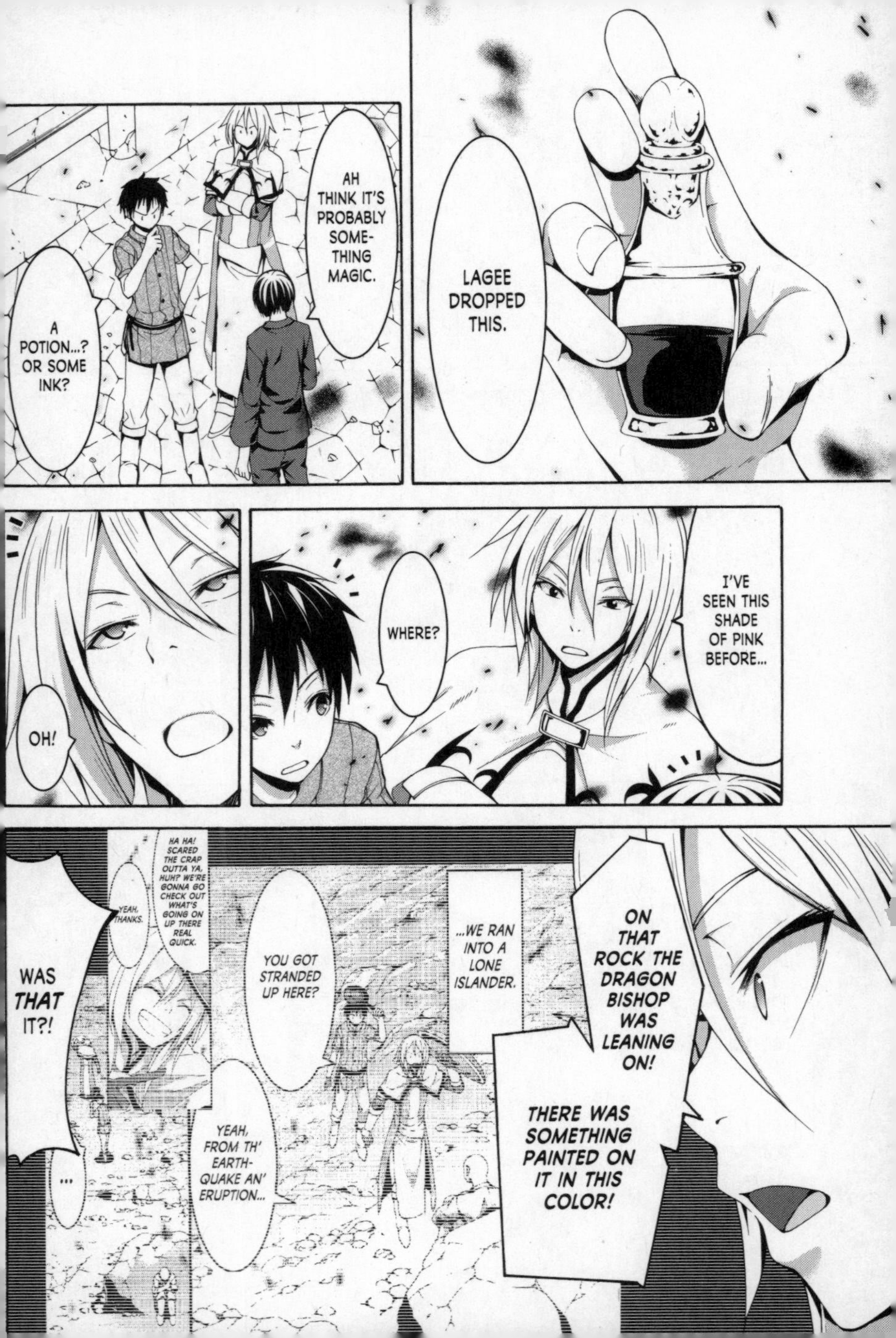
LAGEE DROPPED THIS.
AH THINK IT'S PROBABLY SOME-THING MAGIC.
A POTION...? OR SOME INK?
I'VE SEEN THIS SHADE OF PINK BEFORE...
WHERE?
OH!
ON THAT ROCK THE DRAGON BISHOP WAS LEANING ON!
THERE WAS SOMETHING PAINTED ON IT IN THIS COLOR!
...WE RAN INTO A LONE ISLANDER.
YOU GOT STRANDED UP HERE?
YEAH, FROM TH' EARTH-QUAKE AN' ERUPTION...
HA HA! SCARED THE CRAP OUTTA YA, HUH? WE'RE GONNA GO CHECK OUT WHAT'S GOING ON UP THERE REAL QUICK.
YEAH, THANKS.
WAS THAT IT?!
...

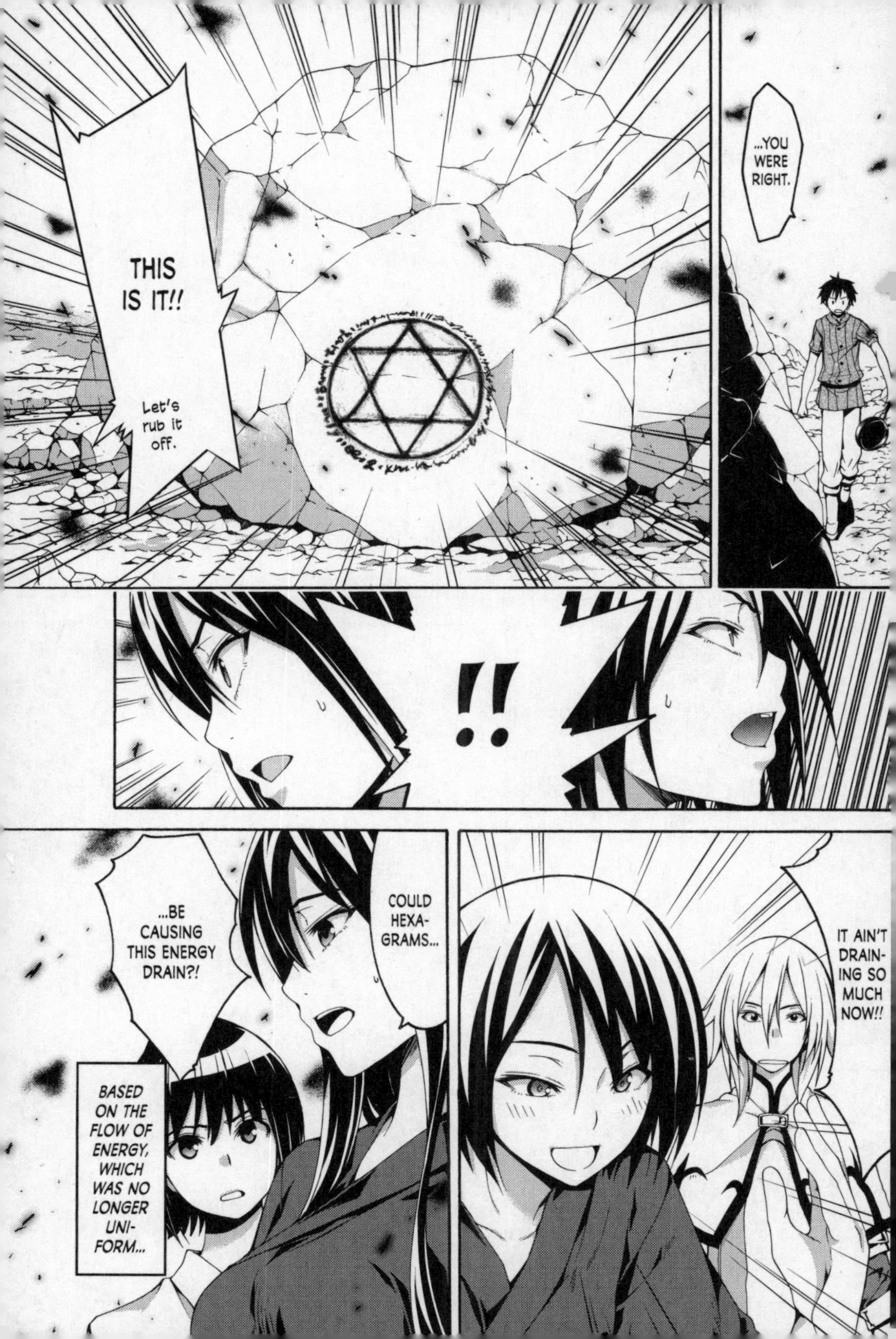
...YOU WERE RIGHT.
THIS IS IT!!
Let's rub it off.
!!
IT AIN'T DRAIN-ING SO MUCH NOW!!
COULD HEXA-GRAMS...
...BE CAUSING THIS ENERGY DRAIN?!
BASED ON THE FLOW OF ENERGY, WHICH WAS NO LONGER UNI-FORM...

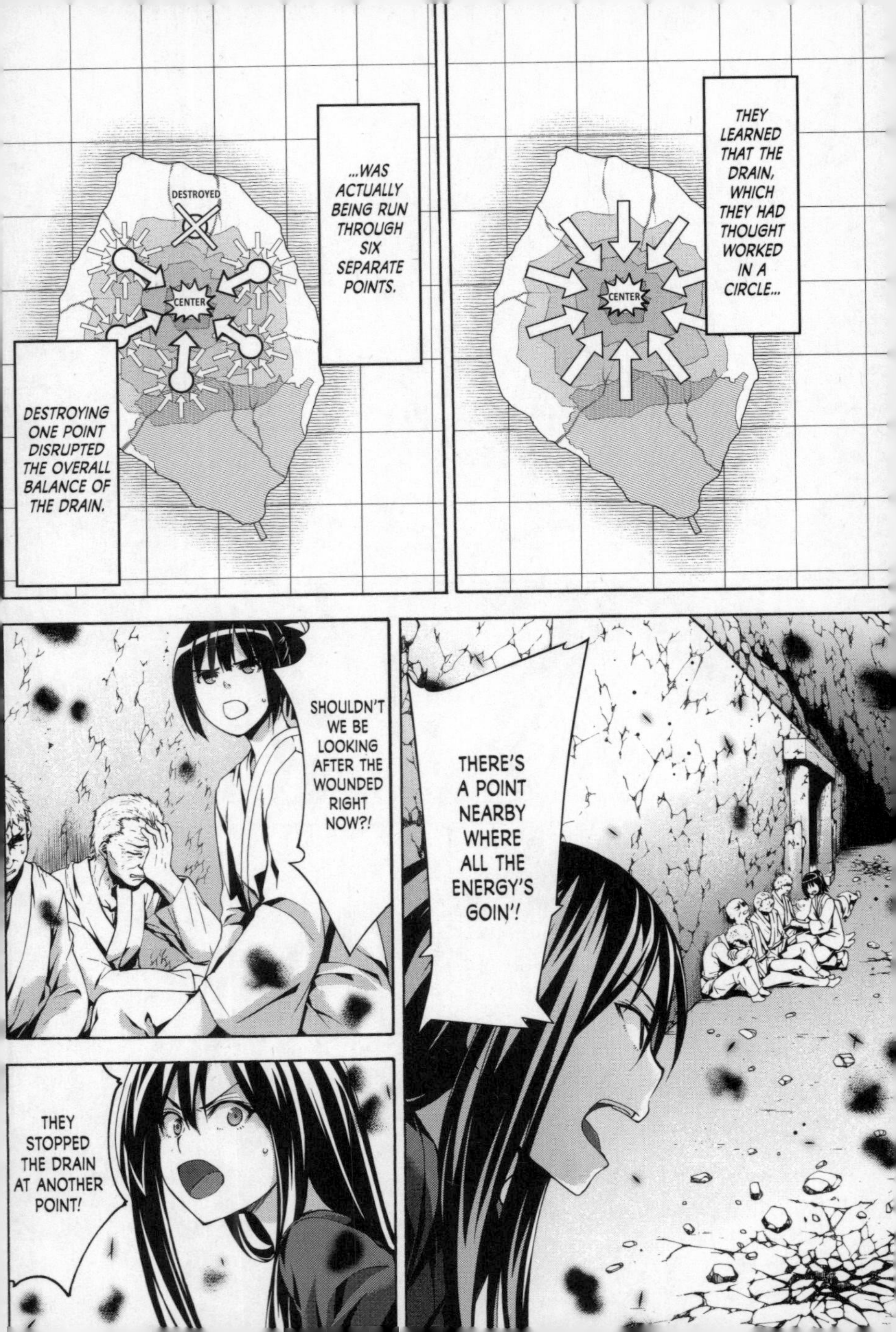
THEY LEARNED THAT THE DRAIN, WHICH THEY HAD THOUGHT WORKED IN A CIRCLE...
CENTER
...WAS ACTUALLY BEING RUN THROUGH SIX SEPARATE POINTS.
DESTROYED
CENTER
DESTROYING ONE POINT DISRUPTED THE OVERALL BALANCE OF THE DRAIN.
THERE'S A POINT NEARBY WHERE ALL THE ENERGY'S GOIN'!
SHOULDN'T WE BE LOOKING AFTER THE WOUNDED RIGHT NOW?!
THEY STOPPED THE DRAIN AT ANOTHER POINT!

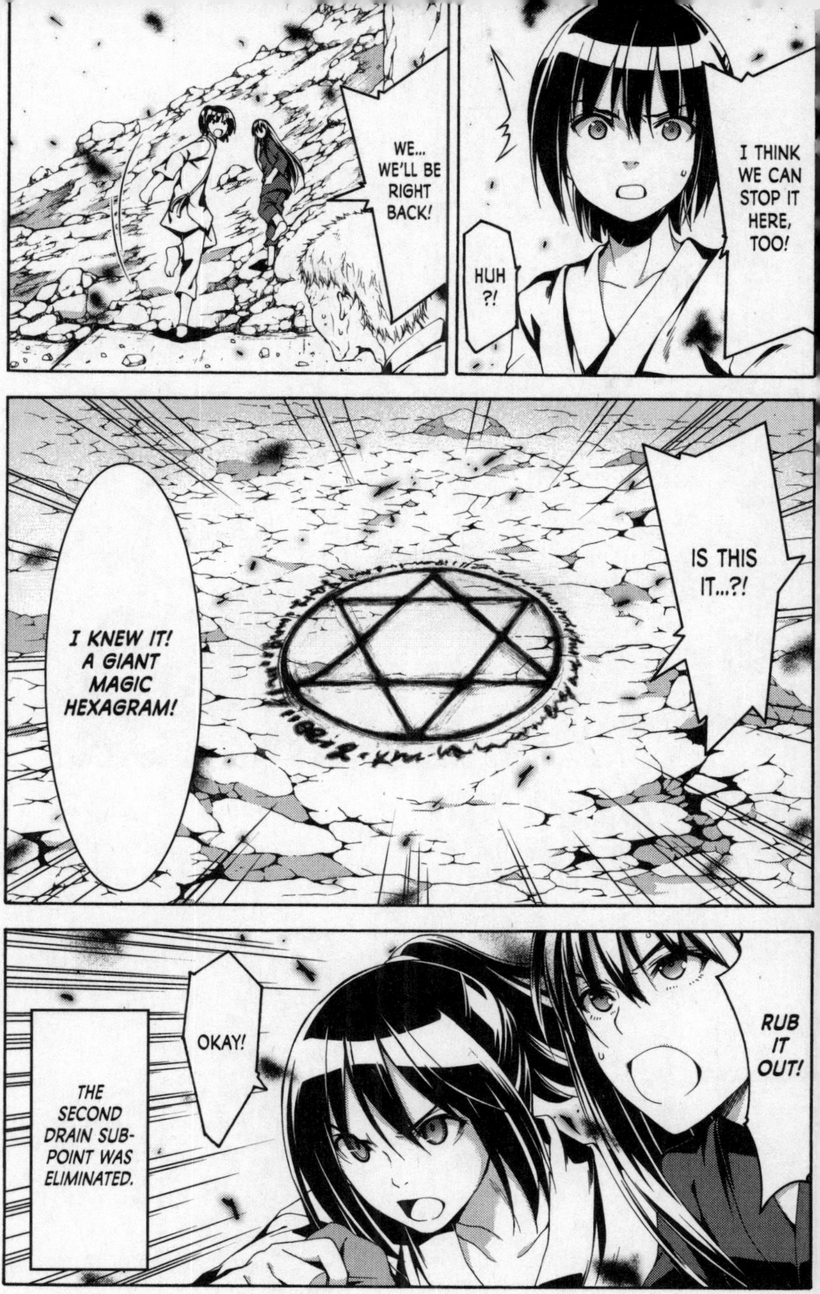
I THINK WE CAN STOP IT HERE, TOO!
HUH?!
WE... WE'LL BE RIGHT BACK!
IS THIS IT...?!
I KNEW IT! A GIANT MAGIC HEXAGRAM!
RUB IT OUT!
OKAY!
THE SECOND DRAIN SUB-POINT WAS ELIMINATED.

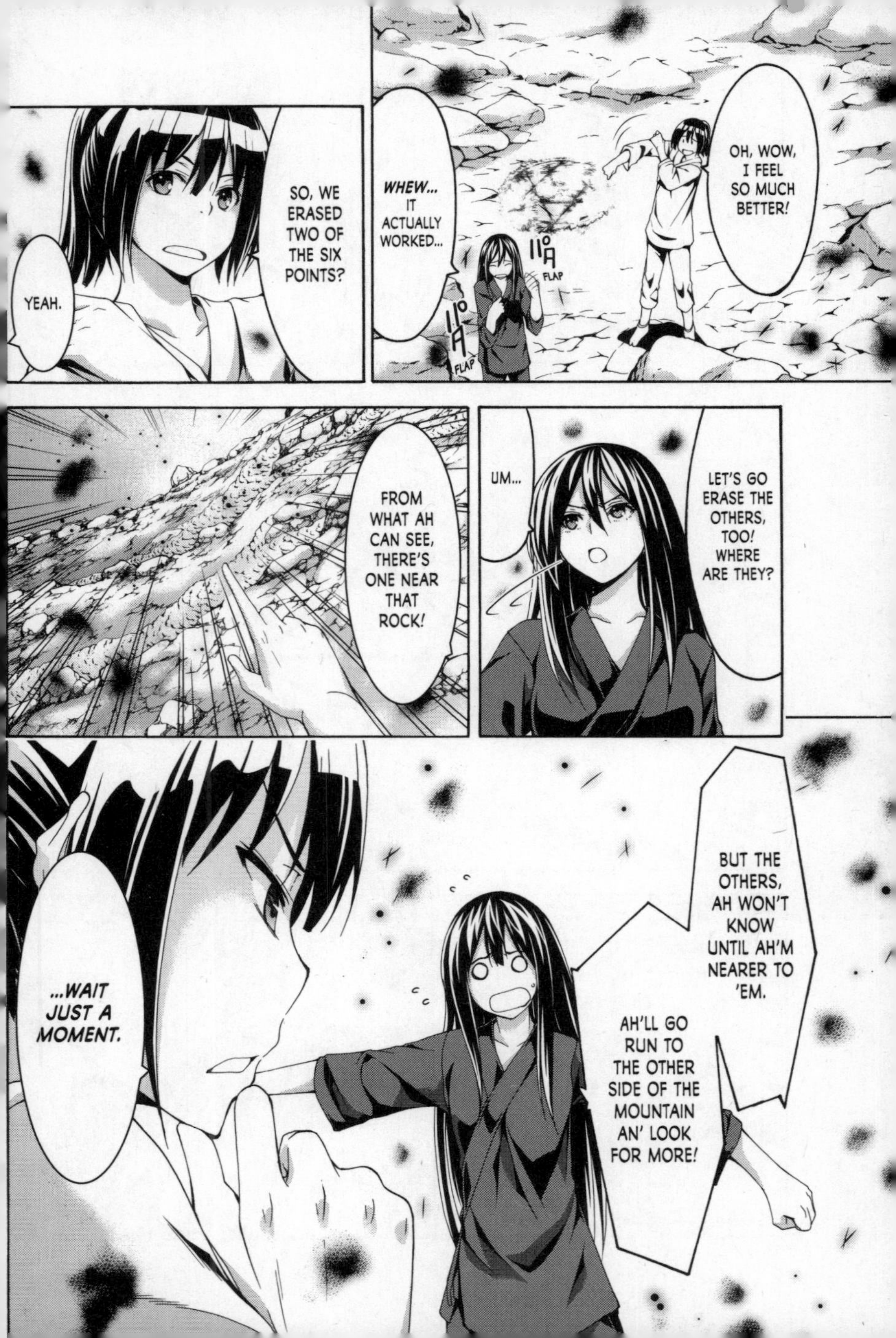
OH, WOW, I FEEL SO MUCH BETTER!
WHEW... IT ACTUALLY WORKED...
FLAP
FLAP
SO, WE ERASED TWO OF THE SIX POINTS?
YEAH.
LET'S GO ERASE THE OTHERS, TOO! WHERE ARE THEY?
UM...
FROM WHAT AH CAN SEE, THERE'S ONE NEAR THAT ROCK!
BUT THE OTHERS, AH WON'T KNOW UNTIL AH'M NEARER TO 'EM.
AH'LL GO RUN TO THE OTHER SIDE OF THE MOUNTAIN AN' LOOK FOR MORE!
...WAIT JUST A MOMENT.

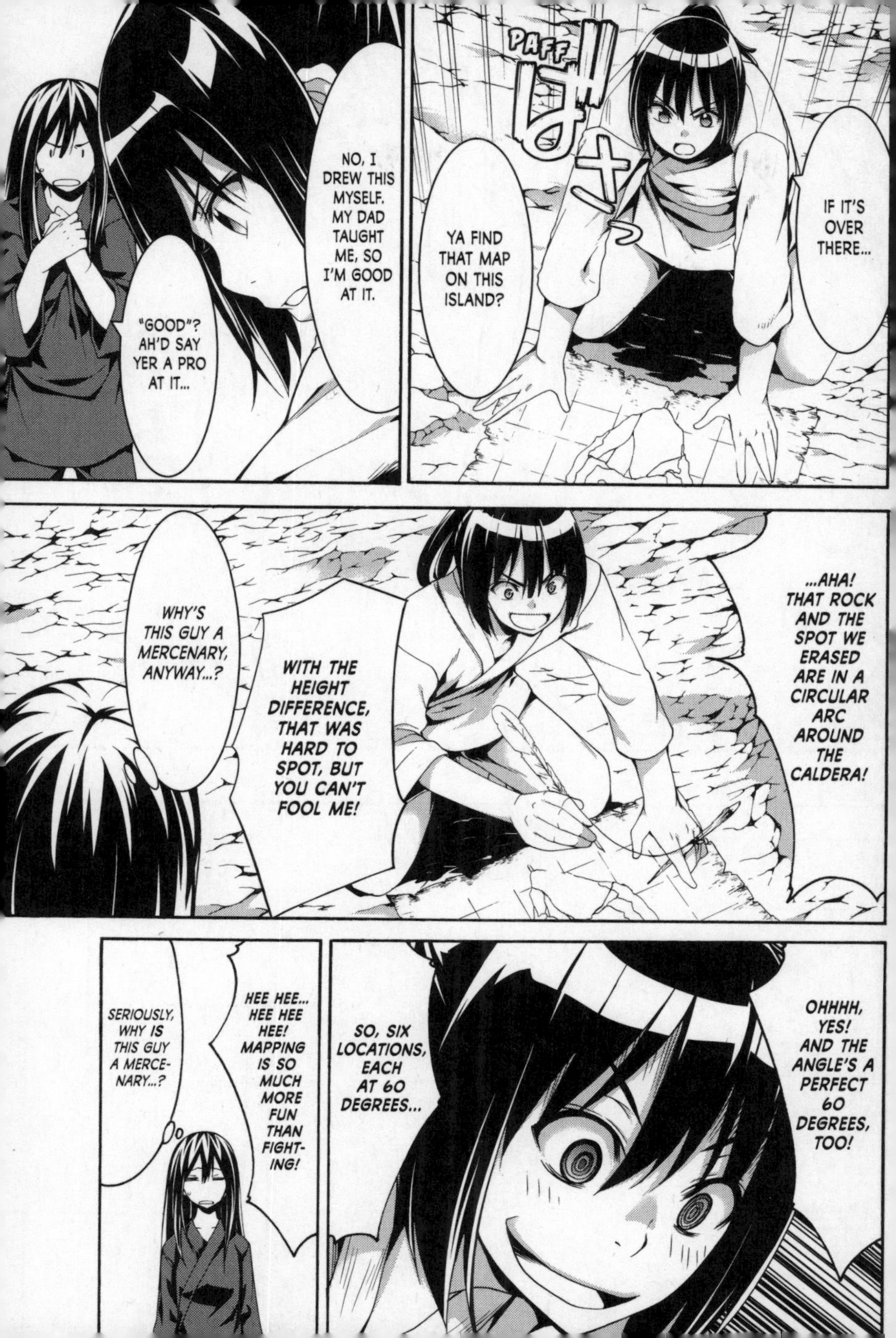
IF IT'S OVER THERE...
PAFF
YA FIND THAT MAP ON THIS ISLAND?
NO, I DREW THIS MYSELF. MY DAD TAUGHT ME, SO I'M GOOD AT IT.
"GOOD"? AH'D SAY YER A PRO AT IT...
...AHA! THAT ROCK AND THE SPOT WE ERASED ARE IN A CIRCULAR ARC AROUND THE CALDERA!
WITH THE HEIGHT DIFFERENCE, THAT WAS HARD TO SPOT, BUT YOU CAN'T FOOL ME!
WHY'S THIS GUY A MERCENARY, ANYWAY...?
OHHHH, YES! AND THE ANGLE'S A PERFECT 60 DEGREES, TOO!
SO, SIX LOCATIONS, EACH AT 60 DEGREES...
HEE HEE... HEE HEE HEE! MAPPING IS SO MUCH MORE FUN THAN FIGHT-ING!
SERIOUSLY, WHY IS THIS GUY A MERCE-NARY...?

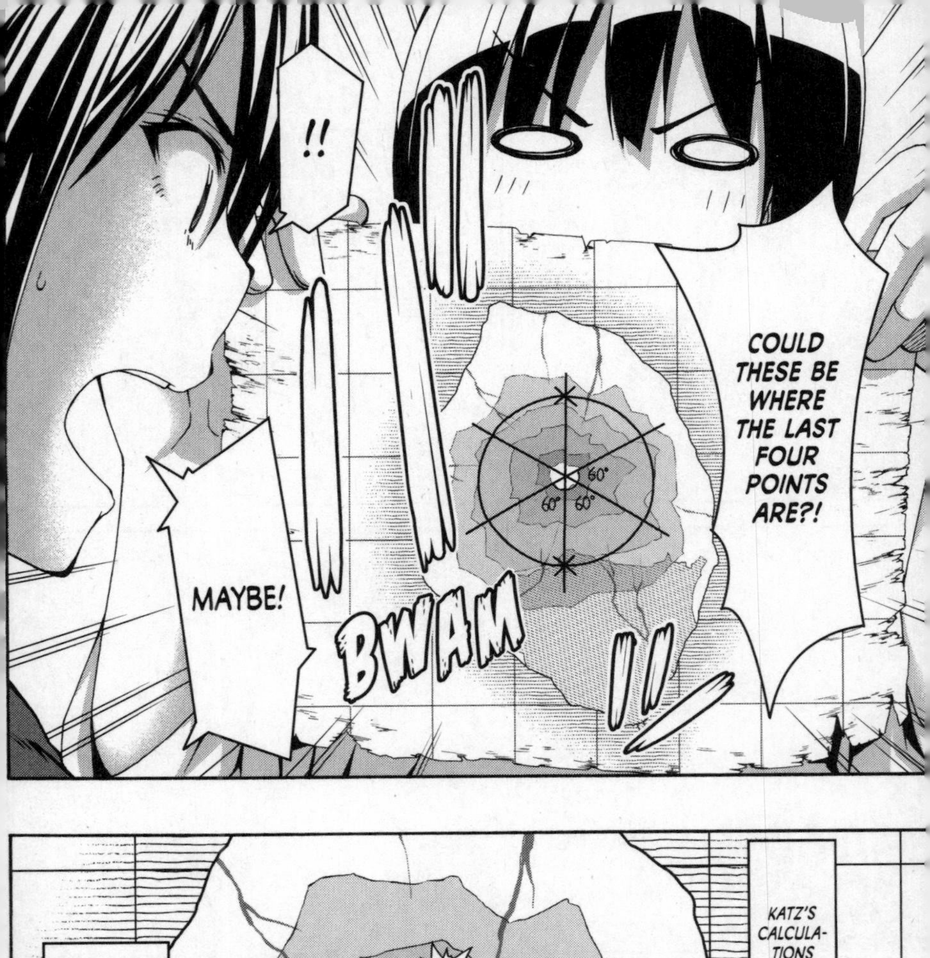
COULD THESE BE WHERE THE LAST FOUR POINTS ARE?!
!!
60°
60°
60°
MAYBE!
BWAM
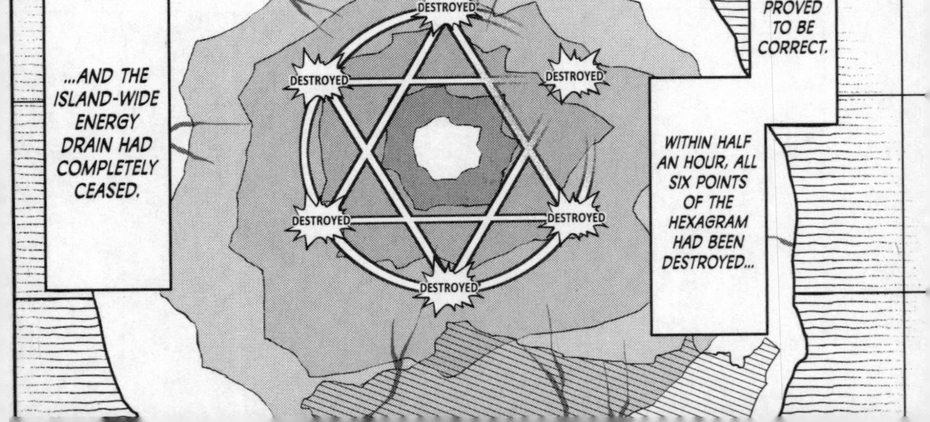
KATZ'S CALCULA-TIONS PROVED TO BE CORRECT.
WITHIN HALF AN HOUR, ALL SIX POINTS OF THE HEXAGRAM HAD BEEN DESTROYED...
DESTROYED
DESTROYED
DESTROYED
DESTROYED
DESTROYED
DESTROYED
...AND THE ISLAND-WIDE ENERGY DRAIN HAD COMPLETELY CEASED.

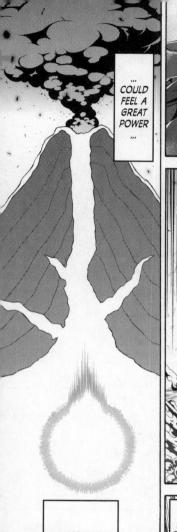

...COULD
FEEL A
GREAT
POWER
...

...

SPLASH

FWOOSH

...MOVING
DOWN
THROUGH
THE
CALDERA,
DEEP
INTO THE
MOUNTAIN.

ALL
FOUR
...

!!

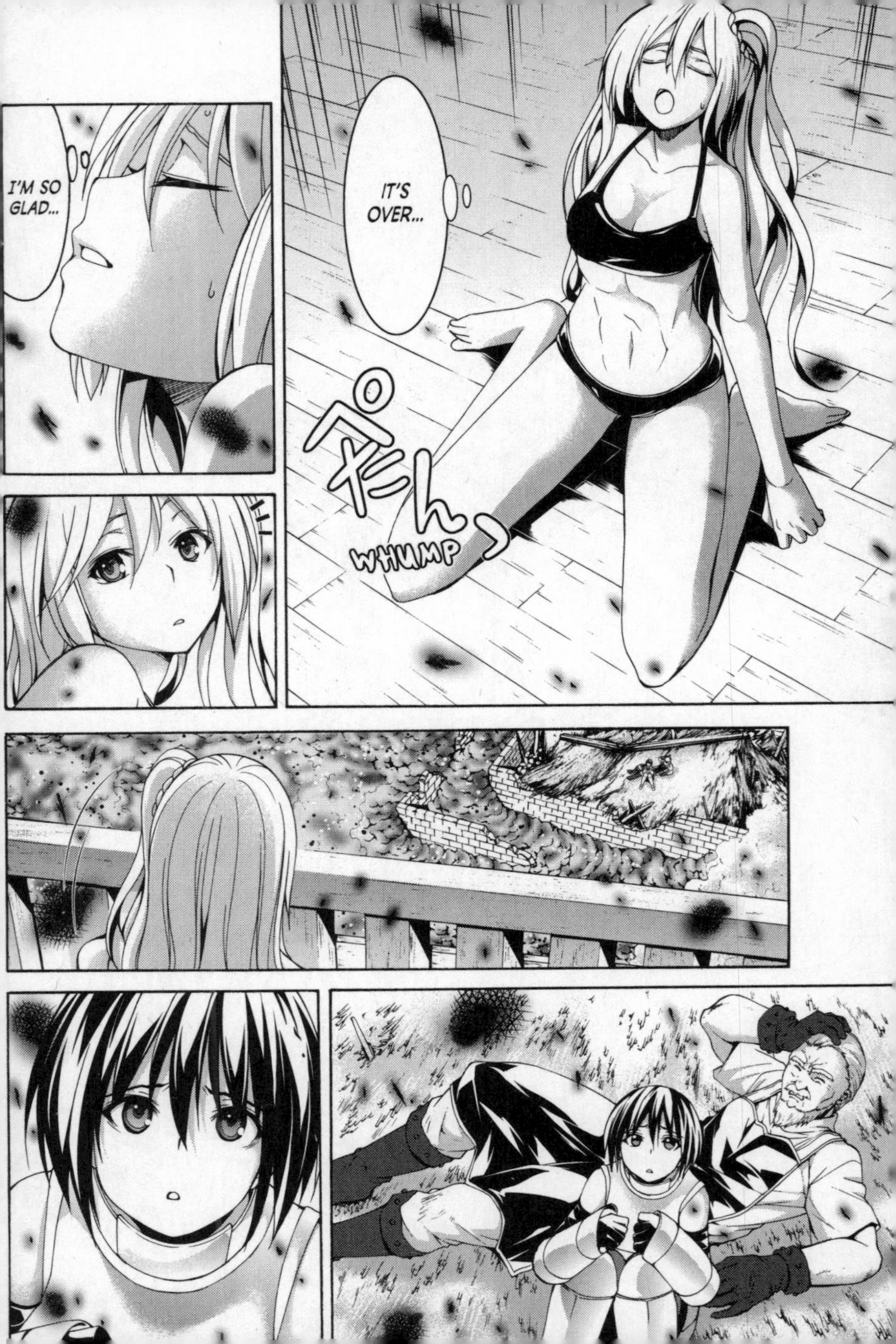
IT'S OVER...
ぺたーん
WHUMP
I'M SO GLAD...

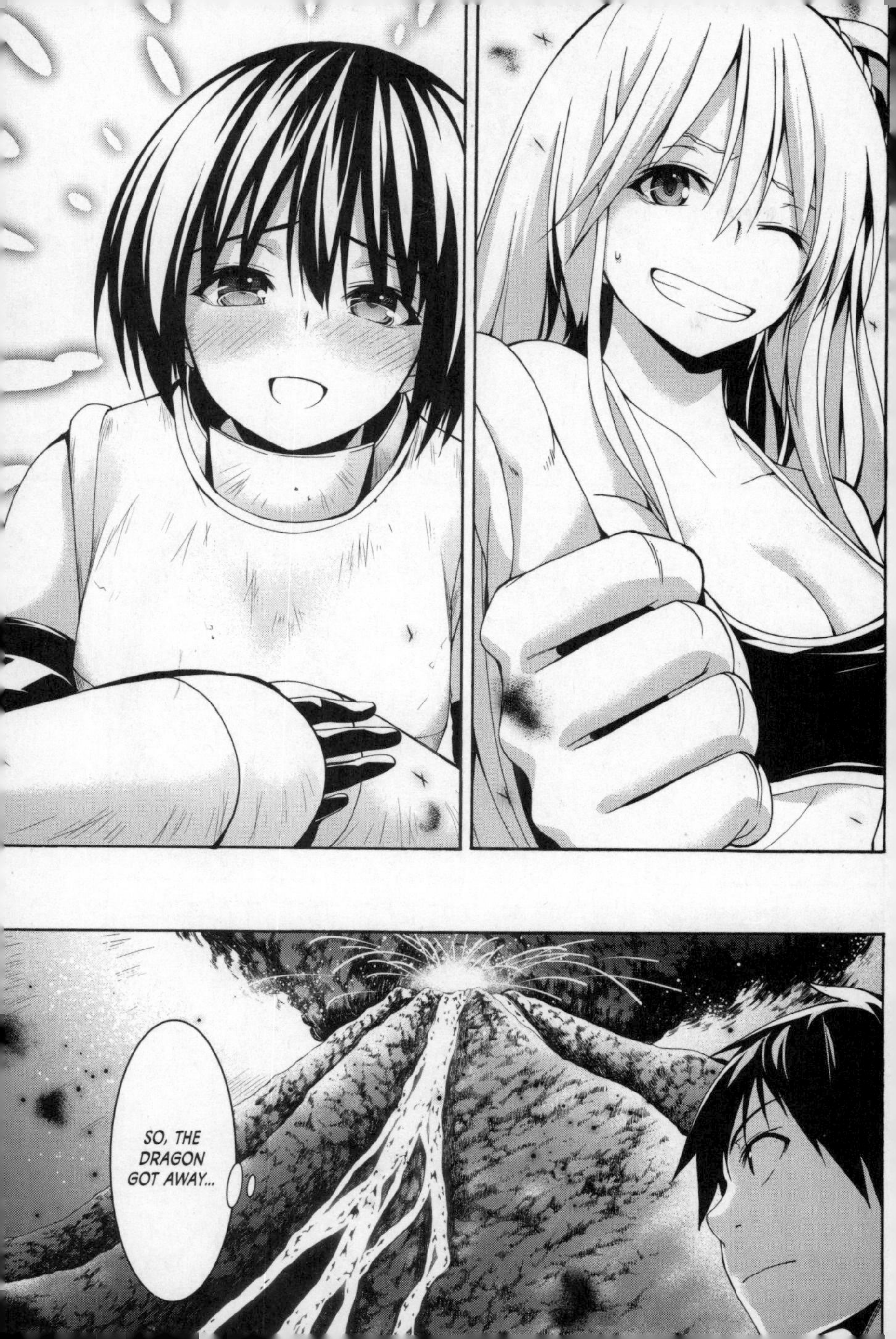
SO, THE DRAGON GOT AWAY...

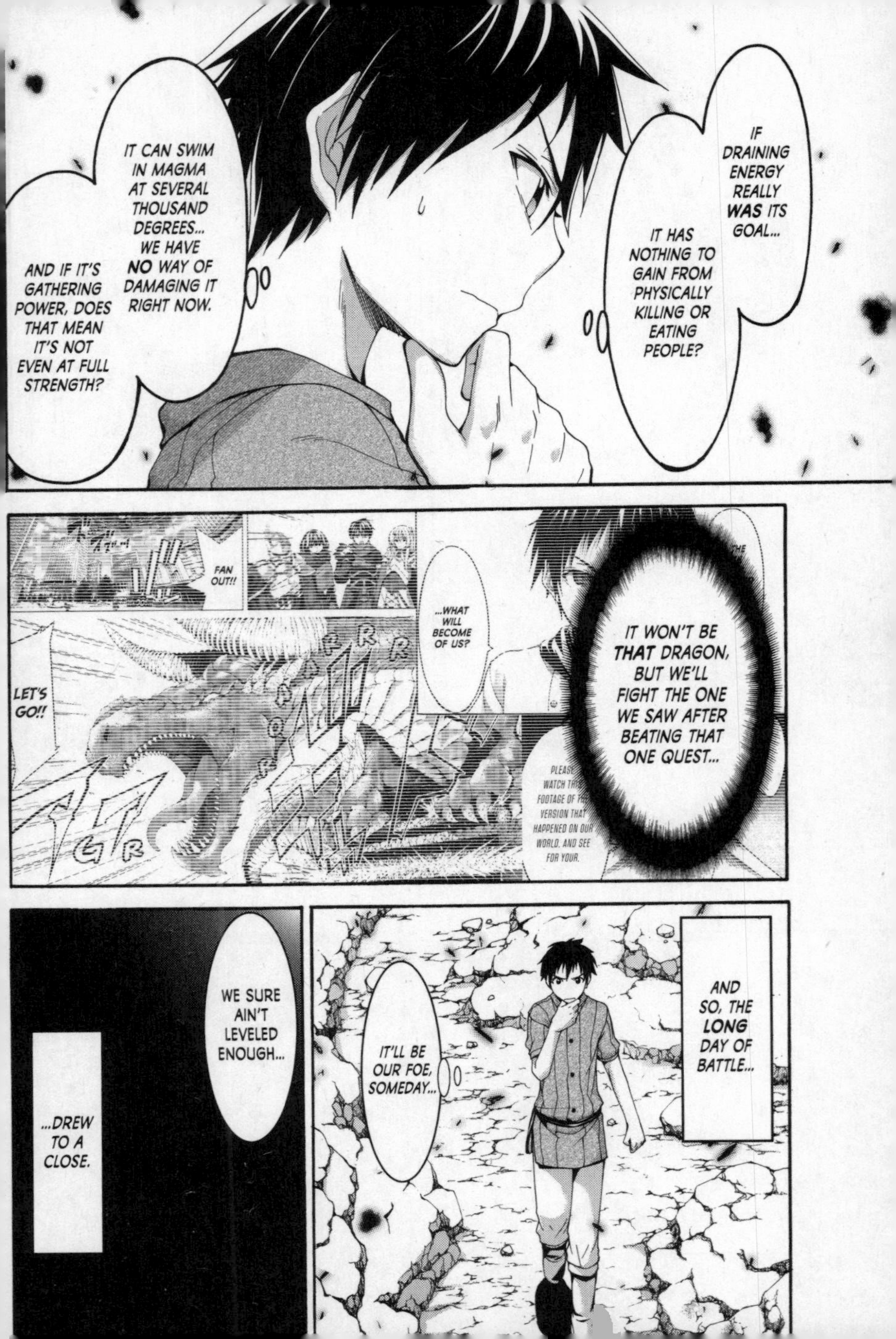
IF DRAINING ENERGY REALLY WAS ITS GOAL...
IT HAS NOTHING TO GAIN FROM PHYSICALLY KILLING OR EATING PEOPLE?
IT CAN SWIM IN MAGMA AT SEVERAL THOUSAND DEGREES... WE HAVE NO WAY OF DAMAGING IT RIGHT NOW.
AND IF IT'S GATHERING POWER, DOES THAT MEAN IT'S NOT EVEN AT FULL STRENGTH?
IT WON'T BE THAT DRAGON, BUT WE'LL FIGHT THE ONE WE SAW AFTER BEATING THAT ONE QUEST...
...WHAT WILL BECOME OF US?
FAN OUT!!
LET'S GO!!
AND SO, THE LONG DAY OF BATTLE...
IT'LL BE OUR FOE, SOMEDAY...
WE SURE AIN'T LEVELED ENOUGH...
...DREW TO A CLOSE.

#24 Interested Eyes, Indifferent Ears

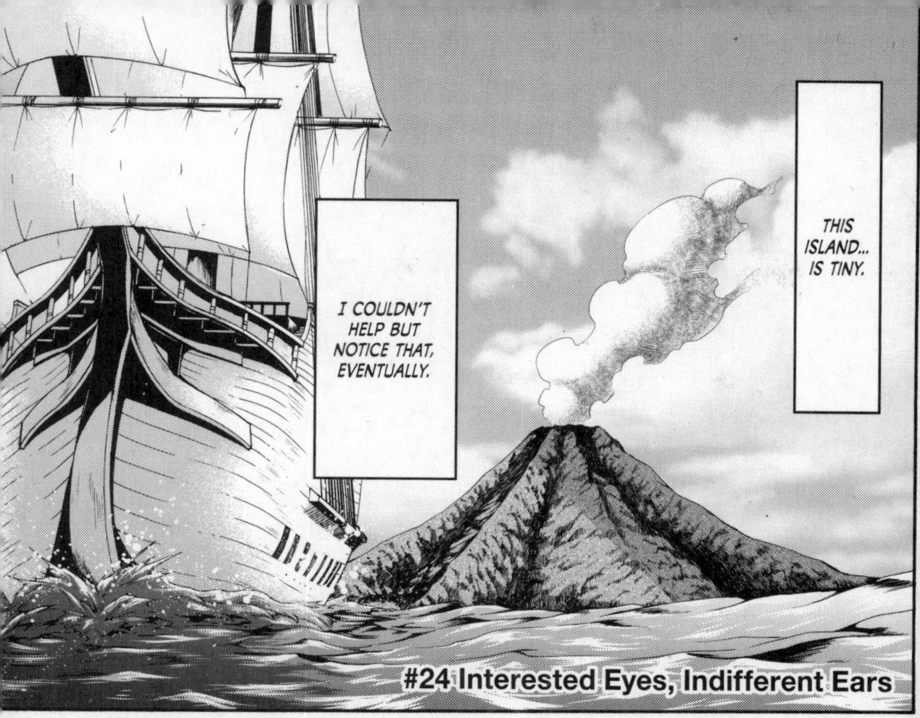
THIS ISLAND... IS TINY.
I COULDN'T HELP BUT NOTICE THAT, EVENTUALLY.
#24 Interested Eyes, Indifferent Ears

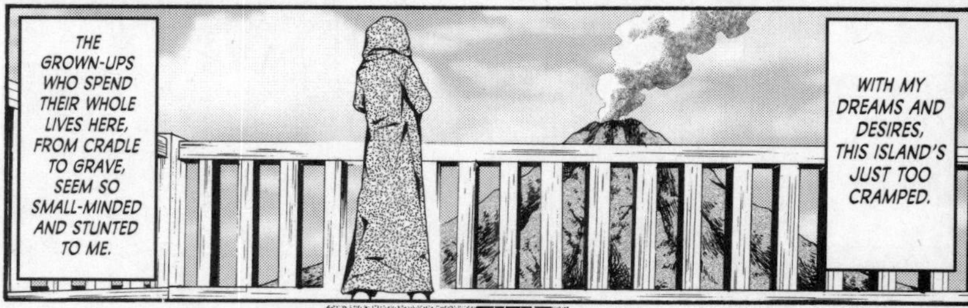
WITH MY DREAMS AND DESIRES, THIS ISLAND'S JUST TOO CRAMPED.
THE GROWN-UPS WHO SPEND THEIR WHOLE LIVES HERE, FROM CRADLE TO GRAVE, SEEM SO SMALL-MINDED AND STUNTED TO ME.

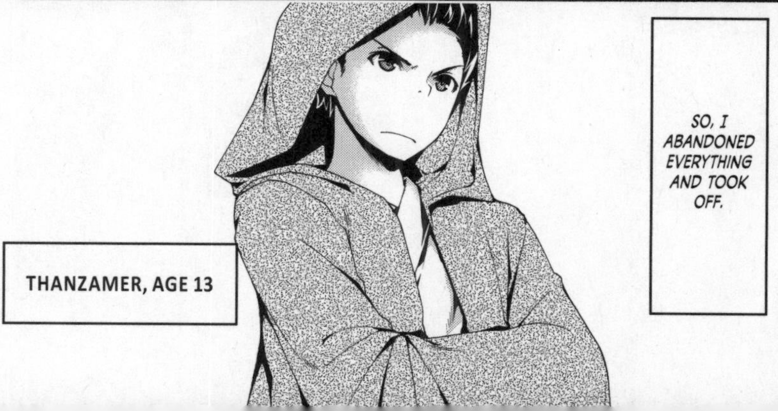
SO, I ABANDONED EVERYTHING AND TOOK OFF.
THANZAMER, AGE 13

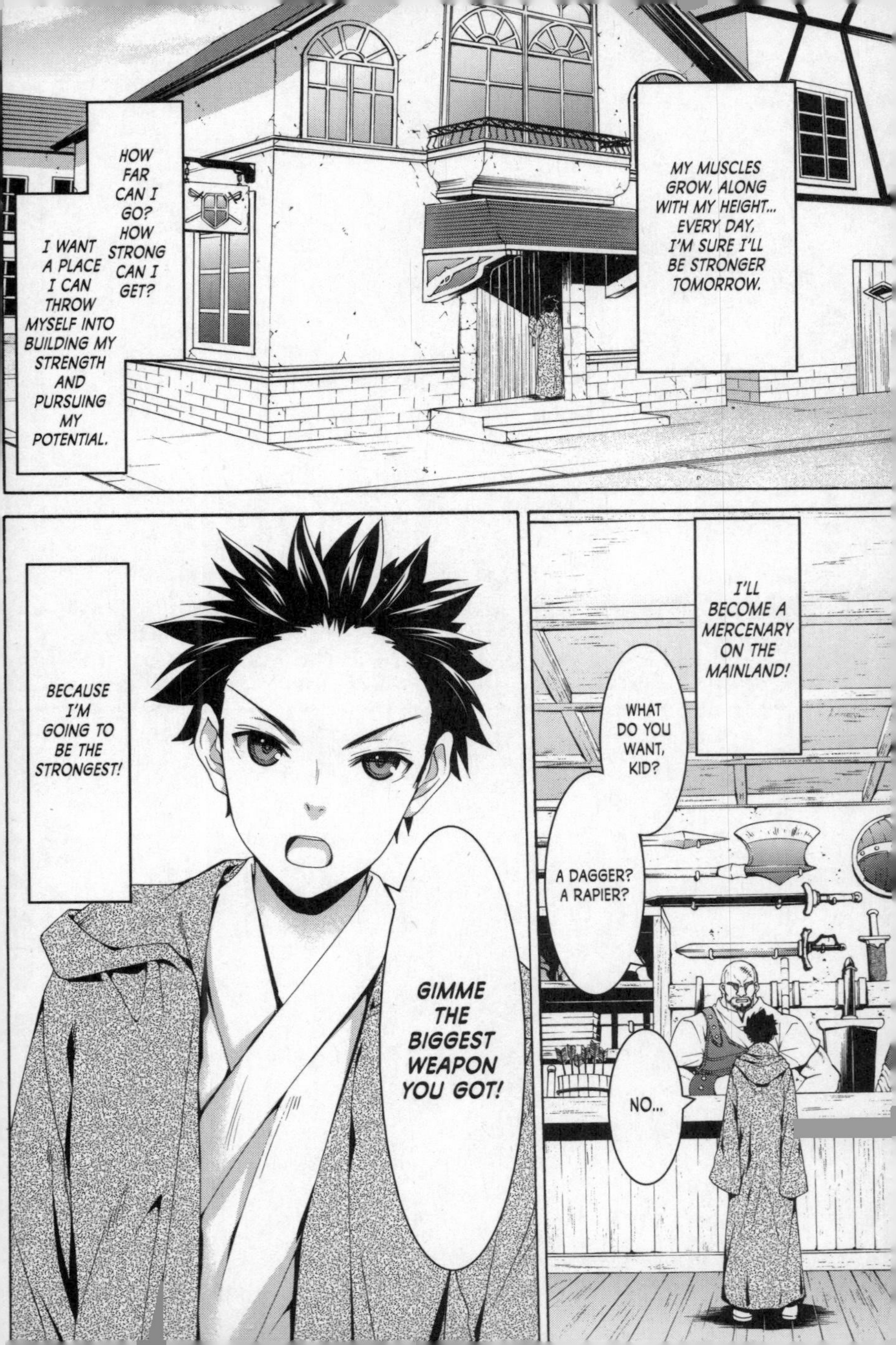
MY MUSCLES GROW, ALONG WITH MY HEIGHT... EVERY DAY, I'M SURE I'LL BE STRONGER TOMORROW.
HOW FAR CAN I GO? HOW STRONG CAN I GET?
I WANT A PLACE I CAN THROW MYSELF INTO BUILDING MY STRENGTH AND PURSUING MY POTENTIAL.
I'LL BECOME A MERCENARY ON THE MAINLAND!
WHAT DO YOU WANT, KID?
A DAGGER? A RAPIER?
NO...
GIMME THE BIGGEST WEAPON YOU GOT!
BECAUSE I'M GOING TO BE THE STRONGEST!

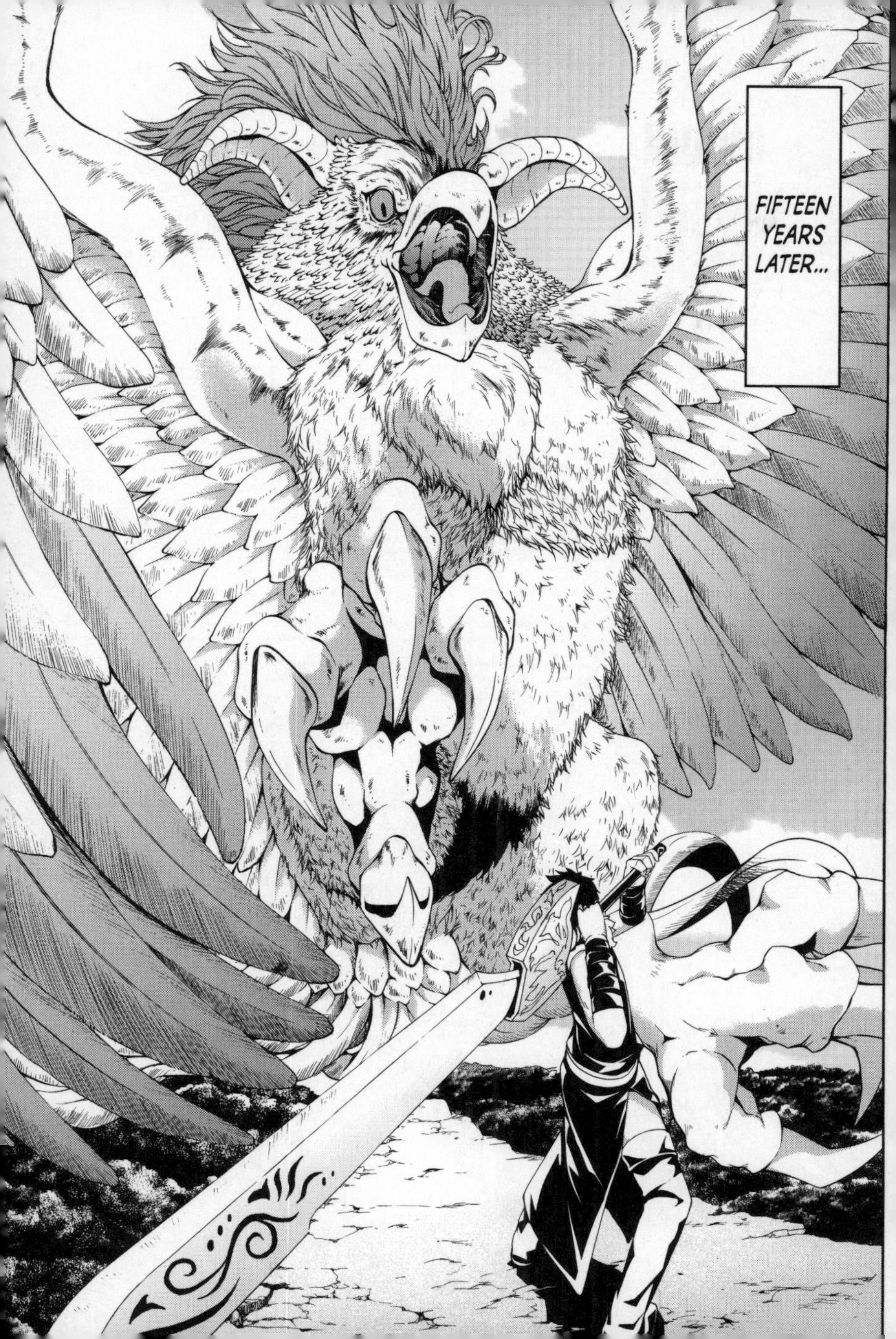
FIFTEEN YEARS LATER...

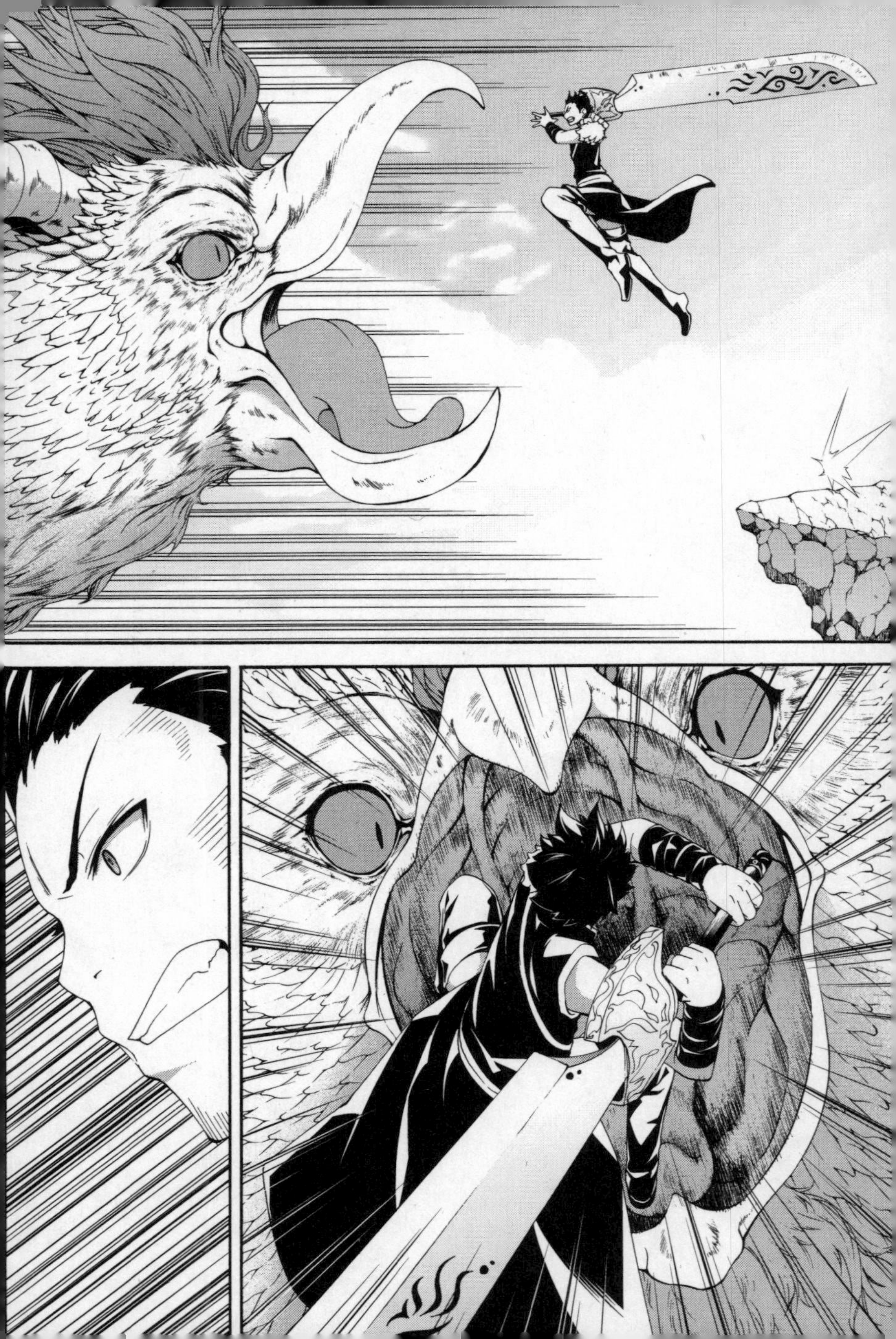

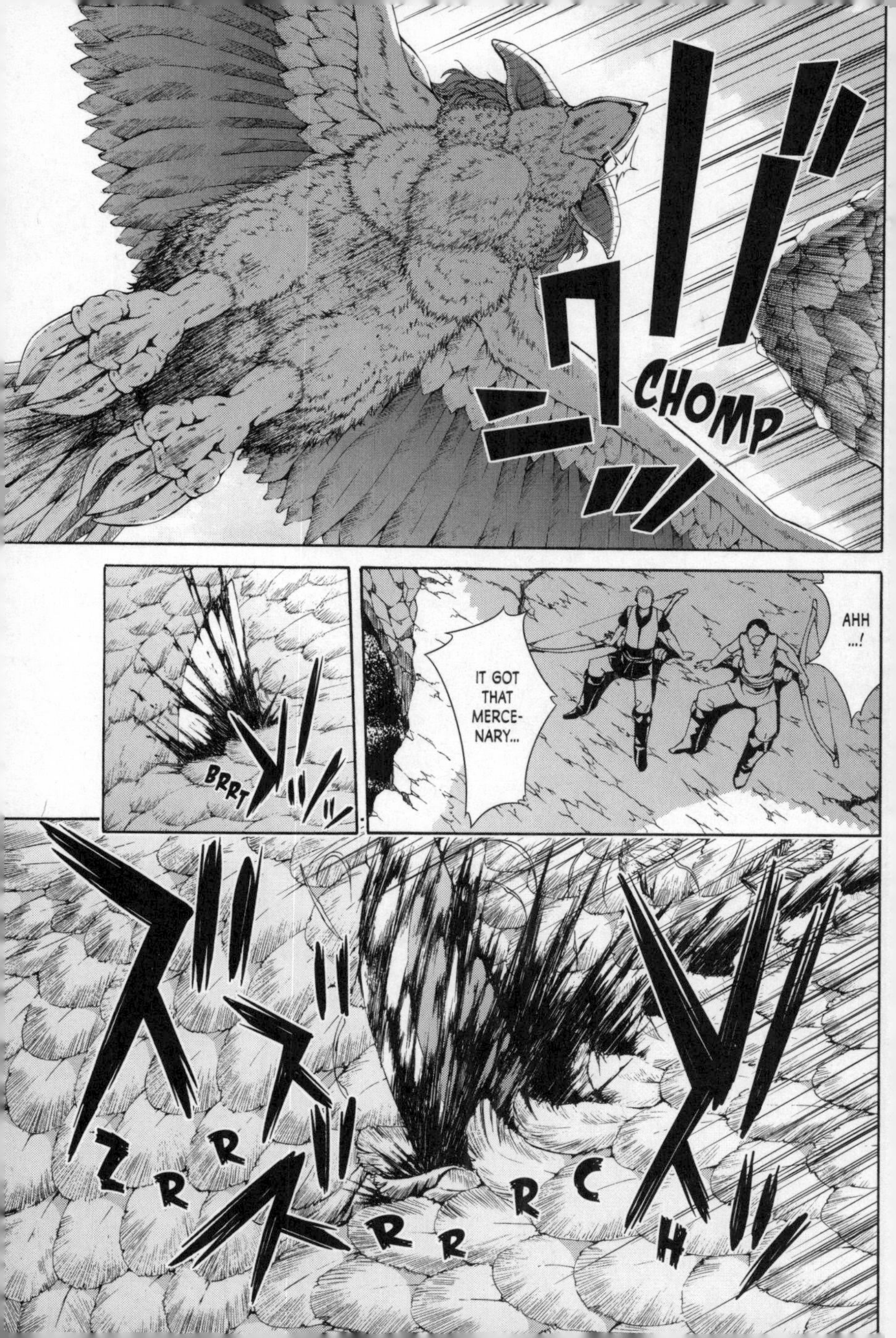
CHOMP
AHH ...!
IT GOT THAT MERCENARY...
BRRT
ZRRRRRCH

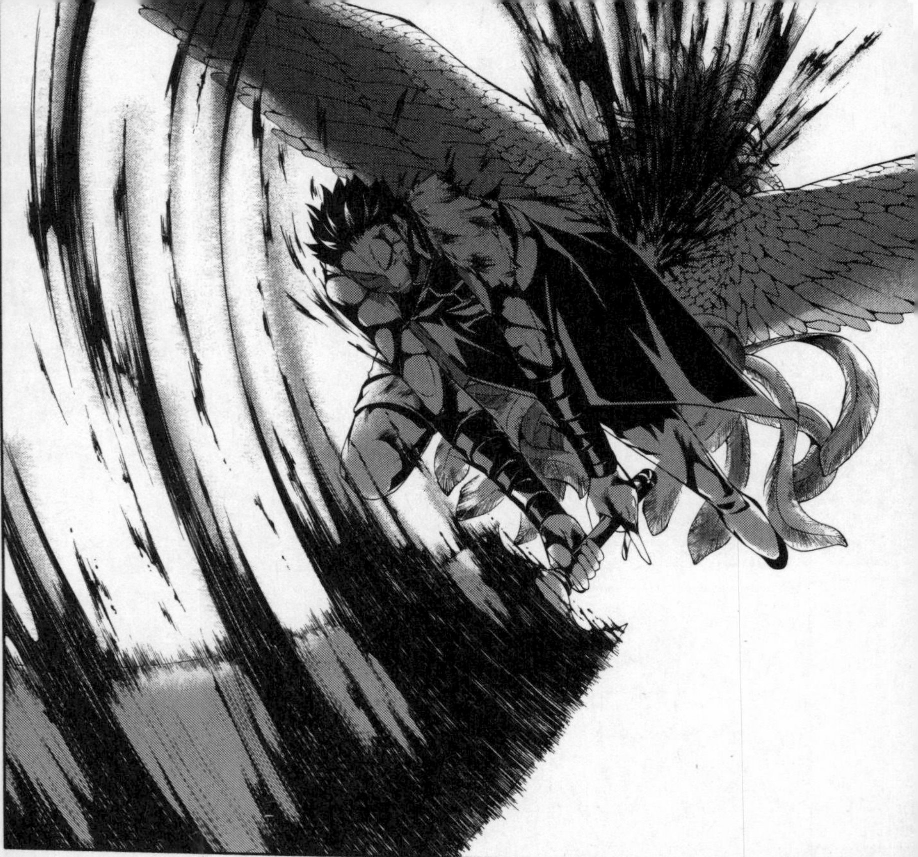
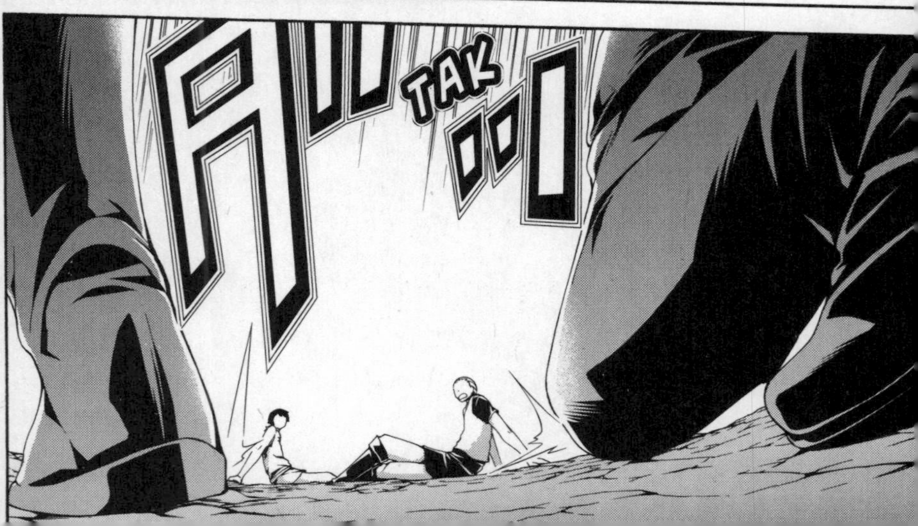
TAK

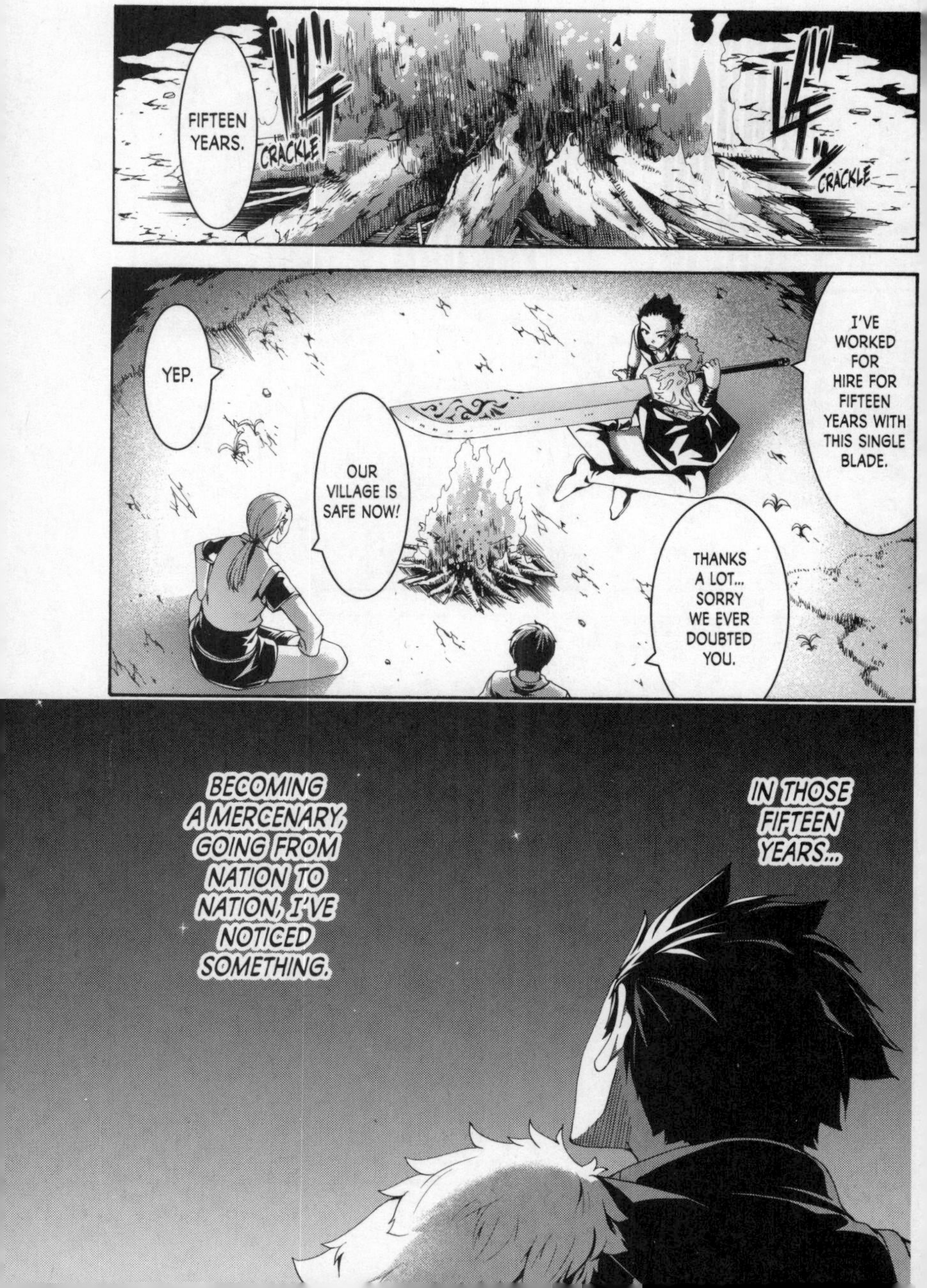
CRACKLE
FIFTEEN YEARS.
CRACKLE
I'VE WORKED FOR HIRE FOR FIFTEEN YEARS WITH THIS SINGLE BLADE.
OUR VILLAGE IS SAFE NOW!
YEP.
THANKS A LOT... SORRY WE EVER DOUBTED YOU.
IN THOSE FIFTEEN YEARS...
BECOMING A MERCENARY, GOING FROM NATION TO NATION, I'VE NOTICED SOMETHING.

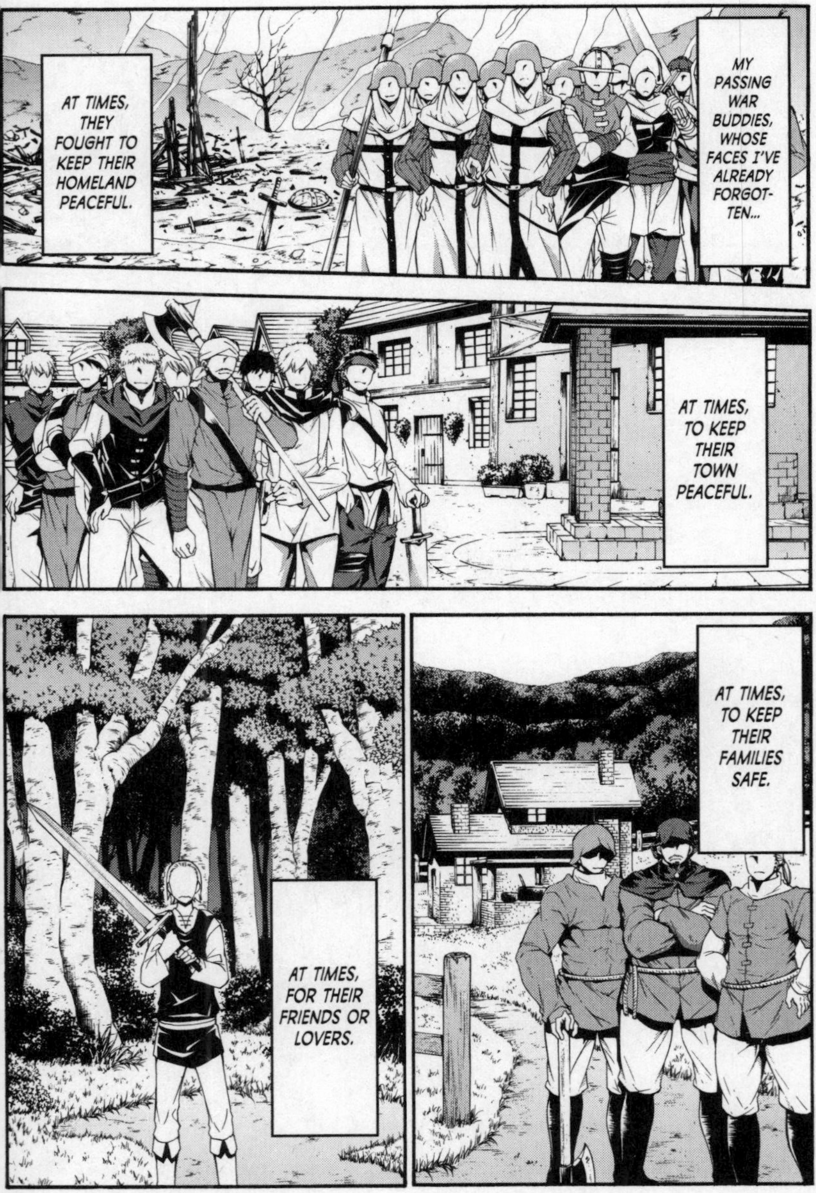
MY PASSING WAR BUDDIES, WHOSE FACES I'VE ALREADY FORGOT-TEN...
AT TIMES, THEY FOUGHT TO KEEP THEIR HOMELAND PEACEFUL.
AT TIMES, TO KEEP THEIR TOWN PEACEFUL.
AT TIMES, TO KEEP THEIR FAMILIES SAFE.
AT TIMES, FOR THEIR FRIENDS OR LOVERS.

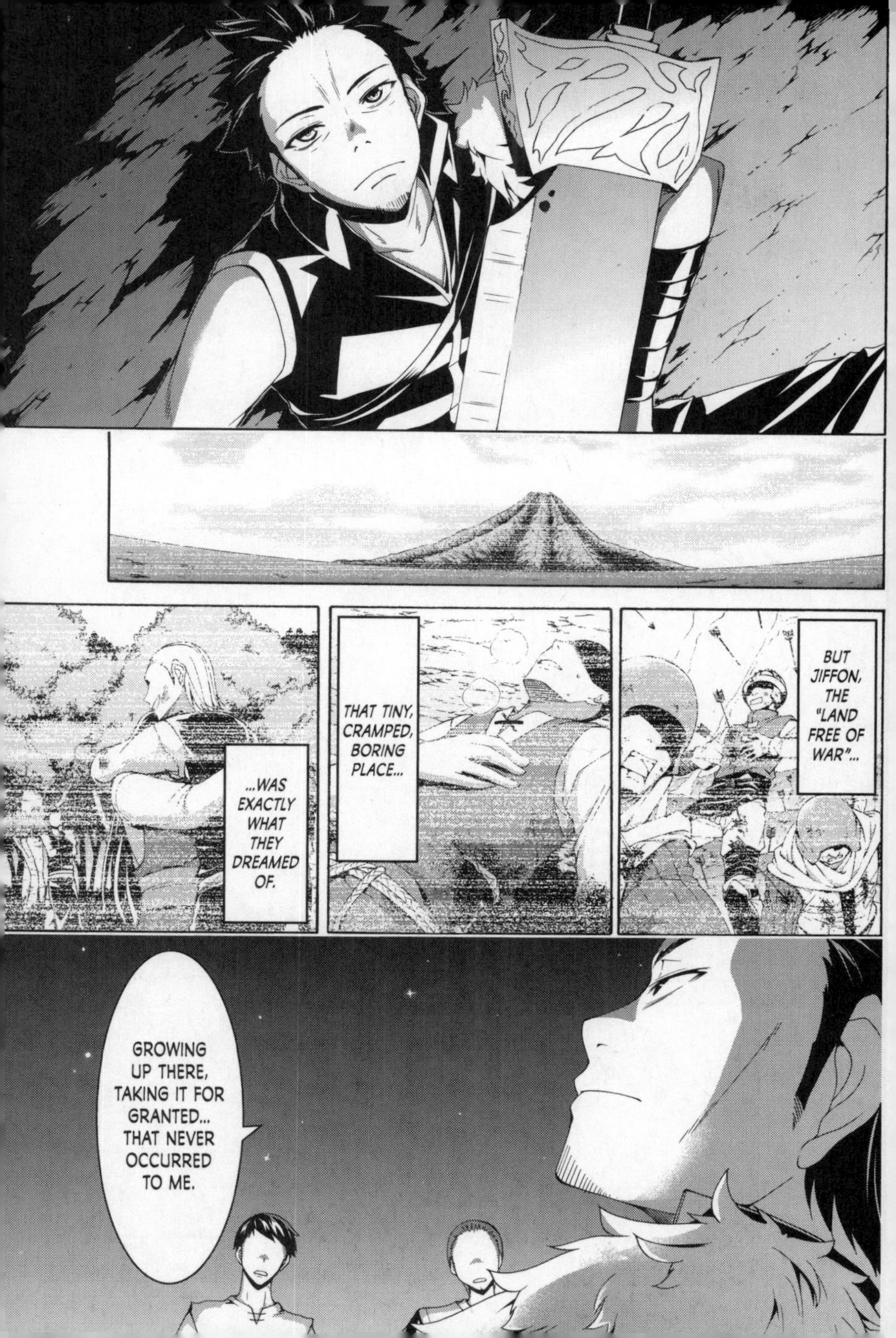
BUT JIFFON, THE "LAND FREE OF WAR"...
THAT TINY, CRAMPED, BORING PLACE...
...WAS EXACTLY WHAT THEY DREAMED OF.
GROWING UP THERE, TAKING IT FOR GRANTED... THAT NEVER OCCURRED TO ME.

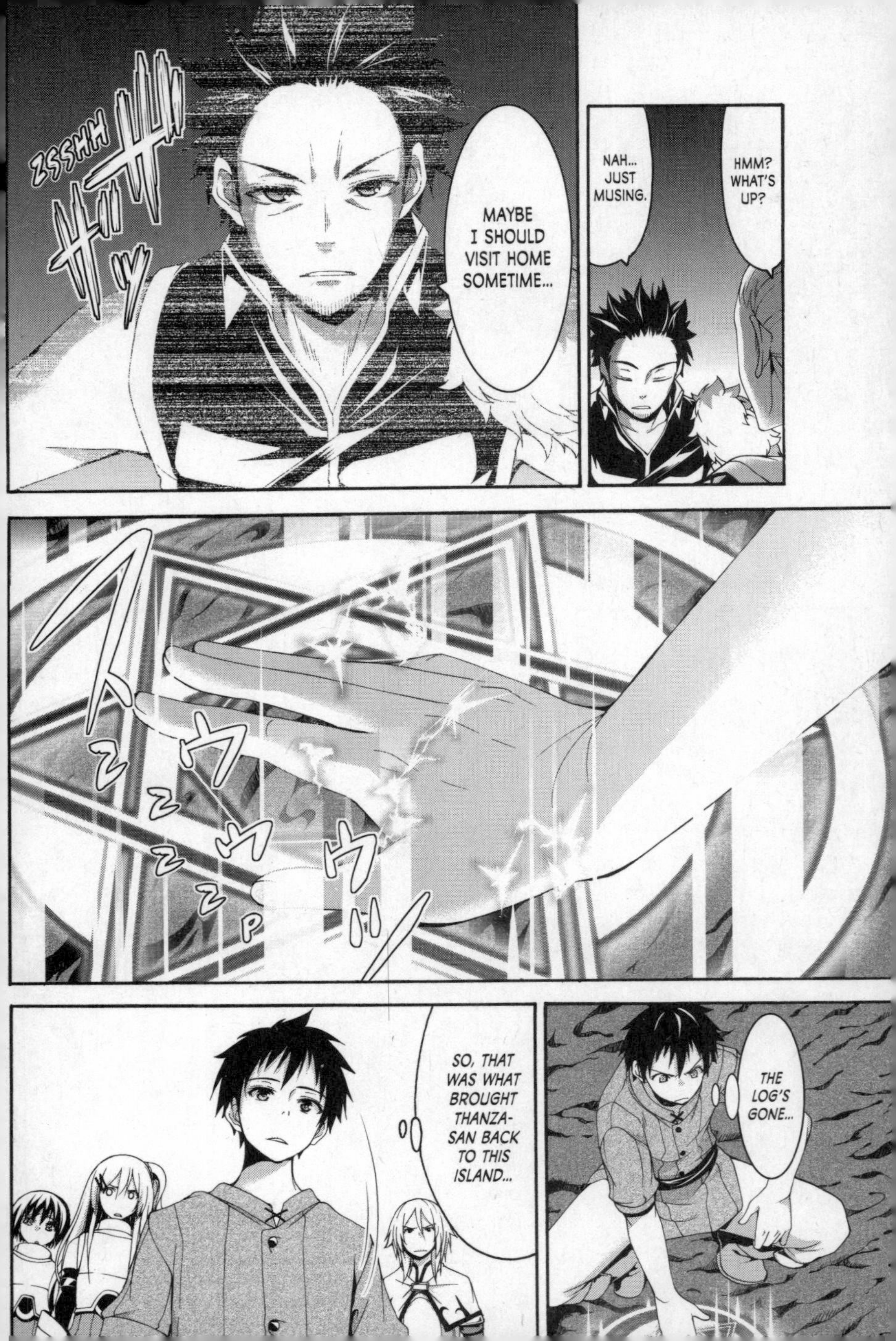
HMM? WHAT'S UP?
NAH... JUST MUSING.
ZSSHH
MAYBE I SHOULD VISIT HOME SOMETIME...
ZZZZP
THE LOG'S GONE...
SO, THAT WAS WHAT BROUGHT THANZA-SAN BACK TO THIS ISLAND...

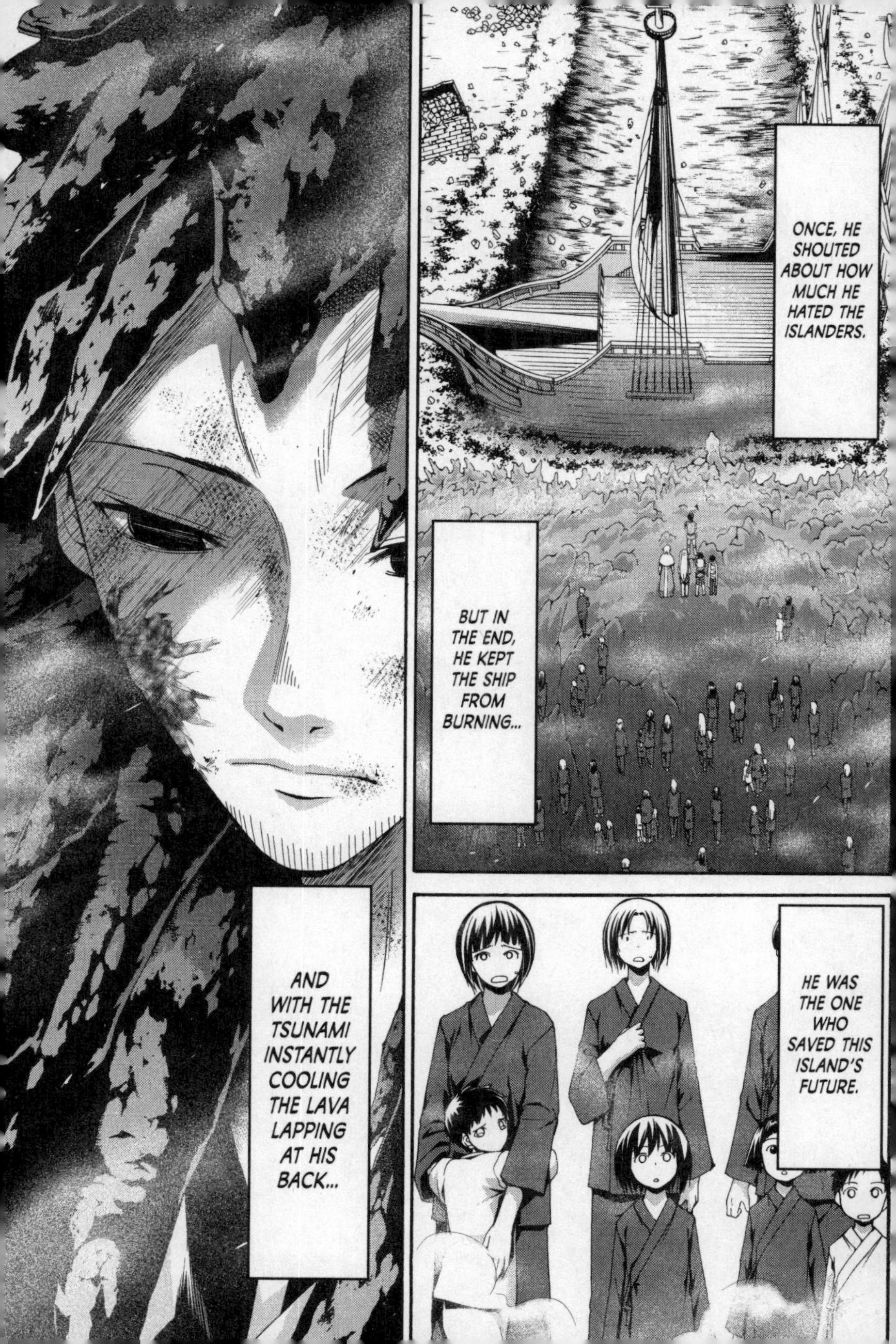
ONCE, HE SHOUTED ABOUT HOW MUCH HE HATED THE ISLANDERS.
BUT IN THE END, HE KEPT THE SHIP FROM BURNING...
HE WAS THE ONE WHO SAVED THIS ISLAND'S FUTURE.
AND WITH THE TSUNAMI INSTANTLY COOLING THE LAVA LAPPING AT HIS BACK...

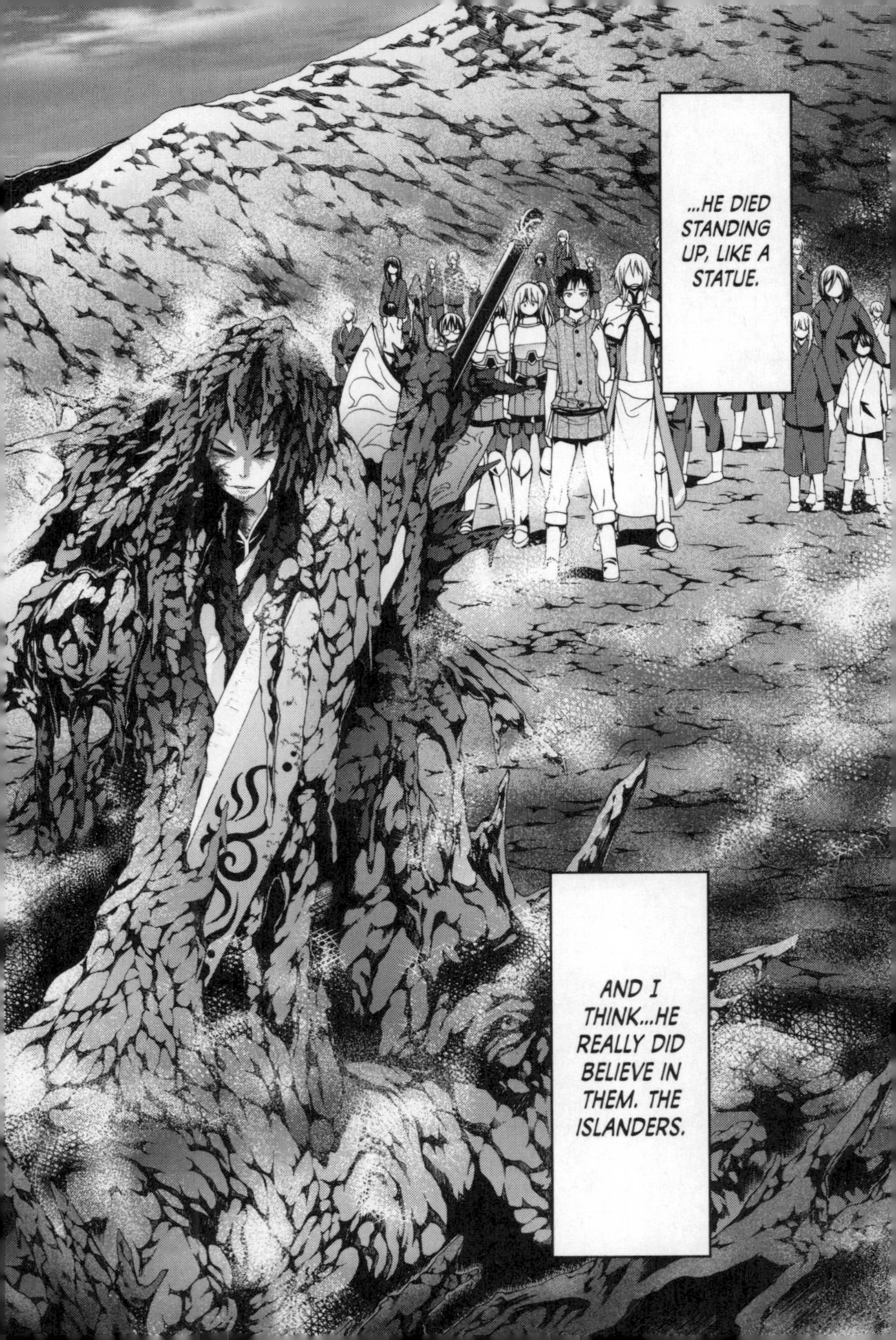
...HE DIED STANDING UP, LIKE A STATUE.
AND I THINK...HE REALLY DID BELIEVE IN THEM. THE ISLANDERS.

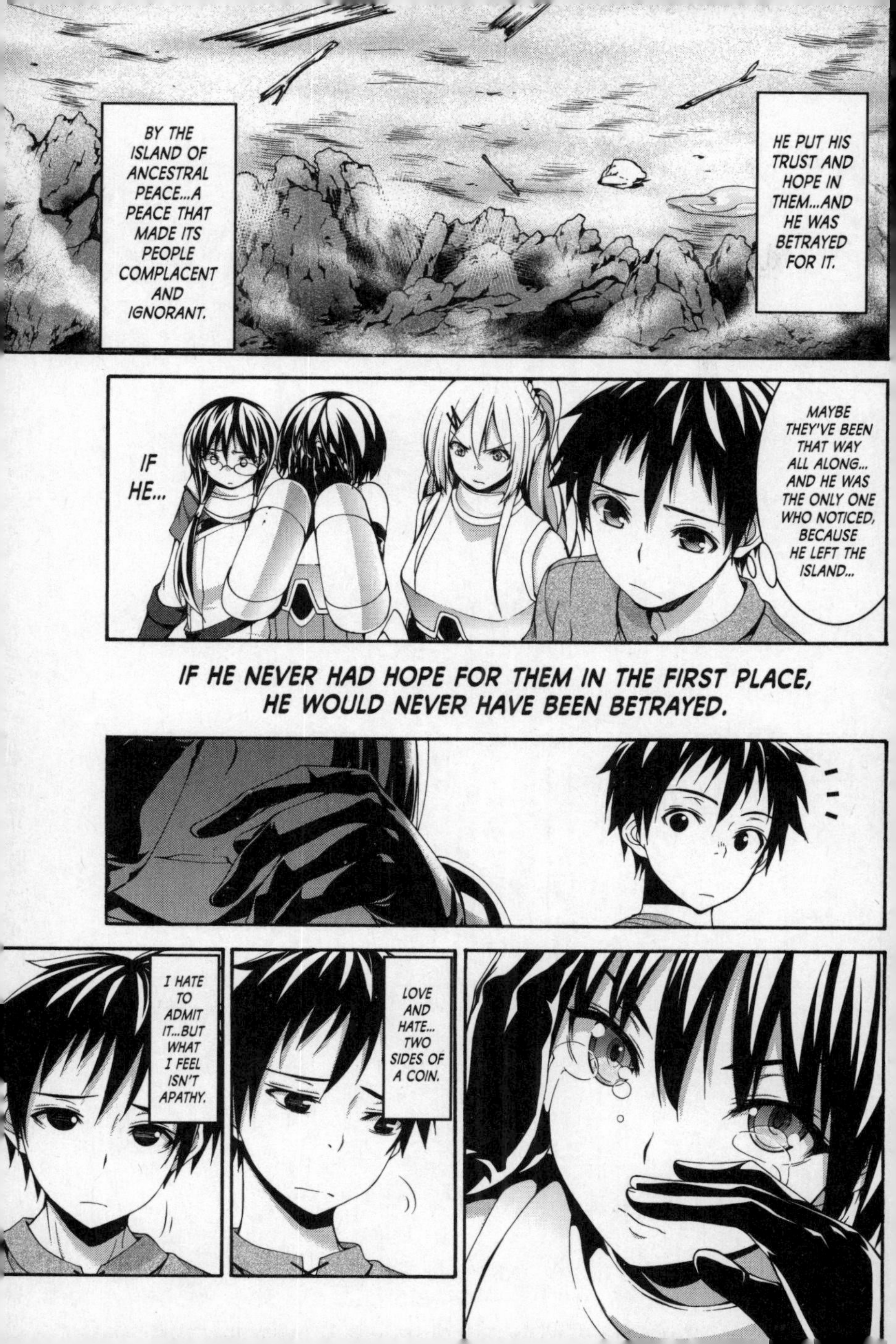
HE PUT HIS TRUST AND HOPE IN THEM...AND HE WAS BETRAYED FOR IT.
BY THE ISLAND OF ANCESTRAL PEACE...A PEACE THAT MADE ITS PEOPLE COMPLACENT AND IGNORANT.
MAYBE THEY'VE BEEN THAT WAY ALL ALONG... AND HE WAS THE ONLY ONE WHO NOTICED, BECAUSE HE LEFT THE ISLAND...
IF HE...
IF HE NEVER HAD HOPE FOR THEM IN THE FIRST PLACE, HE WOULD NEVER HAVE BEEN BETRAYED.
LOVE AND HATE... TWO SIDES OF A COIN.
I HATE TO ADMIT IT...BUT WHAT I FEEL ISN'T APATHY.

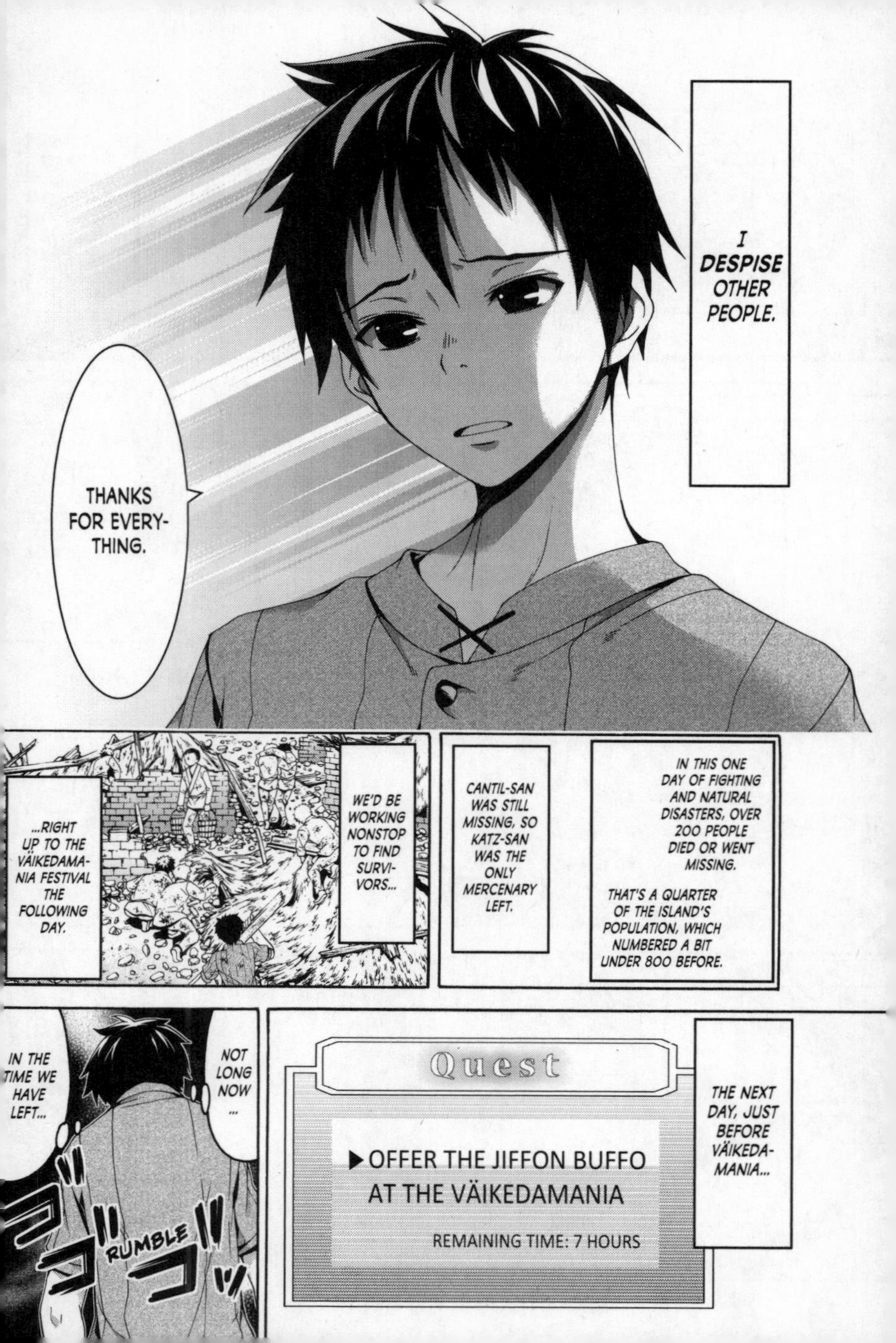

I DESPISE OTHER PEOPLE.
THANKS FOR EVERYTHING.
IN THIS ONE DAY OF FIGHTING AND NATURAL DISASTERS, OVER 200 PEOPLE DIED OR WENT MISSING.
THAT'S A QUARTER OF THE ISLAND'S POPULATION, WHICH NUMBERED A BIT UNDER 800 BEFORE.
CANTIL-SAN WAS STILL MISSING, SO KATZ-SAN WAS THE ONLY MERCENARY LEFT.
WE'D BE WORKING NONSTOP TO FIND SURVIVORS...
...RIGHT UP TO THE VÄIKEDAMANIA FESTIVAL THE FOLLOWING DAY.
THE NEXT DAY, JUST BEFORE VÄIKEDAMANIA...
Quest
▶OFFER THE JIFFON BUFFO AT THE VÄIKEDAMANIA
REMAINING TIME: 7 HOURS
NOT LONG NOW ...
IN THE TIME WE HAVE LEFT...
RUMBLE

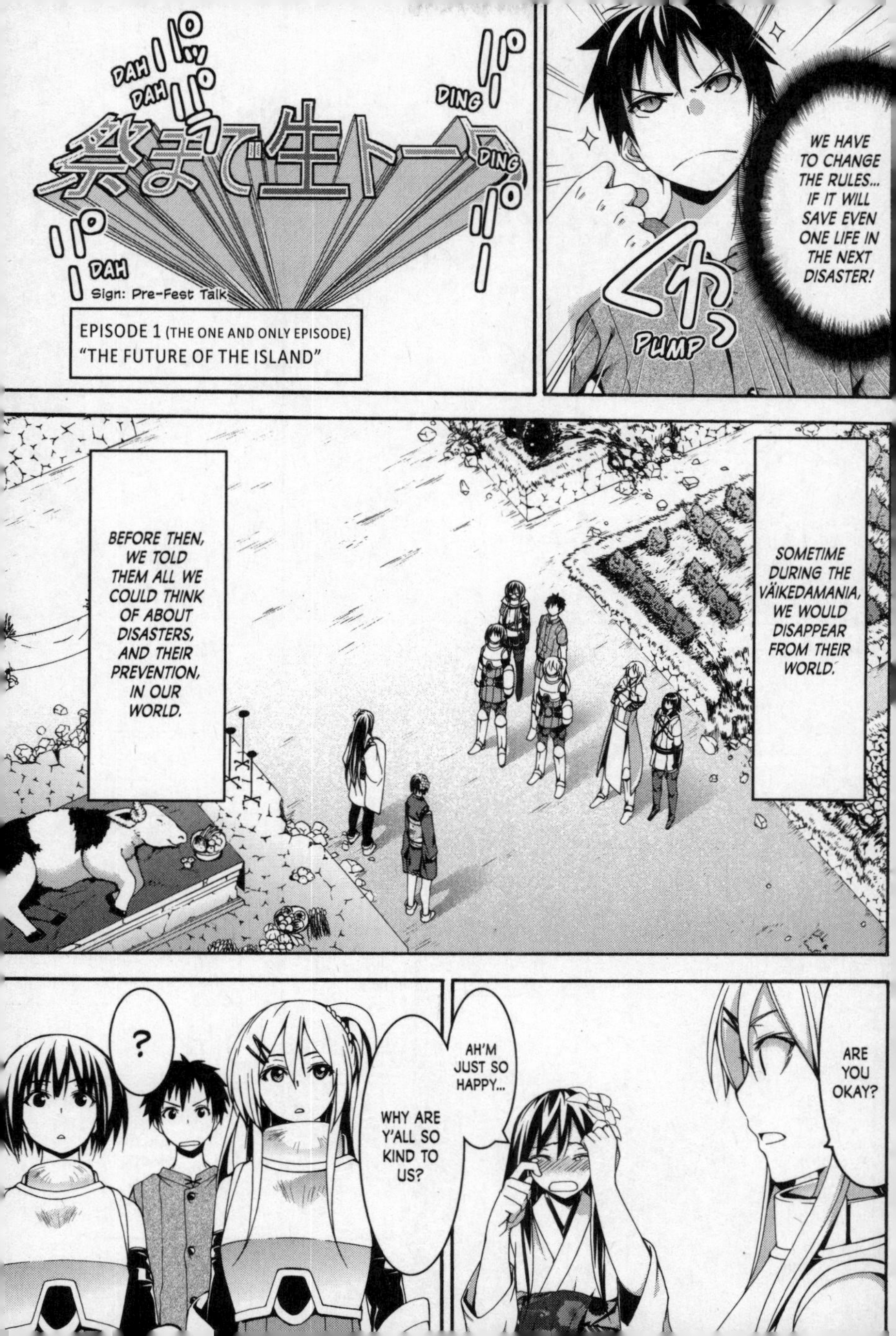
WE HAVE TO CHANGE THE RULES... IF IT WILL SAVE EVEN ONE LIFE IN THE NEXT DISASTER!
PUMP
DING
DING
DAH
DAH
DAH
祭まで生トーク
Sign: Pre-Fest Talk
EPISODE 1 (THE ONE AND ONLY EPISODE)
"THE FUTURE OF THE ISLAND"
SOMETIME DURING THE VÄIKEDAMANIA, WE WOULD DISAPPEAR FROM THEIR WORLD.
BEFORE THEN, WE TOLD THEM ALL WE COULD THINK OF ABOUT DISASTERS, AND THEIR PREVENTION, IN OUR WORLD.
ARE YOU OKAY?
AH'M JUST SO HAPPY...
WHY ARE Y'ALL SO KIND TO US?
?

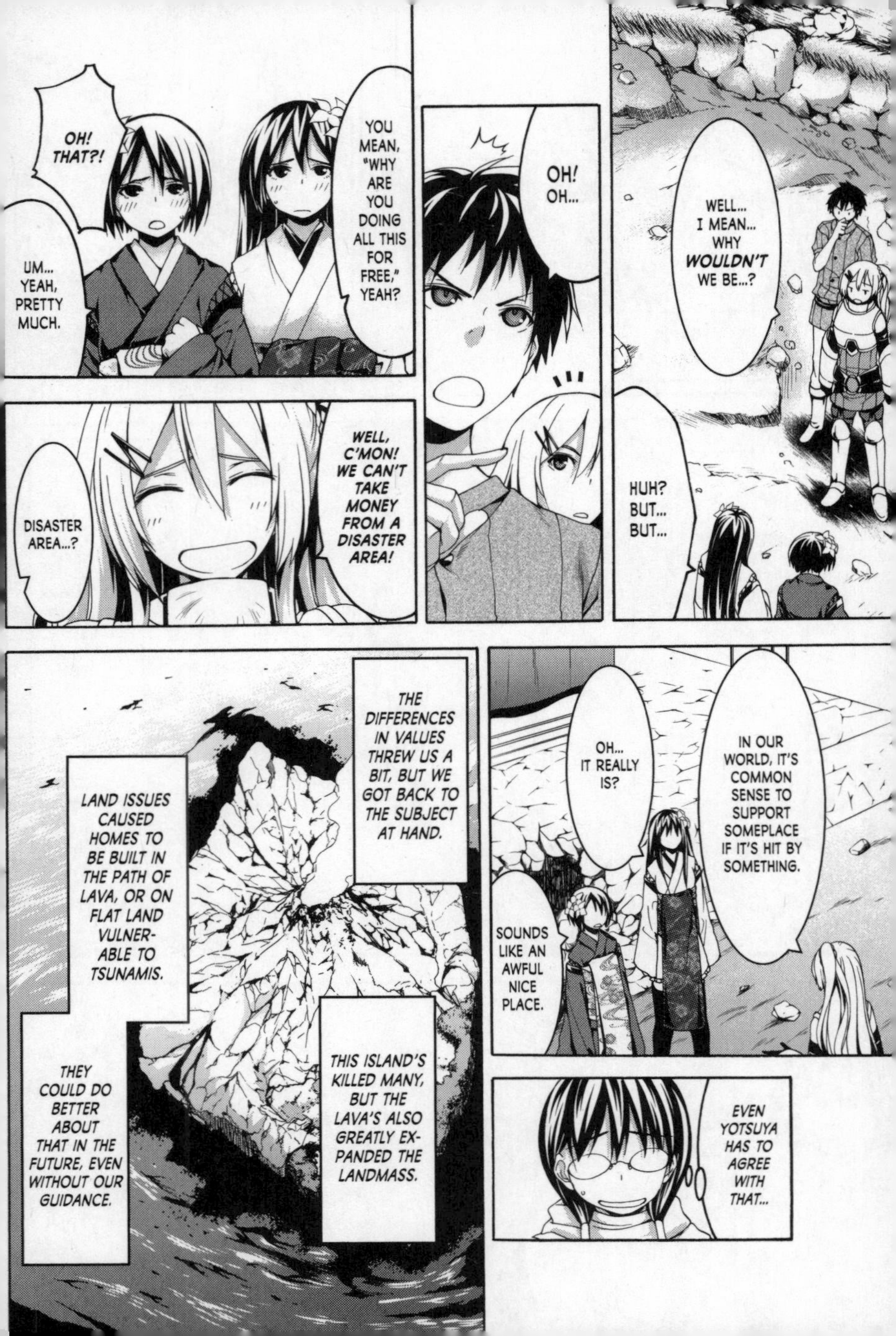
WELL... I MEAN... WHY *WOULDN'T* WE BE...?
HUH? BUT... BUT...
OH! OH...
YOU MEAN, "WHY ARE YOU DOING ALL THIS FOR FREE," YEAH?
OH! THAT?!
UM... YEAH, PRETTY MUCH.
WELL, C'MON! WE CAN'T TAKE MONEY FROM A DISASTER AREA!
DISASTER AREA...?
IN OUR WORLD, IT'S COMMON SENSE TO SUPPORT SOMEPLACE IF IT'S HIT BY SOMETHING.
OH... IT REALLY IS?
SOUNDS LIKE AN AWFUL NICE PLACE.
EVEN YOTSUYA HAS TO AGREE WITH THAT...
THE DIFFERENCES IN VALUES THREW US A BIT, BUT WE GOT BACK TO THE SUBJECT AT HAND.
LAND ISSUES CAUSED HOMES TO BE BUILT IN THE PATH OF LAVA, OR ON FLAT LAND VULNER-ABLE TO TSUNAMIS.
THIS ISLAND'S KILLED MANY, BUT THE LAVA'S ALSO GREATLY EX-PANDED THE LANDMASS.
THEY COULD DO BETTER ABOUT THAT IN THE FUTURE, EVEN WITHOUT OUR GUIDANCE.

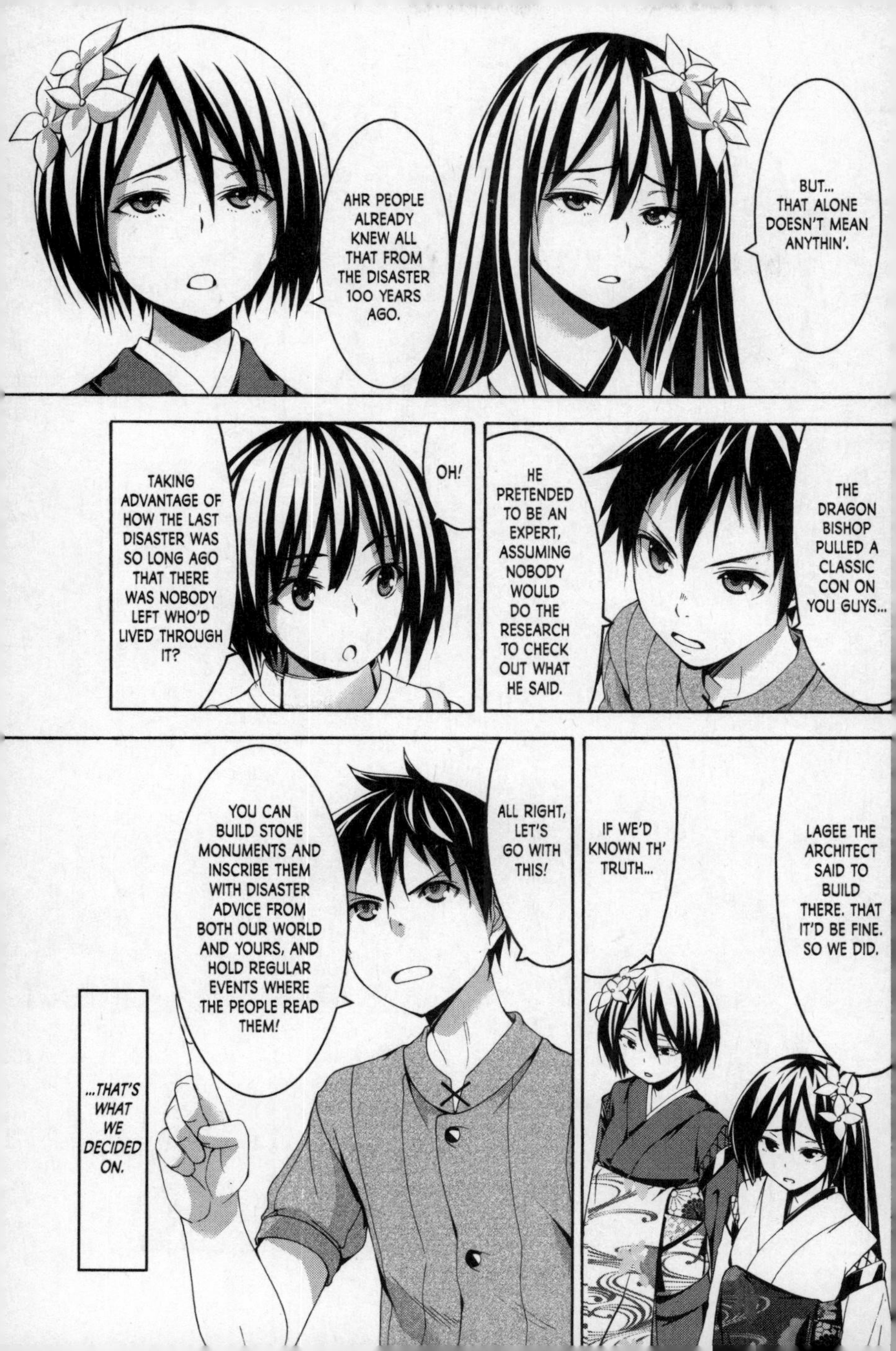
BUT... THAT ALONE DOESN'T MEAN ANYTHIN'.
AHR PEOPLE ALREADY KNEW ALL THAT FROM THE DISASTER 100 YEARS AGO.
THE DRAGON BISHOP PULLED A CLASSIC CON ON YOU GUYS...
HE PRETENDED TO BE AN EXPERT, ASSUMING NOBODY WOULD DO THE RESEARCH TO CHECK OUT WHAT HE SAID.
OH!
TAKING ADVANTAGE OF HOW THE LAST DISASTER WAS SO LONG AGO THAT THERE WAS NOBODY LEFT WHO'D LIVED THROUGH IT?
LAGEE THE ARCHITECT SAID TO BUILD THERE. THAT IT'D BE FINE. SO WE DID.
IF WE'D KNOWN TH' TRUTH...
ALL RIGHT, LET'S GO WITH THIS!
YOU CAN BUILD STONE MONUMENTS AND INSCRIBE THEM WITH DISASTER ADVICE FROM BOTH OUR WORLD AND YOURS, AND HOLD REGULAR EVENTS WHERE THE PEOPLE READ THEM!
...THAT'S WHAT WE DECIDED ON.

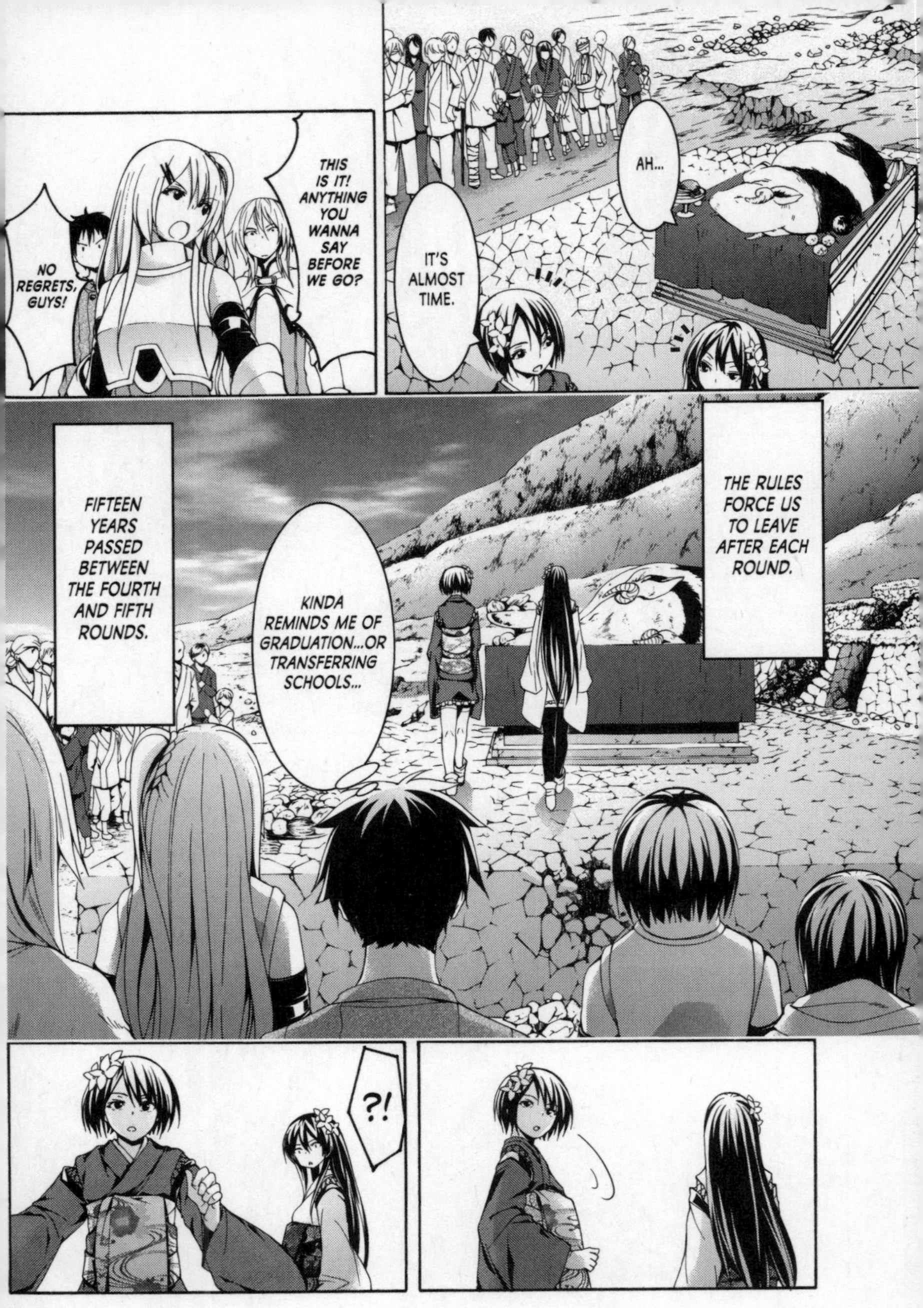
AH...
IT'S ALMOST TIME.
THIS IS IT! ANYTHING YOU WANNA SAY BEFORE WE GO?
NO REGRETS, GUYS!
THE RULES FORCE US TO LEAVE AFTER EACH ROUND.
KINDA REMINDS ME OF GRADUATION...OR TRANSFERRING SCHOOLS...
FIFTEEN YEARS PASSED BETWEEN THE FOURTH AND FIFTH ROUNDS.
?!

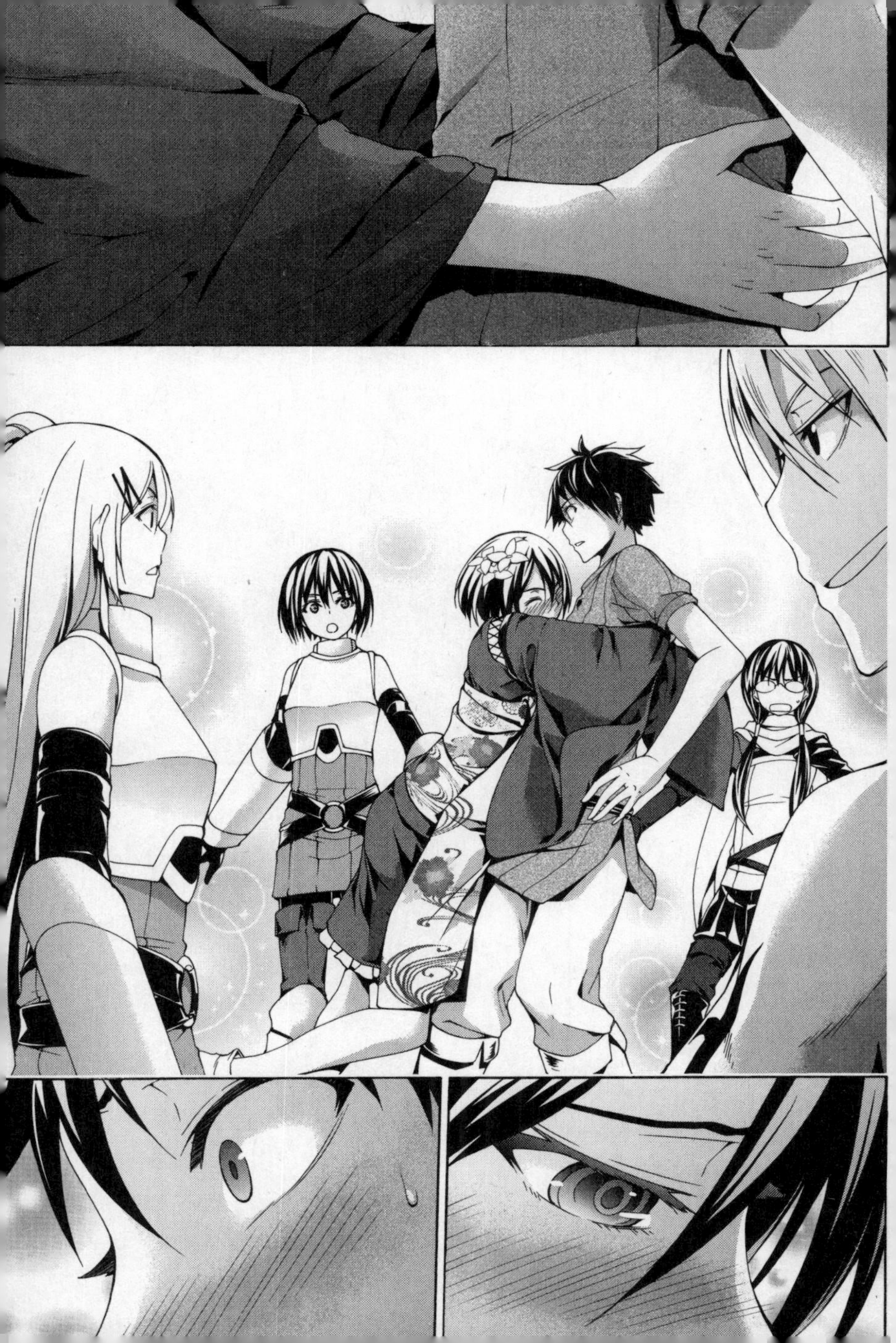

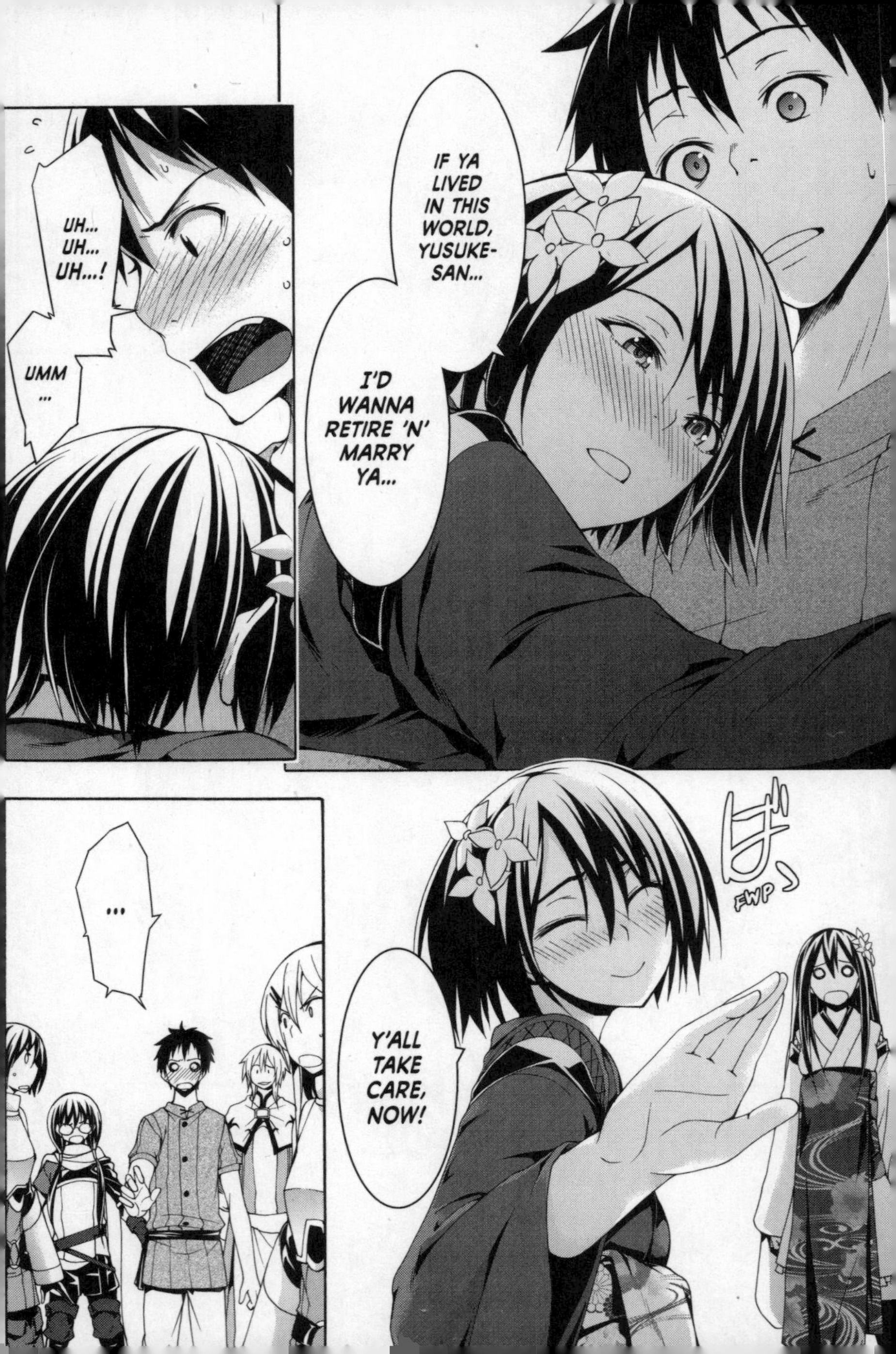
IF YA LIVED IN THIS WORLD, YUSUKE-SAN...
I'D WANNA RETIRE 'N' MARRY YA...
UH... UH... UH...!
UMM ...
FWP
Y'ALL TAKE CARE, NOW!
...

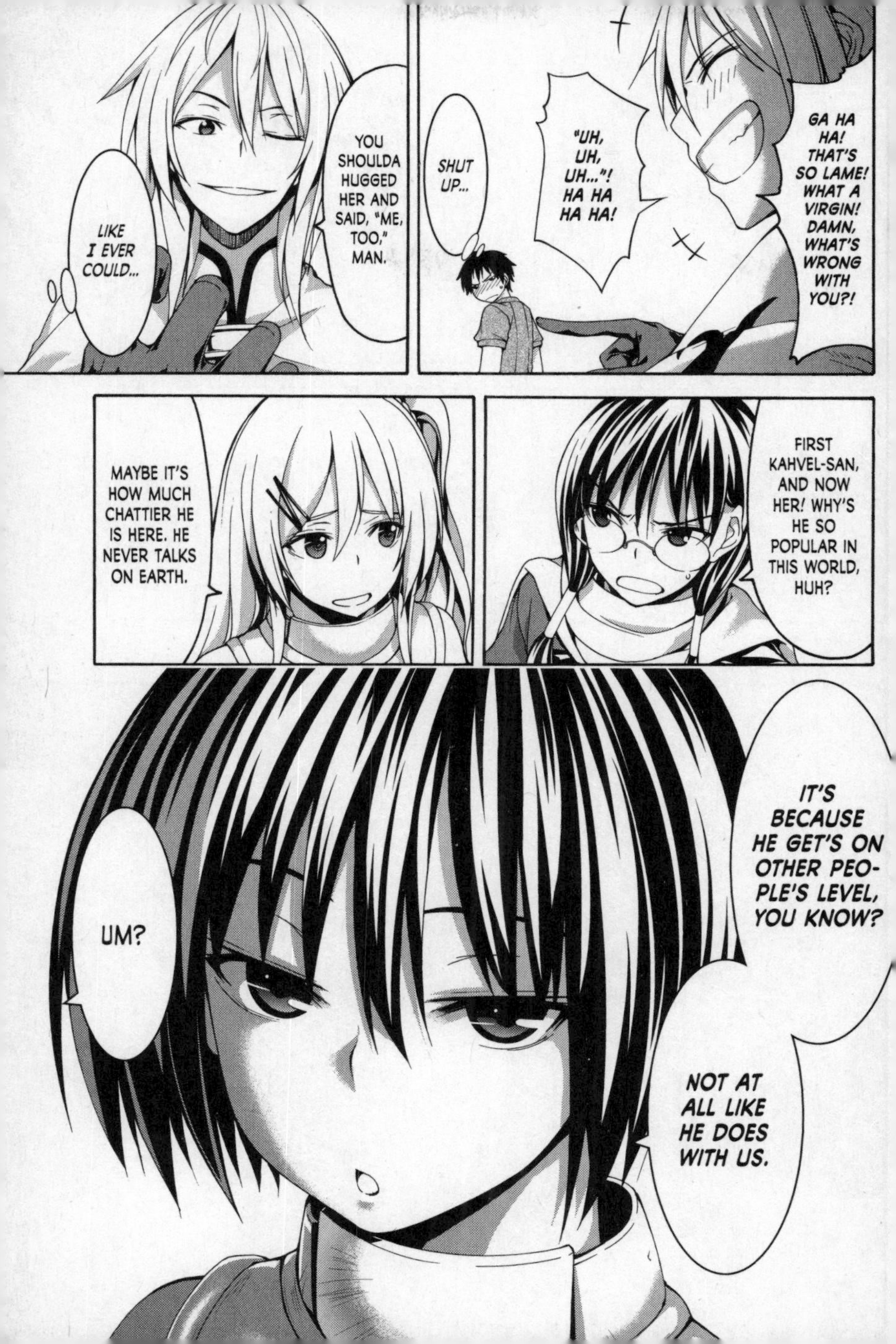
GA HA HA! THAT'S SO LAME! WHAT A VIRGIN! DAMN, WHAT'S WRONG WITH YOU?!
"UH, UH, UH..."! HA HA HA HA!
SHUT UP...
YOU SHOULDA HUGGED HER AND SAID, "ME, TOO," MAN.
LIKE I EVER COULD...
FIRST KAHVEL-SAN, AND NOW HER! WHY'S HE SO POPULAR IN THIS WORLD, HUH?
MAYBE IT'S HOW MUCH CHATTIER HE IS HERE. HE NEVER TALKS ON EARTH.
IT'S BECAUSE HE GET'S ON OTHER PEO-PLE'S LEVEL, YOU KNOW?
NOT AT ALL LIKE HE DOES WITH US.
UM?

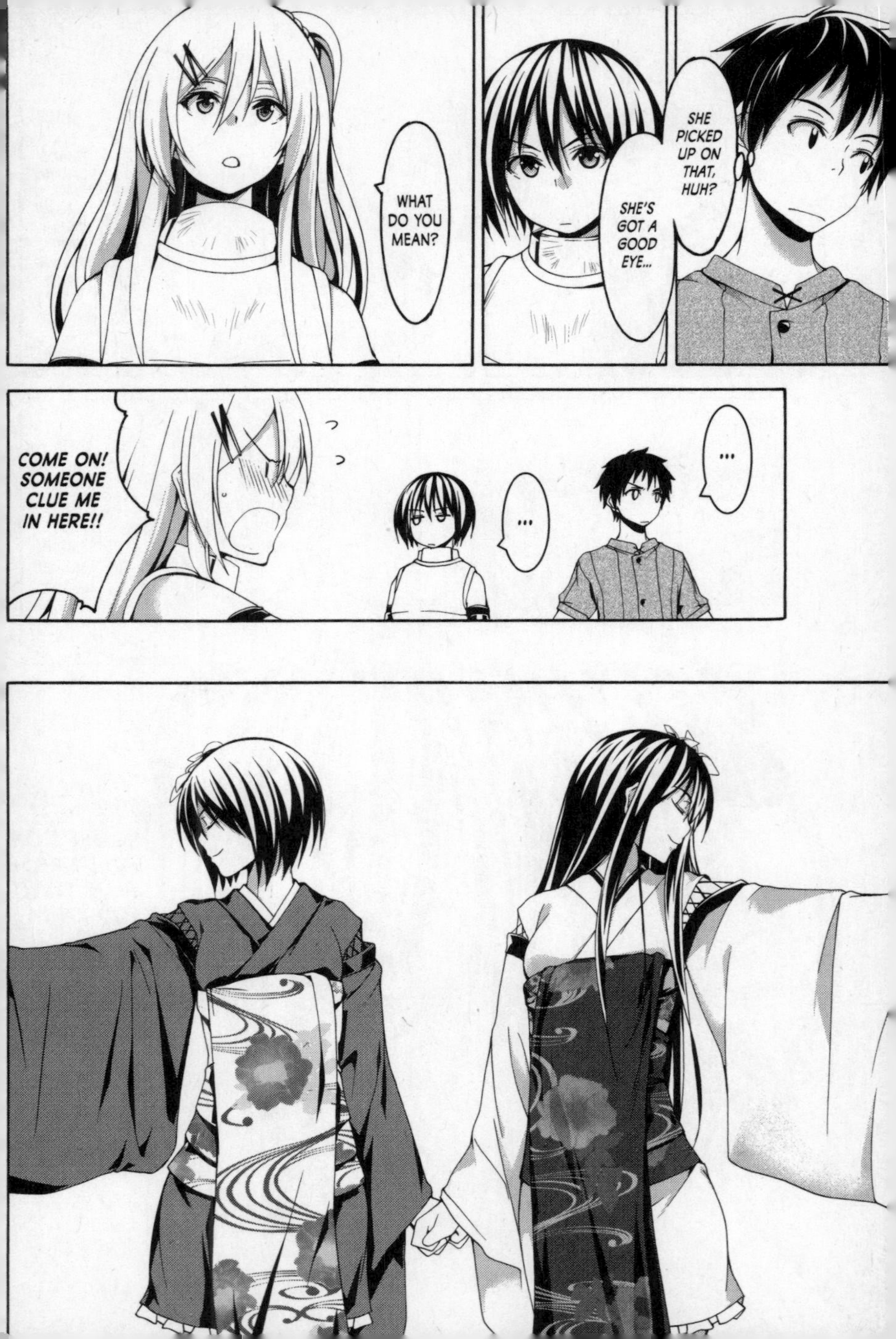
SHE PICKED UP ON THAT, HUH?
SHE'S GOT A GOOD EYE...
WHAT DO YOU MEAN?
...
...
COME ON! SOMEONE CLUE ME IN HERE!!

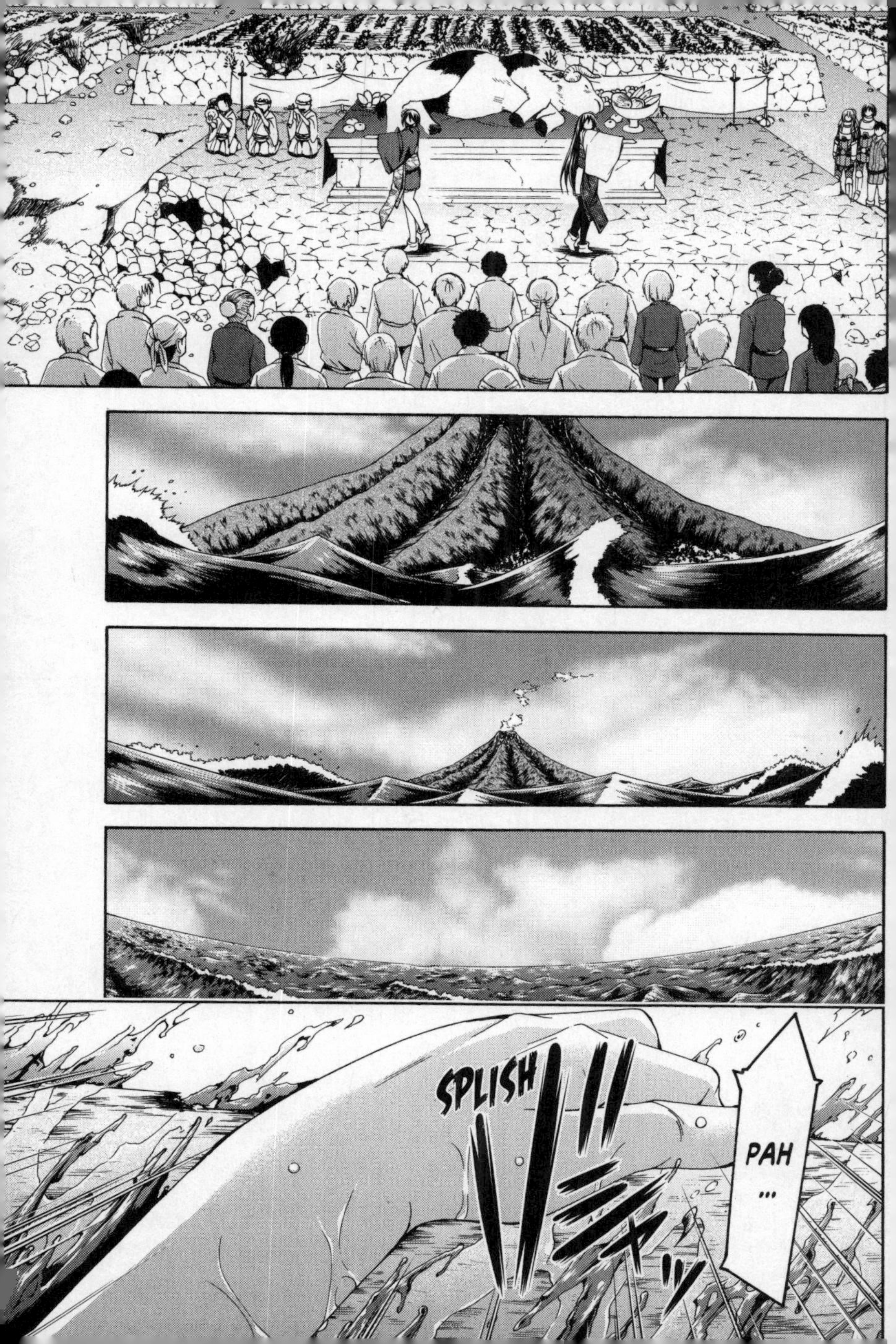
PAH
...
SPLISH

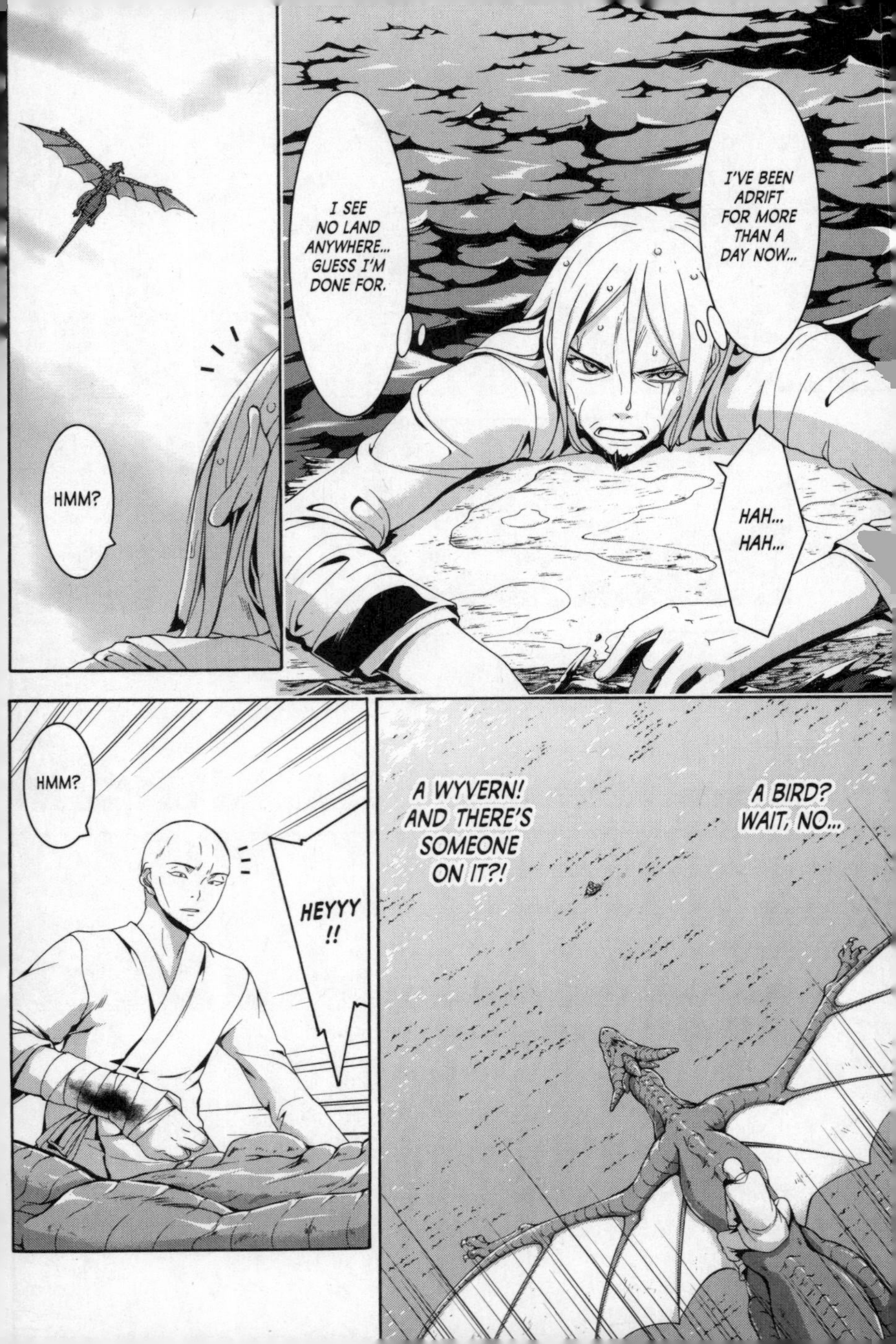
I'VE BEEN ADRIFT FOR MORE THAN A DAY NOW...
I SEE NO LAND ANYWHERE... GUESS I'M DONE FOR.
HAH... HAH...
HMM?
A BIRD? WAIT, NO...
A WYVERN! AND THERE'S SOMEONE ON IT?!
HEYYY !!
HMM?

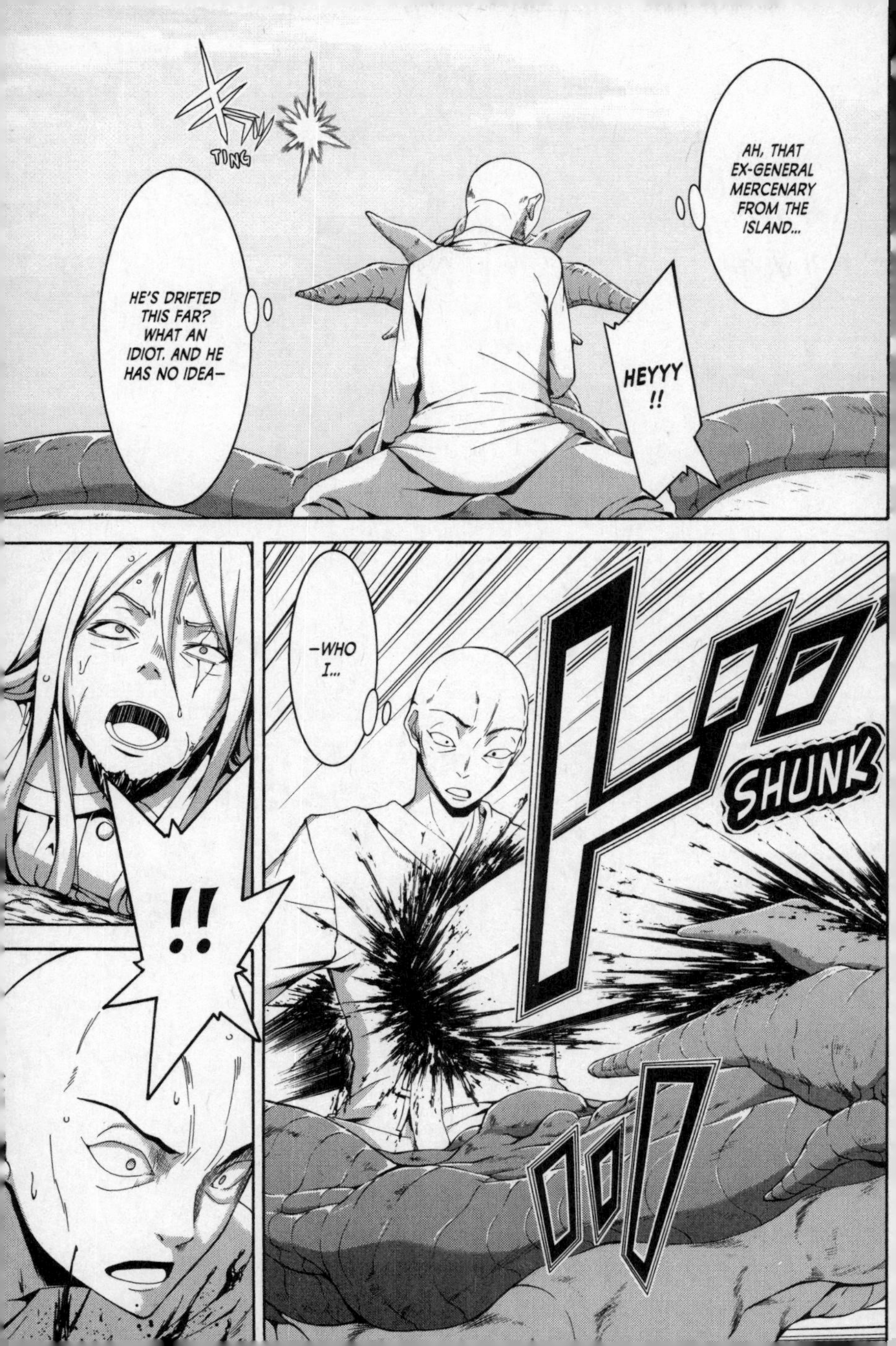
AH, THAT EX-GENERAL MERCENARY FROM THE ISLAND...
HEYYY !!
HE'S DRIFTED THIS FAR? WHAT AN IDIOT. AND HE HAS NO IDEA–
TING
–WHO I...
SHUNK
!!

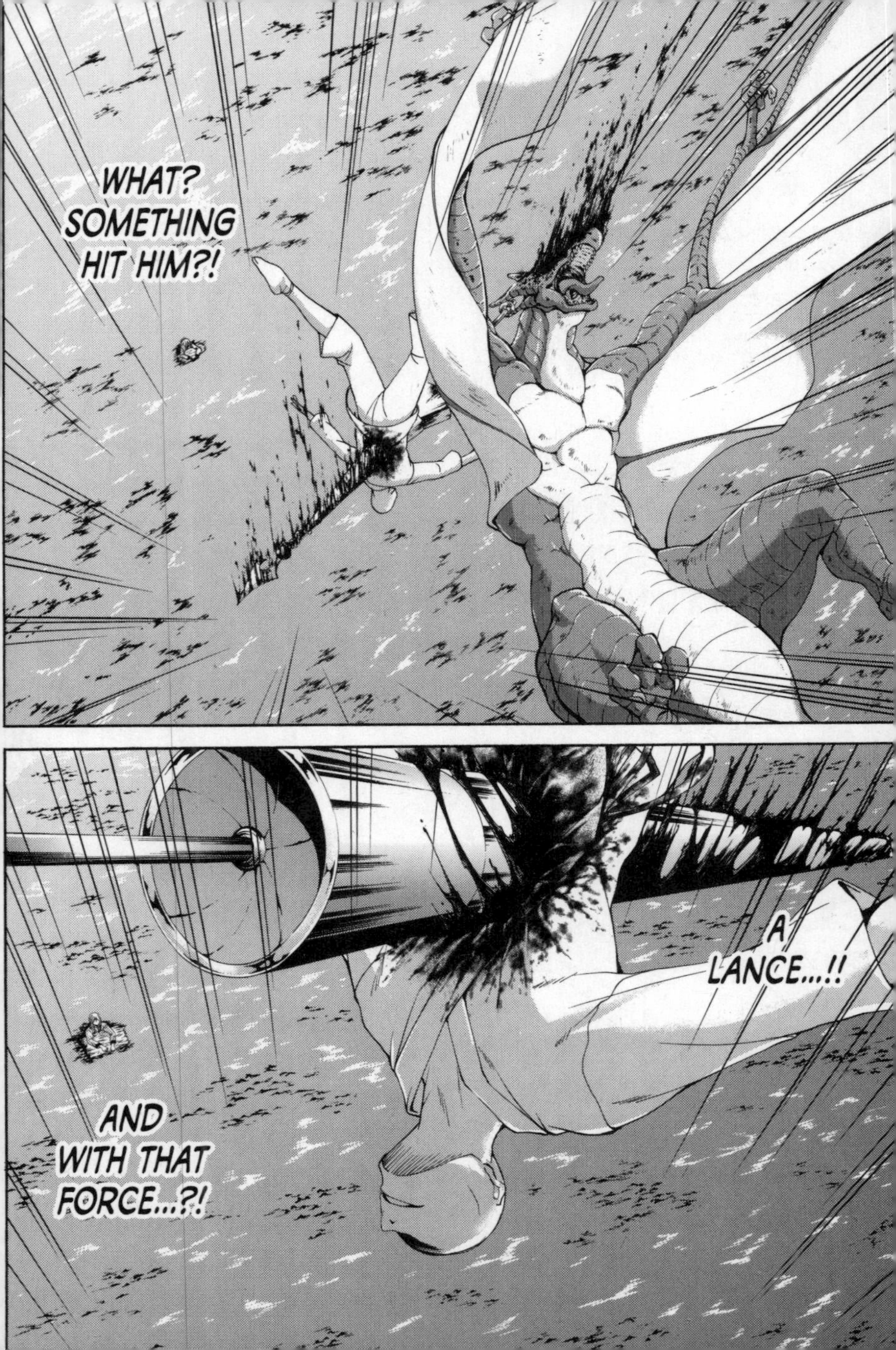
WHAT? SOMETHING HIT HIM?!
A LANCE...!!
AND WITH THAT FORCE...?!

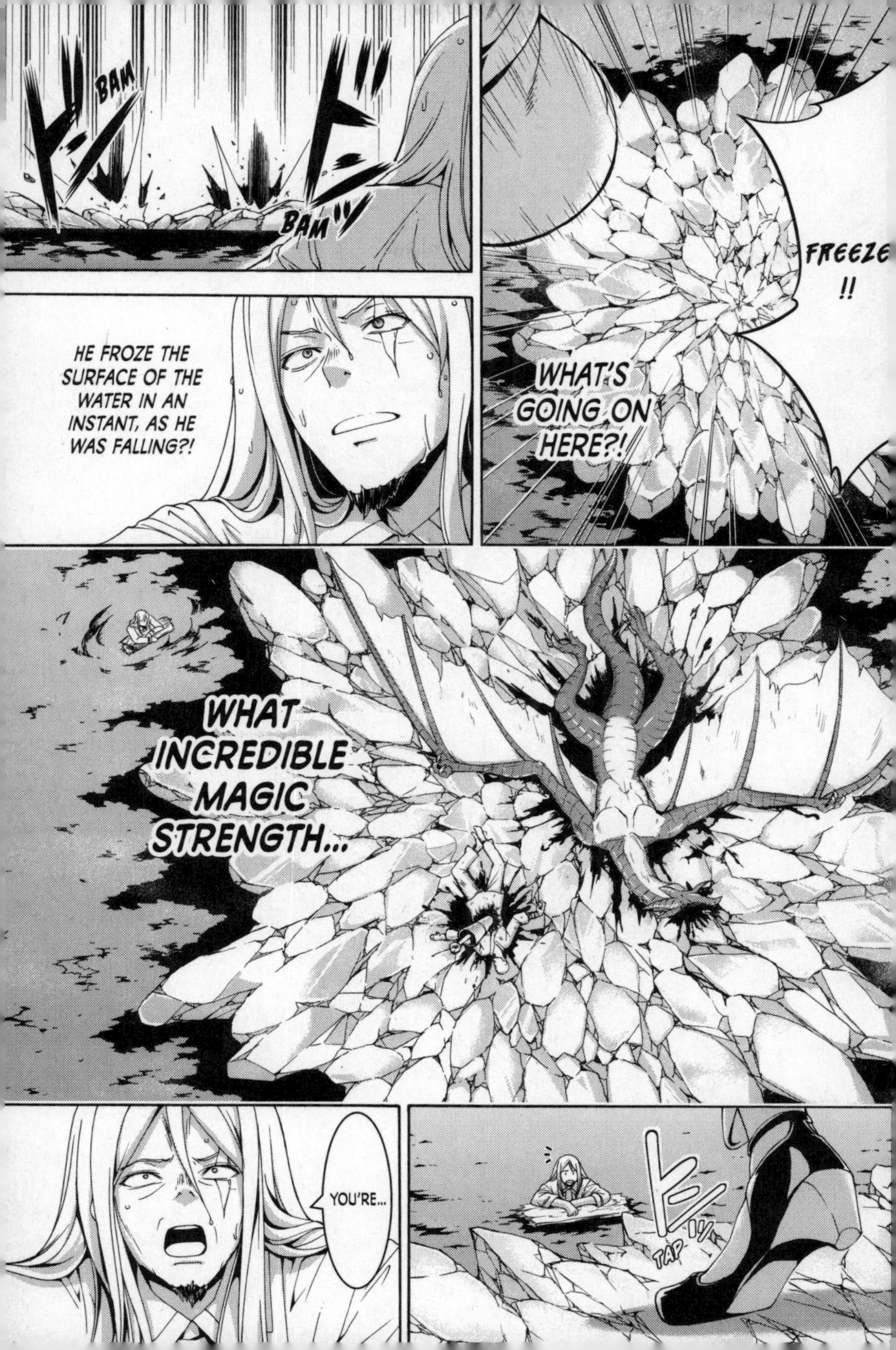
FREEZE !!
WHAT'S GOING ON HERE?!
BAM
BAM
HE FROZE THE SURFACE OF THE WATER IN AN INSTANT, AS HE WAS FALLING?!
WHAT INCREDIBLE MAGIC STRENGTH...
TAP
YOU'RE...

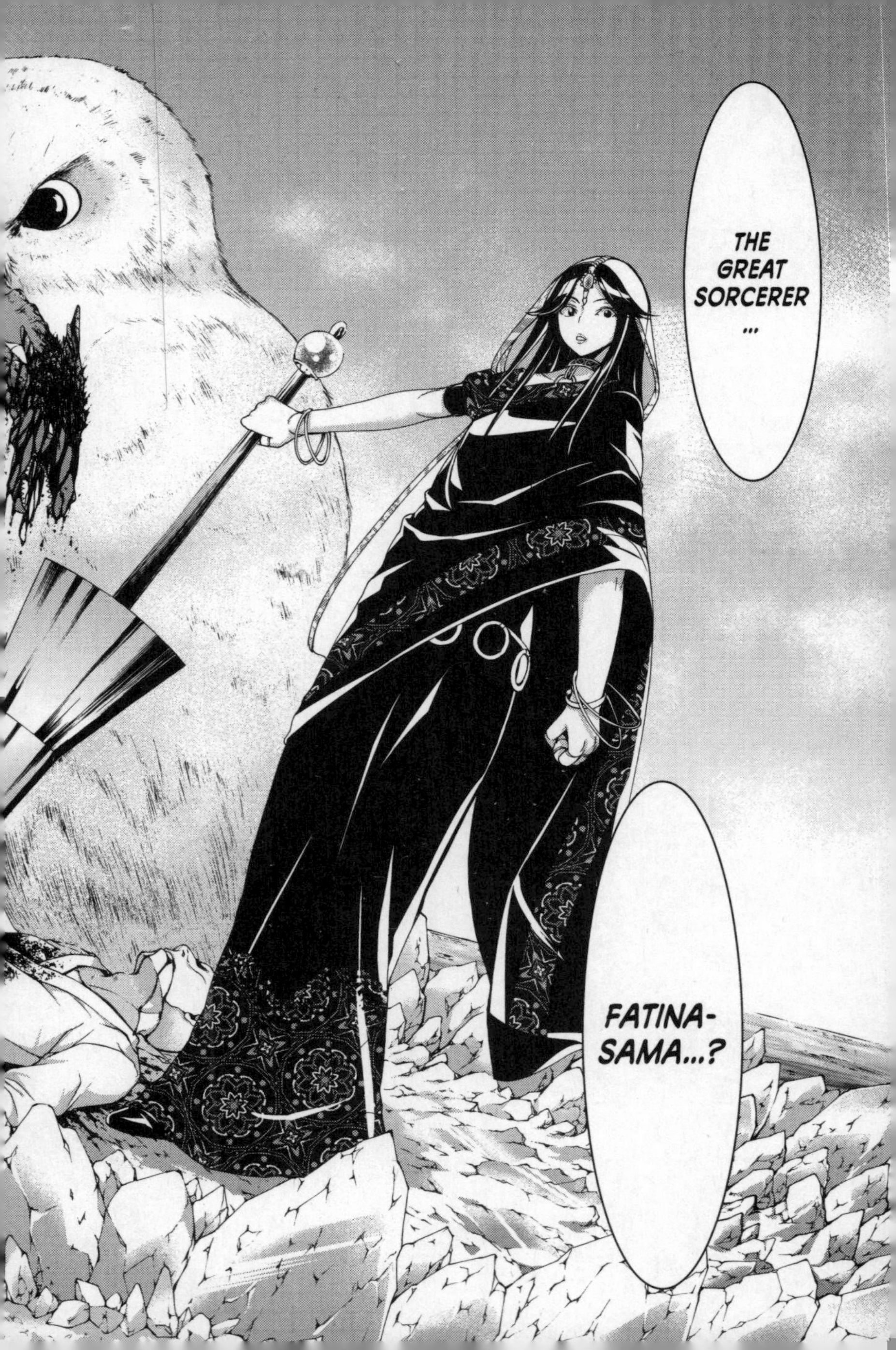
THE GREAT SORCERER ...
FATINA-SAMA...?

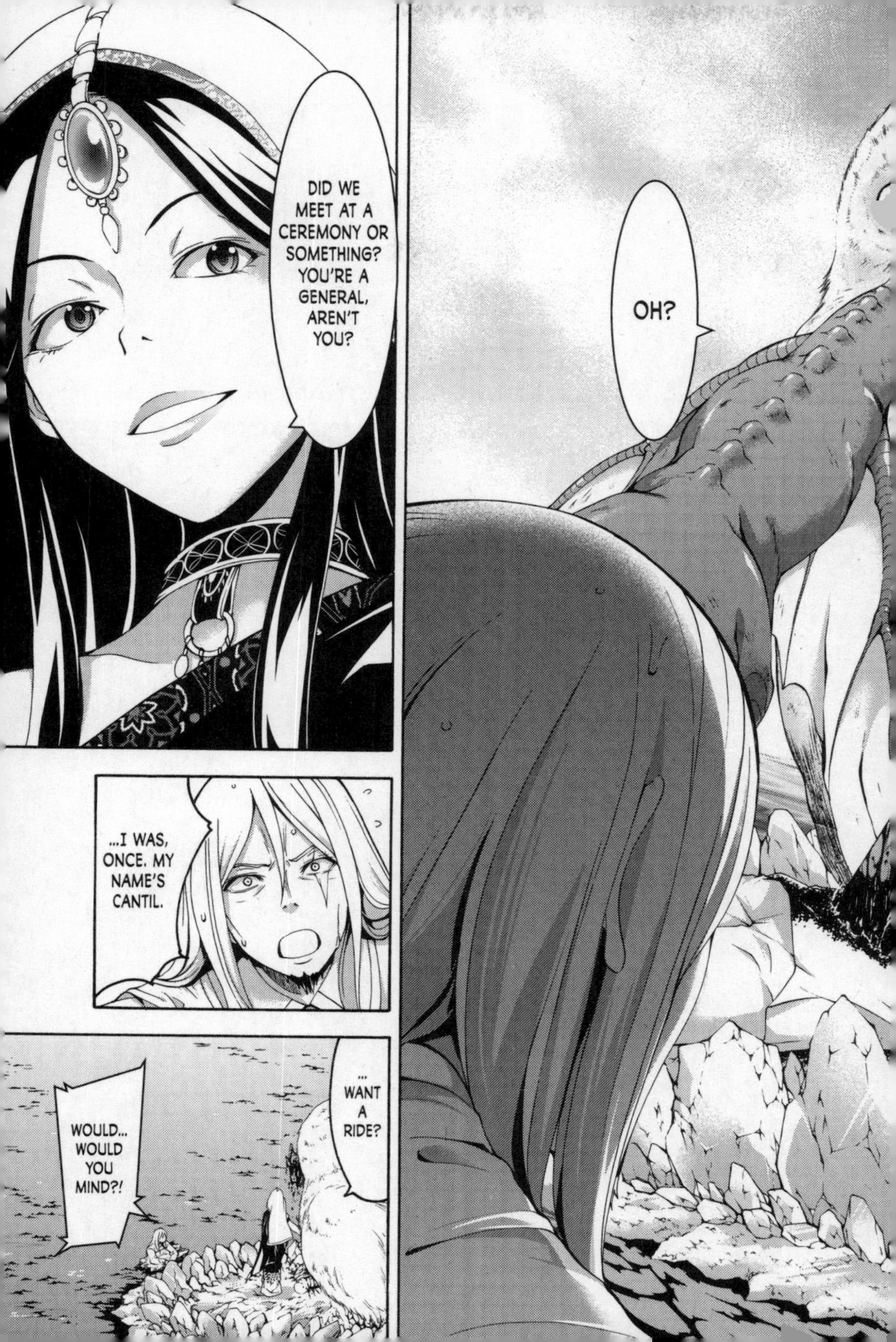
OH?
DID WE MEET AT A CEREMONY OR SOMETHING? YOU'RE A GENERAL, AREN'T YOU?
...I WAS, ONCE. MY NAME'S CANTIL.
... WANT A RIDE?
WOULD... WOULD YOU MIND?!

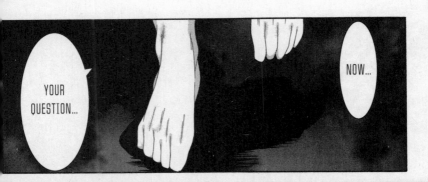

YOUR
QUESTION...

NOW...

...AS A
REWARD
FOR YOUR
ACCOMPLISH.

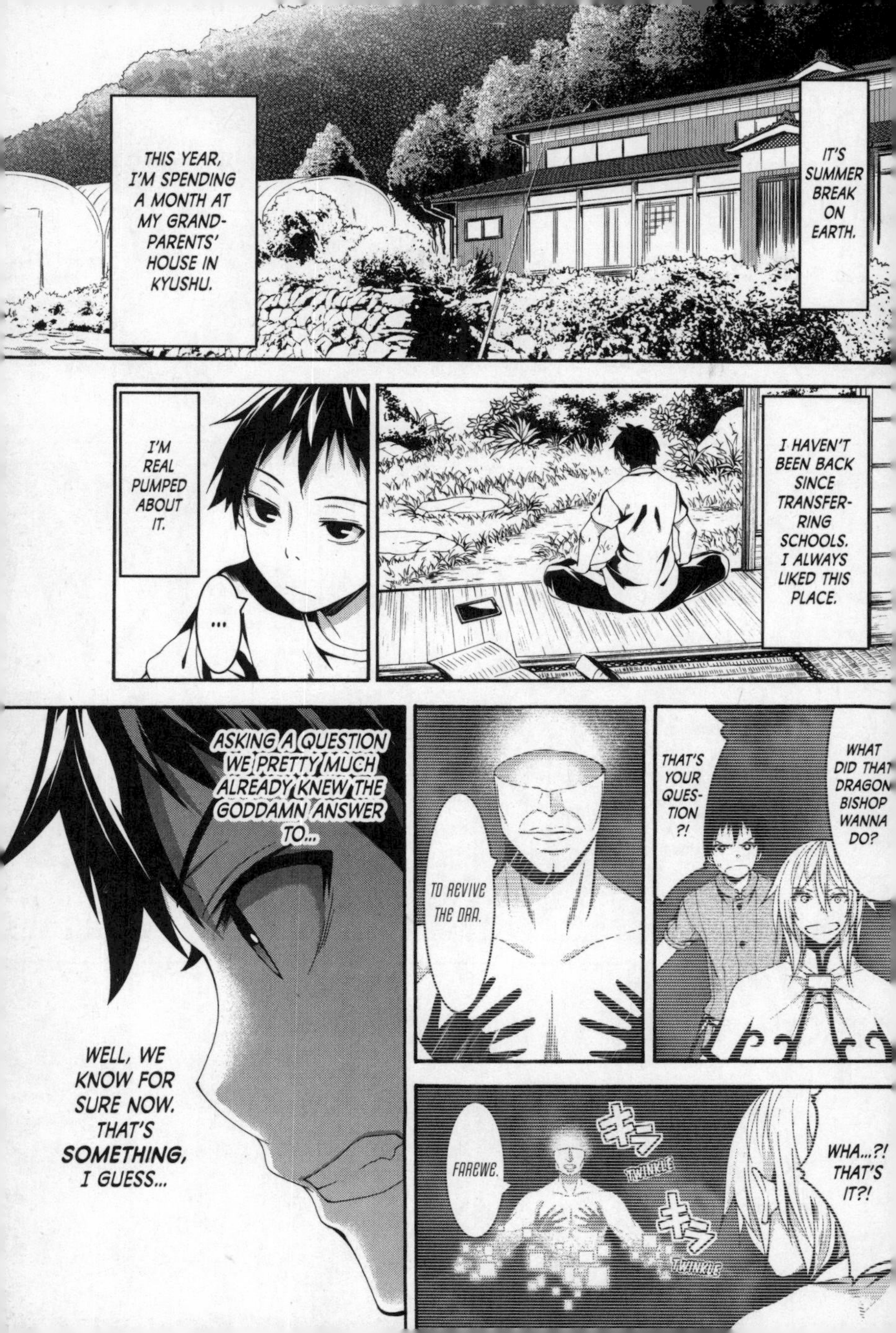
IT'S SUMMER BREAK ON EARTH.
THIS YEAR, I'M SPENDING A MONTH AT MY GRAND-PARENTS' HOUSE IN KYUSHU.
I HAVEN'T BEEN BACK SINCE TRANSFER-RING SCHOOLS. I ALWAYS LIKED THIS PLACE.
I'M REAL PUMPED ABOUT IT.
...
WHAT DID THAT DRAGON BISHOP WANNA DO?
THAT'S YOUR QUES-TION ?!
TO REVIVE THE DRA.
WHA...?! THAT'S IT?!
キラ
TWINKLE
キラ
TWINKLE
FAREWE.
ASKING A QUESTION WE PRETTY MUCH ALREADY KNEW THE GODDAMN ANSWER TO...
WELL, WE KNOW FOR SURE NOW. THAT'S **SOMETHING**, I GUESS...

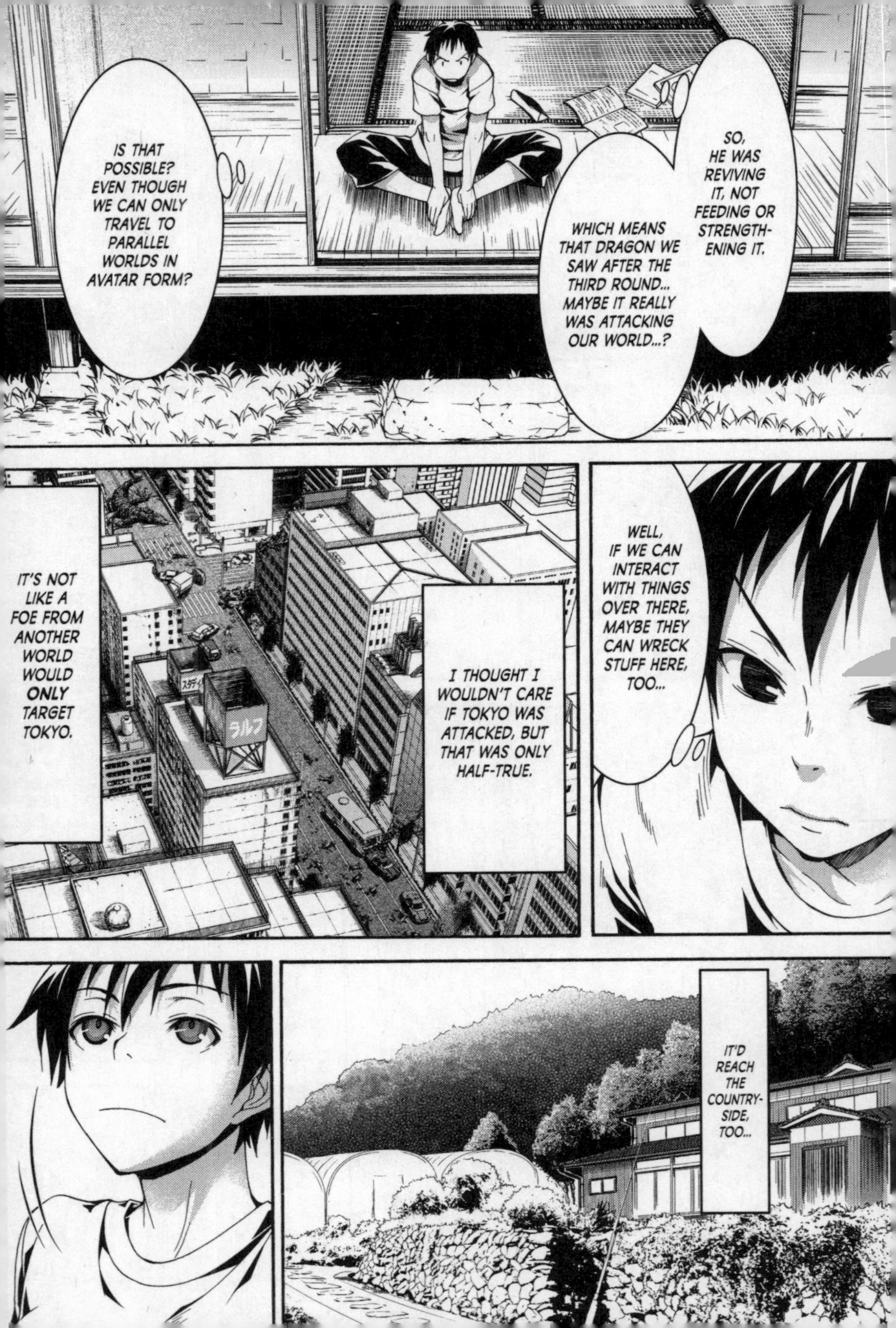
SO, HE WAS REVIVING IT, NOT FEEDING OR STRENGTH-ENING IT.
WHICH MEANS THAT DRAGON WE SAW AFTER THE THIRD ROUND... MAYBE IT REALLY WAS ATTACKING OUR WORLD...?
IS THAT POSSIBLE? EVEN THOUGH WE CAN ONLY TRAVEL TO PARALLEL WORLDS IN AVATAR FORM?
WELL, IF WE CAN INTERACT WITH THINGS OVER THERE, MAYBE THEY CAN WRECK STUFF HERE, TOO...
I THOUGHT I WOULDN'T CARE IF TOKYO WAS ATTACKED, BUT THAT WAS ONLY HALF-TRUE.
ラルフ
IT'S NOT LIKE A FOE FROM ANOTHER WORLD WOULD ONLY TARGET TOKYO.
IT'D REACH THE COUNTRY-SIDE, TOO...

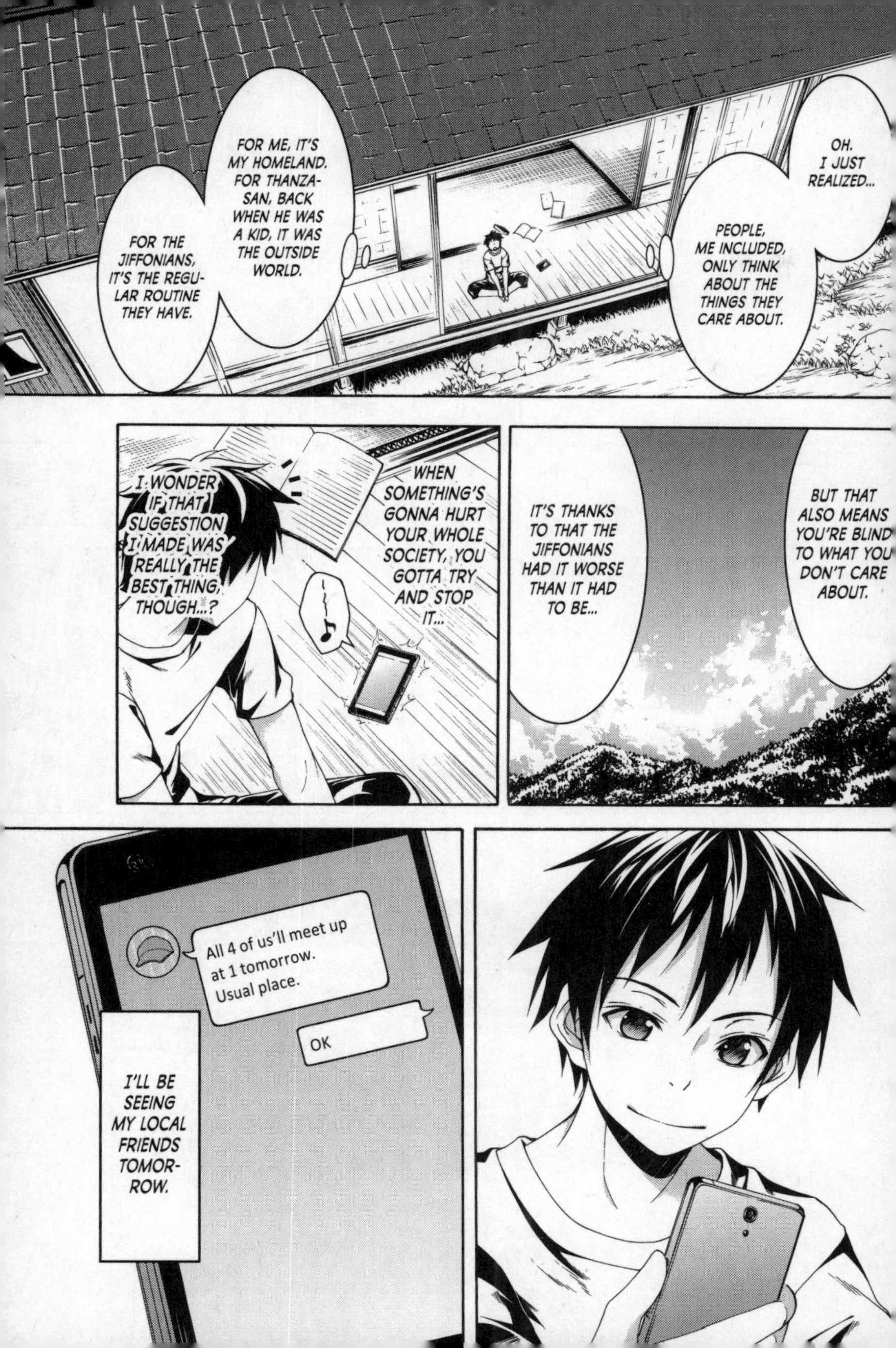
OH. I JUST REALIZED...
PEOPLE, ME INCLUDED, ONLY THINK ABOUT THE THINGS THEY CARE ABOUT.
FOR ME, IT'S MY HOMELAND. FOR THANZA-SAN, BACK WHEN HE WAS A KID, IT WAS THE OUTSIDE WORLD.
FOR THE JIFFONIANS, IT'S THE REGULAR ROUTINE THEY HAVE.
BUT THAT ALSO MEANS YOU'RE BLIND TO WHAT YOU DON'T CARE ABOUT.
IT'S THANKS TO THAT THE JIFFONIANS HAD IT WORSE THAN IT HAD TO BE...
WHEN SOMETHING'S GONNA HURT YOUR WHOLE SOCIETY, YOU GOTTA TRY AND STOP IT...
I WONDER IF THAT SUGGESTION I MADE WAS REALLY THE BEST THING, THOUGH...?
All 4 of us'll meet up at 1 tomorrow. Usual place.
OK
I'LL BE SEEING MY LOCAL FRIENDS TOMORROW.

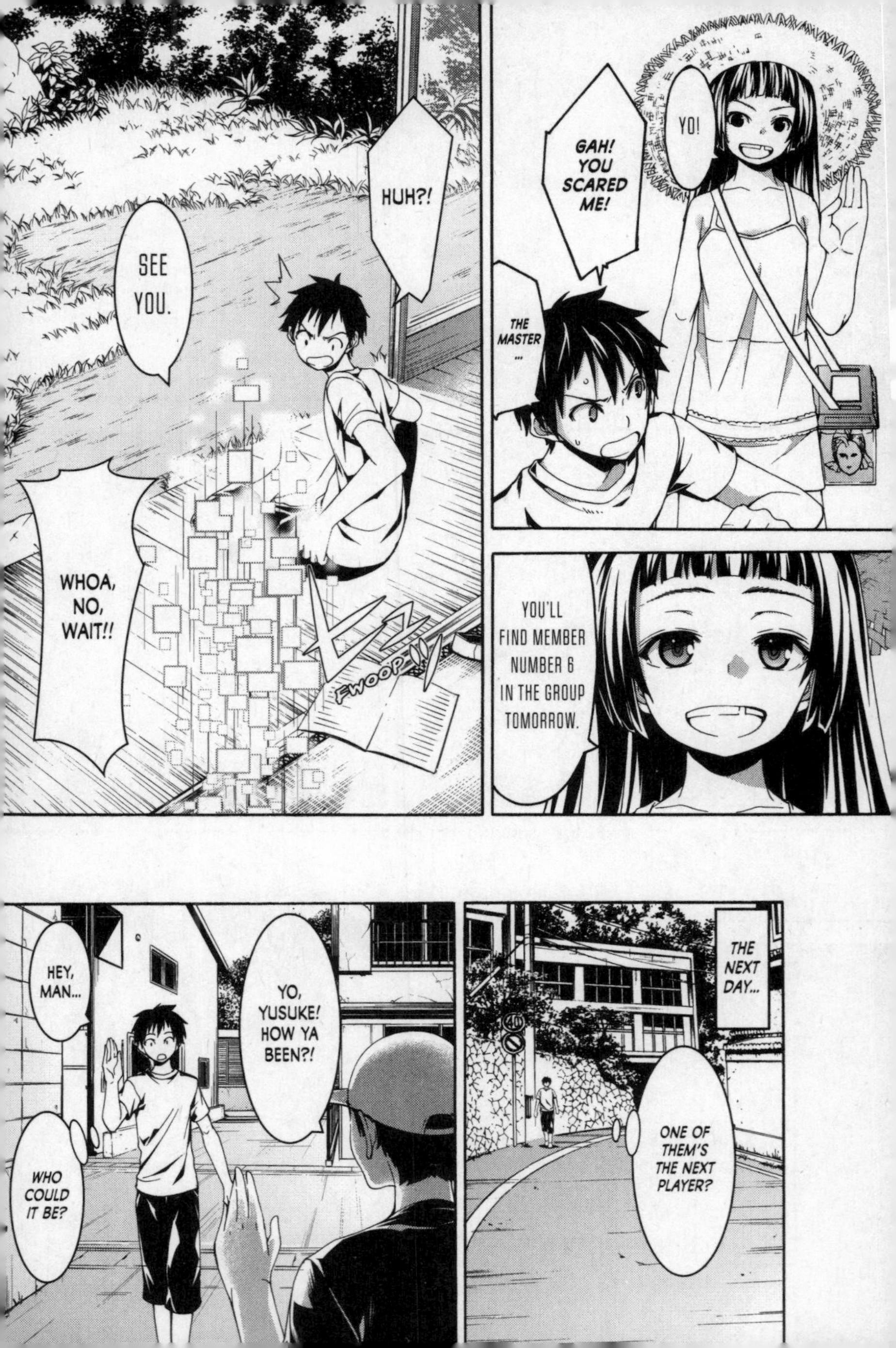
YO!
GAH! YOU SCARED ME!
THE MASTER ...
YOU'LL FIND MEMBER NUMBER 6 IN THE GROUP TOMORROW.
HUH?!
SEE YOU.
FWOOP
WHOA, NO, WAIT!!
THE NEXT DAY...
40
ONE OF THEM'S THE NEXT PLAYER?
YO, YUSUKE! HOW YA BEEN?!
HEY, MAN...
WHO COULD IT BE?

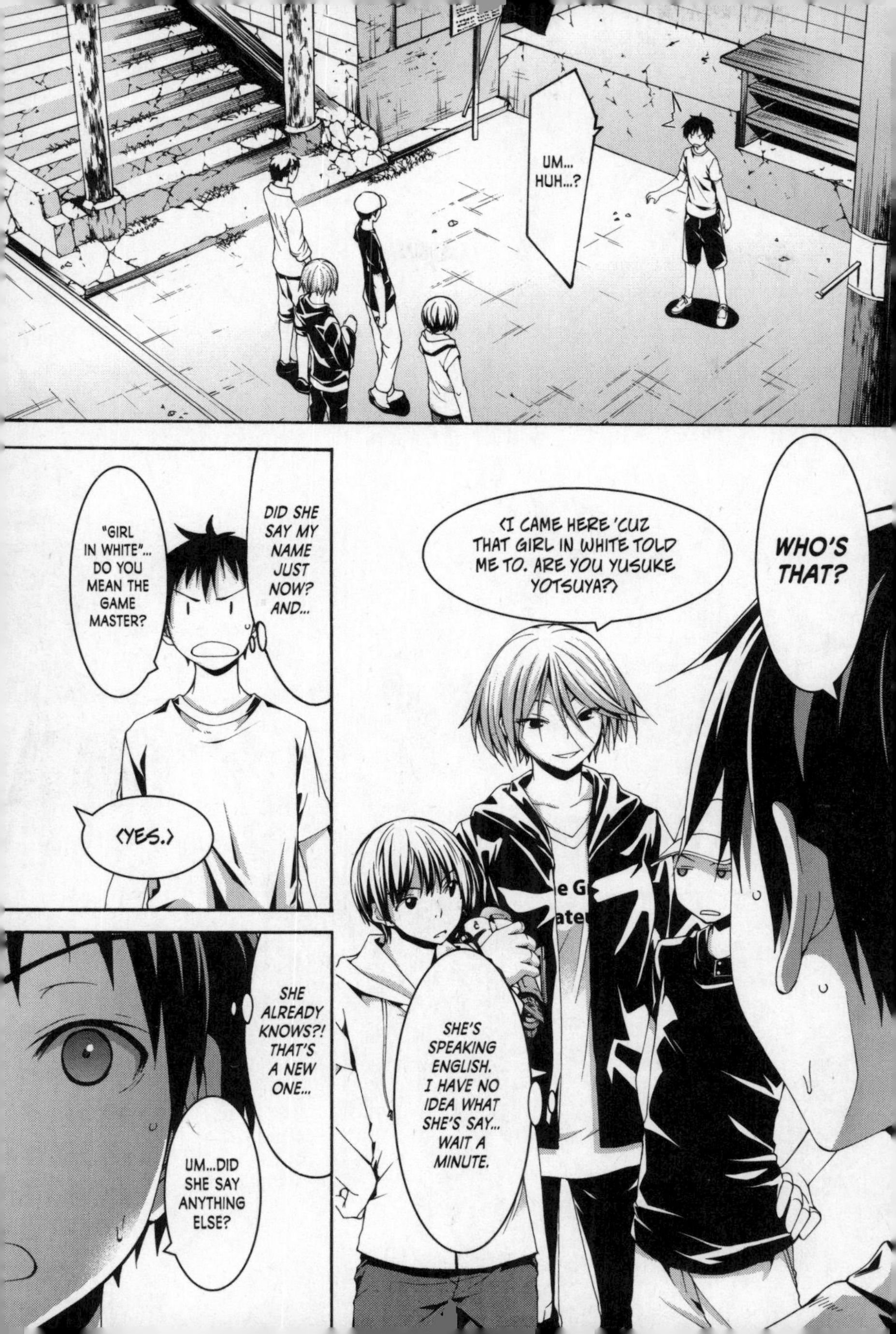

UM... HUH...?
WHO'S THAT?
‹I CAME HERE 'CUZ THAT GIRL IN WHITE TOLD ME TO. ARE YOU YUSUKE YOTSUYA?›
SHE'S SPEAKING ENGLISH. I HAVE NO IDEA WHAT SHE'S SAY... WAIT A MINUTE.
DID SHE SAY MY NAME JUST NOW? AND...
"GIRL IN WHITE"... DO YOU MEAN THE GAME MASTER?
‹YES.›
SHE ALREADY KNOWS?! THAT'S A NEW ONE...
UM...DID SHE SAY ANYTHING ELSE?

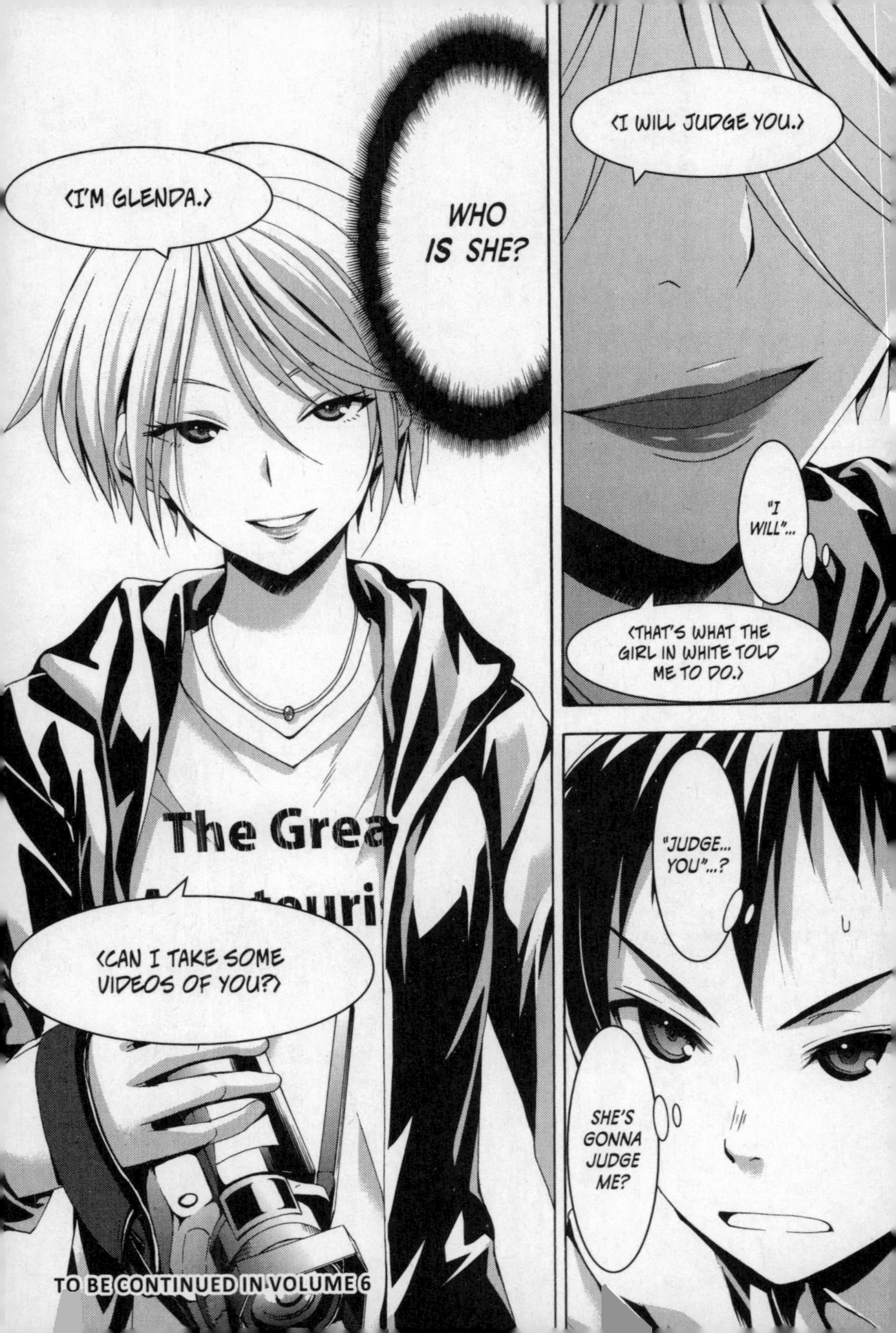
‹I WILL JUDGE YOU.›
"I WILL"...
‹THAT'S WHAT THE GIRL IN WHITE TOLD ME TO DO.›
"JUDGE... YOU"...?
SHE'S GONNA JUDGE ME?
WHO IS SHE?
‹I'M GLENDA.›
‹CAN I TAKE SOME VIDEOS OF YOU?›

TO BE CONTINUED IN VOLUME 6

I'M STANDING ON A MILLION LIVES

KAMOME SHIRAHAMA

Witch Hat Atelier

A magical manga adventure for fans of Disney and Studio Ghibli!

Witch Hat Atelier © Kamome Shirahama/Kodansha Ltd.

The magical adventure that took Japan by storm is finally here, from acclaimed DC and Marvel cover artist Kamome Shirahama!

In a world where everyone takes wonders like magic spells and dragons for granted, Coco is a girl with a simple dream: She wants to be a witch. But everybody knows magicians are born, not made, and Coco was not born with a gift for magic. Resigned to her un-magical life, Coco is about to give up on her dream to become a witch...until the day she meets Qifrey, a mysterious, traveling magician. After secretly seeing Qifrey perform magic in a way she's never seen before, Coco soon learns what everybody "knows" might not be the truth, and discovers that her magical dream may not be as far away as it may seem...

KC KODANSHA COMICS

KC
KODANSHA COMICS

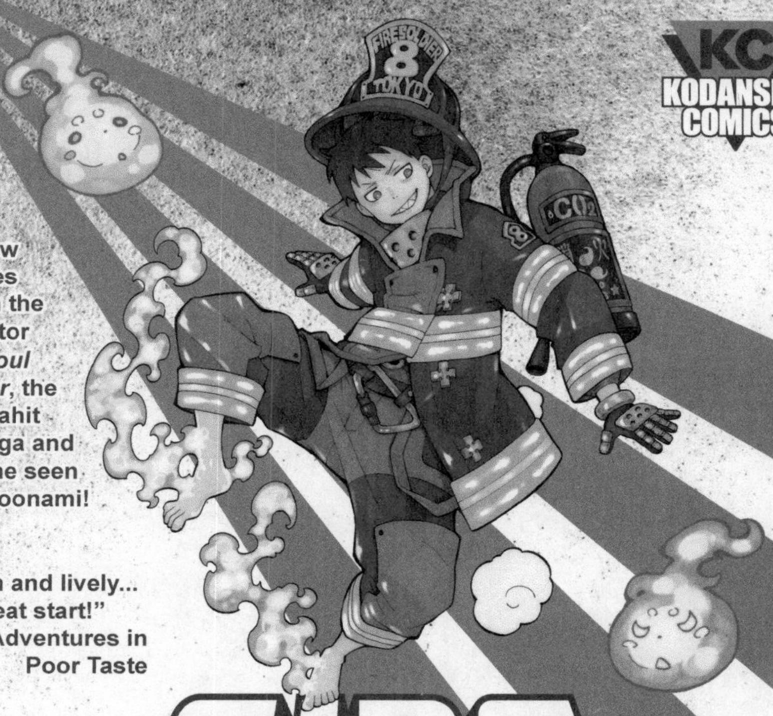

FIRESOLDIER
8
TOKYO
CO2

A new series from the creator of *Soul Eater*, the megahit manga and anime seen on Toonami!

“Fun and lively... a great start!”
-Adventures in Poor Taste

FIRE FORCE

By Atsushi Ohkubo

The city of Tokyo is plagued by a deadly phenomenon: spontaneous human combustion! Luckily, a special team is there to quench the inferno: The Fire Force! The fire soldiers at Special Fire Cathedral 8 are about to get a unique addition. Enter Shinra, a boy who possesses the power to run at the speed of a rocket, leaving behind the famous “devil’s footprints” (and destroying his shoes in the process). Can Shinra and his colleagues discover the source of this strange epidemic before the city burns to ashes?

HIRO MASHIMA IS BACK! JOIN THE CREATOR OF *FAIRY TAIL*
AS HE TAKES TO THE STARS FOR ANOTHER THRILLING SAGA!

EDENS ZERO © Hiro Mashima/Kodansha, Ltd.

A high-flying space adventure! All the steadfast friendship and
wild fighting you've been waiting for...IN SPACE!

At Granbell Kingdom, an abandoned amusement park, Shiki has lived his
entire life among machines. But one day, Rebecca and her cat companion
Happy appear at the park's front gates. Little do these newcomers know
that this is the first human contact Granbell has had in a hundred years! As
Shiki stumbles his way into making new friends, his former neighbors stir at
an opportunity for a robo-rebellion... And when his old homeland becomes
too dangerous, Shiki must join Rebecca and Happy on their spaceship and
escape into the boundless cosmos.

Magus of the Library

Mitsu Izumi

MITSU IZUMI'S STUNNING ARTWORK BRINGS A FANTASTICAL LITERARY ADVENTURE TO LUSH, THRILLING LIFE!

Young Theo adores books, but the prejudice and hatred of his village keeps them ever out of his reach. Then one day, he chances to meet Sedona, a traveling librarian who works for the great library of Aftzaak, City of Books, and his life changes forever...

KC/
KODANSHA
COMICS

A Kodansha Comics Trade Paperback Original
I'm Standing on a Million Lives 5 copyright © 2018 Naoki Yamakawa/Akinari Nao
English translation copyright © 2020 Naoki Yamakawa/Akinari Nao

Published in the United States by Kodansha Comics, an imprint of Kodansha USA Publishing, LLC, New York.

Publication rights for this English edition arranged through Kodansha Ltd., Tokyo.

First published in Japan in 2018 by Kodansha Ltd., Tokyo.

ISBN 978-1-63236-898-0

Original cover design by Tadashi Hisamochi (hive&co., Ltd.)

Printed in the United States of America.

www.kodanshacomics.com

9 8 7 6 5 4 3 2 1
Translation: Kevin Gifford
Lettering: Thea Willis
Editing: Erin Subramanian, Nathaniel Gallant
Kodansha Comics edition cover design by Phil Balsman

Publisher: Kiichiro Sugawara
Managing editor: Maya Rosewood
Vice president of marketing & publicity: Naho Yamada

Director of publishing services: Ben Applegate
Associate director of operations: Stephen Pakula
Publishing services managing editor: Noelle Webster
Assistant production manager: Emi Lotto